THE SOCIAL PROCESS OF SCIENTIFIC INVESTIGATION

SOCIOLOGY OF THE SCIENCES

A YEARBOOK

VOLUME IV – 1980

TABLE OF CONTENTS

Introduction   vii

Contributors to this Volume   xxvii

PART I
Discovery Accounts

MARC DE MEY – The Interaction between Theory and Data in Science   3

KARIN D. KNORR – The Scientist as an Analogical Reasoner: A Critique of the Metaphor Theory of Innovation   25

B. LATOUR – Is it Possible to Reconstruct the Research Process? Sociology of a Brain Peptide   53

PART II
Discovery Acceptance

T. J. PINCH – Theoreticians and the Production of Experimental Anomaly: The Case of Solar Neutrinos   77

ANDREW PICKERING – The Role of Interests in High-Energy Physics: The Choice between Charm and Colour   107

BILL HARVEY – The Effects of Social Context on the Process of Scientific Investigation: Experimental Tests of Quantum Mechanics   139

DAVID TRAVIS – On the Construction of Creativity: The 'Memory Transfer' Phenomenon and the Importance of Being Earnest   165

PART III
The Research Process

MICHEL CALLON – Struggles and Negotiations to Define What is
Problematic and What is Not: The Sociologic Translation   197
JAN PÄRMARK and GÖRAN WALLÉN – The Development of an
In   'isciplinary Project   221

PART IV
Writing Public Accounts

/E WOOLGAR – Discovery: Logic and Sequence in a Scientific
Text   239
NIGEL GILBERT and MICHAEL MULKAY – Contexts of Scien-
tific Discourse: Social Accounting in Experimental Papers   269

PART V
The Context of Scientific Investigation

RICHARD WHITLEY – The Context of Scientific Investigation   297

Index   323

INTRODUCTION:
TOWARD THE EMPIRICAL STUDY OF SCIENTIFIC PRACTICE

The question, "What is science as a human and social enterprise?", has been giving rise to an increasing range and volume of studies in the last 15 to 20 years. This volume marks a new phase of study, the development of the empirical study of the research process itself. From patterns in the long-term growth and change in scientific ideas, to the response of science to its larger social and economic context, to its patterns of institutionalization and professionalization, to processes of the giving and seeking of recognition for unusual contribution, we have only lately finally arrived at the question, "How does scientific work proceed at its core, the research process itself?". Once posed, it seems strange that the question was left until so late. Perhaps that was because research has been seen as being on the one hand self-evident, and on the other mysterious — self-evident in its basic standards of empiricism and logic and a mystery concerning the origin of ideas, how the particular circumstances of research were made to yield universal statements. In either case, self-evident or mysterious, research was not problematic. In studying a respected and even semi-sacred institution, it is not surprising that the sense of the problematic first touched its external and larger features — the economic, class, religious conditions of its countries of origin — and only later its internal and more subtle ones. The former could be done in the institutions' own vocabulary, but the latter has required a new language, a reconception of basic terms in order for there to be any question at all. Given the institutions' own terms and assumptions the reasons for standard practice are self-evident.

The papers in this volume are all in answer to the question "What is scientific practice; how is it done?". They depart from the conventional language

Karin D. Knorr, Roger Krohn and Richard Whitley (eds.), The Social Process of Scientific Investigation. Sociology of the Sciences, Volume IV, 1980. vii–xxv.
Copyright © 1980 by D. Reidel Publishing Company.

of science in different ways and to different degrees, but a major common theme is how the new concerns may be expressed and new observations made. They also move to an array of more specific and more answerable questions: how are problems formulated and selected; how are research opportunities recognized and exploited? How is scientific work presented, received and evaluated by other scientists? And so forth.

The presupposition of these questions is that science is not a category of exception, but elaborated from the same elements as everyday practice, and shares as well as differs in these elements from other specialized cultural activities, whether art, religion, law, journalism, or whatever. The unique features of scientific investigation and communication may then eventually be established. These papers begin to resolve Ravetz's paradox of 1971: how does "the subjective, intensely personal activity of creative science ... (become) the objective, impersonal knowledge which results from it." (1)

The expansion and shift of focus in this questioning process is illustrated by such papers (2) as Knorr and Woolgar who emphasize that the scientists' later and public account of what was done in his/her laboratory is as constructed, is as much a cultural artifact, as the work itself. Harvey also shows that the reasons for rejecting an anomalous experiment change from the contingent and contextual judgements of credibility during the process of evaluation to a reconstruction in terms of evidence and logic ("the errors argument") after the rejection. (160–161). An earlier and more personal account, as in an interview, will give additional, valuable information, but it will also be a partial and selective construction of "what happened". This, in turn, can be usefully supplemented by an observer's account, if he/she is well informed on a day-to-day basis over a considerable period of time. In this view, the phrasing and revision of the scientists' final published account then becomes the object of attention and interpretation in a way impossible if it is seen as the objective and only possible report of logically organized work.

Thus, the investigation and the communication phases are seen to be in deep interaction, and must both be described as they occur if the "results" are to be understood. In fact, one unique feature of science may well turn out to be the degree to which communication with colleagues enters into the creative process, into the formulation of the work, in its anticipation and in the event. On this view the sciences then become a series of sites of local practice, some of which is translated into the standard forms of public discourse, in publication, and then retranslated by readers and adapted again to local practice at self-selected other sites. Less may be left implicit, and additional personal and contextual information is carried, by the "informal" methods of communication which mediate local projects and international publication. But both methods of communication are screens as well as conduits of information.

History and Background of the Volume

When the planning of this volume began in the spring of 1977, it seemed a natural part of the mandate for the *Yearbook*. There had also been a number of more specific calls for deeper studies of research in social and historical context (3). These calls can be seen as giving permission and legitimacy to ask questions otherwise seen as irrelevant, or even disrespectful, and as attempts to develop new perspectives from which to ask and to answer them. The implied and expressed irreverence toward traditions and institutions of great respect may have prolonged this process of initial apologetics. In any case, in May 1977 the theme of 'The Social Process of Scientific Investigation' was proposed to the Editorial Board for Volume IV as "the heart of the subject." That is, the ethnographic and detailed historical study of actual scientific activity and thinking at or close to the work site. The plan called for one or two conferences of authors presenting papers in response to a "theme paper" to be written by the present author. Papers were also solicited by his trip to most of the known centres of social and historical studies of science in the U.K. and attendance at the ISA World Congress in Upsalla, Sweden in August, 1978. The first conference was held in Bielefield, West Germany, in June 1979. As it turned out, there was more work being done than was anticipated, and it was better developed, especially in England. The response was so strong that the volume was filled by the papers given at the Bielefeld conference.

Naturally, all this work, already underway and separately conceived, could not be fully integrated. However, our hope is that the selection and self-selection of authors, their responding to a theme paper, and their interaction during and after the conference has given the papers greater coherence, integration, and improved quality. The editors believe that this set of papers represents the majority of the empirical work on the conduct of scientific research today.

The Phrasing of Issues and the Revision of Assumptions and Language

As mentioned, the first challenges to established conceptions of science raised issues concerned with some of its external features, its institutional and class location and support, its professionalization, etc. Social factors were asserted as important as technical factors, knowledge was supposed related to social conditions rather than absolute, etc. (4) This is not to outline the first set of issues in the emergence of the sociology of science, but rather to point out that they were phrased in the same terms, and made many of the same assumptions, as the perspective they challenged. Both assumed that social factors were clearly separated from technical ones, for example. The argument about whether technical factors were temporally and logically prior to social ones or vice versa was impossible to solve and not very productive. It constrained formation of genuinely new problems and the new observations needed to resolve them. These traditional issues can be grouped into three assumed dichotomies: data/theory, objective/subjective (includes technical/ social and internal/external), and explicit norms versus implicit coutner-norms of science. (5) These issues and terms are reflected in the following papers, but the significant move is the attempt to effectively bypass them. The focus is not now on the priority of data or theory but on pattern conception and recognition (De Mey) and the utility of analogy and metaphor during research (Knorr). The debate over True/False versus relativity has weakened into whether scientific ideas can be treated "symmetrically" with ideas from other cultural areas (Harvey, Pickering). And the technical versus social aspects of research are now seen to be separated *subsequent* to the research by participants in the course of making persuasive claims for its carefully constructed results (Woolgar, Latour). Nor are norms or counter-norms seen as terms of explanation of behaviour, but rather as selectively used terms of persuasion into which accounts of behaviour are rhetorically cast. (Gilbert and Mulkay)

Some authors have gone another step to invent new language to conceive processes that fall outside or cut across existing concepts. Some of these terms have been borrowed or adapted from economics, as "investment", or "symbolic capital"; a scientist is seen to invest his symbolic capital (credibility, reputation) together with other resources in a local research site. While on the one hand this merely extends the use of economic terms already present in scientific vernacular, as in "making an investment" in a line of work, it also allows the identification of elements otherwise separated into technical versus social at the beginning of the analysis. Rejoining them cannot then appear as a problem in the analysis and as a solution at the end. In the same way, "practical reasoning" has been found useful in describing activities somewhere between formal logic and trial and error, or in finding the implicit reasoning occurring within trial and error. And, "account" has been borrowed from symbolic interactionism and ethnomethodology to replace "theory" or "history", avoiding an assumed reproduction or description of what is "really there" or "really happened"; an "account" is someone's version of what is there or happened, neither irrelevant nor absolute.

More improvization of language is evident in "qualitative logics" or "heterogeneous reasoning" in the attempt to pose the question more precisely of just how relationships and patterns among events are perceived and articulated than "hunch", "insight", and "hypothesis" allow. (Latour, 65–66) In the same way an "idea" becomes a "speech form" in order to avoid the assumption that cognition ever was separate from social context, and in order to be able to say that only later, after the event, are elements isolated and attributed to individuals, times and places. (Woolgar, 247) Finally, I will just mention the metaphor of the ventilation of a building for conceptual change used by De Mey. "With the removal of a 'solid soil', the metaphor of founding scientific theories on the rock bottom of observation becomes empty . . . . 'ventilation' would emphasize that observation enters our conceptual edifices at several floors simultaneously." (De Mey, 20) Thus, these innovations become fertile sources of new, more specific questions and observations unavailable in the traditional language.

Contributions of this Volume

The first thematic claim of the present authors, taken collectively, is precisely the need to revise the language by which science is discussed: "idea," "logic," "insight," "theory," "problem," "anomaly," are brought under review. There is considerable variation among authors, with perhaps the minimum claim being that traditional categories, especially "social versus technical factors," should be seen as integrated in the investigative process itself, that factors later identified as "technical" were grounded in and made possible by social factors (Harvey, Pickering, Pinch, Barmark and Wallen). As one example, Pinch points out that in his case, because his protagonist needed a new, expensive apparatus of only temporary utility he needed a strong theoretical rationale, which in turn influenced the design of the experiment, his collaboration with an astrophysicist, and the conception of the results. (84–86)

Other authors are more ambitious in their revision of language, and in fact, taken together, they suggest an outline of a potential perspective which assumes that scientists pay as much attention to the selection and construction of their language as they do to the construction of equipment or any other aspect of the conduct of research. To Callon, Gilbert and Mulkay, Knorr, Latour, and Woolgar, scientists are literally constructing their world rather than merely describing it.

The imagery of the "construction of our world" rather than "describing" or "explaining" it marks a more important shift of assumption than may be apparent. Beneath the face assertion that the verbal and symbolic aspects of culture are not that different from material culture lies a more basic revision of the legacy of "Knowledge" being conceived as a separate verbal and symbolic high culture, autonomous and possessing some special force, the power to reveal, order and enlighten. The present visual and spatial imagery locates "Knowledge" outside of people and outside society, somewhere "out there", a heritage of theological and philosophical traditions. Now, "Knowledge" is being brought down to earth, demystified as a human construction, in the natural as well as the social areas. At the same time, the new imagery revises the exceptional status previously given to natural science knowledge as also "out there", but as closer to physical reality ("more objective"), less distorted by its human vehicle.

This shift of imagery has at least three dimensions. A high/distant/formidible image is replaced by a low/close/everyday one. An abstract/spiritual/perfect image is replaced by a physical/imperfect image. And an impersonal/universal/permanent image is replaced by an image of personal work carrying the marks of the craftsman and his time and location of work, which is assumed to be of temporary utility and validity. All of these dimensions were carried in Ravetz's image of science as craft work, which is why his work was so suggestive for many researchers on science (6).

Knowledge is left to be only a part of a craft skill, existing in a person, at a place and time. Its (printed) means of publication may force it to be formally, abstractly stated, or there may be other advantages in such lean statements. But these forms are clearly not all of the skill of doing science, and cannot communicate the entire skill. This skill can only be recreated by people at work at a place and time, whether from master to student or colleague to colleague.

The ability to translate formal, printed statements into locally useful skills and back again may be as formidable as the skill to invent new skills. We could see then at least three phases: (1) The translation and amplification of formally stated "Knowledge" into particular skills; (2) The revision, invention, and improvement of present skills by new particular skills; (3) The translation and reduction of new particular skills into formal, publishable "Knowledge".

What our authors have done, in effect, is to look at these phases as problematic and contingent, rather than as routine, automatic or logical. This brings into view processes left implicit before, and gives rise to a range of questions never posed before. Our authors give most attention to phase (2), the revision and invention of technique, skill, and accounting for what happened at the work site, previously ignored or underplayed, left implicit or even mystified — "genius", "talent," "hunch" serving to divert the question of origins. Scientists seem to have believed, and philosophers have often stated, that scientists could speak directly — citing evidence and logic — to each other in a published form assumed to autonomously convey "Knowledge". This conveyance is now seen as problematic and complex, and to require much other work — "the social construction of reality."

A second consequence of this expanded problematic is that the possibility is raised that the psychological attitudes required of phase (1), the closest approximation to programmed learning, might hinder abilities necessary at phase (2), as in the commonly cited difference between "problem solving" and "problem finding" abilities. Third, the habits and conventions of phase (3) ("writing") might hinder phase (1) ("reading") becoming so elliptical or deepy coded that only very experienced people can make the translation back to what the article means "in practical terms". Some graduate departments have in fact developed special courses in how to read scientific papers (7).

Finally, an issue implicitly raised by the persistently drawn contrast between "practical reasoning", associated with actual research, and formal logic, associated with published argument (Gilbert and Mulkay, Woolgar, this volume, and Knorr (8, 9) is how significant is the manipulation of forms in extension from and in some independence from practical experience, say by theorists or mathematicians? In what ways and when is it productive and when not?

The papers here also provide opportunities for comparative case studies. They are not formally symmetrical case studies allowing precise or conclusive comparisons, but rather each was done for its own purpose and by its own design. Suggestions do emerge for example from the juxtaposition of cases where innovative or non-orthodox research results in open controversy (Travis, Pickering, Harvey) versus private or informal contention and negotiation over the meaning of results (Pinch). A committed protagonist who believes in his own results carries more potential for controversy, which in the latter case the major parties went to great length to avoid, than one with the posture that the theory "at least deserves a test" (Harvey). Another condition is that when an accepted, respected theory is contradicted by a well-conducted experiment, the experiments may be discounted by the experimenter himself (Harvey, Travis) or they may be allowed to stand (Pinch); the particular circumstances by which the latter may be accomplished without public controversy are described by Pinch. A third, more obvious dimension here is that of methods judged "softer" (Travis) versus "harder" experiments (Pinch, Harvey, Pickering). There are here other, complicating contrasts, the depth of challenge to cultural assumptions, as in the relation of animal to human learning, and unorthodox, humourous, non-serious presentation of findings in the former case.

As a third type of contribution to the sociology of science, our authors make more specific observations relevant along the course of the process of investigation. It is the major point of Callon's paper that "the problem" is not the origin of the research, nor purely cognitive, but rather has also to be created in a "core area of suspicion" where previously separated social versus technical factors are fused for re-analysis; the contrasting purposes of rivals gives rise to sharply different research problems and programs, in spite of their having the same apparent technical givens. The presence of an adversary position, in fact, is often useful to an investigator in formulating his views more completely than he would have otherwise done.

The intimacy of the relation of the intellectual state of a field and the social organization of a large-scale project is demonstrated by Barmark and Wallen's case where an administratively centralized project is mismatched to the cognitive dispersal of the various biological fields involved. Realignment then required considerable struggle and reorganization. The social organization of research also gives rise to special social roles. Barmark and Wallen identify the role of "the generalist" in interdisciplinary groups who must understand both cognitive and social problems in order to translate, mediate, and co-ordinate among the specialties involved (231). This is parallel to the "idea man", known locally and consulted frequently although the importance of his contribution is not reflected in co-authorships or even in acknowledgements and footnotes, and to the "super-technician" identified by Latour and Woolgar (10).

Finally, at the writing end of the process, Gilbert and Mulkay in contrasting the formal, published accounts of research with the far more varied and contextual accounts given in interviews, point out that the published accounts do not aim at genuine objectivity (such as a fair statement of an opponent's arguments) as much as seek a subtle, veiled method of persuasion. Gilbert and Mulkay do not speculate upon why scientific style has the particular form that it does, but this reader is tempted to say that "the best offence is a good defense": to put up a hard shell and not offer any unnecessary openings. For example, all opening for *ad hominem* kinds of suspicion are routinely omitted and thus the burden of raising them rests with the potential critic. (277–278). Thus, formal scientific communication would seem to proceed by implication and inuendo — a "high context" type communication and culture in Hall's terms — and nearly the opposite of its self image as having "the mass of the information vested in the explicit code." (11)

Remaining Issues in the Sociology of Science

The older versions of the internal/external factors debate on the causes of the conduct and progress of science seems here to have been safely bypassed, and the technical/social factors dichotomy has been softened to the point that it no longer appears interesting to insist on the priority of one over the other. Still, this social determinist phase of development in the sociology of science veils a residual problem: What constraint does the perceivable environment put on what can be said about it? We have no systematic account of how the perceivable environment enters its investigation, along with intellectual and professional "interests", "opportunities of success", etc.

If the positive programme for science could be said, for present purposes, to have made environmental objects the sole source of the content of knowledge, the sociology of knowledge (insofar as it was extended to natural science), could be said to have assumed that men could and would make of their environment what they wanted. As a third alternative, the "strong programme" of the Edinburgh school brackets the environment for science, saying that the environment is no more or less available to or closely described by science than by any other area of culture. A fourth "interpretive" or "constructivist" school (Latour, Knorr, Woolgar, Gilbert and Mulkay), if we can give them a name for the moment, account for the opposition of social to cognitive-technical facts as an artifact of the research profess itself. They argue that all possible facts are potentially considered by research strategists, resources at hand, career considerations, the credibility of other scientists' techniques, etc., during the research process. At the moment of a convincing construction of a working artifact, they begin to sort "technical", credible from "social", merely situational or personal elements. After this split, the "technical factors" (professionally convincing) are seen as the primary or exclusive causes of their own behavior and of the derived results. Now, presumably, in this latter case, perceivable, inscribable elements of the environment did enter the complex process of construction, and are partial determinants of its final shape, even if not systematically accounted for. So, we still have the question, what was this role and what constraints did it put on what happened and what was produced? A parallel point holds for the "strong programme". After the descriptions have been given of the various interests or other social factors which entered the process of research, the formulation of results, the presentation of arguments, where are the perceptions made along the way? Are defeated theories (colour) potentially as useful, suggestive, etc. as victorious ones (charm)? Could we go back to Lamark, phlogiston, fixed continents, and made those work too? It is one thing to refuse to put theories into true and false boxes before the search for the occasion of their invention, no doubt a useful heuristic. The risk is at the end of the investigation to insist that they bear an equal or underterminable relation to the environment they purport to describe, and to close off another range of answerable questions. To include the perceivable environment as part of the process of research takes nothing away from its social and cultural nature but would add to the realism and credibility of our accounts in the longer term.

In these last pages, I will try to give some perspective on where we are at the moment in the sociology of science and at the same time some personal worries about possible difficulties. We are now well into a second, corrective phase that is saying that science is like everything else: social, built from the same faculties as common sense, also rhetorical in language, etc. As informative as this has been, eventually we will enter a third phase, asking again "How and why is science different?" Why is it accumulative, in the sense that each success opens new opportunities for further achievements? Why is it coherent, in the sense that many achievements in different specialities have been brought into coherence, and places of contradiction have often been informative? Why and how is science able to change itself, in an apparent bootstrap operation where some more certain aspects are brought to bear on and change others which new knowledge then is brought to bear upon and to change the original certainties? Otherwise said, how are new observations of low confidence brought to bear upon and to change "Knowledge" of high confidence? And, of course, why does science have large practical impact and utility? The items behind the fascination and celebration of the reverent phase of science studies will have to find a (rephrased) place in a third phase.

Another aspect of this problem of dialectic type development in science studies is that while we have had changes in the theory of science we have also had changes in science. This problem is activated by the fact that most of the close data of day-to-day scientific practice is available only through current ethnographic type studies. These have naturally first occurred in large-scale, high-technology research in the core of our current national/professional science system. Now, how many of the features currently being read into the nature of science, e.g. careful calculation of risk, direct concern with recognition as "symbolic capital", high attention to the current trends in the direction of research, etc. are actually particular features of our national/professional system? For example, a large part of the support of science, in some areas virtually all, is poured in through its own prestige system. This is done through the peer review system, and the general system of allocation of funds according to the "reputation" of specialities, universities, departments, and individuals. All resources for research, career, and livelihood being channeled through the prestige system, participants are naturally highly conscious of being recognizable in that system, and, may even be somewhat "agonistic". Perhaps further studies of specialities less tightly geared into the national support system, perhaps such as animal ecology, will serve as a partial corrective (12). Another might be renewed interest in detailed historical studies (13) and the attempt to phrase accounts of scientific practice congruent both with historical and current data.

Several authors have used economic metaphor to describe current science. At least one (Pinch, 77) finds the use of economic metaphor frequent among scientists themselves. "Production and re-reproduction," "investment of resources", "symbolic capital" etc. have made insights available into relations among resources, the exchange and conversion from one kind of research resource, such as scientific "credit", to another, research support, or publication in journals, etc. That is, the economic language has allowed the juxtaposition and interpretation of elements otherwise segregated into "intellectual," "professional", "institutional", "cognitive", etc., categories. Less explicitly, economic language has allowed the translation of the semi-mystified or sacred language of institutionalized science into a secular language. Thus, behind apparent noble motives, "love of truth," or "curiosity" can be detected the down-to-earth motives of seeking recognition, prestige, and career advancement.

I hesitate to see this economic language become too well entrenched. From left to right of the political spectrum it is our natural, conventional habit of mind, and the translation of scientific into economic ideom is being readily worked through. But it allows a limited view of human motivation, reduced to various forms of career interest. In the amateur and academic eras of science, "personal interest", "curiosity", and "significant" were used as pervasively as the terms of career interest are now. Even though phrased in the terms of a then current system, did not these terms point to something (just as "interest" does now)? Are the previous sets of motives, although they might be better described, merely missing now? In short, we tend to assume a professional system of science, and hence use extensively the same basic terms as participants. (Properly and persuasively argued against by Latour and Woolgar in *Laboratory Life*) (14) If the system of science is changing at the same time as the framework we use to describe it, what appears as a theoretical advance and more accurate description can also be participation in the adjustment of its language to new circumstances.

On the other hand, our language for cognition and emotion in science seems less developed than that for exchange and negotiation. Only two papers apply analogy and metaphor (Knorr) and Gestalt psychology and the imagery of artificial intelligence (De Mey) to the empirical analysis of cognition. On the side of the emotional life of science we seem still limited to conventional language of little new informative power, "bias", "commitment", "Interesting", etc. And no paper takes up the topic here, nor was one offered. This seems to me a front for future development (15).

These papers are largely sociological in orientation, and their authors tend to see psychological factors as emphemaral, trivial, or methodologically difficult. Perhaps this is a corollary of the advance of a sociological point of view. But, whatever else it is, science is certainly intellectual work with a high degree of personal involvement. The nature and dynamics of that involvement seems a likely influence on the nature, direction and pace of its development. Most obviously, a particular blend of emotional, observational, and cognitive elements in the origin and emotional dynamics of the process of investigation becomes characteristic of a scientist and his style of work. There is the well known urge to interpret, to see connections, to locate phenomena in a larger picture versus the that to pin down and to test, to be "right rather than interesting". Among observationalists, some prefer to survey, to develop an array of observations while others prefer to make a close study of one or a few cases, as in the field versus laboratory sciences. Among theorists there is the difference between those who want to probe for deep structure, for the mechanism behind the appearance versus those who develop a synthesis, a model to explain a wide range of data.

But these direct satisfactions, reflected in the choice of discipline, speciality, problem and research style and not the subject of as much attention as occupational and career motives. Yet, every personal document by an active scientist I have seen witnesses the strength of direct satisfaction in scientific work. How are personal and instituted motives combined in specific pieces of scientific work? (16) Are strong personal motives related to moves to new specialities, to later but greater achievement, to the length of time research is pursued without tangible success, to the kind of intellectual change that is sought? If one sees creativity as ultimately emotional in origin and in drive, the topic takes on basic importance. These or similar questions seem likely prospects for further phases of research.

At the other end of the social scale from psychological dynamics, case studies of research projects, programmes, or specialities can only with difficulty place their events in a larger social and political context. Barmark and Wallen illustrate some of the constraints and limitations of national planning policy on the design of research programmes. And Pinch is apprehensive about the effects of large size and the high cost of experiments on the openness to challenge of modern physics projects. With rising costs of experiments only people of high initial credibility will be able to do them; they will be too expensive to duplicate, and thus not subject to dispute: " . . . the market for credible information becomes dominated by large and expensive projects which produce almost guaranteed credible information" (103–104). Both Barmark and Wallen and Pinck raise the larger question of what will be the longer term effects of the contemporary concentration and centralization of the support of science. A period of a retrenchment after the growth which put this system into place would seem to accelerate any conservative tendencies of the system. Only at the local level can the subtle effects of such trends be perceived. Other studies here, not explicitly drawing out these implications, might be read in this context.

My final point concerns science as a contradictory process. We may be in some danger of moving from an older straight forward view of correct method producing evidence, and intelligence producing theoretical discoveries, to a new straightforward view of recognition leading to grants leading to purchasing equipment, which produces data, which produces arguments, which produces articles which are read giving recognition, all in a "credibility cycle" (17). But science is historically too late, too rare (one origin point), and too problematic in its discoveries to be produced in such a straightforward way. Science as a contradictory process is brought into view by seeing it as an effort at purposive cultural change. Cultural change is not only sought but also resisted; the sources and occasions of this resistance should be viewed not as irrational deviations but as essential parts of making social life and science work.

Certain of the traditional dilemmas of the interpretation of science can be seen as artificial, as dilemmas of interpretation rather than as inherent to its process. Thus, the division between logic and empiricism stands in the way of a social account of discovery. The problem of the moves between perception and conception has been dealt with through the concepts of "metaphorical innovation" (18) "analogical transfer" (Knorr), "pattern recognition", "ventilation" of observation and conception at several levels, (De Mey, 3), "perspective shifts", and now the current proposal of "metacultural change". These concepts invite attention to changes in terms in which a problem in conceived, to the shift and redefinition of categories as basic events in science. They begin to develop a language for the analysis of scientific advance as not only the addition of items of culture, but also as changes in its basic terms.

A second example is the by-passing of "internalist" (explicit logic and data analysis) versus "externalist" (class, organizational, career) factors for a return to the core topic in science, its cognitive structure, but now in the social and psychological context in which it occurs with concepts which do not force the social/cognitive separation in the first place, such as "opportunities for success", (Knorr), "convergence" of lines of research and "discovery" as an interpretative as well as observational process (19).

Other dilemmas would appear to have a basis in the practice of science and some practical devices or implicit mechanisms have been developed as ways around them. Identifying these dilemmas reveals science as not a natural or easily contrived system, but rather as partly fortunate accident and partly ingenious innovation. Nor need it be seen as automatic once set in place nor necessarily yet complete or perfect.

First, there is a certain tension between the importance attributed to ideas and their being open to empirical challenge. This appears in Lakatos' contrast of the "hard core" of informative ideas and the "protective belt" of auxilliary hypotheses (20). It also appears in Callon's division of a problematic situation into an outer area of unanalysed assumption, an inner "net of certainty", and a core "area of suspicion", where social and technical factors are "fused" and thus open for reconception. In the outer rings the social and technical are separated and thus both are solidified. Concepts felt to be more meaningful, more informative, and interconnected logically are then seen as *barriers* to new perception. This disjunction between the more emotionally significant and the more empirical terms helps to explain the elation people feel on the discovery of terms which both seem significant and are empirically relevant.

There is a parallel tension between emotional involvement in a problem and the ability to obtain perspective on it, to be able to integrate its particulars into one holistic view. Sometimes temporal and spatial distance give also enough emotional distance that another perspective becomes possible and a switch to a more informative image is achieved.

Since the established categories have not solved the problem, this must be a discovered association or invented pattern. One plausible route to a newly recognized association or pattern is a felt or emotionally based similarity. There is dual need for emotional involvement and distanced perspective, the wish to solve the problem and the distance to see the pattern.

The final dilemma to mention is between our need to see in patterns and the need for accuracy. The first images are inevitably vague or incomplete and analogies inexact (21). If initial images are vague and partial, but nevertheless the necessary source of new thought, the problem of resolution between initial image and the empirical and problematic referent must be great.

These dilemmas or contradictory processes make it difficult for two necessary things to happen at the same time. We can here only briefly suggest how these dilemmas are sometimes bridged in scientific practice. First, one could suggest recurrent phases of conviction in newly perceived relations or patterns followed by phases of criticism and reconciliation of the new pattern with new and older data and data taken as given knowledge from neighboring specialities. Safan-Gerard's discussion of the phases of perception, elaboration, expression, and evaluation in art show how empirical relevance can be brought to bear after meaningful insights are obtained, how distance and perspective is later obtained on ideas conceived in passion, and how refined, well elaborated constructions are developed from initial images (22). More obviously, different types of research — exploratory versus developmental — and research strategies — broadly observational versus precise, restricted, specialist research (23) advance one side or the other of the contradictory demands of innovation. The same is true of different types of people and styles of work, for example the difference between people inclined to be enthusiasts or advocates and those inclined to be critics, or the different cognitive styles apparent in those inclined to "social differentiation" versus "remote association" abilities (problem finding versus problem solving) described by Lodahl and Gordon (24). Finally, some of the organizational features of science would appear to play a role, such as the duplication of research, which allows a pattern to be perceived at one time and place and to be established at another. Ben-David's argument for the key role of decentralization of research and its support and the key role of marginal social roles could be linked to these dilemmas in the same way (25).

It is our hope that this first substantive set of empirical studies in investigative practice renews and significantly advances the question, "What is science?". It is renewed by seeing science not as a category of exception defined in advance, but as a human social construction in its elements like any other. This perspective requires some new language for its developing programme of studies, an "alerting framework" for the observation of events previously ignored, but now seen as highly significant. Some older, much argued issues and their language of phrasing will have been bypassed — such as internal versus external factors, social versus cognitive factors, and accumulative versus revolutionary change. And new themes and issues have emerged, — such as the interpenetration of publication and investigative practice, and how the perceivable environment enters the construction of scientific accounts.

As a third phase we can project the development of and hopefully the incorporation of a psychology of science, an attempt to come to terms with the particularities of the contemporary system of the national support and organization of highly professionalized research, and the impact of larger social structures on the special arrangements of scientific institutions and on the details of local scientific practice. It seems that science studies have now decisively entered a new and rapidly moving phase of development.

Acknowledgements

I would like to gratefully acknowledge the support of the Social Science and Humanities Research Council of Canada, including a sabbatical leave grant and research and travel support, the hospitality, office and other facilities during the summer of 1978, given me by the Department of Liberal Studies of Science, Manchester University, and the continuous support of McGill University for the several trans-Atlantic trips this project has involved.

McGill University   ROGER KROHN

Notes

1. Ravetz took the problem and the concept of craftwork as a promising answer from Michael Polanyi. See his *Personal Knowledge*, Routledge and Kegan Paul, London, 1958, and Jerome R. Ravetz, *Scientific Knowledge and its Social Problems*, Clarendon Press, Oxford, 1971, pp. 75–76.
2. Papers in this volume are cited by the author's name only or with a page reference.
3. Helga Novotny, 'On the Feasibility of a Cognitive Approach to the Study of Science', *Zeitschrift für Soziologie* **2** (3), (1973) 282–296.
   Richard Whitley, 'Cognitive and Social Institutionalization of Scientific Specialities and Research Areas'. In R. Whitley (ed.), *Social Process of Scientific Development*, Routledge and Kegan Paul, London, 1974.
   Ron Johnston, 'Contextual Knowledge: A Model for the Overthrow of the Internal/External Dichotomy in Science', *Australia and New Zealand Journal of Sociology* **12** (3), (1976) 193–203.
   Roger Krohn, 'Scientific Ideology and Scientific Process: The Natural History of a Conceptual Shift', *The Sociology of the Sciences Yearbook*, Reidel, Dordrecht, 1977.
   Kenneth Studer and Daryl Chubin, 'The Place of Knowledge in Scientific Growth', given at the American Sociological Association meetings, September, 1977.
4. See Krohn, *op. cit.*, 1977 for an historical outline of these issues in the sociology of science.
5. See *Ibid.* for a discussion of this grouping of issues.
6. Ravetz, *op. cit.*, (1971) 75–108.
7. Rue Bucher and Joan G. Stelling, *Becoming Professional*, Beverley Hills, California, Sage Publications, 1977, p. 90.
8. Karin Knorr, 'From Scenes to Script: On the Relationship Between Laboratory Research and the Published Paper in Science', *Social Studies of Science*, forthcoming.
9. See Karin Knorr, *The Manufacture of Knowledge*: An Essay on the Constructivist and Contextual Nature of Science, Pergamon Press, Oxford, 1980.
10. Bruno Latour and Steve Woolgar, *Laboratory Life*: *The Social Construction of Scientific Facts*, Beverley Hills, California, Sage Publication, 1979, p. 218.
11. Edward T. Hall, *Beyond Culture*, Garden City, New York, Doubleday, 1977, p. 91.
12. Douglas McKegney, 'Large Mammal Field Ecology Research', given at the conference on The Social Processes of Scientific Investigation, Montreal, October, 1979.
13. See, for example, Howard Gruber, 'Darwin on Man: A Psychological Study of Scientific Creativity', together with *Darwin's Early and Unpublished Notebooks*, transcribed and annotated by Paul H. Barrett, Wildwood House, London, 1974. And Edward Manier, *The Young Darwin and his Cultural Circle*, D. Reidel Publishing Co., Dordrecht, 1978.
14. Latour and Woolgar, *op. cit.*
15. See Michael J. Mahoney, 'Psychology of the Scientist: An Evaluative Review', *Social Studies of Science* 9, (1979) 349–376.
16. Roger Krohn, *The Social Shaping of Science, Institutions, Ideology and Careers in Science*, Greenwood Press, Westport, Conn., 1971.
17. Latour and Woolgar, *op. cit.*, 201.

18. Barry Barnes, *Scientific Knowledge and Sociological Thought*, London: Routledge and Kegan Paul, 1974.

19. Chubin and Studer, *op. cit.*;
    S. W. Woolgar, 'Writing an Intellectual History of Scientific Development: The Use of Discovery Accounts', *Social Studies of Science* 6, 1976.

20. Imre Lakatos, 'Falsification and the Methodology of Scientific Research Programmes,' I. Lakatos and Alan Musgrave (eds.), *Criticism and the Growth of Knowledge*, Cambridge University Press, London, 1970, 90–196.

21. Jacques Hadamard, *The Psychology of Invention in the Mathematical Field*, Dover, New York, 1954.

22. Desy Safan-Gerard, 'How to Unblock', *Psychology Today*, Jan., 1973, 80–86.

23. W. I. B. Beveridge, *The Art of Scientific Investigation*, Random House, New York, 1950, 170.

24. Janice Lodahl and Gerald Gordon, 'The Structure of Scientific Fields and the Functioning of University Graduate Departments', *American Sociological Review* 37, (1972) 57–72.

25. Joseph Ben-David, *The Scientist's Role in Society*, Prentice-Hall, Englewood Cliffs, N. J., 1971.

CONTRIBUTORS TO THIS VOLUME

Roger Krohn, *McGill University*.

Marc de Mey, *University of Ghent*.

Karin D. Knorr, *University of Pennsylvania*.

B. Latour, *Conservatoire National des Arts et Métiers, Centre Science, Technologie et Société*.

T. J. Pinch, *University of Bath*.

Andrew Pickering, *University of Edinburgh*.

Bill Harvey, *Napier College of Commerce and Technology, Edinburgh*.

David Travis, *University of Bath*.

Michel Gallon, *GSI, Ecole des Mines, Paris*.

Jan Bärmark, *University of Gothenburg*.

Göran Wallén, *University of Gothenburg*.

Steve Woolgar, *Brunel University*.

Nigel Gilbert, *University of Surrey*.

Michael Mulkay, *University of York*.

Richard Whitley, *Manchester Business School*.

PART I

DISCOVERY ACCOUNTS

THE INTERACTION BETWEEN THEORY AND DATA
IN SCIENCE

Exploring a New Model for Perception in an Application to Harvey's
Discovery of the Circulation of the Blood

MARC DE MEY

University of Ghent

> Nothing is harder to pin down than the way
> we 'see' objects of which we know the shape
>
> E. H. GOMBRICH, *The Sense of Order*,
> Oxford, Phaidon, 1979, p. 164

The theory-laden character of scientific observation in both sociology of science (see e.g. Mulkay (1)) and philosophy of science (see e.g. Shimony (2)) is now generally accepted. However, it cannot be claimed that the details of the interaction between theory and data are fully understood. Somehow, the idea is accepted as a general principle while its application remains puzzling and paradoxical. Based on developments in AI (artificial intelligence) and cognitive psychology, this paper explores new ideas about perception which lead to a model for interaction between theory and data. In order to investigate its potential relevance for science studies, it is applied to a historical case in history of science: the role of theory and data in Harvey's discovery of the circulation of the blood.

Theory-Ladenness

If what we observe depends on what we except to occur, how can we discover anything new? If observation is theory-laden, how can we ever adapt theories to new data? Since the 1960's, the theme of the theory-laden character of data has been widely accepted. Beside Hanson, who coined the phrase *All data are theory-laden*, authors like Kuhn, Polanyi, Toulmin, and Feyerabend

Karin D. Knorr, Roger Krohn and Richard Whitley (eds.), The Social Process of
Scientific Investigation. Sociology of the Sciences, Volume IV, 1980. 3—23.
Copyright © 1980 *by D. Reidel Publishing Company.*

promoted the idea of scientific observation as strongly influenced by large conceptual systems of a more theoretical nature. This is contrary to what has been called the 'orthodox' view of theories. According to that view, scientific theories are free-floating entities which increase in acceptability to the degree they can be anchored to the solid 'soil' of observation. Observation is independent of theories. It constitutes the rock bottom on which scientific theories should be founded (see Feigl (3)).

With respect to the theory-dependency of observations, one can distinguish between a *logical* and a *psychological* approach.

The logical approach goes back on authors such as Duhem, Quine and Feyerabend. It simply states that, even if we can make a neat distinction between the observations and the theoretical statements of a particular theory in science, we always *depend on* an auxiliary *theory* of perception to indicate what we regard as observations. So there seems no escape from circularity. As such, the notion of theory-dependency of observation is a somewhat disheartening principle which extinguishes the hope of ultimate verification and the anchoring of theories in the solid soil of observation.

The psychological approach is more directed by the wish to understand how new knowledge is formed than by the need to justify acquired knowledge. The guiding function of theory is the focus of attention here. It shapes expectations so that perception can be highly selective and specific. If it is, in Einstein's terms "the theory which decides what we can observe" (4) then the question becomes, how do the abstract terms of a theory interact with concrete sensible things? How can a theory penetrate into observation processes? In this paper, we will follow a psychological approach and attempt to clarify the relationship between theory and data by means of some currently new ideas on visual perception.

The Celebrated Exemplars

Demonstrations of the theory-dependency of observation provided by Hanson and Kuhn refer often to the classical ambiguous figures familiar from so many textbooks on perception. One of the most famous ones — the Necker cube — goes back to an authentic experience with scientific observations. Necker hit upon the ambiguity of this image while studying figures of cristalline forms (5). Other celebrated examples are Rubin's figure-ground reversal which alternates between a goblet and a pair of face profiles, Boring's "young girl-old woman" reversal and the rabbit-duck figure developed by Jastrow in 1900 (see Figure 1).

Fig. 1. Jastrow's rabbit-duck figure (1900).

Kuhn repeatedly emphasizes the exemplary nature of these apparently simple reversals for the understanding of conceptual changes in scientific revolutions. In his chapter on such revolutions as changes of world view, he indicates that

scientists see new and different things when looking with familiar instruments in places where they looked before. . . . It is as elementary prototypes for these transformations of the scientist's world that the familiar demonstrations of a switch in visual gestalt prove so suggestive. *What were ducks in the scientist's world before the revolution are rabbits afterwards. The man who first saw the exterior of the box from above later sees its interior from below* (6) (italics added).

Despite the popularity of such ambiguous figures in even elementary psychology textbooks, few of them offer a thorough discussion of the problems involved. In this paper we will combine some lines of research in the psychology of perception (in particular Arnheim, Gibson and Palmer) to suggest a model that could account for the gestalt switch experiences. One of the reasons for the promising character of the model is that it is highly suggestive with respect to how Kuhn's and Hanson's reference to the phenomenon should be understood.

Perception and Knowledge

Among the publications that have emphasized the central importance of such ambiguities as the *rabbit-duck*, E. Gombrich's *Art and Illusion* (7) stands out as a most eloquent and convincing argument for what could be called a *two-component* model of perception. Already in Aristotle's analysis of the notion of experience, observation is described as a combination of sense perception and memory. Perception is the interpretation of sense data on the basis of stored knowledge retained from previous encounters with the object of perception. Current cognitive orientations in both psychology and AI tend to stress the relative contribution of stored knowledge at the risk of loosing sight of the data. Gombrich's book is a penetrating attempt to "disentangle what we really see from what we merely know" in the perception of art. Though pictures should not be looked upon as substitutes for visual objects, we can hope to derive useful suggestions for a theory of perception from an analysis of "the beholder's share in the reading of an artist's image". According to Gombrich "ambiguity — rabbit or duck? — is clearly the key to the whole problem of image reading" (8). In the course of a fascinating study of the development from the conceptual art of Egypt to a "gradual adjustment to natural appearances" in Greek art, the comparable development from schematic medieval art to the "constant search" and "sacred discontent" brought in by the Renaissance, and similar issues in modern art (e.g. impressionism vs. cubism), he accumulates numerous examples to argue for the acceptance of what could be called the *Bartlett-model*. Bartlett's 1932-book (9) studies remembering in human subjects for both verbal and pictorial material. The general result is the notion of a *memory scheme*.

Knowledge is stored in memory in terms of some general *schemes*, accepted conventional representations for various instantiations of objects or events. The scheme embodies the basic conceptual knowledge about objects or events. In memory it constitutes the framework for the reconstruction of what has been seen. In perception, it constitutes the "beholder's share", the skeleton brought in by the perceiver to assimilate the detailed information so generously offered by the perceptual world. This notion of scheme can be found back in current cognitive science under various names and implementations as e.g. Minsky's concept of *frame* (10). Such views express a cognitive trend in that they suggest that the substantial component in an act of perception is brought in by the subject (in terms of knowledge) while local colour and appearance are brought in by the object (in terms of sensations). However, no details are provided with respect to the mechanism of the interaction between knowledge and sensation. Obviously, the cognitive orientation is superior to the uni-directional causal chain model of crude empiricism. There perception is related to events in the outside world which, according to a kind of domino theory, trigger a series of causal connections ending in an event in the brain associated with the mental state of perception. In the cognitive view, the inward bound chain of causal events is supposed to be met by outward bound schemes embodying expectations so that there are indeed contributions from both subject and object. But again, how are we to conceive of their inter- action? Could we think of the subject as a source of expectations irradiating schemes in all directions while bombarded from all sides with data and should we reduce genuine perception to those happy collisions where data fit ex- pectations? Even if the collision model would seem plausible, it does not contribute substantially to our understanding of the perception of ambiguous figures. In that respect, a finding of Leeper (11) is highly significant. Using Boring's *young girl—old woman*, Leeper found that conceptually induced expectations were not very effective in orienting perception towards a specific interpretation of the ambiguous picture. Even when the experimentalist tells his subject to look for a young woman, the subject might hit upon the old woman interpretation and remain temporarily unable to find any other possibility. How then do perceptual data and conceptual entities interlock? A more subtle model is needed than just a scheme to be augmented with detail.

The New Perceptual Elements

The notion of point-like sense-data as the micro-units of perception has been criticized from several sides. Gombrich does away with it as the untenable *mosaic* approach, however without providing a clear and workable alternative. Like the gestalt psychologists, Gibson, for several decades the most acute student of perception, rejected these units of analysis already in his 1950- book as "nothing but geometric fictions" and "sensory elements" that "could never be specified" (12). In his more recent publications and especially in his new book *The Ecological Approach to Visual Perception* (13), one of the major units of analysis is the "ambient optic array" which is in all respects, the antipode of the isolated sensation. We discuss the perception of objects as if the *figure-ground* separation is an automatic and unproblematic achievement of our perceptual system. But it is as much a challenge to explain how an object is identified and separated out of the enormous complexity of a visual array as it is to construct an object from elementary sensations. The new approach which we discuss in this paper is compatible with the array-approach and leans on what Gibson discusses as the principle of nesting, in particular nested visual angles.

In order to appreciate the new ideas about visual perception, it is instructive to review the recent history of pattern recognition and picture processing in AI.

In a very orthodox empiricist way, computer picture processing started with the mosaic model that turns out to be so misleading. In fact, our current T.V. sets still operate on that basis. Scenes are recorded by means of a camera and the recorded picture is projected on a grid-like structure. There the image is decomposed into a huge number of matrix cells which register in terms of a single value the recorded intensity of light for that particular cell. Images are reconstructed by reproducing the light intensity corresponding to the registered value in a similar matrix element. As with photographs, the quality of the reconstruction is considered directly related to the size of these granular elements. The finer the grain, the more precise the image. However, perception is not the encoding and reconstruction of images and developments in AI have shown that low level of resolution information is as important as high level of resolution information. Lipkin and Rosenfeld's collection on picture processing (14) distinguishes between three classes of relevant variables: contrast and border, shape and geometry, and texture. Roughly, these variables correspond to three different levels of resolution and/or visual angle. The psychologist Palmer (15) has in line with AI experience, convincingly demonstrated that object perception involves a combination of such levels.

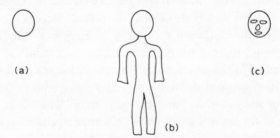

Fig. 2. Apparently meaningless forms such as (a) acquire a quite definite interpretation when embedded in a larger figure as in (b) or when filled in with details as in (c) (after Palmer, 1975).

Take an elliptical structure as exemplified in Figure 2(a). In principle, it can represent a variety of objects with that kind of outline, e.g. a boulder, an egg, a head, a kind of fruit. However, if it is joined to the shape indicated in Figure 2(b), ambiguity disappears and it clearly becomes the representation of a head. The same occurs however when the elliptical form is filled in with the kind of detail indicated in Figure 2(c). On its own, each of the forms involved is highly ambiguous and abstract. Used in combination, specifying entities at different visual angles, they allow for the straightforward identification of an object. Palmer (16) has generalized this scheme in terms of three levels of units involved in the pictorial representation of objects:

– the *whole* figure specified in terms of a closed edge or outline;

– the multisegment *parts* specified in terms of internal contours or edges;

– the individual line segments specified in terms of texture, i.e. the uniform granular aspect of surfaces.

According to this scheme, each object can be seen as a concatenation of forms related in terms of part-whole relationships which are of a conceptual nature. Triggered by some particular features suggesting a specific local interpretation at some level, recognition can be thought of as extending along a conceptual ladder in order to generate specific expectations at another level. If some dots and dashes in a confusing picture suggest two eyes and a nose, we should look out for the circular shape of the head at a more global level and the texture or colour (17) of skin at a more detailed level. Let us illustrate this process for an ambiguous figure so that we can explore how it could illuminate gestalt switch as well as gestalt perception.

Data-driven and Concept-driven Processes in Gestalt Perception

Consider the drawing used by Fischer (18) (see Figure 3). It represents the face of a man or a sitting girl. Depending on what forms are extracted as most salient, a partial interpretation of either the outline or an internal part or some textural element (e.g. the hair) or a combination of some of these activates a semantic network. This is a system of concepts represented by nodes which are linked by means of labeled, i.e. specific relations. The semantic network for face contains as nodes *face, eyes, nose, mouth, ears, hair*, etc., and these are linked in terms of part-whole relationships. Eyes are part of a face, so are ears, nose, etc ... The semantic network for *mouth* contains as parts *lips, teeth, tongue* .... In short, the semantic representation contains, in terms of a hierarchical tree, the conceptual decomposition which we mention while discussing the empiricist model of perception. One or more particular forms activate some of the nodes at some level in this hierarchy and further exploration is then guided by upward and downward exploration within that conceptual hierarchy. In the older empiricist language it could be phrased as follows: When a particular form suggest the idea of a mouth, this idea, being part of a network of knowledge elements, suggests the idea of a face as a superordinated unit and the idea of teeth as a subordinated unit. Since each of these ideas is supposed to have some pictorial form(s) associated with it, in addition to its links with other nodes, ideas or concepts, it can provide concrete suggestions for perceptual search (19). When I have tentatively interpreted some forms as eyes, nose and mouth, an elliptical shape of a certain size should indicate the boundary of a head and I may actively look for it. Four types of subprocesses combine in this activity. Some abstract perceptual forms in certain configurations trigger conceptual nodes somewhere in a semantic network. They might be called *data driven*, since they originate, in principle, in the data, events in the outside world. Within the conceptual system of the semantic network, explorative processes might develop from part to whole, i.e. *bottom up* or from whole to part, i.e. *top down*. Finally, the nodes thus activated generate mental image like elements, *concept driven* production of forms that orient search for additional data in a precise and specific way. The final "percept" contains both concept driven (knowledge based) entities and data driven entities so that knowledge and data interlock and constitute together a "solid" object.

There are several intriguing aspects to this new way of looking at perception. One is that it dissolves the old riddle of Gestalt psychology that "the whole is more than the sum of the parts". That riddle can only arise within an approach that requires the seeing of parts in order to see a whole. In the new approach, the whole is accessible to perception independently of the perception of parts. One can discriminate the elliptical outline of a head without recognizing some smaller entities as parts of a face. In this sense, the whole is indeed more than the sum of its parts because the whole is an additional part with its own perceptual representation. Confusion arises from conflating two senses of "whole", a perceptual sense and a conceptual sense. The second sense of "whole" is the transversal connection between several

Fig. 3. Fischer's man-girl figure.
Triggered by data-driven identification of either a global shape and/or some internal
edge(s), contour(s) or texture(s), a conceptual framework is activated that allows
for the generation of concept driven expectations by means of bottom up and top
down conceptual processes. Arrows pointing from figure to labels are meant
to give examples of data-driven linkings between forms and concepts. Arrows
pointing from the label to the figure indicate concept driven links whereby
specific 'figural' expectations are derived from an activated conceptual node.

levels of analysis which is achieved, as we have illustrated, by means of a
conceptual network. Seeing the whole in that second sense comes down to
knowing the part-whole connections between perceptual forms at various
levels of analysis (at various visual angles, various levels of resolution).

It should be clear that we have now sketched an *interactive* theory of
perception which is superior to the collision model suggested by the cognitive
approach. Both expectations and data can be expressed in the same language
of forms so that an object of perception is built up of entities that dovetail
rather than collide. In its layered structure, data driven and concept driven
forms combine into a whole held together by a conceptual hierarchy of
functional relationships. It might seem far-fetched to invoke this conceptual
knowledge as 'theory' penetrating perception in the case of our daily objects
and the simple drawings which compose the ambiguous figures. However, in its
application to genuine cases of scientific observation, such an interpretation
of the new scheme does not seem improper. In an analysis of Harvey's discovery of the circulation of the blood we will try to indicate how it could
apply to both cases of minute description and brilliantly wide vision.

Galen and Harvey, Two Keen Observers

In line with the positivist image of science, Harvey's discovery of the circula-

tion of the blood (1628) is usually depicted as one of the most typical victories of the scientific method over medieval speculation (20). It is presented
as if all that was needed was someone who looked more carefully and systematically at the facts than at the books of predecessors in order to disclose
the truth. However, when reading Galen (129—199), the creator of the
rival model of the vascular system for more than fourteen centuries, one is
confronted with an author who is a strong defender of careful observation. In
refering to his emphasis on sense perception in science, N. W. Gilbert calls
Galen's doctrine of science "an astonishingly modern doctrine of logical
empiricism" (21)! From the pages of Galen's descriptions, one retains the
conviction of reading an author with great skill in anatomy and an enormous
practical experience. Graubard rightly rejects observational ability as a
criterion to distinguish Galen from Harvey and argues for a psychological
approach which seeks "to determine how brilliant minds operate" (22), both
Galen's and Harvey's.

Another trait, in addition to dedication to observation, which Galen and
Harvey have in common, is their need for an adversary position to push off
against. For Galen, the opponent is Erasistratus whom he blames for making
"rash assertions without observing" (23). Harvey, more careful and understanding that "habit or doctrine once absorbed . . . become second nature" is
convinced to surpass Galen. Though both are keen observers, the conceptual
scheme of an opponent has apparently been a major device for orientation and
direction in a complex area. Obviously the intriguing question is: how can such
a scheme that has been instrumental in seeing be overthrown by new observations? Where do the latter come from and how can they upset the scheme?

However, before we consider whether Harvey's discovery can be looked
upon as a gestalt switch, we should inquire whether it is legitimate to see
Galen's and Harvey's descriptions of the vascular system as related in terms
of the duck and the rabbit of our celebrated example.

Angiological Duck and Rabbit

The gist of our argument has been that perception involves the use of perceptual forms selected at various levels of resolution which are combined and
hold together by a conceptual network. To illustrate the potential use of this
conception for an analysis of observation in science, we should be able to

indicate how particular perceptual forms retained from observation at various levels combine with specific conceptual systems to yield the type of integrated view that also typifies the seeing of an object.

Anyone who has ever been obliged to put to practice his anatomical knowledge drawn from books and pictures knows how bewildering reality can be in comparison to the clear and simple schemes of the books. Both Galen's and Harvey's model are attempts to arrive at a clear picture of the complicated system of organs and tubes which we now know as the respiratory and circulatory systems but which to an apprentice anatomist should be comparable to the meaningless patchwork of black and white blotches that characterizes a first confrontation with pictures such as Porter's hidden man or R. C. James' dog (24).

Galen's model is characterized by a distinction between a system for alimentation (the veins) and a system for ventilation (the arteries). The introduction of a ventilation system based on blood — arterial blood — is a feature of Galen's system which distinguishes it from others which considered arteries to be comparable to the trachea filled with air or spirit. He rejects a classification of arteries as windpipes though retains a ventilation function through aerated blood. At various levels, Galen can claim clear perceptual indicators to justify his conceptual distinctions:

— venous blood differs from arterial blood in colour and viscosity; venous blood is blueish red and thick, arterial blood is highly red and thin and vaporous;

— veins differs from arteries; arteries are harder, have a coating differing from the coating of veins and can be up to five times thicker; furthermore arteries are distinguished from veins by their pulsation which Galen considers their prominent feature;

— both systems seem to have their own major organ: the position and the connection of the portal vein with respect to the liver is comparable to the relationship between the aorta and the heart;

— pulsation as a rhythmic alternation of inhalation and evacuation is a feature of both the respiratory system and the arterial system. It is noticed at the level of arteries, the heart, and the lungs and becomes a major organizational principle in Galen's model apparently allowing him to make the connection between the two systems. It is often referred to in terms of the so called *tidal* model with an ebb and flow rhythm.

A major anomaly which Galen struggles at pains to explain away is the structure of pulmonary vessels. In a scheme that considers venous blood as alimentation produced in the liver and distributed through the veins, the arterial structure of the vessel that connects the right ventricle to the lungs (the pulmonary artery) is at odds with the fact that it contains venous blood. The introduction of an arterial vein (pulmonary artery) and a venous artery (pulmonary vein) is the major weakness in the Galenic model.

Obviously, there are many more important aspects to Galen's description but we need not to consider them here. Our only claim is that his model can be seen as a conceptual system which combines perceptual features withheld from the study of some tubular parts of the body at various levels of analysis into a unitary view.

Confronted with the same tangle of tubes, Harvey arrives at another picture. He too can claim clear perceptual indicators to justify his conceptual distinctions:

— venous valves suggest a centripetal rather than a centrifugal blood flow;

— ligatures of the veins show an emptying between the ligature and the heart while in arteries the opposite is true: swelling occurs between the ligature and the heart;

— contrary to Galen's description, the active moment of the heart is the contraction and not the expansion; rather than sucking in blood, the heart propels it away;

— the total quantity of blood is apparently fixed and from the amount pumped away at each contraction of the heart, one has to infer that it moves around in a circle.

Many more ingenious and subtle observations can be found in Harvey's work, but the ones we have retained are among the most important. Notice how again, they specify perceptible attributes at various levels of aggregation: valves as parts of the veins, the level of the vessels, the level of the heart, some perceptually specifiable attributes of the overall system: the total amount of blood in an organism.

Presented in this schematic way, both Harvey's and Galen's model for the vascular system qualify as integrated conceptual entities which relate in a functional way subparts, parts and wholes which have each at their own level, perceptually accessible forms. In that sense, they might seem to relate as the rabbit and duck of the famous ambiguous figure. However, such schematized presentations are to scientific observation what pictures are to "real" perception. And as Gibson indicates, we should beware of taking the reading of pictures as representative of the observation of a real scene or object. Even under poor perceptual conditions few people will confuse real rabbits with real ducks. In contrast to cartoon-type drawings, real objects allow for a "closer look" which means that additional levels of analysis are accessible and can be added or interposed. Do such "closer looks" account for the dynamics of one scheme into another?

Origin of Gestalt Switch: New Theory or New Data?

A conceptual scheme offers the possibility of seeing unity and coherence in an otherwise puzzling multitude of perceptual forms. In the way we have presented them, both Galen's and Harvey's allow for the interactive kind of perceptual process we dealt with above. However, when dealing with science the challenge apparently is to explain either how observations give rise to *new* expectations or how expectations give rise to *new* observations. How and why was the one system abandoned and replaced with the other? The case of Harvey is interesting in that several alternatives have been documented for locating the origin of his discovery ranging from the observation of an apparently minor detail to purely speculative general ideas (25).

It can be argued that first the new idea arose, a concept that had to be elaborated "downward" to the level of observation in disregard of the perceptual attributes used in the accepted scheme. It is indeed obvious that Harvey ignores or minimizes the relevance of some of the observable differences exploited by Galen. He ignores the difference between venous and arterial blood. He argues against emphasizing the difference between arteries and veins: "in many creatures, . . . , a vein does not differ from an artery by the thickness of its coat" (26). Where Galen sees two major organs, the heart and the liver, each governing their own subsystem, Harvey sees but one. He describes the heart as "the first principle of life and the sun of the microcosm, just as the sun deserves equally to be called the heart of the world" (27). One could argue that it is a conviction of this kind, a general idea about the central role of the heart and the unity of the blood, that set off Harvey's revolt against the Galenic view. Such ideas, including the high esteem for circular motion as the main force of the cosmos at large are, according to Pagel, entirely compatible with Harvey's admiration and adherence to Aristotelian notions. Pagel, who has done some of the major studies on Harvey, would consider these as "philosophical, mystical or religious 'side-steps' of otherwise 'sound' scientific workers" and he sees it as the task of the historian "to uncover the internal reason and justification for their presence in the mind of the savant and their organic coherence with his scientific ideas" (28). But if such ideas are at the origin of Harvey's innovation, the problem is not so much whether they are scientific or not. The problem is to see how they can guide observation.

According to Harvey's own account of his discovery as reported to Boyle at some time, it was the observation of the venous valves that made him rethink the whole of the vascular system. Whitteridge (29) has considered this a crucial element for the construction of an interpretation that stresses "observation" rather than "ideas". This could equally be made a nice illustration of another type of "external" (30) factor: a teacher-pupil relationship. During his stay at the major medical school of his time, the university of Padua, Harvey studied with Fabricius, the discoverer of the venous valves. This biographical element could be a sufficient reason for providing to this particular observation a special and prominent status in Harvey's mind. But again, if this is the spark, what did it set in motion? Why should one develop the need to overturn the Galenic system by scrutinizing the venous valves?

It should be clear that as long as it is phrased in terms of *either* ideas *or* observations which set a discovery on its way, the question remains puzzling. Observations and concepts interact all the time and cannot be taken apart, neither in the course of scientific investigation nor in the case of simple object perception. Pagel is well aware of this in his general appraisal of possible origins for Harvey's discovery:

> . . . we cannot separate the single 'spark', in his case the venous valves, from the tangle of ideas which seem indissolubly bound up with it and form the complex background of his discovery. Nor would it be easy to say which came first: idea or observation, or even philosophy or observation, . . . there is support for the view that indeed the idea came first. Harvey had been a staunch Aristotelian all the time – by up-bringing as well as by inclination. Perhaps this and all that it had taught him about the heart and the blood *influenced the way in which he looked upon the venous valves* (30) (italics added).

This is the challenge and this is what the new model of perception should achieve: to determine how general ideas influence the way one looks at specific objects.

In a later treatment of the subject, Pagel unambiguously opts for the primacy of the *idea* explicitly stating "that the discovery was at first an *idea* which called for the provision of evidence in order to be proved and demonstrated rather than a conclusion drawn from evidence already available 'en masse'" (32). In his conclusions, he uses the term "a 'hunch' or idea that formed the challenge to produce such evidence *de novo*" (33).

Besides some indirect support for such confusing notions as that ideas are general and of a wide range while observations are small and needed in great number before they count, these statements do not explain very much. Where does a hunch come from? Are no observations involved in its construction? And once it has been installed, how does it control the search for evidence, how is it transformed into specific expectations? Somewhat surprisingly, in the same monograph (34) Pagel seems to approve of Bylebyl's *two-step-model* although the latter seems to allow for a more subtle analysis of the commerce between observation and ideas.

Gestalt Switch in Two Steps

According to Bylebyl (35), Harvey's celebrated monograph *An Anatomical Disputation concerning the Movement of the Heart and Blood in Living Creatures* (1628) has been written in two quite distinct phases. The part on the motion of the heart and arteries should be considered as written years before the part on the movement of the blood. Harvey first developed his theory on the movements of the heart as an extension of the old view, i.e. an augmented Galenic scheme to which Harvey, in a sense, thought to contribute by making local corrections and adding detail. The conspicious "detail" he thereby noticed was the substantial amounts of blood necessarily transmitted by the heart within even relatively short periods of time. Once it was abundantly clear for him that the blood *moves*, that it moves fast and massively, this movement became something Harvey felt he had to account for. The discovery of the *movement* of the blood as a consequence of the movement of the heart is *phase one*, not necessarily incompatible with the older scheme though generating very serious questions. *Phase two* is the disclosure of *circulation*, the discovery that the blood moves in a circle, a revolutionary new idea. The crucial step in arriving at this idea is apparently a conceptual jump. Here the Bylebyl-model can be connected to Pagel's who emphasizes Harvey's sympathies for Aristotelian concepts in which circular movement is considered the ideal type of movement containing both preservation and change.

On a global scale, the two-step-model of Bylebyl is compatible with the gestalt switch associated with ambiguous figures. It would however oversimplify issues to look upon the first stage as observational, largely "data-driven" and the second stage as theoretical or "concept-driven". On the level of details, the interactive mode of perception seems to apply in stage one in the same way as in stage two. Bylebyl's account does not separate the "data" from the "ideas" in any specific way. What are we to conclude from this?

Conclusions

Unlike the simple line-drawings of tricky figures, which offer a very restricted number of levels of analysis, the objects of observation in anatomy offer opportunities for analyses at many levels. Between Galen and Harvey, several discoveries have been made which modified and corrected the Galenic view substantially. Nevertheless, although these discoveries resulted in important local revisions, they have not led to a global reorganization of the view on the vascular system. It required Harvey to reconsider the consequences of the movements of the heart, in order to arrive at the idea of a revolutionary reorganization at the global level. Abstracting from the preparatory discoveries by others, Bylebyl's two-step-model for Harvey's discovery corresponds to the two-step-model for gestalt switch exemplified in the celebrated figures. Observations at some particular levels suggest a local reinterpretation which upsets the conceptual system in such a way that global reorganization results from it.

It would however be totally inappropriate to consider local reinterpretations as purely observational while taking the global reorganization as purely theoretical. The observations expressing Harvey's understanding of the heart are of the same nature as those expressing his discovery of circulation. In each case we find the same integrative and interactive perceptual process whereby a perceived object is constructed as an amalgam of forms whose coherence depends on a conceptual network that specifies their relationships. The major difference is that the first one remains at an intermediate level within the conceptual network while the second one expresses a reorganization of the network at top-level. But still the basic question remains, how do new observations arise in the old schemes?

Only one answer seems plausible for confronting this question: new observations are imported from other, apparently unrelated areas. On the level of the global reorganization, we have already mentioned the Aristotelian concepts on the perfection of circular movement. That this is an "imported" conceptual network can be argued on the basis of Pagel's remark that Harvey should be considered "a kind of split mind" or "a dweller in two worlds" (36). One world is an Aristotelian one, the other is the world of modern anatomy. However, also on the intermediate level and the level of detail "external" schemes intrude and lead into less spectacular but not less important changes. As we have indicated, the heart in the system of Galen is a different object form the heart in the system of Harvey. In Galen it is like bellows, drawing in blood in a way similar to and coupled to the way in which the lungs draw in air. In Harvey, it is a pump-type organ which actively propels blood through the vascular system. As far as the pump-analogy has influenced Harvey's perception (37) it is equally a scheme imported from yet another conceptual realm. Analogies like this one seem particular apt to express a newly observed relationship between two levels of analysis. Notice that with respect to the central insight of the circle, Harvey points to the inspiring analogy of the vapour-rain-water-cycle. Without exploring whether the analogy is only a way of expressing a newly discovered relationship or also an important instrument in finding it, we should recognize its capacity to function as a vehicle for importing new local conceptual schemes from areas outside the guiding conceptual framework. Though, considered that way, new schemes can only enter piecemeal, they can enter, in principle, at many levels. This implies an unexpected openness of scientific theories.

The major shift brought about by recognizing the hierarchical dimension in perception of simple objects is the abolishment of the notion of "solid soil of observation". Perceptual entities can penetrate conceptual pyramids at many levels. It seems indicated to think in terms of a continuum between vision as encountered in the perception of objects and creative vision as expressed in scientific innovations. With the removal of a "solid soil", the metaphor of founding scientific theories on the rock bottom of observation becomes empty. If a new metaphor is needed, the notion of *ventilation* could replace the notion of *foundation*. It would emphasize that observation enters our conceptual edifices at several floors simultaneously. Though our analysis might seem predominantly involved with problems in psychology of science, it is not without consequences for sociology of science issues.

The openness for observations at many levels means also an openness at these levels for fragments of conceptual schemes from foreign areas, whether from other areas of science, or technology, or down to earth daily routines. As we have seen in studies on Harvey, his new vision on the global system might stem from his Aristotelian background, his view on the heart couples to a technological device such as a pump and the valves in the veins are seen as flood-gates. Even casual observation of a meaningless action such as blowing in a glove can harbour the seed of innovation as is manifest from Harvey's observation of the pulse in arteries. These are all observations that originate in schemes that are *external* to the dominating conceptual network of the scientific discipline. They constitute so many apparently innocent but nevertheless efficient entries for letting in the *new*.

Illustrating the creeping way in which new observations penetrate into the old conceptual network, the scheme we have explored allows a new analysis of the intertwining of (partly redefined) internal and external factors. Obviously, many questions remain. One of the most intriguing ones is why a scientist is looking for the new. Why would an observer with a Galenic outlook on the vascular system feel inclined to improve upon the scheme? Why first extend it and later on reorganize it? From where this unsatisfiable need to improve upon what one has? Though this is a most basic question pertaining to the equilibruim and the dynamics of conceptual systems, it is beyond the scope of this analysis on the relationship between theory and data (38).

Notes and References

1. M. J. Mulkay, *Science and the Sociology of Knowledge*, Allen and Unwin, London, 1979, pp. 27–49.
2. A. Shimony, 'Is Observation Theory-Laden? A Problem in Naturalistic Epistemology', in R. G. Colodny (ed.), *Logic, Laws and Life*, University of Pittsburgh Press, Pittsburgh, 1977.

3. H. Feigl, 'The 'Orthodox' View of Theories: Remarks in Defense as well as Critique', in Radner and Winokur, *Minnesota Studies in the Philosophy of Science, Vol. IV*, Univ. of Minnesota Press, Minneapolis, 1970.

4. Einstein quoted in W. Heisenberg, *Physics and Beyond*, Allen and Unwin, London, 1971, p. 63.

5. L. A. Necker, 'Observations on an apparent change of position in a drawing or engraved figure of a crystal, an optical phenomena which occurs on viewing a figure of a crystal or geometrical solid', *Philosophical Magazine* 1, 329–337 (1832). Excerpt in W. N. Dember, *Visual Perception: The Nineteenth Century*, Wiley, New York, 1964, pp. 78–80.

6. T. S. Kuhn, *The Structure of Scientific Revolutions*, University of Chicago Press, Chicago, 1962, p. 110.

7. E. H. Gombrich, *Art an Illusion: A Study in the Psychology of Pictorial Representation*, Phaidon, London, 1977[5].

8. *ibid.*, p. 198.

9. F. C. Bartlett, *Remembering: A Study in Experimental and Social Psychology*, Cambridge Univ. Press, Cambridge, 1967[5].

10. M. Minsky, 'A Framework for Representing Knowledge'. In P. H. Winston (ed.), *The Psychology of Computer Vision*, McGraw-Hill, New York, 1975, pp. 211–277.

11. R. W. Leeper, 'A Study of a Neglected Portion of the Field of Learning – the Development of Sensory Organization', *Journal Genetic Psychology* 46, 41–75 (1935).

12. J. J. Gibson, *The Perception of the Visual World*, Houghton Mifflin, Boston, 1950.

13. J. J. Gibson, *The Ecological Approach to Visual Perception*, Houghton Mifflin, Boston, 1979.

14. B. S. Lipkin and A. Rosenfeld (eds.), *Picture Processing and Psychopictorics*, Academic Press, New York, 1970.

15. S. E. Palmer, 'Visual Perception and Knowledge: Notes on a Modal of Sensory-cognitive Interaction', in D. A. Norman and D. E. Rumelhart, *et al., Explorations in Cognition*, Freeman, San Francisco, 1975.

16. S. E. Palmer, 'Hierarchical Structure in Perceptual Representation', *Cognitive Psychology* 9, 441–474 (1977).

17. In this new approach, the recurrent element at each level is *shape*: contour as shape of the whole, internal contours as shapes of parts, texture as revealing the shape of micro-parts. Colour fits into this hierarchy too when considered a limit case of texture.

18. G. H. Fischer, 'Ambiguity of Form: Old and New', *Perception and Psychophysics* 4, 189–192 (1968).

19. With respect to systems for the representation of knowledge, the idea is to have links to pictorial elements at several conceptual levels and nodes in the semantic network, somewhat along the line suggested by A. L. Glass, K. J. Holyoak, *et al., Cognition*, Addison-Wesley, Reading, 1979, p. 21. However, where they put complete pictures into the semantic network, we would emphasize more simple and elementary shapes. It is a central theme of R. Arnheim, *Visual Thinking*, University of California Press, Berkeley, 1971[3], that visual representations – pictures – are made up by means of a restricted number of elementary shapes: circles, ovals, straight lines, arches, angles, rectangles. Following Pestallozzi, he considers these

elements as constituting the *alphabet* of the *shape* of objects. Pictures are like words or sentences written in circles, rectangles and arches. Ignoring aspects of size, it is indeed surprising to realize how the great variety of shapes that we know can be reconstructed with so few elements. And when size is taken into account, it is surprising to realize how flexible the system is. A few dashes or dots within a circle make. up a face. Perception can cope with a wide variety of distortions: tilted ovals, alongated ones, flattened ones .... They are all handled as different tokens of the same type, just as the widely differing handwritten forms of a character represent one single type. Apparently, there are standard perceptual representations constructed out of a limited number of pictorial elements depicting the structure of objects along two or more levels of a conceptual hierarchy.

20. See, for example, M. Kirchner, *William Harveys Verdienste um die Entdeckung des Blutkreislaufs*, Schade, Berlin, 1878, p. 6.

> Mit Harvey begann eine neue Art zu forschen. An Stelle aprioristischer Speculation trat Beobachtung und Experiment, an Stelle blindgläubiger Teleologie die mechanische Erklärung.

21. N. W. Gilbert, 'Galen'. In P. Edwards, *The Encyclopedia of Philosophy*, Vol. 3, Macmillan, New York, 1972[2], pp. 261–262.

22. M. Graubard, *Circulation and Respiration: The Evolution of an Idea*, Harcourt, Brace and World, New York, 1964, p. 56.

23. If not otherwise indicated, quotations from Galen stem from the selections in Graubard, *op. cit.*

24. P. B. Porter, 'Another Puzzle Picture', *American Journal of Psychology* 67, 550–551 (1954). The photograph by R. C. James can be found in P. H. Lindsay and D. A. Norman, *Human Information Processing. An Introduction to Psychology*, Academic Press, New York, 1977[2], p. 12.

25. As a major source with respect to Harvey's discovery and the various theories offered to explain it, we have used W. Pagel, *William Harvey's Biological Ideas: Selected Aspects and Historical Background*, Karger, Basel, 1967, W. Pagel, *New Light on William Harvey*, Karger, Basel, 1976, J. J. Bylebyl (ed.), *William Harvey and His Age*. John Hopkins University Press, Baltimore, 1979.

26. W. Harvey, *An Anatomical Disputation concerning the Movement of the Heart and Blood in Living Creatures*, trans. with introduction and notes by Gweneth Whitteridge, Blackwell, Oxford, 1976, p. 76.

27. *Ibid.*, p. 76.

28. Pagel, *op. cit.*, 1967, p. 82.

29. G. Whitteridge, in W. Harvey, *op. cit.*, introd., xxvii–li.

30. The first type of external factors mentioned are what Pagel calls "philosophical, mystical or religious 'side-steps'".

31. Pagel, *op. cit.*, 1967, 210.

32. Pagel, *New Light on William Harvey*, Karger, Basel, 1976, p. 5.

33. Pagel, *op. cit.*, 1976, p. 172.

34. Pagel, *op. cit.*, 1976.

35. With respect to Bylebyl's theory, see Bylebyl, 'The growth of Harvey's De Motu Cordis', *Bull. Hist. Med* 47, 427–470 (1973). Also Bylebyl, 'William Harvey'. In Gillespie (ed.), *Dictionary of Scientific Biography, Vol. IV*, 1973, pp. 150–162,

and Bylebyl, 'The medical side of Harvey's discovery: the normal and the abnormal', in Bylebyl (ed.), *op. cit.*, 1979, pp. 28–102.

36. Pagel, *op. cit.*, 1976, p. 1.
37. The importance of the scheme of "pump" in Harvey's discovery cannot be considered as established. According to Pagel, the reference made to it by Harvey "occurs more as an aside than as an idea of principal importance", Pagel, *William Harvey's Biological Ideas*, Karger, Basel, 1967, p. 80.
38. Parts of this paper have been presented at the 'International Conference on Knowledge and Representation' held at NIAS (Netherlands Institute for Advanced Studies) Wassenaar, Netherlands, March 8–10, 1979 and at the conference on 'Social Process of Scientific Investigation' held at ZIF (Zentrum für Interdisziplinäre Forschung), Universität Bielefeld, June 17–19, 1979.

Though many improvements have resulted from suggestions and remarks made at both meetings, not all important comments have been dealt with in the reworked version. For a more extensive treatment of the topic and complete acknowledgements, see M. T. M. De Mey, *The Cognitive Paradigm*, Harvester Press, Brighton, in preparation.

THE SCIENTIST AS AN ANALOGICAL REASONER: A CRITIQUE OF THE METAPHOR THEORY OF INNOVATION

KARIN D. KNORR

University of Pennsylvania

Summary

Recent, well-known explorations of the role of models in science suggest a theory of scientific innovation which links innovation to a creative extension of knowledge brought about by the invokation of a metaphor. At the same time, concrete evidence about actual procedures of scientific investigation have for the first time become available from anthropological observation studies of scientific laboratories. This paper draws upon one year of observations done in 1976–77 in a group working on chemical, microbiological, toxicological and technological aspects of plant proteins and plant protein generation at a research institute employing more than 300 scientists in Berkeley, Ca. and upon interviews done with scientists of various other groups at the same institute. The paper attempts to reconsider the role of metaphor in the light of the observer's account of the research process in the laboratory, and in the light of the scientists' accounts of research efforts they considered innovative. Both the scientists' and the observer's account suggest that reference to metaphor needs to be extended to include, in accordance with some earlier conceptual investigations, the more general phenomenon of analogical reasoning. At the same time they suggest that the metaphor- or analogy-theory needs to be restricted in its claim to account for innovation, and that innovation must be linked to the active constructions of the process of production and reproduction of research.

1. The Metaphor-Theory of Innovation

It is probably no exaggeration to say that the question of scientific innovation

Karin D. Knorr, Roger Krohn and Richard Whitley (eds.), The Social Process of Scientific Investigation. Sociology of the Sciences, Volume IV, 1980. 25–52.
Copyright © 1980 by D. Reidel Publishing Company.

has in the past received most attention in a host of issues relevant to the process of scientific investigation: the 'context of discovery' is considered significant mainly in as far as it produces scientific innovation and much ignored with respect to anything else. The collection of papers brought together in this volume illustrates the narrow-mindedness of such a conception. Yet the data we have now on the process of scientific investigation also allow us to reconsider the question of scientific innovation. In recent years, the most relevant and illuminative account of scientific innovation has been given by the metaphor-theory of innovation. In the following, I will discuss the metaphor-theory of innovation in the light of material which comes from the direct observation of and talk to scientists at work. Rather than to start from a product which is a declared scientific innovation and to search for its explanation, we will look at the process of production from which 'scientific innovation' emerges. In contrast to the question of discovery acceptance treated in Section 2, the focus here will be on discovery accounts which are given by the scientists as well as by the observer of scientific investigation. While other papers in this section emphasize the cognitive-perceptual basis of such accounts, their formal organization, or the situational logic of the underlying process, my interest here is in the dynamics of research as implied by what we will hear. The question of scientific innovation has mainly been conceived of as a question of the origin of ideas. It is the purpose of this paper to link scientific innovation to the process of research production. I will begin with a discussion of the metaphor theory of innovation.

Imagine a bag-lunch in a small laboratory connected with a scientist's office room. Two scientists chat about the progress of the protein work, and one takes his protein samples from the shelf and shows them to the other. The first scientist had just told his colleague that he did not know how to account for the different volumes they had obtained in a series of experiments on proteins exposed to different degrees of temperature. The other says that the hardness of the protein particles might be a relevant factor there, and continues to elaborate about particle size and particle behaviour. The first scientist turns the 'worst'-looking sample in his hands as if closely inspecting it: "Well, this protein really looks just like sand!" he responds.

Similes such as the above have found some attention in recent literature because of the role which is attributed to them in scientific innovation. "If the protein looks like sand" the scientist in charge of the samples went on to reason, "it must be denatured. If it is denatured, it's effect will be to dilute the samples, and nothing else. Thus if it does dilute the samples just like sand would, we will have the proof of the 'dilution-theory', in which everybody seems to believe. But if it does not have the same effect as sand, I can finally disprove this crap of dilution, and propose my own interpretation"(1). Three hours later the scientist had dropped whatever he had been doing originally; he had gone to the storage room and found some chemically pure sand; he had set up a 'quick and dirty' experiment designed to compare the behaviour of sand- and protein- samples under heat treatment; and he had almost ruined a blender in which the particles of the sand left unremovable scratches. But he had also built a strong argument for his interpretation, since the behaviour of the sand-diluted samples turned out to be indeed significantly different from that of the protein-diluted samples. To be sure, the results were preliminary because of the quick and dirty character of the test. Yet the comparison between protein and sand eventually led to a new theory of protein additives as well as to an elaborate investigation of protein particle behaviour.

The metaphor theory of innovation assumes that figurative comparisons such as the one between protein and sand are the very source of conceptual innovation (2). Through metaphor, two phenomena or concepts which are usually not associated with each other are suddenly perceived to have some kind of correspondence. Through this intimation of similarity between hitherto unrelated con/cepts or phenomena the systems of knowledge and belief associated with each conceptual object can be brought to bear upon the other conceptual object. This is the source of creative extension of knowledge. The example above is slightly more complicated since the similarity invoked between protein and sand suggested an experimental way to expose a presumed underlying un-similarity between the respective particles with respect to the property of denaturation. Yet it did so by bringing to bear knowledge about the properties of one phenomenon (sand) upon another phenomenon (protein) whose properties were up to investigation. In the literary use of metaphor, the same effect is achieved through the systems of associations which we combine with a conceptual object. In Dante's "hell is a lake of ice" for example (3), the images and ideas we combine with a lake of ice are a source of creative extension of the picture we may have had of hell up to reading the metaphor. This creative extension of ideas is not limited to the conceptual object under consideration; in principle, the image invoked to illuminate this object will also change through an extension of ideas associated with the object. Not only does hell become more like a lake of ice as a result of the similarity classification, but a lake of ice does also become more like hell. Conceptual *interaction* as a basically symmetric relationship is considered to be the core of the metaphor-theory of innovation.

However, conceptual interaction and symmetry of influence do not only characterize metaphoric classifications. They are part of analogical reasoning in general, or of similarity classifications. Analogical reasoning is based upon a logic of resemblance in which the notion of similarity is described as logically basic and primitive: basic in the sense that it is presupposed from the very beginnings of language learning onwards, and primitive in the sense of its apparent irreducibility to analytic criteria (4). It appears that metaphoric classification can best be differentiated from other kinds of analogical reasoning by the degree of *distance* or independence between the two conceptual systems brought together through similarity classification. In the limiting case of 'primary recognition' (5), we can no longer distinguish between the two conceptual systems. Primary recognition refers to our seeing something as something, that is to the recognition of differential segments of our natural and social environment by identifying them in our natural language or in a professional idiolect. Our scientist's remark "the stuff has gone white" when he looked at his protein samples is an example from the laboratory in which a given stimulus is identified as an instance of a certain kind. Note that the definition of primary recognition in terms of similarity gives credit to the 'theory-ladenness' (Feyerabend) of observation (6).

A second form of similarity classification is involved when we 'interpret' a situation or when we 'account' for a phenomenon. For example, the scientist might have said, when he saw the white colour of the samples, that "the protein was precipitated", for it was this interpretation of his recognition that the stuff had gone white upon which he based his further procedures. When we determine that a given situation fits into an interpretation, we are in a sense determining that the current situation is analogous to those situations from which the interpretation was originally derived. In other words, the original situation serves as a kind of paradigm case against which the new situation is matched when we interpret it. More important here, we are apt to make inferences about unobserved aspects of the situation for which we account from the accounting situation. This making of inferences is, in principle, symmetric, since the contexts of association of both the interpreting and the interpreted situation can potentially influence each other. In the laboratory for example, this can be seen when the outcome of a recalcitrant experiment suggests a modification of the covering interpretation which in itself had created the expectations in terms of which the experiment had been conducted. What is important here is that the classifications involved are intended and used in a *literal* way, which means that the observed situation tends to get absorbed in the similarity class applied to it. Despite this tendency toward assimilation, the classified situation retains independency as long as it is independently describable, and so does the interpretation. This becomes obvious when an interpretation is modified, revised or extended. In the above example, the protein was found to be not only precipitated, but also otherwise affected by the means of precipitation used. When no decision is reached between different kinds of interpretation, interpretation is impending, but sustained for the time being. Given the basic independence between an interpretation and the situation it classifies, we can also say that this kind of similarity classification involves a greater distance than primary recognition.

Metaphor can now be seen as the form of similarity classification which involves the greatest distance between the conceptual objects classified as similar, in the sense that it would be absurd or false to take the conjunction proposed *literally*. Primary recognition makes an occurrence recognizable as something. Interpretations classify an occurrence as 'really' an instance of something else. Metaphors classify occurrences as similar, but really *not* the same. In the example cited in the beginning, protein was obviously not considered really to be sand. For the time being, we should add, since a metaphor can become a literal interpretation over time, or for some specific reasons. According to Hesse (7), even primary recognitions do not provide "a stable and independent list of primitive observation predicates". Nor do, of course, interpretative or metaphoric classifications establish a similarity relationship which could not be de-established or changed with respect to the degree of distance it originally implied. Needless to say, much of the scientists' work goes into demonstrating why and to what degree some object is or is not an instance of a certain kind. Similarity relationships are not just perceived; nor are they hidden to be discovered once and for all as seems to be suggested by Koestler (8). The scientists' suddenly recognized similarities include an element of decision and of persuasion, and consequently also of change (9). In that sense, the similarities which underly a metaphor or an analogy are complex rather than primitive, fragile and temporary rather than basic and stable.

Because of their figurative character, metaphors show this perhaps more clearly than literal interpretations. But the important point about metaphor as exemplified in the beginning was not the figurative character of the similarity relationship it established between the objects brought together, but the conceptual interaction and subsequent extension of knowledge to which it led. This conceptual interaction, however, is not limited to the use of metaphor, as indicated before. Rather, conceptual interaction appears to be a routine feature of 'displacements of concepts' in general (10). Conceptual objects are regularly transfered to instances beyond their original range of application. They are displaced to contexts which differ from the situation of their established use. They are extended to problems which are clearly distinguished from those which they have previously solved. It is this difference of some sort which is reflected in distinctive descriptions of the two objects brought together, and it is this difference which is bridged by analogical reasoning. Conceptual interaction emerges from the different universes of knowledge or belief associated with the distinctive descriptions brought together by a presumed similarity. While an analogy needs to be made in order to allow for conceptual interaction, it need not be made in a figurative sense: when two situations or problems become seen to be really similar the knowledge we have of one will be extended to the other, just as it will be in the case of a figurative similarity. In the process of extension, this knowledge regularly becomes modified according to the particularities of the new situation, and the result of this process will transform the interpretation of the original situation.

2. The Scientists' Accounts of Innovation

The argument of the last paragraph suggests that the social scientist's account of innovation in terms of metaphor must be broadened to refer to analogical reasoning in general, since conceptual interaction and the extension of knowledge it breeds cannot be limited to figurative similarity relationships. The argument here is that the scientists' own accounts of innovation display such a broadened perspective, since they link innovation to the making of analogies in a much more general sense than postulated by the metaphor-account of innovation. When scientists were asked to tell the story of the origin of an idea or of a research effort which they considered to be innovative, they regularly displayed themselves as analogical reasoners who built their 'innovative' research upon a perceived similarity between hitherto unrelated problem contexts. Let us consider the story of a biochemist who told me about his work on the isolation of hormones in a mold, a line of research which he traced back to the idea of a colleague that steroids might be involved in the transformation processes which the mold undergoes. The colleague, a biologist (*B*), appeared to be attracted by the problem of the slime mold

She is not the only one who is interested in this mold. Many biologists like this mold because it is a model of differentiation. It changes from an animal to a plant as the result of some hormone stimulation.

B was aware of the fact that steroids are involved in the reproduction of many forms of life. When she became pregnant, it 'occurred' to her that the hormone which stimulated the transformation of the mold and which was unknown at the time might be a steroid

Her original discovery was that when she was pregnant, she used some of her urine (which contains steroids) to stimulate the mold to undergo this conversion. – The idea that steroids are involved in reproduction even in the lowliest forms of life is not new . . . although most biologists still don't accept it. Anyhow, she uh – tried some, and it worked. I mean what happens is very spectacular. These bugs are like amoeba, they crawl around on a plate of agar, and one of them will make a hormone which they call a (inaudible), but the nature of which was unknown at that time. And, when one creature makes this hormone the other creatures congregate. Or collect around this individual. In other words, this substance acts as an attractant. And after they all get together, they undergo this phenomenal transformation from ameboid animal-like creatures to a regular mold, you know . . .

In the laboratory, the isolation of the hormone became complicated by the fact that the attempts to stimulate the mold with pregnancy urine did not work out. According to the biochemist

– it was not a real effect. No one could ever repeat (it). But she had a good hunch that steroids were involved and she had the wrong observations.

Consequently, the biochemist turned to a more direct way of trying to isolate the hormone

So anyhow, she brought this pregnancy urine, and I was working on uh steroid hormones
in urine among other things and I knew how to isolate them and I used my methods, and
what I got out her urine didn't work at all. And I have had some hormones that I had in
the lab in pure form and they didn't work either. And then I had the idea of going to the
mold directly. During that time that this aggregation, this congregation of individuals
takes place there must be more of this hormone present. So I thought that if we, uh, go
to this mold directly and then isolate from it the fraction that is biologically active, that
causes this attraction, we will find out what this hormone is. So we did this, and using
methods that I had developed over the years . . . you have to use fractionation methods,
you know. And in deciding which fraction to keep and which one to throw away you
have to have a bioassay method. So — after your separation you take the individual
fractions and test them and see whether they cause aggregation. And we did that together, and low and behold, one of the fractions had . . . the ability to cause aggregation.
And this happened to be a steroid, and since then some other steroids have been isolated
from all kinds of mold. They also have sex hormone activity. They are not related to the
sex hormone that women have in pregnancy. They are steroids, but they are in a different
class of steroids.

The similarity which underlies the biologist's attempt to stimulate the mold
with the help of pregnancy urine is that between the transformation of the
mold and reproduction in other forms of life. Since the latter often involves
steroids, the biologist had "the good hunch" that steroids would be involved
in the transformation of the mold too. In the scientist's account, the idea
that the unknown hormones could very well be steroids is based upon the
establishment of a similarity between two contexts and the transfer of one
element from one context to another.

The following story shows a similar pattern. It was told by the same
biochemist and involves the group which he supervised

This happened during a time when we already had a small group. And I was interested in
finding out how steroids are synthesized in plants. These are plant steroids, and there are
all kinds of theories on how they are made and nobody really knew. So we were working
away, and doing pretty pedestrian stuff, until one of my colleagues found . . . a lot of
radioactivity incorporated in a particular fraction which was present in such minute
quantities that we couldn't identify the material. But talking among ourselves we came
to the conclusion that it could be cholesterol. There was another man in the group who
was working on unrelated problems and had a similar observation . . . And then they
pooled their resources and, uh, of course mine too and we together came up with the
conclusion that this was cholesterol. And this opened up a whole series of experiments
which culminated in the fact that cholesterol which was up to then considered to be a
real animal product that wasn't even present in plants is actually the substance from
which all plants steroids are made. And this is, uh, very significant, we can now trace
the biosynthesis of plant steroids very easily by administering radioactive cholesterol

and seeing what transformations it has to go through before it becomes one of those many many steroids that occur in plants.

When I asked him how they had arrived at the respective conclusion the scientist said

You see, I had been working on people up to then. And, although it wasn't very clear at the time I started it, it became increasingly evident, during the time – from both my own work and that of other people, that cholesterol in animals and in people is the key substance from which all the other steroids are made.

But it was known at the time that "plants do not contain cholesterol". So there was the discovery by my colleagues that the radioactivity accumulated in a certain fraction ... *The link* (between the observation of accumulated radioactivity and the idea that this was cholesterol) *was that in animals that's what you would expect.* That's what we as well as other people had previously observed. But that the same thing could happen in plants was completely unexpected, because until that time nobody knew that plants even contain cholesterol. (emphasis added)

The observation of accumulated radioactivity in a certain fraction of the plant material together with other aspects of the problem and procedure provided a context similar enough to that of cholesterol-formation in animals to suggest the 'idea' that cholesterol was formed in plants too, despite of the ruling contrary opinion (the attractiveness of the idea derived at least partly from its being in opposition to established beliefs). Thus we have again a report of a transposition of one element from one context to another which displayed itself as sufficiently similar to the original context to suggest and warrant the transfer. The examples above can also be considered from the point of view of the result of the transfer: in both cases, the scientists found an explanation for a phenomenon by assimilating it to known phenomena, that is to the operation of steroids in reproduction and of cholesterol in animals. Other stories of the origin of research results which the scientists held to be innovative did not invoke the context of explanation, yet they implied the same pattern of analogical transfer.

In the following account which is a summary of various comments a scientist had made during the period of observation, an enzymatic procedure is the element transposed. The scientist (*K*) who worked on plant proteins had found a certain plant protein to contain an expectably high amount of toxic solanine. During the later part of my observations, he more or less intentionally ignored the problem, as it had no immediate bearing on the research underway or on projected publications. He remained bothered by it, however, and occasionally talked about the need to eliminate or reduce the solanine. At one point in time, he wondered whether he could not make the elimination of solanine a byproduct of some other, more pressing experiments

He discussed his plan with a colleague (*H*) who had worked on solanine for many years. *H* felt that the method showed no promise of success, but mentioned that his laboratory had recently been successful in eliminating a similar toxic compound from another plant by using an enzymatic procedure, a work which was as yet unpublished.

K immediately picked up on the 'idea' to use *H*'s enzymatic procedure to eliminate the solanine from his proteins

"I think I have the advantage of being the only one who got the message (about the existence and the success of *H*'s enzymatic procedure), and the only one to understand its implications" (for the elimination of solanine). Both scientists deemed it to be highly probable that some equivalent enzymatic procedure would work in the case of *K*'s plant material too. *H* was 'not interested' to do the necessary research himself. He was 'too settled on chromatography and his own projects' according to his colleague. For the latter, *H*'s disinterest appeared as an excellent opportunity not only 'to solve the problem', but also to distinguish himself by exploiting an idea which would otherwise not be used.

Note that when *K* heard about the enzymatic procedure, he immediately responded to it as the key to solving the problem of solanine elimination, despite of the fact that the procedure had been established for a *different* plant and a *different* toxic compound. The contextual similarities between the problem of solanine elimination in *K*'s proteins and the problem for which the procedure had worked out originally were appealing enough to suggest the transfer of the 'idea' of such a method. Naturally, what we called 'transfer' involved modification and adaptation, for example working with different enzymes. It thus required an actual *transformation* of the procedure involved.

There are many more examples of this kind which I encountered during the period of observation

One of the scientists involved in the plant protein generation got a report from the head of his group who had just returned from a visit of several research groups in industrial and nonindustrial settings in different European and American countries. The report mentioned in passing, as the scientist told me, that "the people at NN try to enrich soft drinks with protein and that they found that the protein colour of the samples used became lighter when citric acid was applied in the process". The samples had been sent to them by the head of the group for the respective protein-additive tests.

Since the scientist was interested in obtaining a protein powder which was as light as possible, the idea of using citric acid as a coagulant which would not pollute the proteins appeared promising enough to be tried out immediately in a series of experiments.

Again, both contexts resembled each other to a sufficient degree to warrant the transfer of the procedure, although they involved different proteins, different goals, and a variety of other differences. At an earlier point in time, a similar transfer of a method had given rise to a whole new line of research

The scientist mentioned above was looking for a way to generate large amounts of protein needed for bioassay tests which involved feeding the protein to rats. At one point in time, he happened to read a paper in which the use of ferric chloride was reported as an effective means of precipitation when removing protein from waste water. In general, precipitation of protein which is an important step in protein recovery is done by using heat coagulation methods which involve high temperatures and result in a strongly denatured protein.

In the context of an energy shortage, the use of ferric chloride instead of heat co-agulation appeared as an excellent alternative for protein generation in general: because of the low protein content of the source material, the energy consumption associated with heat coagulation was enormous. Thus by transferring the use of ferric chloride from the context of waste water cleaning to that of protein generation from plants the scientist had solved the problem of generating a sufficiently large amount of protein for the intended bioassay tests. At the same time, he had initiated a new line of research which was based upon the appeal of a low-energy method resulting in a higher quality protein at a time of a generally recognized energy shortage and of an increased quality awareness.

While the last examples illustrate the transfer of a method or procedure from one context to another, the following account refers to the transfer of a kind of solution. The example comes from the food engineering group of the institute in which the observations were done. The group leader told me the story of the origin of one of the group's current research efforts which he considered innovative

As described by the research leader, in sweetcorn processing "corn is cut with a knife, (and in) doing so you make a tremendous amount of effluent during the washing step and you loose all of the flavour of the product". He said that "this is something every-body is aware of (who has) worked in the food industry and seen corn processing plants".

The scientists started to look at this process "as a group upstairs said you guys should be working on a big project". The head whose background is in chemical engineering

continued: "So we said OK, we will show you that we can do a big project . . . (and) we
formed a group and started to look at ways of changing the process completely . . . It is
intuitively obvious that you have to keep the corn kernel intact, because if you break it
open everything is leached out. So we immediately had to go to a process that stripped
the kernel off the cob without damaging the body of the kernel. And . . . we did go to
the literature and found the patents, 1600 or 1700. People had frozen the cob and
broken off the kernel, (there were) a number of cutting techniques, etc . . . R came up
with the idea of splitting the cob in half and then wiping the kernels off with a belt.
Well, they started out with a belt like this and they went through 800 different types
of belts and they finally ended up with a belt made out of (unaudible). So we now have
a technology at least in its infancy that can produce unit kernels. But right after the start
of the project, after the first season we realized that the corn cob itself was designed to
frustrate the removal of kernels by a rolling or plucking action as we called it.

The scientist was well familiar with the type of solution that had played a key
role in mechanical harvesting problems. This familiarity accounts for the
transfer of the solution

In the tomato industry, mechanical harvesting with tomatoes was successful only because
they were able to get a variety that *could* be mechanically harvested. And the thing that
occurred to me to do was to check around − to find out whether there (was) a corn that
is loosely held and that is suitable for mechanical . . . stripping as we were talking about.
I made a few phone calls around the country to people I had worked with in the past
who knew something about sweetcorn. And in two or three calls they directed me to one
of the key corn breeders in the country.

So it turns out that this fellow had been breeding corn for 25 years to get a, . . . a
variety which was very loosely held. It was for fresh market consumption. But it was a
sweetcorn without the little pieces of tissue at the base of the kernels which get stuck
in your teeth. And he had bred corn with two rows, four rows, square cobs. And he pulls
out (this corn) and shows (it to) me, and it is the type of thing when it is at the proper
maturity for processing, the kernels roll right out. (He was just at the point) where he
had increased the seed to where he could go to Florida that winter and grow the first
handful for commercial testing. So we got the first handful and this year we got the first
pound of the seed. We have been able to evaluate it, and indeed it is the type of raw
material that will allow . . . (mechanical) processing.

There is no need to quote further accounts of innovative research in order to
illustrate the kind of analogical reasoning outlined in the beginning. It will
also be clear that there is an extension of knowledge based upon interaction
in the sense of a basically symmetric influence of the instances brought
together in similarity classification. For example, not only did the familiar
operation of steroids in the reproduction of certain forms of life suggest that
steroids might play a role in the unclear situation of the transformation of the

mold, but the knowledge of the hormone itself changed too. It changed to include a series of steroids which were subsequently isolated from all kinds of molds, by the fact that the steroids present in human pregnancy turned out to be not identical with the steriods of the slime mold, and by a variety of other results which emerged from the research. Similar changes occurred with regard to the substance of cholesterol, with respect to the enzymatic procedure proposed to remove toxic compounds from certain plants, or with respect to the bleaching and precipitating effect of citric acid. From the accounts given it will, however, also be clear that these transformations did not just result from *conceptual* interaction; instead, they resulted from a process of production and reproduction.

3. The Conservatism of Scientific Innovation

Usually, the beginning of a piece of research is when something strikes a spark on one's imagination: something one does not know seems a particularly fascinating thing to try and find out. Partly, the thing itself seems important and fascinating in its own right, partly, one has intimations that one can find it out. That is where the spark comes in – the intimation that one actually can find it out gives one a particular thrill that is irresistible. There is a flash, and as with love one knows that one is in it.

Let us look now at the scientists' stories of innovation from a different angle. Consider these stories as accounts of happenings in the process of research production. What does the happening of an 'idea' based upon an analogical influence mean in this process? The first thing to note is that the 'ideas' which mark an analogical transfer or the occurrence of a metaphor have the character of *solutions*. We have said that the very significance of analogical reasoning in this context is that it brings to bear knowledge from a familiar, well-know, clear case upon an unclear, less familiar, problematic situation. Thus, the analogy relation relevant here mobilizes a resource which creates an opportunity for success: since the knowledge mobilized by the analogy or metaphor has worked in a similar context, it holds the promis that it can be made to work, given appropriate modifications, in the new situation. It is precisely this *promise of success* to which Albert Woods refers when he says, in William Cooper's tale of an experimental chemist quoted above (11), that it is the intimation that one actually *can* find it out which gives one a particular thrill that is irresistible. And it is this promise of success associated with the 'unsatisfied capacity' (12) of the scientists' analogical transfers which lurks behind the scientists' talk of 'the interest' of an idea.

A second point to note refers to the difference between the 'ideas' of the laboratory and the hypotheses of the methodologists' vernacular. If the 'ideas' which mark an analogy relation are unrealized solutions holding promise of success, the research associated with these ideas assumes a peculiar post hoc quality, since the investigation is made *after* the solution has been hit upon. The conception of such ideas as unrealized solutions contrasts sharply with the notion that these ideas are, logically speaking, hypotheses, that is ex ante conjectures about a phenomenon subjected to test in the research process. Hypotheses are tried against data, with the ultimate goal that they stand up as either true or false, or one of their weaker substitutes such as confirmed/disconfirmed or tenable/untenable. They require the data which they take to be collected through research to be independent arbiters of the propositions they contain. With ideas that are unrealized solutions mobilized by an analogy relation no such independence can be assumed. Unrealized solutions are not tried against data; instead they are made to work by scientists who are actively engaged in constructing the results anticipated by the solution. They are made to work differently by different scientists depending on practical circumstances, and they are made to work with different degrees of success. The suggestion here is not that to realize a solution is a simple, smooth or short undertaking. The suggestion is rather that to make a solution work rises other questions than those which are specified by the language of hypothesis-testing. The standards against which the ideas of the laboratory are measured do not refer us to the world of theoretical interpretation. Instead they refer us to a world of instrumentation and collaboration, of chances of publication and of the investments at stake. In short, they refer us to a process of production whose products are specified by what *can* be done. Unrealized solutions do not eliminate problems, search processes or outright failures from the process of research. But they turn the open ground of unresolved research problems into the closed program of a production line. It is the unrealized solutions, not the problems which take the lead in this process of production. It is the power associated with unrealized capacities which drives the research process forward, and it drives it in whatever direction the capacities lie.

The scientists' tendency to respond to 'ideas' as 'solutions' and the post hoc character of the investigations initiated by these solutions refers us to a third-point to mention here, the scientists' 'risks'. As suggested (13), solutions are problem translations which are themselves problematic in that they require further problems to be solved. To realize the idea that steroids are involved in the transformation of the slime mold posed the problem of isolating the steroids, and of identifying the right kind of steroids. A scientist's hunch as to how such subsequent problems can be solved is not always correct, as we have seen in the case of the slime mold. When attempting to realize a solution, the scientist faces a certain risk. Furthermore, problems may have to be attended to independent of whether an attractive or reasonably satisfactory solution is in sight. To paraphrase Albert Woods (14), scientists cannot always lay themselves open for something to strike a spark on them − they may have to strike a spark on it and to do so within a limited amount of time. This also implies a certain amount of risk of being unsuccessful. Scientists at the institute observed were well aware of these risks. When talking about a new idea, they displayed a full range of circumstantial reasoning within which these risks appeared to be evaluated. The appeal of an idea were the chances of convincing the research leader of it, of recruiting laboratory assistants, of finding the necessary equipment, of being the first to publish, of having time to do the work, etc. As a chemist told me in the context of his story of innovative ideas he had produced:

− You try to discriminate. You can get one idea a day, or . . . (in) two days, or one a week, and you discriminate (in terms of) your time and your ability to use it. You know, we have idea files, either in your mind or on paper, but you can't spend a lot of your time on things you don't have the opportunity to perform, or to prove, or to verify. *So you try to limit your interest to the idea in which you know you are going to be most productive as quickly as possible within the frame of facilities you got at your hands.* (emphasis added)

A biochemist's version of this was as follows:

We always calculate our risks although we don't know how to calculate. It's just that feel, you know, and I am very good at this by now (through the) many years of experience. I can more or less tell what I should drop and what I should pick up. I think this is a problem with a lot of unsuccessful scientists, that *they are not dumb, they just work on the wrong things* . . . Another thing is, if you are up against a terrific competition, there is no sense in struggling. (emphasis added)

"By now", he added, "I can gage these success factors, and my secret of

success is that I work on things that aren't too unlikely to work out." The
scientists I listened to were not only aware of the risks associated with their
analogy-based 'ideas'. They displayed a concern with keeping these risks at a
low level. We have said that the scientists' analogical transfers represent
unrealized solutions which the scientists seem eager to exploit if local circumstances allow for it. When the scientists follow the lead of an unrealized
solution, they do not foolishly committ themselves to a journey of unknown
destination, of unknown arrival time, and of unknown chances of getting
anywhere. Instead, they choose a path of known destination on which they
have a good chance to arrive at their goal, and on which they have a good
chance to arrive there first and fastest. This implies that there is no reason
to believe that scientists are, by nature or by necessity, devoted to risk taking.
To say that research is a high risk enterprize may reflect the feelings of those
who finance research in order to get a very specific result, with no apparent
success. It does not reflect the reasoning of the scientists in the laboratory.
Scientists can built *their* success on many a 'solution', provided they have
the opportunity to follow its lead and provided they can make it work.
Consequently, many of their arguments focus on securing these opportunities,
and on sorting the circumstances which will allow them "to be most productive as quickly as possible within the frame of facilities" they got at their
hands, as we have heard above. Analogical transfers form a firm ground for
controlled rather than uncontrolled risks, since they mobilize a solution
which has been proven to work, albeit in another context.

   The scientists' analogy-based innovations imply a conservative strategy in
more than one sense. They imply that one starts from an unrealized solution
rather than from an open problem, and that one follows the leads of ideas
which hold promise of success rather than to expose oneself to unknown risks
and uncertainties. Most generally speaking, they imply that the interest of an
'innovative idea' is not that it is new, but that it is old in the sense that it
draws upon available knowledge as a source for producing knowledge. In this
process, previous selections are extended to new areas rather than being
invented, and they are thereby *reproduced* and solidified. Scientific "consensus" emerges from such processes of reproduction. The notion of scientific
consensus is misleading in that it suggests some process of public opinion
formation among scientists, a process which results in unanimous decisions
about certain knowledge claims and which thereby transforms these claims

into 'accepted' or 'rejected' knowledge. What we have instead are the practices of ongoing research within local research scenes in which certain selections get reproduced, and through reproduction are expanded, reinforced, and perhaps petrified to become the solid rock of what counts as true. In as far as analogy-based 'discovery' is a form of spatial expansion of previous selections to new territories it is part of 'consensus formation', or better of the process of solidification and petrification of knowledge. The 'discovery' of the role of steroids in the transformation of the slime mold and in plants as described by the scientists illustrate this process of solidifcation through expansion, as do the other stories of innovation presented above.

If practical reproduction characterizes this process, this also means that the hallmark of analogical extension of knowledge is not just 'conceptual' interaction. It is the mobilization of resources for making things work in the ongoing process of laboratory production, and the transformation of the selections transferred through this process of production. These resources are not just 'ideas'. As indicated before, they refer to available instruments and to source materials which can be obtained from colleagues. They refer to laboratory lines of action which have been effective or to scientists to be consulted. They suggest timings and quantifications, or composition formulae which have been successful. In short, they refer to the mobilization and instantiation of means of production. In the case of the slime mold, the idea that the hormones involved are steroids suggested an array of methods of isolation and a laboratory which had the instruments. It suggested a group of scientists 'interested' in the work and a journal in which to publish the results. It triggered the idea of using purified hormones and led, through laboratory work, to the result that the steroids involved were different from those found in pregnancy urine. In subsequent research, it resulted in the discovery of steroids in all kinds of molds, and in the identification and exploration of the characteristics of these kinds of steroids. Just as the analogies relevant here are not just 'ideas', so the 'conceptual interaction' is not just 'conceptual'. The new results initiated by the making of an analogy are not just derived from the associations invoked by a striking and unexpected similarity, as they are in the literary use of analogical reasoning. They are grounded in the transformations of knowledge which results from laboratory reproduction. The process is material, and it has material consequences.

4. Ethnotheories of Innovation or the Assumptions behind Accounts of Innovation

You asked me where is the origin — I remember the origin of everything because it isn't something you simply drift into! (In research) you have a concept based on somebody else's work, you would be standing on somebody else's shoulder, you are putting two pieces of something else together. But when an idea comes, it comes. It's not something that develops from a series of routine investigations!

There are may be half a dozen developments that we have been involved in, and I think each one has its own origin. *There is no pattern to the origin of ideas!* (emphasis added)

So far we have looked at the logic of sciences' metaphor account of innovation, and we have seen that it needs to be extended to include a more general form of reasoning by analogy. We have heard the scientists stories of the origin of some of their research efforts, and we found analogy-based 'ideas' to be indeed pervasive in work the scientists considered innovative. We have been confronted with the social scientist's interpretation of the role of metaphor and analogical transfer in research production. And we have seen this analogical reasoning qualified as 'conservative' in the sense that it implies a reproduction and solidification of previous selections and the controlled risk of transformations which result from territorial extension rather than from invention. We will now return to metaphor and analogy as the core of a theory of innovation. To begin with, let us look at some of the ethnotheories the scientists themselves hold about innovation.

The above quoted statements come from a chemist who had made his reputation by developing a microbiological assay of proteins using the microorganism *Tetrahymena pyriformis W.* during the first minutes of an interview in which he described the origin of this research. In a nutshell, the theory of innovation contained in these statements is a version of the 'lightning' theory of creativity which claims that ideas hit and strike out of the blue rather than to emerge as the (logical) result of previous investigations. When the first half hour of the interview was completed, the scientist had woven two more theories of innovation into his account. He said for example,

... as far as the innovations are concerned I think it means ... perceiving what the state (of affairs) is and taking what in your mind is the next logical step ... May be that's what creativity is, the summation of everything and putting it together and get a new answer ... *It's a logical, a logical sequence of events* which may not (look) so logical to someone else, and they end up with being "creative". But I think most of it is going down the path and exploring and prospecting the road as you go along. (emphasis added)

And he added, when he came to talk about the group's 'fortuitous' observation that there was an optimum where they had expected a linear decreasing relationship in an experiment on a physical effect of humidity

So this was an anomaly, right. So *the trick in all this*, in all these what I call, *what you might call innovations is observing the anomaly* – what is different about this set of characteristics. And I think if you characterize any of the accomplishments (of science) it says: you tried something, you did something, and you found an anomaly, and (you investigated) what was the reason for the anomaly. Investigate the anomaly! (emphasis added)

In addition to the lightning theory of innovation, we are exposed to a 'logical' theory of innovation in which a discovery appears as nothing more than a step in a logical series of events. And we are exposed to an 'anomaly' theory of innovation in which the occurrence of unexpected events and relationships breeds innovation. These ethnotheories of innovation appear to contradict each other, especially since they were promoted within the context of one and the same question by one and the same scientist. Yet there is no necessary contradiction. 'Ideas' can be triggered off by anomalies which require explanation. The occurrence of an 'innovative idea' is a hit-and-strike chance-event if one tries to predict it, and a step in a logical sequence of events if one reconstructs a research problem after the fact. The scientist selectively looked at a process from different starting points when he promoted his theories, and he paid attention to different aspects of this process. He also answered somewhat different questions in each of his theories of innovation.

Let us now consider the social scientist's theory of innovation by reference to metaphor or to analogy. It adds to the picture painted by the above ethnotheories in that it tells us something about how an 'idea' leads to a creative extension of knowledge, that is by mobilizing knowledge we have from a different context. Yet like the ethnotheories of innovation, it proceeds selectively. For example, it does not address the question of *when* an innovative idea tends to occur, a question answered by the anomaly theory of innovation. Nor does it consider the question of how an innovative idea relates to the immediately *preceding* research, a question addressed by the logical theory of innovation. More important, the metaphor-or analogy-account of innovation is based upon a series of assumptions which tend to obscure rather than to illuminate the process of practical research. A theory of innovation which draws upon metaphor and analogical transfer is streamlined in terms of a successful end-product of investigation which is clearly identified. It starts from the assumption that an innovation has been made which has a name and an author and which is located in time through publication or through participants' accounts. In other words, it assumes that the 'who', the 'when', and the 'what' of an 'innovation' or 'discovery' are settled or can be settled upon further inquiries, and it answers the question of 'how' by reference to conceptual interaction and extension of knowledge induced by the establishment of a similarity relationship. However, 'innovations' are embedded in a past and a future of constructive − and consequently also of destructive − work. When we look at this process in sufficient detail, we see that questions of date and authorship are not settled by the sheer existence of a phenomenon called an innovation, nor do they seem to get settled through close empirical studies of the phenomenon. Instead, clearcut answers to these questions require decisions to be made about what is and what is not significant with a view to the end product of innovation. For example, in the process of investigation the person who invokes an analogy, the person(s) who work out the experiments and those who gain credit for the work are often not the same. In the example of the simile "this protein really looks just like sand" mentioned at the beginning of this paper, the similarity was invoked by a scientist who had nothing to do with the respective research in the context of a chat between colleagues who belonged to different research units. Needless to say, the question of the authorship of an 'idea' is by no means settled among the scientists themselves. One need not go to disputes over priority in the published literature to see this illustrated. In the stories of 'their' innovations they told me, the scientists often shifted and blurred what they had to say about the origin of these innovations. For example, the biochemist who told me about the discovery of cholesterol in plants started out by saying "they (his colleagues) pooled their resources and, uh, of course mine too, and we *together* came up with the conclusion that this was cholesterol" only to end up by saying, some 15 minutes later, "in order to accept *my* idea that cholesterol is present in all plants . . . "

Questions of authorship and of the timing of innovation are the established battlefield of historians of science, and as such they need not bother the theorist interested in the logic of conceptual interaction. To a degree they will bother the social scientist who observes a process of research. Is (s)he to credit the scientist who jokingly invoked a similarity or the one who linked the picture to a workable procedure? The post doc who performed the experiment but not the technicians and the research leaders? And what does (s)he count as the 'origin' apart from the question who was original? Why not the observation that pregnancy urine stimulates the transformation of the slime mold rather than the 'idea' that steroids might be involved in that transformation? Of course these questions are of analytic rather than of practical nature. In practice, the necessary decisions are routinely made in an ad hoc way, and they will differ over different purposes and observers. The metaphor or analogy theory of innovation does not specify which decision criteria it prefers in these cases. And the observer of laboratory research does not yet dispose of the integrating principle of an acknowledged and identified 'innovation' for which history can be reconstructed. This brings us to a second point about the assumptions implicit in the metaphor or analogy theory, and one which is relevant as long as this theory claims to be a theory of innovation. The metaphor- or analogy-theory of innovation aims at explaining the (conceptual) origin of innovation. As indicated before, it does so by starting from the successful endproducts of research, from those who get qualified as 'innovations'. Thus it presupposes innovation as a given, unproblematic phenomenon from which it jumps to an "origin" located in the conceptual sphere. We can also say that it *identifies* innovation with the conceptual occurrence of the invocation of an analogy or metaphor, since it ignores virtually completely the process of research production which lies between this invocation and a research product's acknowledgement (15) as an 'innovation'. We have seen that questions of timing and authorship refer us to this process, yet they are only part of the more general question of how a research result becomes an 'innovation'. It is hard to see how this question could be attacked without due consideration of the process of production and reproduction of research. It is this process through which the ideas of the laboratory are turned into 'innovations', and it is his process in which a theory of innovation will have to be grounded.

5. A Metaphor- or Analogy-theory of Failure and Mistake

To expound the thesis, let us suppose for a moment that we are not interested in a theory of scientific innovation, but in a theory of scientific failure and mistake. The laboratory provides ample examples of such failures. Indeed all we have to do is to take one of the stories of 'innovation' presented before and place it into an ever enlarging context of ongoing research which surrounds this innovation. We will end up with a kind of genealogy of failures which at one point looked like, or were for some time, successful innovations. For example, the transfer of ferric chloride as a means of protein precipitation cited before was embedded in a whole chain of similar 'ideas', all involving analogical transfer. Most of these 'ideas' were accompagnied by specific research efforts. If we choose an arbitrary cutting point and do not look into the prehistory of the research, the first such transfer involved phosphoric acid:

The method had just been published and had been documented to work in a biochemical context. It appeared particularly attractive since the main author of the method worked at the same institute as the scientist who said it could be the solution to his problem of protein generation. Access to the author of the method meant the opportunity of a quick transfer of know-how resulting in an easier process of adaptation. It could also mean collaboration, and hence access to equipment, material and laboratory-assistance pretrained for the purpose.

However, after a period of further exploration the scientist appeared to become less convinced of the method. The context in which the method had worked did not match the new situation. The scientist complained that the experiments needed to be done under nitrogen which was difficult in the large scale laboratory which had to be used since large quantities of protein were needed. Some paper found suggested that phosphoric acid would generate toxic side effects. For large quantities, the method could become expensive. Nevertheless, the method was pursued until the scientist who wanted the protein happened to read about ferric chloride and immediately qualified it as a much 'better idea'.

The 'discovery' of ferric chloride not only sealed the fate of phosphoric acid as a non-solution, it also marked a change in the research focus. As we have heard earlier, protein generation became a research topic in its own right which replaced the original interest of doing biological assay tests with rats, an interest for which the large amounts of protein were needed. Thus one of the major lines of the group's research became the development of methods of protein generation from the respective plants. Ferric chloride was made to work in subsequent experiments. The resulting proteins had a high nitrogen-solubility, a property considered highly desirable.

Thus ferric chloride proved to be a success and remained so throughout the period of observation, as indicated by a quickly published paper dedicated to the promotion of the method. More specifically, it remained a success from the point of view of protein generation. This success was threatened, however, as long as the protein could not be adequately purified. Consequently, quite a bit of effort went into solidifying the success by attempting purification. One idea to achieve purification was suggested in a somewhat ad hoc way when, at the eve of a large scale experiment, it was found out that there was nothing left of the adsorbent agent needed in the laboratory, and moreover, that the 'storage room' had run out of it too.

Since the date of the experiments had been fixed and could not be changed, not enough time was left to order the chemicals. In the somewhat nervous discussions which followed, a colleague suggested an adsorbent which he had used in his own previous research on proteins, where it had worked. The scientists did not appear to be intrigued by the idea, expecting difficulties with removing the adsorbent agent from the proteins. Nevertheless once they got started, attempts to purify the protein with this adsorbent agent went on for several weeks and months.

At one point in time the results were described enthusiastically as "better than anything achieved so far", with an implicit reference to another group of the institute which was said to have failed 'for 25 years' to isolate and purify protein of similar properties from a different plant. However, this success was short lived: after they had looked at the results of chemical composition tests, the scientists qualified it as an artefact. Shortly afterward, the attempt to work with this adsorbent agent was abandoned altogether.

During the time when efforts to use this adsorbent agent were still under way, the scientists picked up the 'idea' of using citric acid from a travel report of the research leader, as mentioned before. As it turned out, citric acid could not only substitute for the use of the above adsorbent agent as an alternative method to change the disturbing properties of the proteins. It could also substitute for ferric chloride as a method of protein generation. The experiments were done in the fall of 1976, toward the end of my observations. They mark the beginning of the deconstruction of the success of ferric chloride. This deconstruction was not completed until about 18 months later, when some of the data on citric acid were finally analyzed and reported in a paper which shows the advantages of this alternative method over ferric chloride. Some such deconstruction had been anticipated when the scientists moved to using aluminium sulphate instead of ferric chloride, an 'idea' which came up in a discussion with a visitor from Israel who suggested that it had been used in the context of environmental research in his country. Since the resulting proteins had a lower nitrogen solubility and other less desirable properties than those obtained from ferric chloride, the method had been qualified as a failure, which did not prevent the scientists from publishing the results in a paper comparing several methods. At the time, the failure had strengthened rather than threatened ferric chloride.

Two other 'ideas' relating to protein generation have been pursued in the meantime. One involves the chemical modification of the protein molecule, a procedure which allows for the engineering of the properties of the proteins. This has the consequence of a potential deconstruction of all 'successful' methods above in the sense that the protein-properties generated by these methods are no longer decisive for their success or failure. Note that this potential deconstruction again did not hinder the scientists to promote citric acid as a successful coagulant through publication (the paper is currently submitted). The second 'idea' involves an enzymatic weakening and a subsequent mechanical destruction of the cell walls of certain molds in order to obtain the protein found in the cell juice. Since the mold can be generated in indefinite quantities from sources such as oil, the potential of this procedure implies a similar change in the fate of the use of ferric chloride, or its present substitute, citric acid.

The last two procedures are to new to determine their fate although there are indications that the chemical engineering of protein-properties will be abandoned again because of the hazards it involves (16). Let us adopt another arbitrary cutting point and consider the development of protein generation research up to the use of citric acid. As shown by the fragments of this process presented above, there is no need to go outside the laboratory to observe the demolishing and replacement of what previously was a successful innovation: the scientists themselves constantly engage in the deconstruction and transformation of their 'innovative' results. In addition, many of the ideas of the laboratory which appeal to the scientists as 'innovative' and 'promising' of success do not work out under given practical circumstances, or are abandoned before bing tried out experimentally. Our genealogy of methods of protein generation which starts with the projected use of phosphoric acid and continues with ferric chloride and its ramifications to the use of aluminium sulphite and citric acid includes both kinds of failures. All methods involve at some origin marked by the scientists analogical transfers or a 'displacement' of knowledge from one context to another. So why not propose a theory which traces the origin of scientific failure and mistake back to the occurrence of analogical reasoning?

The point here is simple but consequential. Analogical transfers of 'ideas' as well as metaphors are routine features of scientific as well as everyday reasoning. They occur not only in the case of innovative success, but also in the case of 'blind alleys', 'degenerative problemshifts', or simple failures to make something work. Thus, a theory of innovation which limits itself to accounting for innovation in terms of conceptual interaction induced by analogy relations must recognize that it is at the same time a *theory of failure and mistake*. It does not discriminate between the differential success analogy based 'ideas' encounter in the process of research. Without due consideration of this process, the fate of 'ideas' remains opaque. 'Ideas' based on metaphor or analogical transfer were said to orient research in terms of the resources they mobilize and in terms of the investment opportunities they open up. Closure of this process is achieved through the *active constructions* of the laboratory, that is through negotiation and instrumental fabrication. Innovations are not the beginning, but the *transient and temporary end-product* of this process.

6. Conclusion

What, then, are the conclusions we can draw with respect to the metaphor theory of innovation? We have heard how invoking a metaphor or an analogy mobilizes a source-model (Harre) which serves to illuminate a new situation. Without doubt this is why ancient rhetoric, demagogy and more generally the art of persuasion have long made systematic use of analogy relations (17). Yet the invokation of a metaphor or of an analogy is not in itself a piece of 'scientific innovation'. Research products which are classified as scientific innovations include a crucial element of success: success in working out in the laboratory, success in being used by other scientists, success in convincing others that some research product is an 'innovation'. The metaphor-theory of innovation does not look at the fabrication and negotiation, at the construction and deconstruction which establishes and demolishes a research as a 'scientific innovation'. We have said that the metaphor account of innovation needs to be extended to include analogy in general. But it also needs to be *restricted* in its claim to account for scientific innovation. Reference to metaphor and analogy tells us something about the sources and consequences of problemshifts and about the circulation and transformation of selections in scientific — as well as everyday — practical reasoning. It suggests why scientists are intrigued by analogy-based 'ideas' which they qualify as 'solutions', and why they let their research be oriented by the 'opportunities' they provide. But reference to metaphor or analogy tells us nothing about whether the problemshifts will be, in Lakatos' terms (18), progressive or degenerative, whether they will be called a failure, or an innovation. Studies of metaphor and analogy in science have in mind only those similes and conceptual shifts which have made their way in the literature. The process of research production and reproduction is more complex than the equation of metaphor and innovation suggests.

Notes and References

1. This and the following examples drawn upon one year of observations done in 1976–1977 in a group of scientists working on plant protein generation at a research laboratory employing more than 300 scientists in Berkeley, Ca., and on interviews done with members of other groups at the same laboratory. The laboratory is oriented toward basic and applied research in chemical, physical, microbiological, toxicological, technological and economic areas. Most of the scientists hold degrees in biochemistry and in one of the above areas. The plant-protein work observed most closely covered a variety of questions involving a series of disciplinary approaches, such as the generation and recovery of protein, its purification, explorations of its biological value and of the structure of protein particles, or questions of texture and of the use of protein additives. Reports, comments and citations are based upon my notes and upon tape recordings made during discussions and interviews. The preceding quote comes from a member of the plant protein group who told me what he had thought after the simile had been brought up. For more detailed discussions of the data and the methodology of the study see the monograph: K. Knorr, *The Manufacture of Knowledge. Toward a Constructivist and Contextual Theory of Science*, Pergamon, Oxford, 1980.

    Needless to say, in depth studies such as the present do not constitute a solid basis for generalizations. The examples given can serve as no more than illustrations for the kind of experience in which the points that are made are grounded. Yet the issue at present may not be to arrive at 'statistically representative' results. The issue may be to use whatever limited basis we have.
2. For a summary of the metaphor-theory of innovation, see M. Black, *Models and Metaphors*, Cornell University Press, Ithaca, N. Y., 1962; D. A. Schon, *Displacement*

of Concepts, Tavistock, London, 1963; For the distinction between metaphor and analogy see particularly M. Hesse, *Models and Analogies in Science*, University of Notre Dame Press, Notre Dame, IN, 1970. See also R. Harre, 'Models in Science', *Phys. Educ.* **13**, 275–278 (1978). An overview over recent discussions of philosophical, cognitive and semantic aspects of metaphor is found in the 'Special Issue on Metaphor,' *Critical Inquiry* **5**, (1978).

3. The example is cited in Hesse, *op. cit.*, 1970, Note 2, e.g. p. 167.
4. In spite of numerous suggestions for definitions, the notion of similarity has been notoriously repugnant to precise explication. The attempt to define the resemblance between two objects in terms of the quantity of properties they have in common leads to the difficulty that on the level of comparative similarity almost any two things could count as common members of some broader kind. If a set theory definition is chosen which holds all members of a set to be more similar to one another than they are to other things outside the set, than Goodman's difficulty of imperfect community comes in. For example, all red round things, red wooden things, and round wooden things would meet the definition, yet we would not want to admit round dinner tables and red rubber balls as belonging to one kind. For a more extensive discussion of this see W. V. Quine, *Ontological Relativity and Other Essays*, Columbia University Press, New York, 1969, Chapter 5; or N. Goodman, *The Structure of Appearance*, Bobbs Merril, New York, 1966, 163 ff. According to Quine, similarity classifications are pervasive: The notions of induction, of causality, and of a disposition to react are all definable in terms of similarity classes. See Quine, *op. cit.*, 1969, 125 ff. and 144 ff.
5. M. Hesse, *The Structure of Scientific Inference*, University of California Press, Berkeley, Ca., 1974, Chapter 1. Hesse approaches the problem of the relationship between theory and observation from the perspective of a logic of resemblance without requiring that we can ultimately say in what the primitive resemblance of properties of two objects consist.
6. For a summary of what cognitive psychology has to say to the interaction between theroy and data in science see M. DeMey, 'The Interaction between Theory and Data in Science. A New Model for Perception Applied to Harvey's Discovery of the Circulation of the Blood', this volume.
7. For a general discussion of shifts of meaning and particularly of shifts in the degree of 'entrenchment' of terms used in primary recognition in our natural language see Hesse, *op. cit.*, 1974, Note 5. 14 ff. Similarity on Hesse's account is "primitive but at the same time complex since it comes in varying degrees and relates pairs of objects in respect of different property dimensions". See page 67.
8. A. Koestler, *The Act of Creation*, Pan Books, London, 1969.
9. For a discussion of what is involved in seeing something as something, and particularly, for the need to presuppose an institution of seeing cf. E. Gombrich, *Art and Illusion*, Pantheon Books, New York, 1960. For pictorial representation and resemblance see also N. Goodman, *Languages of Art*, Bobbs-Merrill, Indianapolis, 1968.
10. The notion of 'displacement of concepts' was introduced by Schon and used by Mulkay to refer to the transfer of ideas which comes about when scientists change their research network. Both Schon and Mulkay identify the notion of displacement of concepts with a metaphoric extension of ideas, although Mulkay's examples,

if I understand them correctly, involve literal rather than figurative similarities. This is probably due to Schon's tendency to identify metaphor with analogy in general. Cf. Schon, *op. cit.*, 1963, Note 2; and M. Mulkay, 'Conceptual Displacement and Migration in Science: A Prefatory Paper', *Science Studies* 4, 205–234 (1974).

11. W. Cooper, *The Struggles of Albert Woods*, Penguin Books, Harmondsworth, Middlesex, 1966, p. 229.

12. In this sense Small's classical definition of an interest as an 'unsatisfied capacity' fits the case. A. W. Small, *General Sociology*, Chicago-London, 1905, p. 433.

13. This suggestion comes from M. Callon, J. P. Courtial and W. Turner, *Les actions concertees chimie macromoleculaire. Sociologique d'une agence de traduction*, unpub. report of the Ecole Nationale Superieure des Mines, Centre de Sociologie de l'Innovation, Paris, 1979.

14. Cf. W. Cooper, *op. cit.*, 1966, Note 11, p. 230. Albert Wood has the problem of creating an 'innovation' he has already announced in public, but not yet worked out. In the book it says: "Albert had two things against him; the first, that he could not lay himself open for something to strike a spark on him – he had got to strike a spark on it; the second, that his obsession could not take its natural course – completion and perfection had got to be reached in a couple of months if not earlier."

15. Disregarding the question of whether unanimous acknowledgement of some scientific research result as an 'innovation' ever occurs.

16. According to the personal communication of members of a group which works at present in this area.

17. There are other elements not considered here which add to the popularity of analogy and metaphor in persuasive discourse, e.g. the pictorial element of referring to something of which one has a concrete picture in mind.

18. I. Lakatos, 'Criticism and the Methodology of Scientific Research Programmes', in I. Lakatos and A. Musgrave (eds.), *Criticism and the Growth of Knowledge*, Cambridge University Press, Cambridge, 1970.

IS IT POSSIBLE TO RECONSTRUCT THE RESEARCH
PROCESS?: SOCIOLOGY OF A BRAIN PEPTIDE

B. LATOUR

STS, CNAM Paris

When social scientists started studying the details of the scientific research process, they first tried to phrase their observations in the then traditional framework provided by sociologists and historians of science, i.e. how internal and external factors contributed to the production of science. The term 'external' refers to concepts invented by social scientists and economists such as 'group', 'profession', 'institution', 'culture', 'influence' and so on. Terms considered 'internal' were folk terms used by scientists and some philosophers such as 'coherence', 'logics', 'problems', 'objectivity', 'rules of method' and so on. A few concepts also had to be invented such as 'paradigm', 'themata' or 'episteme' in order to account for observations that did not fit inside the internal/external frame of reference.

Soon, however, it was evident that most of the terms employed in order to describe 'internal' factors, were actually amenable to sociological analysis and accounted by concepts so far used to describe 'external' factors. The notion of replication of an experiment was reduced by H. Collins (1) to the sociology of controversies; the writing of an article was explained by Latour (2) and Knorr (3) in rhetoric or semiotic terms; the notion of 'proof' had been further reduced to social factors by Pinch (this volume) and Harvey (this volume). Even the small word 'problem' had been made amenable to sociological explanation by Callon (4) (this volume). Indeed, the whole process of fact construction has been shown to be accountable inside a sociological framework.

No matter what one could think of this wealth of new studies dealing with the research process, it is clear that they cannot be located within the internal/external frame of reference, since all the so-called 'internal' concepts have now been re-explained in sociological terms. Although it is not yet clear

53

*Karin D. Knorr, Roger Krohn and Richard Whitley (eds.), The Social Process of
Scientific Investigation. Sociology of the Sciences, Volume IV, 1980. 53–73.*
Copyright © 1980 by D. Reidel Publishing Company.

what new framework will replace the obsolete internal/external one, it is possible to survey briefly the terms that have been found most useful to account for the details of the research process. In this article I present these various concepts in action, so to speak, by using them in accounting for the devising of analogs of a brain peptide named 'somatostatin'.

Presentation of the Case Study

For several years, a large laboratory of neuroendocrinology described at length in another study (5) had looked for a hormone coming from the brain that would trigger the release of another hormone responsible for the regulation of the body growth. This Growth Hormone Releasing Hormone (GHRH), was demonstrated in various cell assays. But in 1971, two young physiologists started stumbling on contradictory results. Instead of increasing the release of growth hormone in their assays when injecting their precious samples of purified brain extracts, they got instead a decrease of growth hormone. Their results were dismissed as mere artefacts by the head of the group. However, the two physiologists soon gathered enough data to make it impossible for the head of the laboratory to doubt their results. This was made easier, because the neuroendocrinology paradigm could accommodate an inhibiting hormone as well as a releasing hormone. After a few more months, they purified a substance they called 'somatostatin' because, they believed, it blocks the release of growth hormone.

A neurohormone can be compared to a one sentence order the brain conveys to a group of cells. To understand the meaning of this order, one has first to isolate it out of the background (this is called purification), then to decipher which letters are used in the sentence (the letters are made of aminoacids and this is called aminoacid analysis), and eventually in which order the letters (or aminoacids) of the sentence are assembled (this is called sequencing). After much debate, the laboratory decided to chose one sequence of aminoacids as being the natural sequence of somatostatin; in the aminoacid transcription the somatostatin sentence reads;

H−Ala−Gly−Cys−Lys−Asn−Phe−Phe−Trp−Lys−Thr−Phe−
1   2   3   4   5   6   7   8   9   10   11

Thr−Ser−Cys−OH
12   13   14

Each letter symbol stands for one of the 20 aminoacids that make up all proteins of the body. The meaning of this specific short protein − called peptide − was said to be: "Stop releasing growth hormone". The publication of this sequence was deemed a major achievement inside the neuroendocrinology profession (7).

In this article I will take for granted the production of all the facts dealing with somatostatin itself, and focus only on the modifications of the original sequence. Once a sequence is decided, it is possible to synthesize it from commercially available aminoacids, but it is also possible to *alter* the original sequence and to modify one, or two or all the aminoacids. These synonyms, homonyms, or antonyms, are all called *analogs* and their fabrication is one of the major tasks of the laboratory I studied. Each analog gives the cells a different order, and by studying the different responses of the cells, one can study the exact content of the message as well as the behaviour of the cells. In this article I will talk only about one aspect of the analog production: the number of *possible* analogs of this 14 aminoacid sequence is 2.6×10^{22}. The synthesis of each microgram of analog costs anywhere between $ 100 and $ 500 and several days of work for two to three researchers putting to use a two million dollar technical lay out. Since all the analogs could not possibly be tried, *what process led* the laboratory workers to choose the few hundred modifications they eventually produced? This is the case study I will use to reconstruct the characteristics of the research process.

Methods

From the protocol books used by the chemists, a chart was set up of all the analogs devised between 1971 and 1976. At this date, only 286 analogs had been made, which is a tiny portion of all the possible analogs but a major effort for the laboratory. Chemists were then asked to write down the reasons they had to devise this or that specific analog. All the articles reporting analogs, were gathered and studied according to methods developed earlier (8). Of the 286 analogs only 70 were reported in the literature. Whenever possible, patent applications were added to the corpus of papers. Earlier drafts of the present paper were written in collaboration with *JR*, the peptide chemist in charge of the analog programme. Reactions to earlier drafts by other members of the group were used as another source of material.

The Research Process is Contextual

It is an old scientific saying that a statement holds true only in the conditions set up for the experiment. Contextual means more: a statement draws its meaning from where, when and by whom it is uttered. Scientific statements have been shown to be as contextual — or as indexcal (9) — as any other statement. This is particularly clear in the case of somatostatin analogs. In the first laboratory the 14 aminoacid structure meant an order from the brain to stop releasing growth hormone. However, by sending samples of this substance all over the world to other investigators in different contexts, a vast array of new unexpected meanings started to be generated for the same substance. If you test somatostatin not only for its action on growth hormone, but also for its action on thyrotropin releasing hormone, the meaning is modified and reads now: "stop releasing growth hormone, trigger thyrotropin releasing hormone". In 1974, for instance, a new group of investigators started testing somatostatin inside their own local layout and linked it to their own personal interests, obsessions, drives and equipment. Somatostatin comes from the brain, they tried it in pancreas cells; it was supposed to stop growth hormone, they tried to show that it inhibited insulin and glucagon as well.

This change of context dramatically modified the very nature of somatostatin. Blocking growth hormones is not very useful in medical terms, (except to make dwarfs!) or more usefully, to cure some forms of acromegaly. However, affecting glucagon and insulin, is affecting a multi-million dollar business: diabetes research. Immediately, an enormous pressure was exerted back on the original laboratory; the initial interest in growth hormones became secondary, and the name 'somatostatin' made arbitrary. What now counted was to devise an analog that would block glucagon — dangerous for diabetic patients — but not insulin which was already deficient. Of all possible analogs, the ones that have to be devised in priority are the ones able to mean: "block glucagon, release insulin", because each of them is worth millions of dollars if it could be of some help in treating diabestes. Each analog was patented and the research followed month after month by the biggest pharmaceutical companies.

Everytime a new investigator uses somatostatin within a new research programme, that is within a new material lay out, the meaning of the original molecule, and then the very nature of this molecule, is modified and recreated.

There is no way to stabilise this change of meanings except by stopping the research and making routine the use of that substance inside a few networks.

The Research Process is Heterogeneous

The genesis of a scientific statement may be purified afterwards but it is never pure; many factors, coming from many parts of the social world, contribute to the production. This is what is meant by heterogeneous; no matter how close one tries to be from the research process, no homogeneous set of factors, that could be called 'internal' or 'purely internal', is visible. This multiplicity of factors is obvious when one looks at the interviews of *JR*:

All the Alanine modifications had been done . . . From the literature it is known that Tryptophane is important biologically . . . There is also a gut feeling . . . I just had received some D-Trp (dextrorotatory form) for LRF (another substance studied in the laboratory) . . . I tried the first D-modification (instead of the levoratatory form only existing in nature. It turned out that I hit right in the bull's eye.

Or, in this other case, where micropower structures are used to make sense of the making of another analog:

There were tensions in the laboratory . . . also I had trouble to cyclize somatostatin . . . something seemed to be missing. Then I supposed that the structure of natural somatostatin was not the published one and that homocysteine was necessary; the synthesis would have been made easier and I would have proven that *X* (his chemist competitor in the lab.) was wrong . . .

The multiplicity of factors is visible in the interviews by the constant jumps from one line of reasoning to another (jumps marked here by blank, silence, or copula), but is made still more visible by the *differences* between one scientist's accounts. When *W* read the account given above in the first excerpt by *JR* he was incensed:

It is not by chance at all! *N* came with a model of the molecule; he gave a seminar or something; his molecule was folded at the eight position; *I* immediately suggested to put a D-Trp at this position; that was the only way of reinforcing the molecule, probably, *N*'s model was wrong, we know that now . . . Anyway, we would have done it sooner or later. That was systematic. But we saved, maybe a year by doing it in the first place.

This is not only to show that the process of analog making is heterogeneous, but also to show that the origin is always lost in a swarm of contradictory accounts. *JR* said it was chance; *W* that it was logical; *JR* said it was his idea, *W* that it was his; *JR* points out the availability of a component, gut feeling, habits of work, *W* points out a friend's model, the occasion of a seminar, a system and so on. When you get closer to the research process, the multiplicity and the chaos increase.

It is an apparent paradox that the inner core of the research process is full of so called 'external' factors, but this is not surprising when you realize the number of outside professional groups that impose constraints on the devising of these analogs. Physiologists need a molecule that can be radioactively labelled for their radioimmunoassay, the radio labelling is convenient only on the aminoacid named tyrosine. Since there is no tyrosine on the newly discovered somatostatin, *JR* is asked to devise analogs with a tyrosine somewhere. Investigators all over the world need more somatostatin, so that *JR* has to devise new ways of synthesizing more of the native substance and more analogs. It is known by neuroendocrinologists that some analogs can be made from the former peptides by more potent and longer acting than the native molecule. It is known that deletion of one aminoacid, or addition of an alanine, or the substitution of an alanine to each aminoacid, might increase the action or the potency. Lawyers are also asking for more specific analogs in order to protect further important analogs through patents (10). Chemists in other, more basic, departments, are interested not only in the primary structure (already known), but also in how it is folded in three-dimensional space, or how it binds with other molecules; to know that, they need specific analogs with modifications they ask *JR* to tailor. *JR* and his colleagues, have to integrate all these heterogeneous demands coming from many professions, demands that are weak or strong, that are changing almost constantly in time.

There is no better way to show the heterogeneous character of the research process, than to read one page of the chart (see Figure 1). As in the interviews, the lines of reasoning are interrupted so many times that no clear cut pattern emerges. Modification 167 combines two former successful modifications des-Asn^5 and D-Trp^8 (11). Then the alanine series is resumed — as it is constant throughout the years — positions 11 and 9, but then is interrupted: "because the chemical company mis-labelled the aminoacid threonine used at position 12, and so the batch had to be discarded". Since a few days later, a paper is

Modification

No.	Add	1 Ala	2 Gly	3 Cys	4 Lys	5 Asn	6 Phe	7 Phe	8 Trp	9 Lys	10 Thr	11 Phe	12 Thr	13 Ser	14 Cys
No. 167						Delete									
No. 168									D-form			Ala			
No. 169										Ala					
No. 170					D-form										
No. 171	Add 3 Gly							D-form							
No. 172	Add 3 Tyr							D-form							
No. 173	Add 3 Gly				Delete			D-form							
No. 174		N E W S A M P L E S O F S O M A T O S T A T I N													
No. 175										Ala					
No. 176					D-form										
No. 177						D-form									
No. 178					Ala										
No. 179											Delete		Delete		
No. 180											D-form				
No. 181	Add 3 Gly											Ala			
No. 182							Delete	Delete							
No. 183							Delete								
No. 184					Delete										

Fig. 1. The 14-aminoacid structure of somatostatin is written at the top of the figure. The modifications are inscribed in the columns beneath each aminoacid. This figure allows the sociologist to see at once which position is modified and what are the analogs invented (each analog is designated by a number coming from *JR*'s protocol books. For instance the analog No. 168 is the original somatostatin except for its 11th position that is now an Ala instead of a Phe.

published which proposes to extend the native molecule by three glycine residues, *JR* immediately manufactures these analogs. He tries them three times (modification 171, 173 and 181) and combines them with his pet analog (D-Trp^8); in his later papers, these three analogs are said to have been a dead alley: "they have not been found to be active in our hands". Then three different programmes are mixed: the deletion one, the alanine series, and the replacement of a levorotatory form by a dextrorotatory form. Each programme interrupts the other, or suddenly they coalesce as in modification 173.

JR and his colleagues get by through this turbulent context of heterogeneous pressures and demands; the process is less and less pure, less and less 'internal', and, once again, could not be purified or stabilised except by stopping it entirely or making it a routine.

The Research Process is Opportunistic

To cope with this turbulent context of heterogeneous demands, is neither a fully orderly, nor a disorderly process; it is an opportunistic one. If you listen to the scientists the first time you meet them, they will claim that the whole process is the strict unfolding of a reasoning out of a few premisses. *W* for instance, told me:

If you give me a peptide, I could devise several hundreds of analogs, just from what is already known in the literature: the D-series, the Alanine series, the replacement by Gly; the deletion series; all that is known, it is logical.

But then he adds:

When intuition arrives, it is for new combinations; OK, for choosing what to do, I mean in which order ... that's where guess, logics, intuition come into the picture that's not systematic.

The same rupture appears in *JR*'s first presentation of the analog making. He first presents the different rules of transformation summarised by *W*, and then adds:

But see you have to be systematic *and* opportunistic this little word 'and', is the reason why *JR* so much despises 'industrial scientists':

They do everything systematically; they screen everything; just screen; it's not science; it's just a computer job.

To understand the research process one has to look exactly in the *middle* of order and disorder. There are rules — borrowed from previous experience — but they are followed *or not* according to the circumstances. In this case they cannot be followed since the number of possible analogs is too high. On the other hand, it is wrong to think like Feyerabend that 'anything goes'. The choice of the 286 analogs is not made at random. If opportunism means that one reacts to circumstances and timing, what *W* and *JR* do is to create local circumstances in which small chains of reasoning lead from one analog to the next, and invent precarious and provisional rules of transformation to sustain the reasoning for a while.

Let us look again at the page of the chart shown in Figure 1. For instance, modification 167 combines two modifications invented earlier. One of the rules is to delete one after the other each aminoacid and see what happens. One of the other programmes is to replace the levorotatory form that exists in nature, with a dextrorotatory form. From these two rules however, you cannot *deduce* modification 167, because they cannot be obtained through systematic screening except by manufacturing thousands of analogs. The modification 167 is not a chance encounter though. In the interview excerpted on page 57, I showed why *JR* and *W* were interested in the modification called D-Trp^8, it increased enormously the potency of the molecule. On page 56, I showed why the new context created for somatostatin pushed *JR* to devise analogs that inhibit glucagon but not insulin. Deleting asparagine at the fifth position, creates, they had found earlier in their work, a dissociative activity; the pancreas cells 'understand' the altered version of the molecule as meaning "release insulin, block glucagon". *JR* makes up a small rule: "combine successful modification"; and then follow another explicit constraint: "go to the analogs that are the most helpful for diabetes — and so justify our one million dollar grant". So, they devise des-Asn^5 D-Trp^8 that is understood by the cells as a 'strong' injunction to stop glucagon and release insulin and is immediately patented by the lawyers of the non-profit institute in which *JR* works.

The modification 167 cannot be deduced systematically from previous ones, but is not random either. Locally it makes sense given the time, the circumstances, and the modifications already made. 'Anything goes' but only inside local contexts and not everything is kept. What is kept however, you can push as hard as you want and combine as much as you can with the few

other successful modifications you already have, but push it only in the
directions that are 'the order of the day'. This 'obstinate opportunism' so to
speak is well marked in the four other modifications of the same page. 168
resumes a programme that is acting throughout the corpus; replacing each
analog by an alanine and seeing what happens; 169 goes on but skips one
position — the tenth — and so cannot be deduced from the former at the
eleventh position. The modification 170 shifts abruptly to another programme
and applies it at position 4. Then, as we explained earlier, a paper appears
that proposed adding three glycine to the native molecule. Again, *JR* suddenly
changes direction, jumps on that new modification and tries it. The modification 173 is particularly interesting. *JR* goes on in his makeshift rule
that advises him to "combine all successful modifications" and fabricates a
monstrous analog with the three glycines learned from the newly published
paper, the deleted asparagine at position 4 and the dextro form at position
8. Since this analog is inactive, *JR* shifts again and invents a new locally
consistent rule to get as much as he can of his few hundreds of analogs.

There is no one rule that could explain all the analogs that the laboratory
devised; but the process is not without reason, or more exactly, it is not
without heterogeneous, short lived, circumstantial reasons. The research
process cannot be described as a game — since there is no rule — but cannot
be described as a chaos of random moves and lucky guesses. It is a game 'à la'
Humpty-Dumpty: make up the rules by closely following the unfolding of
the previous moves, and try to persuade yourself — as well as the other
partners — that you have not made up the rules but observed or followed
them. It is a very soft rule indeed, but that explains why, like in a game of
Go (12) from a random point of departure a coherent and logical process
can be obtained. This process is not without similarity with 'bricolage' or
tinkering (13). Tinkering is always opposed to 'rational' or 'scientific' reasoning, although it best approximates the way scientists work, and, according
to Jacob (14), the way life itself functions.

The Research Process is Idiosyncratic

Tinkering opportunistically amidst a turbulent heterogeneous context is a
process that makes sense only if one looks at the local place of work, that is
the laboratory. If the history of the production of a scientific statement is

told, only dismembered and contradictory accounts can be found. What leads these accounts from one to the next is a set of material and local circumstances, most of them tacit, that Knorr described as 'idiosyncratic' (15). The chart that summarises all the analogs is a mixture of chaotic moves interrupted by short lived systematic chains that are in turn slashed by contradictory lines of reasoning. What holds these analogs together, and makes them something more than random, is the material life of this specific laboratory.

JR is able to manufacture analogs, and even to think about the possibility of manufacturing them, because a few years earlier the laboratory adopted the controversial solid phase synthetic method, invented by Merrifield (16). This method is still despised as a dirty, impure, "unscientific" method by the partisans of the liquid phase synthesis. The main advantage of the Merrifield method, however, is to be fast and entirely automated in one small piece of furniture: the Automatic Peptide Synthetizer (17). The major shortcomings of this method is that the degree of purity of the final product is not guaranteed. But, in this specific laboratory, *JR* can draw on *X*'s instruments of analytical chemistry which, at the time, are said to be the best in the country. By using these heavy and very sensitive tools, *JR* can check that each product of the synthesis is pure enough, checks that no other laboratory can afford to get. With pure, easy to produce analogs, *JR* can swamp the physiologists with many samples to test. Here again, the local conditions are crucial. The very existence of these substances — that is their detection and meaning — is based on their action in fragile biological systems. Each system — called assay — is an idiosyncratic construction that cannot be replicated anywhere else. A 'good' laboratory in this field, is essentially a laboratory that is known for its 'highly sensitive' bioassays. Without them you cannot even detect that a sample of brain extract decreases growth hormone, or you cannot observe the difference between an analog that delete the fifth aminoacid and the native molecule. In this specific laboratory, subtle differences between analogs can be detected; elsewhere, they would be different or invisible. To say that the process is idiosyncratic, is to say that the analogs exist at the *intersection* of these local lay out — synthetic chemistry, analytical chemistry, physiology — and cannot escape from it.

Idiosyncrasy not only points out the local conditions for the definition of an analog, it also points out the material existence of a laboratory. Devising an analog is an intellectual activity only for an outsider; inside the laboratory, it is the black art of chemistry, the cooking of substances, the manipulation of instruments, the reading of literature, the discussions with grant agencies or lawyers, the constant phone calls, the injection of diluted substances, the bleeding of white rats . . . The links between analogs that appear on the chart as meaningless or absurd can be made by the proximity in a cupboard of two vials of different aminoacids; or by the use of a tacit rule known and practised only inside the group; or because a lecturer just happened to suggest that people in Switzerland had tried this modification on another substance. If you tear apart the circumstances, most of the steps leading from one analog to the next seem as many *non sequiturs*. If you re-introduce them, one step follows the other, through a long detour that cuts across the whole material life of a laboratory.

Opportunism and idiosyncrasy best designate these turbulent mechanisms that end up with only 236 analogs out of billions. There is some coherence between the few hundred modifications, a weak kind of coherence that is understandable given the specific group and the specific pressures exerted upon this group by other actors. Like a *culture* the group produced only a few artefacts that are linked only if one looks closely enough to the local setting and becomes familiar enough with its peculiar material conditions.

The Research Process is a Fiction-building

The research process never appears as I have described it so far. The tinkering through changing conditions in order to locally create some provisional pockets of meaning, is constantly re-created and re-ordered by many writing activities. Everytime *JR* or *W* writes an article or answers an interview or discusses with one of their colleagues, creditors or competitors, they build up a new version of how the analogs are linked to one another. It is clear that the process of devising the analogs is neither logical nor rational, but it is also clear that it is constantly *made* logical and made rational.

One easy way to show this re-ordering process is to look at the many interpolations as shown in Figure 2. On the right of this diagram I inscribed the analogs the way *JR* neatly arrayed them in one review paper; in the middle I listed the analog according to the date at which they were fabricated; on the left, I grouped them according to the most 'logical' programme they were

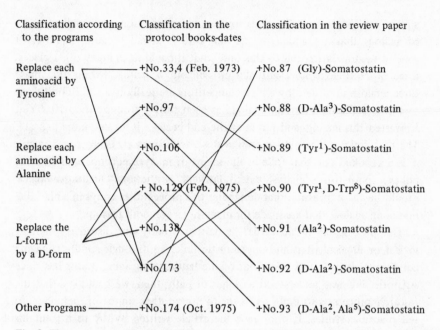

Classification according   Classification in the   Classification in the review paper
to the programs   protocol books-dates

Fig. 2. The analogs number 87 to 93 in a review paper are written on the right side; then in the middle column is recorded the date of their fabrication and the number in the protocol book. In the left column analogs are grouped according to the program that best describe them. Lines linking the same analogs help visualizing the interpolations from one classification to the other.

supposed to follow (see excerpts page 60). The arrows linking the analogs allow the reader to easily follow the interpolations from one type of order to the next. Modification 174, made in 1975 appears first in the classification; however it was made a few days after another one 173, that is 'caused' by an entirely different programme which started two years earlier and 'caused', among others, modification 33 that is classified two steps below the first one. Each order mobilizes the others according to the new rule of classification that is for the time being the most useful.

This is not to say, however, that the rule is followed in any strict and straightforward manner. If you now read the drafts where *JR* wrote the classification that is shown on the right hand column of Figure 2, you find that no specific rule is applied consistently. The starting rule was to list all the modifications at the first position, then all the modifications at the second and so on. The draft, however, is covered with corrections and small packages of analogs that are added or deleted. One is added because, said *JR*: "I wanted to draw attention to this one", but it could fit in many other places; three other analogs are eventually crossed out because: "I think that these three analogs published by . . . (a competitor) are really bad and I don't want to embarrass him". Another analog has been shifted from position 10: "Yes, I inverted this analog, and put it at the end because it seemed more logical". The path linking the analogs, even in this *post hoc* review is far from straight; it is a crooked one that follows the seams of many preoccupations (journal policy, competitor's claims, patent lawyers, aesthetic). 'Qualitative logics' should be the expression that designates this process that arrays in a plausible reasoning analogs that are made for many heterogeneous reasons.

The process, as I said earlier, is neither orderly nor disorderly, neither logical or illogical, it is an opportunistic tinkering through rapidly changing conditions. If logic was taken out of the laudative meaning that it has since Aristotle and was understood as logos or path, then, we could say that the research process is to build paths or, to use another source of metaphor, to tell plausible stories. If one reads the article written by *JR* to present his analogs, it will be clear: (a) that his reconstruction has no relation whatsoever with the various orders followed in making them in the laboratory (18); (b) that his reconstruction is deeply different from the ones provided in other papers written by him or his colleagues; (c) that his formulation of the logics in the making of analogs is no more straightforward than any of the others. I reproduce in Figure 3 one paragraph of this review paper. If the reader disregards the 'technical' terms and concentrates on the argumentation only, the story-telling character of this paragraph will immediately appear (19).

Temporal markers invent a temporal framework which is as realistic as that of the fairy tales; it is not written: 'once upon a time', but "the early observations" (. . .) "we then looked", (. . .) "we knew that from then on", etc. As in any other fiction, actors are made up that undergo transformations or are supposed to be the authors of various actions; this making up is achieved by using words like 'we', 'one', or impersonal actors like 'the Ala[1] Gly[2] chain' or 'the early observations'. Then causes are fabricated that link transformations with one another; "the early observations *lead* us" (. . .) "*to* test this hypothesis, we synthesised" (. . .) "*to* account for . . . one might consider", etc. Writing devices are used to dramatise the text; "it was therefore a surprise

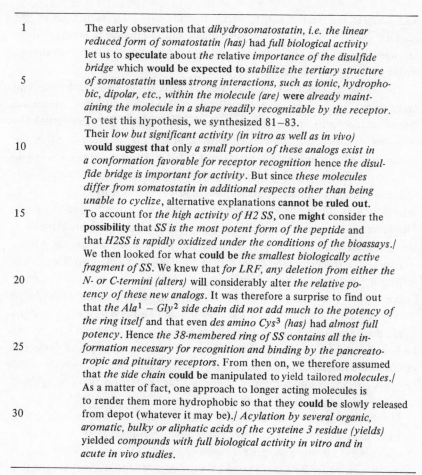

1   The early observation that *dihydrosomatostatin, i.e. the linear*
     reduced form of somatostatin (has) had *full biological activity*
     let us to **speculate** about *the* relative *importance of the disulfide*
     bridge which **would be expected to** *stabilize the tertiary structure*
5   *of somatostatin* **unless** *strong interactions, such as ionic, hydropho-*
     bic, dipolar, etc., within the molecule (are) **were** *already maint-*
     aining the molecule in a shape readily recognizable by the receptor.
     To test this hypothesis, we synthesized 81–83.
     Their *low but significant activity (in vitro as well as in vivo)*
10   **would suggest that** only *a small portion of these analogs exist in*
     a conformation favorable for receptor recognition hence *the disul-*
     fide bridge is important for activity. But since *these molecules*
     differ from somatostatin in additional respects other than being
     unable to cyclize, alternative explanations **cannot be ruled out.**
15   To account for *the high activity of H2 SS,* one **might** consider the
     possibility that *SS is the most potent form of the peptide* and
     that *H2SS is rapidly oxidized under the conditions of the bioassays./*
     We then looked for what **could be** *the smallest biologically active*
     fragment of SS. We knew that *for LRF, any deletion from either the*
20   *N- or C-termini (alters)* will considerably alter *the relative po-*
     tency of these new analogs. It was therefore a surprise to find out
     that *the Ala^1 – Gly^2 side chain did not add much to the potency of*
     the ring itself and that even *des amino Cys^3 (has)* had *almost full*
     potency. Hence *the 38-membered ring of SS contains all the in-*
25   *formation necessary for recognition and binding by the pancreato-*
     tropic and pituitary receptors. From then on, we therefore assumed
     that *the side chain* **could be** manipulated to yield tailored *molecules./*
     As a matter of fact, one approach to longer acting molecules is
     to render them more hydrophobic so that they **could be** slowly released
30   from depot (whatever it may be)./ *Acylation by several organic,*
     aromatic, bulky or aliphatic acids of the cysteine 3 residue (yields)
     yielded *compounds with full biological activity in vitro and in*
     acute in vivo studies.

Fig. 3. This paragraph of a review paper has been treated to separate the modalities
(**bold** letters) and the assertions of fact (*italics*). In parentheses are the verbs and
the tense that would be required if the sentence were not modalized.

to find out", and many modalities to qualify statements and make the story
still less rigid. The writing process puts to use elementary logical devices like
a simple table of presence and absence (lines 5–10), a classic analogical step
(line 19), but in mobilising analogs, logical tools, rhetorical devices, fictional
tricks, it eventually builds up a whole world. In this specific paragraph, *JR*
invents a history – a micro one of course – and epistemology (observations

lead people; steps are taken to verify hypothesis), a representation of the research process (people do things to check out alternative hypothesis; there are scientists led by observations) and also a plausible story to link analogs within an acceptable logic.

The fictional character of this specific reconstruction — and indeed of every scientific account — is immediately visible if the different articles are taken into account in which *JR* presents his analogs. Fourteen articles — including 5 abstracts — have been written in the chosen period — that use analogs to make points in the literature (20). According to which article you consider, different analogs are mobilised as arguments to make various points and the reasons to make them will be modified accordingly. First of all, in several articles, *JR* is not even allowed to write any reason for making them. The same analog can be a chemist's story — and then physiologists are used in the technical part of the text to state the potency of the analog — or a physiologist's story ... and then chemists are allowed only two lines in the technical part to state how they made the analogs. One paper for instance (number 168) was written by *JR* in collaboration with a young physiologist post doctorate: "I wrote the article very fast and before *B* — the physiologist — had done anything; so I included all the physiology in the technical section; he is still a freshman, he co-signed the article, but he could have made it a physiological paper". Having an author writing his own reconstruction of the research process is not a given; it is already the result of a fierce struggle to define *who* will make up the fictional account.

If I limit myself to the articles in which *JR* succeeded in being the first author, many more interpolations can be seen. For instance the story about des-Ala^1 Gly^2 being a surprise (Figure 3, line 21), appears only in this paragraph. In paper 339 it is presented only as a way to understand the role of the disulfide bridge. In still another paper (367), the same analog is used not to show the small role of the N-ter-minus, but to explain why a longer acting somatostatin is possible. For other arguments, on the contrary, the same sentence is repeated over and over again through all the papers and only the modalities (or the style) are adapted. Of course, there are many good rhetorical reasons for these modifications. For instance, an analog taken as a systematic one in several chemistry papers is suddenly dramatised in a new paper written, this time, for clinicians: "in view of the considerable hindrance that represents this character in the prospective clinical uses of somatostatin" and then follows an analog 'caused' by this tactical clinical reason. In the various papers analogs are grouped, eliminated, clumped again not according to any *one* rule, but much like troops and tanks in a battlefield: for tactical reasons wherever someone thinks they could be used to make a point stronger.

The various writings when compared do not offer a quieter or more rational picture of the research process than the observation of this process or the interviews of the scientists engaged in it. Each interview, each manipulation of analog, each writing is, in a way, a reconstruction. This does not mean that there is something 'wrong' or 'dishonest' with this process, because there is nowhere any account of the research that could be something more than a fiction. We constantly make sense of the world and build paths leading points to one another and convince people that a particular path is more straightforward than any other. It is useless to say that the accounts provided in this volume, and the present account, obey the same mechanisms (21).

A New Conception of Order

I chose the example of these analogs of somatostatin only because it was the dullest, most mechanical, most systematic and most straightforward process I could observe in the laboratory I studied. If such a straightforward process can be shown to be so chaotic, illogical, opportunistic, contextual and constantly reconstructed, the reader can get a vague idea of what the research process can be when one studies more interesting, more original and less routinely made pieces of a science. If a dull piece of puzzle-solving science is made through such noise and disorder, one can imagine the 'story full of noise and furore' that is heard when one listens to a paradigm shift. Actually, everyone *knows* this noise; it is the noise of *history*. By an old privilege, science was supposed to be less disorderly, less noisy, less fictional than the rest of history. The new wealth of studies on the research process have one main consequence; they put an end to this age old (actually Greek-old) privilege. The research process is nothing *more* and nothing *less* than the rest of our daily world and daily stories of fictions and disorder (22).

The strings of words that have been chosen to describe the research process (from 'contextual' to 'fiction') all aim to end the privilege of science by using precisely the words that ought to be eliminated when passing from 'history' to 'science'. These words, however, have been chosen haphazardly for most of them and with polemical or negative connotations. There is not yet any coherent framework – but is this possible or desirable – that would describe the research process without maintaining the former privilege. The only attempt has not been made by sociologists of science, but by isolated scientists dealing with information, or with turbulent phenomena. The works of Brillouin (23) and the recent book of Prigogine and Stengers (24) together with the philosophy developed in France by Michel Serres (25), convinced me that a new framework is already at hand to understand and rephrase our observations on the way science is made. In the old framework, disorder, turbulence, agitation, circumstances, were to be *eliminated* for a world of order, logics and rationality to appear and be maintained. In the new framework, order is nothing but local circumstances obtained from, maintained by, dissolved from time to time in *disorder*; if you eliminate the opportunism, the context, the fiction building, the agitation, the reconstruction, the rationalisation you get *nothing* at all; if you introduce them you understand how the scientific facts, discoveries and theories emerge and are maintained. More importantly, in the old framework, since disorder was to be eliminated, the factors dug out by historians, sociologists and psychologists, always appeared as 'external' to the main process of science, and hence the sterile but convenient paradigm that phrased the research process within 'internal' and 'external' factors. In the new framework, since disorder is the main component and, so to speak, the *substance* of the final orderly product, the factors dug out by historians and sociologists are not 'external' anymore. They are, to use a religious term, consubstantial to the science produced. In consequence, it is now possible to account for the very content and nature of the objects produced by scientists (26). As important is the methodological consequence that should be drawn when working in this new framework. As I have shown elsewhere (27) since disorder is the substance of science the factors and events we reveal to the scientists are not threatening to them; sociologists and scientists both feed on fiction, disorder, circumstances and, from time to time, logical stories. In the old framework, we had to observe scientists from the outside, to threaten them, or worse, to give up studying and pass inside their fortress to worship them or become their servants. Now that we are all equally inside the heterogeneous opportunistic, fictional science that is built, new alliances are possible that are much more interesting than the boring 'tête à tête' of scientists and their observer.

I am not able to fully describe this new framework, and have only shown (28) how it works when one accounts for the research process in laboratories. One thing is clear however; although we all haphazardly invented words to describe this process, they all seem to fit if we modify the conception of order we used to have. Immediately, words like circumstances, random, opportunism, fiction, idiosyncrasy, rationalisation stop being a derogatory criticism of science and rationality or a claim for relativism. If we modify the conception of order these same words start expressing the very nature of the scientific objects. The interest of micro-studies of the research process in science, is to provide the best possible ground to test this 'new alliance' that Prigogine and Stengers are advocating, and to help in what they call 'metamorphosis of science' (29).

Notes and References

1. H. M. Collins, 'The seven sexes: a study in the sociology of a phenomenon' *Sociology* 9 (2), 205–224 (1975).
2. B. Latour, 'Including citations counting in the systems of actions of a scientific text', First Four-S Meeting, Cornell, Ithaca, 1976.
3. K. Knorr, 'From scenes to scripts: on the relationship between research and publication in science', Institute for Advanced Studies, Vienna, 1978 and *Social Studies of Science*, (forthcoming).
4. M. Callon, 'De problèmes en problèmes: itinéraire d'un laboratoire universitaire saisi par l'aventure technologique', 1978 Cordes, Paris.
5. B. Latour and S. Woolgar, *Laboratory Life: The Social Construction of Scientific Facts*, Sage, 1979.
6. *Ibid.*
7. P. Brazeau, W. Vale, R. Burgus, N. Ling, J. Rivier and R. Guillemin, 'Hypothalamic Peptides that inhibit the Secretion of Immunoreative Pituitary Growth Hormone', *Science* 170, 77–79; J. Rivier *et al.*, 'Review on the Design of Synthetic Analogs', in *Peptides 1976*, Editions de l'Universite de Bruxelles, 1977 Bruxelles, pp. 427–452.
8. Latour, *op. cit.*, Note 2; Latour and Woolgar, *op. cit.* Note 5, Chapter 11; B. Latour and P. Fabbri, 'Pouvoir et Devoir dans un article de Sciences Exactes', *Actes de la Recherche*, Février 1977, pp. 81–95.
9. B. Barnes and J. Law, 'Whatever should be done with indexical expressions', *Theory and Society* 3 (2), 223–237 (1976).
10. The only analog that was invented in my presence was the result of a lawyer coming into the laboratory with the draft of a patent application. The other analogs were devised through a sort of quantic process that I was never able to document directly. I was always one day, one hour or one minute too late to add my own observations to the stories fed to me by the scientists. It is why I do not use my observer's note in this paper like I did in the other cases I could follow continuously.

11. "Des" means that the aminoacid has been deleted; the small figure indicates which position in the 14 aminoacid structure is modified. "D" means that the levorotory form that is the only form existing in nature, has been replaced by its mirror image, the dextrorotatory form that is created artificially. When a substitution is made the new aminoacid is indicated as follows: the Thr[8] Somatostatin, which means that the naive analog Cys at the third position has been replaced by the analog Thr. Of course, no knowledge of peptide chemistry is necessary to understand the paper; except for these few writing conventions, the analogs can and should be taken by the reader like the proper names in novels. What they really mean is uninteresting and no more effort is required than recognising Russian names in a Dostoievsky's novel.

12. Latour and Woolgar, *op. cit.*, 1979, Note 5, page 246. The game of Go is certainly the best model to test the various components of the research process especially because the basic rules are so few and the complexity at mid-game is so baffling.

13. Levi-Strauss, *La Pensée Sauvage* Plon, Paris, 1962.

14. F. Jacob, 'Evolution and Tinkering', *Science* **196** (4295), 1161–1166 (1977).

15. K. Knorr, 'The research process: Tinkering toward success: Prelude to a Theory of Scientific Practice', *Theory and Society* 8, 347–376 (1979).

16. R. B. Merrifield, 'The automatic Synthesis of Proteins', *Scientific American* **218**, 56–71 March (1968).

17. The instrument manufactured by Beckmann has been studied in a one-month side project of the main field study. For presentation of the importance of the instruments, see Latour and Woolgar, 1979 *op. cit.*, Note 5.

18. This is not surprising since the aim of a scientific paper is not to reproduce reports on what happened in the laboratory but to act on the literature; see Latour *op. cit.* 1976. Note 2: Knorr *op. cit.* p. 197, Note 3, and P. Medawar: 'Is the scientific paper fraudulent?' *Saturday Review*, August 1964, pp. 42–43.

19. The analysis is very crude indeed. For a full semiotic treatment of a scientific text, see F. Bastide; 'Le foie lavé. Approche semiotique d'une texte de sciences expérimentales', *Documents* No. 7 1979 EHESS-CNRS Paris.

20. For the review paper, see J. Rivier *et al. op. cit.*, 1976, Note 7. For specific examples with JR as first author, see J. Rivier, 'Somatostatin Analogs. Relative Importance of the Disulfide Bridge for biological activity', *Journal of Medicinal Chemistry* **18**,123–124 (1975); or J. Rivier *et al.*, 'D-Trp[8] an analog of somatostatin more potent than the native molecule', *BBRC* 6, 746–748 (1975).

21. There is nothing self destructive in this obvious consequence. 'Fiction' is not taken as synonym of 'empty', 'false' or 'fraudulent'. It is the word that describes the construction of paths and plausible stories; what count are the *effects* of the story on the readers. One of these many effects is that the story 'is true'. This effect can be studied and deconstructed – or contructed – like any other.

22. The work inspired by ethnomethodology tries to reach the same conclusions through very different techniques, see Woolgar (this volume).

23. L. Brillouin, *Scientific Uncertainty and Information*, Academic Press, New York, 1964. See also H. Atlan, *L'organisation biologique et la Theorie de l'Information*, Paris 1972, Hermann.

24. I. Prigogine and I. Stengers, *La Nouvelle Alliance*: *Metamorphose de la Science* Paris Gallimard, 1979.

25. M. Serres, *La Naissance de la Physique dans le Texte de Lucrece: Fleuves et Turbulences* Paris. Editions de Minuit, 1977. I cannot even summarise the arguments of Serres in this article.

26. This is why the major objections of microsociologists to the former brands of sociology of science was their disregard for the contents of the sciences they studied. They talked about external factors and really thought — like some scientists — that these factors were indeed external. The new framework helps to seize a new idea: these factors are the essence of the produced science and then a full study of the scientific facts is possible.

27. B. Latour, 'Who is agnostic or what could it mean to study science'. In H. Kuclick (ed.), *Sociology of Knowledge Science and Art*, 1980.

28. For a still shy and awkward tentative, see B. Latour 1979, *op. cit.*, Note 5, Chapter VI, especially the middle part.

29. Prigogine and Stengers, 1979, *op. cit.*, Note 24.

PART II

DISCOVERY ACCEPTANCE

THEORETICIANS AND THE PRODUCTION OF
EXPERIMENTAL ANOMALY: THE CASE OF
SOLAR NEUTRINOS

T. J. PINCH

University of Bath

Introduction

In-depth studies of the development of particular pieces of scientific knowledge form the hallmark of recent work in the sociology of science (1). Broadly
informed by a relativist approach, the authors of such case studies have
attempted to explain scientific development in a fully sociological manner.
That is, the main explanatory weight is given to the social world rather than
to the natural world.

The emphasis of these case studies has tended to be on either experimental
or theoretical controversies. However, it is also important to consider cases
where both theoreticians and experimentalists are involved. In particular
we need to know what role is played by theoreticians when a controversial
experimental result appears which does not fit their theories. It is this type of
question which I address below by drawing on a study made of solar-neutrino
science − an area where there is an experimental result which conflicts with
theoretical expectation.

Theoreticians and Experimenters

Theoretical and experimental work, in physics anyway, is largely carried out
by two different and clearly identifiable groups with different work environ-
ments, publication patterns, career structures and rewards (2). Although
there are some exceptions, large areas of modern physics have a well defined
division of labour between theory and experiment.

On a recent round of interviews of American scientists working in the field

Karin D. Knorr, Roger Krohn and Richard Whitley (eds.), The Social Process of
Scientific Investigation. Sociology of the Sciences, Volume IV, 1980. 77−106.

of solar neutrinos some of these differences were apparent (the differences noted here may only be local to this branch of physics – high-energy physics, for instance, has much larger teams of experimentalists and theoreticians). I noticed, for example, that I was more likely to encounter a theorist in the privacy of his office on the upper floors of the physics building, whilst an experimentalist was usually to be found on the ground floor or basement, either near or in his laboratory (many theoreticians 'look down' on experimentalists simply because the large and complex pieces of apparatus used by experimentalists are more conviently housed in the lower levels of buildings). Experimenters were more likely to be surrounded by post docs., graduate students and technicians, whilst the theoreticians seemed to favour working alone in the sanctity of their offices. Interviews with experimenters were often conducted amidst an assortment of instruments and odd pieces of hardware in various stages of assembly. This contrasted with the array of books, periodicals, computer programmes and the blackboard covered with formulae which greeted me when I entered a theorist's office – these were of course, the instruments of *their* trade.

It is clear that theorising and experimentation are very different activities and require quite different competences. The theorist constructs and manipulates the esoteric formalisms characteristic of most modern physical theory, whilst the experimentalist constructs and manipulates the sophisticated pieces of measuring apparatus found in today's physics laboratories. Yet, despite obvious differences in the two types of activity, at some point they must interact – and the exact nature of that interaction has been the problem which has been taken up in recent work in the philosophy of science (3). The problem I find with such philosophical work is that the issues are discussed in the abstract. For example, philosophers might consider the relationship between a particular observation and theory without any consideration for the setting in which they were produced. It seems to me that in science theory and observation are brought together not in some abstract world (such as Popper's 'World three' (4)) but in a particular scientific and social setting.

The approach that I favour for investigating the interaction of theory and experiment is to trace the parts played by theoreticians and experimenters in the development of a concrete area of science – in this case solar-neutrinos. By outlining the activities of the two groups and in particular their relationship, hopefully we will gain some insights as to their contributions to the production of scientific knowledge.

The Solar-Neutrino Anomaly

Solar-neutrino science has been dominated by one outstanding problem – the solar-neutrino anomaly. This arises from a clash between the theoretical prediction of the flux of neutrinos coming from the Sun and the experimental measurement of this flux.

The possibility of detecting solar neutrinos and thus confirming nuclear fusion as the Sun's motor, first became a realistic enterprise in 1958, when it was pointed out that the sun produced a rare branch of neutrinos whose energy spectrum was sufficient for them to be detected on earth. In 1964, at a cost of \$ 600 000, a detector was built in a gold mine in Lead, S. Dakota (a mile of rock shields out cosmic rays). The detector was based on a large tank of cleaning fluid (perchloroethylene) containing chlorine-37 atoms with which incoming neutrinos would interact to produce radioactive argon-37. This could be extracted and detected by its characteristic Auger electron decay. By 1967 the flux of solar neutrinos was being monitored. The reported detection rate has always been lower than theory predicts. Although there have been fluctuations in both the theoretical prediction and experimental result, the discrepancy has remained and there is now a growing consensus that the result is correct.

It is this discrepancy between theory and experiment which forms the basis of the present study.

The investigation which I undertook had both sociological and historical dimensions. The main sociological data came from tape-recorded interviews with as many of the scientists who had made significant contributions to the field as were accessible geographically and within the logistics of the project (most of the interviews were conducted on one fieldwork trip to the U.S. in November/December 1978). Interviews were also conducted with scientists on the fringes of the field (for instance, those connected with funding). In all forty interviews took place. In addition to this 'oral history', the traditional History of Science sources, provided by the primary and secondary literatures of the field, were used. A substantial amount of correspondence between some of the leading solar-neutrino scientists was also collected, and this provided a further source of data.

The history of the solar-neutrino anomaly can be conveniently divided into two parts around the date of August 1967, when the first experimental result was reported. I will describe the activities of experimentalists and theoreticians and their relationship pre-1967 and post-1967.

PART I

The Activities of Experimentalists and Theoreticians Pre-1967

The pre-1967 period can be further divided, into the time up until 1958, when the main experimenter worked largely alone, the time between 1958 and 1964, when several theoreticians became interested, and, finally, the period 1964—7, which was characterised by an intense interaction between the experimenter and one theoretician. I will discuss each of these periods in turn.

The Early Situation — Very Much an Experimental Problem

Until theoreticians became directly involved in 1958, solar-neutrino detection was largely an experimental problem. The attempt to detect solar neutrinos was preceded by an experiment to measure the flux of neutrinos produced at a nuclear reactor. The chlorine-37 radiochemical technique, which was used in both experiments, was first proposed in 1946 (5), but it was not until 1954 that Raymond Davis, Jr., of the Brookhaven National Laboratory, was able successfully to build and operate such a detector. No earlier attempt had been made because it was thought the background effects would swamp any signal.

The first detector consisted of two 500 gallon tanks and was set up to measure the neutrino flux produced at the Savannah River nuclear reactor in 1956. However, events in nuclear physics overtook the experiment when it was discovered that there were significant differences between the neutrino and its anti-particle, the anti-neutrino. Unfortunately for the experiment it turned out that only anti-neutrinos were produced at reactors, and, as the detector was only sensitive to neutrinos, only background counts were registered. At the same time as Davis, using radiochemical techniques, was getting nothing, Reines and Cowan, also working at Savannah River, but with a direct counting array, produced the first direct experimental evidence for the existence of anti-neutrinos. Despite the negative result, there was some interest in what Davis had done because it provided a confirmation of the difference between the neutrino and anti-neutrino.

The aim of Davis's research programme was the detection of neutrinos and, after the reactor experiments, he began thinking in earnest about other sources of neutrinos, in particular the Sun.

Davis was very much a loner at this time in thinking about the possibility of solar-neutrino detection. The elusive nature of the neutrino (it only interacts weakly with matter) meant that most people neglected it as a possible probe of the Sun. The consensus amongst theoreticians was that the predominant energy cycle in the Sun was the proton-proton cycle of reactions and that it did not produce any neutrinos of sufficient energy to trigger Davis's detector.

Davis's attitude, however, was that it might be worth putting a large tank in a mine just to see what signal there was. However, there were obstacles to doing this as such an enterprise would inevitably be expensive. Given the largely negative attitude towards the possibility of detecting solar neutrinos which prevailed at that time, it is unlikely that he would have got funding for an experiment looking 'on the off chance'. Davis needed some sort of further justification for doing his experiment, and it was towards theory that he looked.

Davis's interest in theory can be seen from his attitude towards one of the theoretical possibilities. This concerned a nuclear reaction in the sun, the conversion of ^{3}He to ^{4}Li by proton capture. The ^{4}Li formed would then decay by the emission of a very energetic neutrino which Davis should be able to detect. Most theoreticians considered this reaction was unlikely to occur. Davis, however, was more enthusiastic about the possibility because it gave him something to test. He explained the situation as follows (6):

Kuzmin [A Soviet physicist] posed this . . . he pointed out it was possible, you don't know – that kind of argument. And *Z* [a nuclear physicist] said 'Oh hell, lithium-four can't be stable'. He talked about the nuclear structure 'It is absolutely out of the question' . . . So you had these two viewpoints. For me it was interesting because at least someone posed something you could test.

I will break off from my account of the development of the solar-neutrino problem here in order to outline a schema of analysis which will prove to be useful in describing events.

Cycles of Credibility

Thus far the relationship between the experimental program of neutrino
• detection and theoretical concerns would appear to be unexceptional. Indeed the activities of the experimentalist seeking a theory to test critically seem to fit well with the Popperian model of science (7). As mentioned earlier, my objection to philosophical approaches (such as Popper's) to the relationship between theory and experiment is that the particular developments under discussion are frequently divorced from their social setting. In order to clarify my criticism of the philosophical approach I will set it against a sociologically informed analysis of science, outlined recently by Latour and Woolgar (8). This approach was developed from an anthropological study of a scientific laboratory (the aspect of Latour's and Woolgar's study drawn on here is not the central thrust of their argument – for that the reader is advised to consult the original work).

In order to make sense of inter-relationships between individual scientists, the laboratory, and other laboratories, within the overall context of the production of scientific facts, Latour and Woolgar found it useful to talk about 'cycles of credibility'. In a departure from the pre-capitalist system of scientific reward developed by Hagstrom (9) and, to a lesser extent, the capitalist economy of scientific authority outlined by Bourdieu (10), the authors conceived of scientists as investors of credibility in a market in which there is a demand for credible information. Credibility can take on different forms and individual scientists are best described as being engaged in a cycle of credibility whereby different currencies of credibility (or capital accumulations) are converted one to the other. The activity of producing scientific results will enhance the overall credibility of the scientist, provided, of course, that he produces credible results. The production of credible results enables the scientist to get more resources, such as funding and equipment, which can, in turn, be converted into more credibility by producing yet more results. Scientists can thus be seen as investing their previously acquired credibility in the hopes of getting a return by producing credible information.

One benefit of this picture of science is that it enables what have traditionally been seen as disparate themes to appear alongside each other; there is a correspondence between, for instance, economic and epistemological terms. It can be seen that it is quite possible for scientists to be making crucial tests of theories *as well as* furthering their own careers. To conceive of the scientific enterprise in terms of merely the testing of theories is as onesided as to picture scientists as opportunist careerists. Neither explanation is alone sufficient to describe the full richness of scientific activity.

If scientists are engaged in a struggle to maximise their credibility then we can expect them to exploit the specialization of modern science to further their investment strategies. By forming partnerships it is possible for individuals with quite different areas of scientific expertise to come together and make a joint investment. Latour and Woolgar cite many cases where one scientist or group will give money or equipment to another in the expectation that they will produce results that are of use to the first group, thus enabling the first group to boost their credibility. Clearly the recipients of the equipment and money will also boost their own credibility by producing reliable information for the first group. It is this type of joint enterprise which has been important in the development of the relationship between theoreticians and experimenters in the area of solar neutrinos.

If we look at Davis's career in terms of investment strategies we can see that by 1958 he had reached an impasse. He had devoted most of his career to the development of the chlorine-37 neutrino detector. His investment in this form of experimentation had shown some return with the results of his experiments at reactors and, by 1956, he had built up a substantial capital of credibility in this field. However, if he was to further increase his credibility he had to find other sources of neutrinos to detect (after the successful experiments of Reines and Cowan there was little point in continuing with reactor experiments). The only source that might be usefully detectable with this type of equipment was solar neutrinos and hence it would be a natural extension of his investment strategy to explore this avenue. The problem Davis faced, however, was that it did not seem there were enough detectable neutrinos to warrant the rest of the scientific community investing the large sums of money needed for such an experiment. Davis had to persuade others that it was worth investing in his experiment. His hope was that theoretical astrophysicists and nuclear physicists, who studied the nuclear reactions in stars, might be persuaded to view his experiment as a test of their theories and thereby support his effort. If such a 'deal' could be struck then both groups would benefit. Davis would get the money for his experiment and the opportunity to further his credibility, and the theorists would have an opportunity to test their theories of the nuclear reactions in stars – a test, which if successful, would undoubtedly enhance their reputation as producers of credible information.

One of the merits of using an economic metaphor to describe scientific developments is that scientists themselves often speak in these terms. Latour and Woolgar found many scientists explicitly referred to their investment strategies. In my own conversations with solar-neutrino scientists, I, too, found that economic language was prevalent. In my continuing account of the solar-neutrino problem we will find that the description in terms of credibility cycles is in close resonance with how the participants themselves viewed the situation. This gives us some encouragement that the account offered here is at least not as divorced from real scientific activity as that offered by philosophers.

Let us now return to the solar-neutrino story and see how it was that the other component in the partnership – the theoreticians – became interested in going into business with the experimentalist.

1958–64. The Entrance of the Theoreticians

The theoretical justification that Davis hoped for came about in 1958. The cross-section (probability of nuclear interaction) for one of the nuclear reactions which could possibly occur in the Sun, ^{3}He + ^{4}He → ^{7}Be + γ, was found to be much larger than expected.

The significance of this result was that ^{7}Be was formed, which, by another reaction (the capture of a proton), could go on to produce ^{8}B, which would in turn decay by emitting a high energy neutrino – a neutrino which could be detected in Davis's proposed experiment. Although the ^{7}Be proton capture had never been measured, calculations showed that there should be a significant cross-section. Two nuclear astrophysicists, William Fowler and A. G. W. Cameron, made the necessary calculations and in early 1958 they both wrote separately to Davis informing him that he might be able to detect ^{8}B neutrinos and indeed that he might be doing so already.

The importance of the new result to Davis was, of course, that now he had good reasons to do the experiment. However, he did not plan the experiment in the expectation that he would exactly confirm the theoretical prediction. As he told me:

I guess this is an experimentalist's attitude. What do you use the theory for? . . . You use the theory for guidance as to whether it makes sense to do the experiment. . . . And so you say at least I've got the theoreticians telling me that now's a good time to do the experiment. But if you do the experiment you may or may not find what they say.

Davis's primary goal was the detection of solar neutrinos. This is what he hoped would give him credibility in his field. He could achieve this goal by testing astrophysical theories. However, the test, as such, was for him only a means to an end. For the nuclear astrophysicists, however, the test itself was the crucial thing. If the test of nuclear astrophysics was successful they would boost their own credibility. Thus the performance of a solar-neutrino experiment served the interests of both groups.

Of the two scientists who wrote to Davis in 1958 pointing out the Boron-eight possibility, the most significant for the development of the experiment has undoubtedly been Fowler. Although Cameron continued to be interested in the solar-neutrino possibility and calculated some neutrino fluxes, his interest came more from astrophysics as a biproduct of his general concerns with stellar evolution. Fowler's interest, on the other hand, came more from nuclear physics. Fowler, who heads a group of nuclear-astrophysicists at CalTech, orientated his research program around the slogan that 'more can be learnt about stars by studying nuclear reactions than by looking down telescopes'. One outcome of this programme was a celebrated paper, published with Hoyle and the Burbidges (11), in which they produced their schema for the synthesis of the elements by tracing the evolution of stars through the various stages of nuclear burning. By the early 60's, Fowler thus already had considerable scientific achievements, and the detection of solar neutrinos, which would provide the first direct test of the nuclear reactions thought to occur in stars, would have been, as one respondent put it, 'the icing on the cake'.

Clearly if the nuclear astrophysicists were to take an interest in Davis's work they had to think he was capable of producing reliable information concerning the solar-neutrino flux. It can be seen that Fowler, anyway, had a high regard for Davis's work. An extract from his letter to Davis in 1958 reads (12):

Permit me to conclude by expressing my great admiration for your beautiful work on
this problem.

That Fowler should have a good opinion of Davis is almost a precondition for
his interest in the experiment as a test of nuclear astrophysics. Clearly if a
fruitful partnership was to be entered into each party had to regard the other
as capable of producing credible information. The nuclear astrophysicists
would have nothing to gain from an incompetent test of their theories, in
the same way Davis would be left with a costly white elephant (an olympic
swimming pool of cleaning fluid a mile below the Earth's surface) if it turned
out there were no ^{8}B neutrinos to detect.

The aim of the partnership developing between Davis and the astrophysicists was, like in all business agreements, to produce a return for the investments of both parties. Such returns would only come when a successful
solar-neutrino experiment was under way — it was towards this goal that both
parties now worked.

With the theoreticians telling him there was a detectable flux of neutrinos
from the Sun, Davis proceeded to 'convert' his apparatus into a solar-neutrino
detector. He did this by moving his tanks from the Savannah River nuclear
reactor to the Barberton mine in Ohio, where the rock would provide the
necessary cosmic-ray shield. At the same time Fowler's group at CalTech
started to make the first experimental measurements of the crucial ^{7}Be-
proton capture cross-section. As it turned out this cross-section was lower
than expected and it seemed unlikely that Davis's 500 gallon tanks would
be big enough to see anything. Davis's move to the Barberton mine was,
however, important because it enabled him to demonstrate the feasibility
of this sort of detection technique for a solar-neutrino experiment.

Out at CalTech Fowler continued to make calculations of the solar-
neutrino flux. He got a stellar-model specialist, R. D. Sears, to make some
computations but it was becoming increasingly obvious that whether or
not there was a detectable flux of Boron-eight neutrinos depended on very
detailed and complex calculations. And working through the problem in
the detail required was going to be a fairly major undertaking. It was here
that Fowler's influence was important because he drew Davis's attention
to a physicist who might be capable and willing to work on the problem.
This physicist was John Bahcall. If solar neutrinos were to be Fowler's

'icing on the cake', they were for a while, any way, to be John Bahcall's 'bread and butter'.

Bahcall's interest was stimulated by a letter from Davis. He was at the University of Indiana and was acquiring a reputation as an expert in the calculation of stellar nuclear reactions. Davis wrote to Bahcall in the hope that he would be willing to make some calculations. John Bahcall described his reaction to the letter as follows (13):

> The reason I decided to work on it, is the result of a conversation with [a colleague] . . . We got into a discussion about this letter I got from Davis, and I had to decide whether I would spend the time, once I saw that it was some time to calculate . . . so we got into a discussion about how unique or fundamental the experiment would be . . . I became convinced that it was . . . really a unique way of testing an otherwise very fundamental theory.

It can be seen that Bahcall had to weigh up whether to make the necessary investment in the venture. Clearly doing the required work would be demanding and time consuming, but it is equally clear that, after receiving advice from his colleague, he thought the scientific rewards (which would be co-extensive with a boost to his own capital of credibility) provided by a test of stellar evolution, made the proposition put to him by Davis worthwhile.

Having decided to make the necessary calculations, Bahcall kept in touch with Davis by letter, reporting on his progress. Although it turned out that this particular calculation did not show any great promise for the feasibility of Davis's experiment, Bahcall was now enthusiastic about making further calculations. He was able to do so by virtue of a post. doc. place at CalTech in Fowler's group.

It was now in the late summer of 1962 that intense theoretical work on the solar-neutrino problem started at CalTech. In order to make a sufficiently detailed calculation, several different types of theoretical expertise were needed. It first of all required someone who could calculate all the nuclear reaction rates (both in the Sun and in the experiment) — this was Bahcall's particular expertise. Experimental values of the nuclear reaction rates, where they were obtainable, were also required — these were provided by Fowler and the nuclear physicists working with him in the CalTech, Kellogg Radiation Laboratory group. Finally a detailed model of the Sun was required, into which the nuclear reaction rates could be plugged. The production of solar models is a complex theoretical activity in its own right and requires a massive computer program. A sub-routine of this program gives the neutrino fluxes. The generation of such models for stars in general had become a well established branch of astrophysics and two CalTech scientists, R. D. Sears and Icko Iben, were experts in this kind of computation. It was Bahcall's job to put all the different parts of the calculation together – not an easy task as the stellar-model scientists could see little point in working out the Sun in the detail required and were more interested in the late stages of stellar evolution. Indeed Bahcall required Fowler to use his institutional position as head of the group in order to set things in motion.

Eventually the detailed calculations were made by Bahcall in collaboration with Fowler, Iben and Sears, but again the results did not look over promising for the solar-neutrino experiment. As Bahcall wrote to Davis (14):

These results suggest the experiment is extremely difficult. Do you think it is possible?

Davis's reply was more optimistic (15):

It would be possible to observe a rate as low as this . . . However, an experiment of this magnitude would be quite expensive, a rough estimate would be $200,000 . . . I have started some exploratory discussions on the possibility of carrying out the experiment.

The reactions of Bahcall and the CalTech group can be seen from Bahcall's next letter to Davis (16):

We were all pleased to learn . . . that you have started exploratory discussions . . . Please keep us informed of your progress and let us know if we can be of any help.

It can be seen that the experiment, although expensive, was now perhaps feasible.

The joint venture that Davis and the CalTech group had entered, like all business ventures, required financing. Solar-neutrino detection is a costly business, especially as it results in only one number. Whereas the CalTech nuclear astrophysicists had a powerful and influential figure in Fowler as head of their group and were able to command the necessary resources for their side of the venture, Davis, who in any case required much more funding, was not in as good a position. He was based in a chemistry department and this type of experimentation was far more costly than the normal run-of-the-mill chemistry. A special application for funding to the Atomic Energy Commission would have to be made. Fowler was able to help Davis with this application by writing to the chairman of Davis's department, who happened to be an old friend and former colleague of Fowler's. Fowler not only wrote in support of Davis but also offered to assist further up the funding chain.

It would be wrong to see these negotiations over funding as in any way scurrilous. All parties were acting with the highest scientific ideals. The point is that the struggle for scientific credibility cannot be divorced from the struggle to gain funding. It is the nature of modern science that attempts to further scientific knowledge appear alongside what might seem to the uninitiated as fairly crude money wrangles.

Bahcall continued to spend a large amount of time on the solar-neutrino calculations. In the summer of 1963 he visited the Niels Bohr Institute, in Copenhagen, and it was there that he made the breakthrough that was to prove decisive for the future of the experiment. Working with an idea given him by Nobel Laureate, Ben Mottelsohn, Bahcall was able to show that there was a special state in the chlorine-37 system — the analogue state — which would greatly enhance (by a factor of about twenty) the probability of boron-8 neutrinos interacting with chlorine. Bahcall described what happened next:

I went back to CalTech and calculated things very accurately . . . I gave a seminar . . . and people got very excited about it, so I called Davis. He then invited me to come to Brookhaven to give a seminar there. I think that was the first time we met.

Bahcall's new calculations were, of course, important because they boosted the number of neutrinos which Davis could expect to detect. The analogue-state discovery was also important for other reasons, as can be seen from Bahcall's account of what happened when he came to Brookhaven to give the seminar:

He [Davis] had arranged for us to meet the director of Brookhaven . . . we had to sell [the director] or else we wouldn't get the experiment. This nuclear-physics trick [the analogue state] would be something that [the director] would be turned on about, because he was himself a very bright nuclear theorist amongst other things . . . so we decided to sell him the experiment based mainly on this. Then more or less that worked.

The significant thing here was that the support of the director of Brookhaven was needed before any application for funds could be made. And Bahcall, being a nuclear theorist, could assist Davis in convincing the director of the merits of the experiment.

Shortly after this there was a conference held in New York where Bahcall presented his calculations, based on yet more computations by Sears, and Davis gave a short account of the experimental possibilities. These presentations formed the basis of the first major papers stemming from the collaboration. Again Fowler's influence was important; he was pulling strings in the background to try to get the experiment funded and he advised Bahcall and Davis to get something into print quickly in order to draw the attention of the rest of the scientific community to the proposed experiment. Eventually two papers, an experimental one by Davis and a theoretical one by Bahcall, were published 'back to back' in *Physical Review Letters* in March 1964 (17). I asked Davis why they preferred to publish separate papers rather than producing a joint publication; he told me:

See the topics were very different . . . I can't say anything about solar models, and the cross-sections . . . To do the experiment, how to do the experiment, I know all about that.

As we shall see below this publication format is especially significant. This is because, although reflecting the common-ends of the joint venture, it also maintains a boundary between the two very different types of expertise involved.

1964–7. The Years of Close Collaboration

Shortly after the appearance of the articles, two events of significance happened. The calculations made by Bahcall of the analogue state were indirectly confirmed by measurements made on the ^{37}Ca system (18) and the necessary funding for the experiment was made available by the Atomic Energy Commission.

Davis now had to choose a mine and develop plans for constructing the apparatus. There were lots of experimental problems to be solved and contractual details to be sorted out. Eventually, after much negotiation, excavations were started in early 1965 in the Homestake gold mine, in Lead, South Dakota.

On the theoretical front there was plenty of work to be done in refining the calculations. Several new experimental measurements of the relevant input physics were being made and these new results had to be fed into the model predictions. Other theoreticians, such as Cameron, were also making calculations, so Bahcall was faced with the task of comparing these calculations with his own and sorting out any differences which appeared.

Relationships between Bahcall on the west coast and Davis on the east coast required delicate handling as each felt his way into the collaboration. This can be seen from their reaction to two episodes where reporting of the collaboration gave the impression that only one of the two groups was responsible for the experiment. In a letter to Bahcall, written in early 1964, Davis expressed concern about a report in *Time* magazine (19):

> The article, in *Time* magazine, seemed quite good but I was disappointed that there was no mention of your paper and the CalTech contribution. I, of course, like the idea of the experiment being a joint effort.

Later it was Bahcall's turn to express concern when a report appeared in *Scientific American* which seemed to attribute the whole project to him – the author of the article being under the impression that Davis was the technician supervising the building of the experiment! After Bahcall complained to the Editor, *Scientific American* published an *erratum* (20). Perhaps the somewhat delicate nature of the relationship between Bahcall and Davis at this stage can be seen from Bahcall's recollection of the Editor's comment when they first met:

> He said it was unique in his experience at *Scientific American* that somebody complained about getting too much credit!

As the construction of the experiment neared completion, the contact between Bahcall and Davis increased. As Bahcall told me:

> I went to visit the site ... I didn't have much useful to say but I wanted to be involved in that ... I used to go back continually to talk to him about theoretical things, advise him how often to take samples, current levels of theory ... and in the language I was the house theorist.

Bahcall was now clearly committed to the experiment and was even giving advice on matters of experimental detail. Arrangements were made for Bahcall to become a Brookhaven consultant. Bahcall was thus truly the 'house theorist' – he was paid for his services by the same house!

The relationship between Bahcall and Davis now encompassed more than mere technical matters. As Bahcall told me:

I was also the guy that encouraged him . . . We were good friends, he's much older than I but we had both more or less staked our careers on this. I had staked my career on my ability to predict the response of the instrument, that the instrument would work and be sensitive in the way I said it, and he in spending his major, almost his entire, effort in building the equipment.

It can be seen that career investments and personal relationships appear alongside each other — they are all integral parts of scientific activity. Bahcall's comment about having 'staked his career on this' shows the degree to which he had invested his credibility in the enterprise. It was not unnatural for Bahcall to feel increasingly apprehensive as the date when Davis would make measurements drew near. He recalled his attitude:

I can remember being enormously nervous before the results came out . . . I was then a young research fellow whose emotions and scientific advancement depended in a large part on my correctness in what I was asserting.

It can be seen that even the psychological state of the researcher is tied up with the enfolding drama.

By the stage Davis was ready to make his first measurements we can see that a lot of time, effort, and money had been invested in the experiment. In particular, it was the partnership between theoreticians and experimentalists which was so important in preparing the way for the first measurements. In a sense it was Bahcall's and Davis's scientific careers which were as much at stake as the flux of neutrinos.

PART II

1967–Today. The Appearance of the Anomaly

In this part of the paper I will look at how the solar-neutrino anomaly became established. That is how the consensus developed that this experimental result, which stood out against theoretical expectation, was worth taking seriously. Obviously results can only be anomalous in a given theoretical context and if theory could be brought into agreement with experiment, then we would no longer have an anomaly. In the case of solar neutrinos, however, the attempts to accommodate the result within standard theory have so far been unsuccessful. Although I will be paying close attention to the attitude of the theoreticians to the experiment. I will not here be discussing theoretical developments *per se*.

In my discussion of the reception of Davis's experiment, as in my account of earlier developments, I will try and set events in a wider context. I, thus, do not share the view that the success or otherwise of experiments can be understood independently from the wider scientific and social setting in which they appear. In this particular case my main concern is to outline why Davis's experiment has managed to achieve credibility in the face of a hostile theoretical climate. The question is particularly pertinent when we consider that other experiments which clash with theory (the most relevant example here is perhaps Weber's claimed measurement of large fluxes of gravitational radiation) have lost credibility and are not generally believed (21).

In discussing the reception of the experiment it is useful to distinguish three groups — firstly, nuclear chemists and radio chemists familiar with the particular technique Davis used; secondly, astrophysical neutrino detection experts with other techniques; and finally, the nuclear astrophysicists whose work is directly impinged on by Davis's result.

The Reaction of the Chemists

When Davis got his first indication of a low result in August 1967 his initial task was to convince himself that he had made a good measurement. As he told me:

The thing that concerned me most was whether I was getting the right answer, . . . was there something wrong with the apparatus?

Davis was particularly worried because of his relative isolation. He worked alone, and, although he had assistance from two scientists in the design and the construction of the experiment, there was no other experimental scientist directly involved as he started to make measurements (there were, of course, technical staff). Thus, one of the first things he did was to get two of his immediate colleagues from Brookhaven to check over his work.

As Travis has stressed it is important for scientists to be seen to be acting correctly (22). Many respondents have commented to me that they have been most impressed by Davis in this respect. He has all the qualities of an ideal experimenter – he appears to be careful, modest, and very open with his results. Indeed Davis has told me that he has made it a deliberate strategy to be open with his results because it is unlikely the experiment will ever be repeated. He has not only been open to suggestions but also has attempted to check many of the possible uncertainties in the experiment (possibilities which he himself might regard as highly unlikely) by running more tests of parts of the experimental technique.

After Davis had received the blessings of his immediate colleagues he felt confident enough to notify a wider audience of his results. He presented his initial results to a meeting of the American Chemical Society in September 1967.

The reactions of chemists to Davis's result has been that as far as they are concerned he is just doing standard chemistry – admittedly on a slightly larger scale than is usual – but, nevertheless, standard chemistry. Also the chemistry of argon is considered to be particularly simple.

Two other reasons may be important in understanding the acceptance which Davis's result has gained amongst chemists. Firstly, his result can be seen as posing very little difficulty for chemistry – it conflicts with astrophysics not chemistry. Secondly, Davis had been doing experiments of this sort (but on a smaller scale) for the previous decade and, thus, it is unlikely that chemists should only now be concerned about his techniques after being quite happy with them earlier. In other words Davis's previously acquired credibility in this field may have been enough to see him through.

The Reaction of the Astrophysical Neutrino Experimenters

Apart from Davis, the other main astrophysical neutrino experimenter is Fred Reines, of the University of California, Irvine. Reines had built two solar-neutrino detectors in the mid-sixties (23). One of these experiments, located in a mine in S. Africa, was actually operating in August 1967. Reines favoured direct counting techniques, similar in principle to those which he had used to detect neutrinos at a nuclear reactor. Reines and Davis were not only the two principal astrophysical neutrino detection experimentalists, they were also close friends.

When Davis got his low result, Reines got in contact with him to see whether it was worth pursuing his own solar-neutrino detection program. His detector in S. Africa was already encountering a very large background and he had to decide whether to do a lot more work, perhaps building a shield, to try to get down to the sensitivity which Davis had achieved. After a lengthy discussion with Davis, Reines decided there was no point in continuing this experiment. The other detector that he had built, in the expectation of a much larger solar-neutrino flux, was never put into operation, again because it was unlikely that he could get down to the necessary sensitivity (24).

Reines has a very high regard for Davis and his assessment of this particular experiment was that it 'has been done with exquisite care, thoughtfulness and humility' (25). Again it is important to bear in mind that Reines was familiar with Davis's techniques from his earlier reactor work. Davis's Savannah river result, although a negative one, was consistent with Reines's own positive result. Thus Davis had already established his technique as far as Reines was concerned and Reines had every reason to trust his solar-neutrino results.

In view of the conflict between Davis's results and astrophysical theory, it might seem surprising that other experimenters have not placed a greater emphasis on checking Davis's result by an independent experiment (the experiment has never been repeated although the Soviets are building a similar detector). Clearly the huge cost and time-consuming nature of the experiment is an important constraint. It was also pointed out to me by many respondents that there is little scientific reward to be gained from a 'me too' negative result. Such reasoning seems to me, however, to beg the question, because it assumes Davis is correct. If he had made a mistake, and there were neutrinos there to detect, then another experiment could be highly significant. Another factor in the reluctance of experimenters to embark on replications may be their sceptical attitude towards astrophysical theory. As indicated already, Davis himself saw no reason why he should see exactly what the theoreticians predicted. This attitude was also shared by Reines who considered it to be up to the theoreticians to bring their theory into line with the experimental result.

In general then the attitude of other experimentalists to Davis's result has been that they are confident he is correct – a confidence which has grown stronger over the years as he has continued to report a low result and make further improvements and checks on his experiment. The clash with astrophysical theory does not seem to have been a reason for undue scepticism.

The attitude of the nuclear astrophysicists, whose theory would seem to be in conflict with Davis's result, has, however, been somewhat different.

The Reaction of the Nuclear Astrophysicists

I will start by looking at the reaction of the most involved theorist, John Bahcall. I will then go on to consider the attitude of the wider community of theorists.

Bahcall, unlike Davis, took the theoretical prediction very seriously. To him Davis's result was not just an anomaly, it was a personal disaster. He told me the following anecdote which perhaps illustrates the depth to which Davis's result affected his scientific life:

> Ray Davis . . . came to CalTech and gave an informal seminar and Richard Feynmann was there . . . it was clear there was just absolute conflict and afterwards I was enormously depressed . . . I think that was really the low point of my feeling about science . . . after that seminar Feynmann . . . when he saw I was pretty much destroyed by this . . . was really very nice and told me 'Don't worry, you've done nothing wrong, nobody has found anything wrong in your calculations . . . if there's a discrepancy it's all the more important' . . . Even though he spent a lot of time with me, it took me quite a while to get over that . . . well it was a big blow . . . that it came out wrong. I think now that I was mistaken for the reasons that he said . . . the result is more important because it is in conflict, but at the time I was expecting something very different.

Bahcall's dismay is perfectly understandable. His ability to produce credible information was in doubt. Of course, as Feymann pointed out, in the long term the failure of the theory might turn out to be to his advantage if a major change was needed. To have gone for a major, possibly revolutionary, change in the theory (what Bourdieu refers to as a subversion investment strategy (26)) would have entailed a substantial risk. After all, major changes in physical theory are comparatively rare events. It is clear that Bahcall himself preferred the safer bet of an incremental gain in credibility provided by a confirmation of the theory (a succession investment strategy) rather than the possible fame and glory of instigating a radical change. In any case it is not clear that there is much credibility to be gained from merely showing that a theory is incorrect, and any subsequent revolutionary change would, of course, throw the whole previous economy of credibility into disarray.

In view of Bahcall's commitment to his prediction, was he sceptical of

Davis's results? He could not recall for me his immediate reaction, but he told me that it would not have been unreasonable to have shown some initial scepticism:

I can remember being certain that the experiment was right a few years later, expressing myself publicly that way . . . I think it would not have been unnatural . . . at the time, to have wondered if I had invested the crucial years of my research development on a project that was going to go away . . . that I'd spent the four years which I had to prove myself, before I got a good assistant professorship or a poor assistant professorship doing a problem that was irrelevant . . . If you couldn't do the chemistry or couldn't get the atoms out or whatever, then I would have made a bad professional choice and I would have been much further out of the stream than I was . . .

Bahcall certainly seems to have gone over Davis's work with a fine-tooth comb. For instance, in the context of another anecdote about his relationship with Davis, he told me:

He came to CalTech . . . and I talked to him so forcefully and at such length about analysing his data statistically in detail . . . he got a headache, and my wife told me I had better lay off him!

Davis also recalled the attitude of Bahcall when he first learnt of the result:

I remember going to CalTech and giving a seminar on the result . . . going to John Bahcall's house . . . and he used to argue why I was so sure, and what are the arguments, and how did I know that . . . the nuts and bolts of the whole thing.

Bahcall still had worries in early 1968 as Davis prepared the first major publication of his result. Again this was to be an experimental paper alongside a theoretical paper by Bahcall and his collaborators. Davis sent Bahcall a copy of his paper; in the accompanying letter he wrote (27):

I tried to answer your worry about chemical trapping of ^{37}Ar.

This refers to the possibility that the argon was formed in the tank in the expected amounts but was not properly extracted because it bound with something in the tank and was hence 'trapped'. Most chemists thought this was unlikely; however, a number of theoretical physicists, including Bahcall, has worried about the possibility.

Having sent his paper to Bahcall, Davis spent the following weekend at CalTech. Bahcall then sent a letter to Davis on the Monday, in which he expressed further worries about the experiment; it commenced (28):

I am even more convinced ... that the simplest explanation of your results is that the background counter was hotter than the counter which contained the sample.

There were several pages of accompanying calculations where Bahcall attempted to establish this point. The worry here was that the background rate was really lower than Davis measured it to be and hence that the signal in the counter from ^{37}Ar was really much larger because too many background counts were being subtracted from the total signal.

This claim, it seems, was soon answered by Davis to Bahcall's satisfaction and no further reference to it appears in the correspondence to which I had access. Eventually Bahcall's worries were all allayed and he was able to express public confidence that the result was a good one.

Bahcall's initial concern over the correctness of the result is again perfectly understandable when we consider what he had invested in it. As he himself has pointed out he had put the key years of his scientific career into making the necessary calculations and helping ensure that the experiment was funded. He had a lot to lose if it turned out that some experimental error was responsible. His careful checking of what Davis had done was facilitated by the joint nature of the project. He was able to put his worries to Davis directly without having to go through more formal channels – a process which might well cast suspicion on the experiment. Also he did not have to stick his neck out immediately and embrace the result. The publication format of separate papers that he and Davis had established allowed him to reserve judgment. In the theoretical paper that accompanied Davis's 1968 paper (29) nothing directly is said about the validity of the result – the ultimate responsibility for the correctness of the experiment was left in Davis's hands. But, as time went on and Bahcall continued to do theoretical work associated with the experiment, and thus continued to make further investments, it was increasingly likely that he would stand by the result in public, as was eventually the case.

Other theoreticians, apart from Bahcall, have been interested in the result of the solar-neutrino experiment. Many of these have connections with CalTech, which reflects the influence which Fowler's group have had. The particular importance of convincing Fowler and the CalTech group of the correctness of his experiment was recognised by Davis. When discussing scientists who had examined the experiment, he stressed the significance of the visit of CalTech nuclear physicist:

I always welcomed someone from their lab coming. You see he has a lot invested in this, Fowler, . . .
I wanted to be sure that he was thoroughly satisfied that we were doing things right.

Although many scientists, especially those at CalTech, had made investments in the experiment, none came close to Bahcall in the amount invested (with the possible exception of Fowler). It would thus appear that the rest of the nuclear astrophysicists had little to lose if the experiment became discredited and further it would save any embarassment in the domain of theory. The attitude of the wider group has somewhat mirrored that of Bahcall in that most of them at one time or another have indeed been highly suspicious of the experiment. However, as yet, they have not been able to make any of their suspicions hold water. Many of them have been content to voice general worries in informal settings such as seminars, or the informal solar-neutrino conference held at U. C. Irvine in 1972 (30), but few have been prepared to come out with a public attack on the experiment.

The impression to be got is that the theorists' comments have been put forward in the guise of friendly criticism rather than hostile attacks. This may again have been important for the reputation of the experiment. Openly antagonistic criticisms in the mainstream literature would almost certainly have damaged the experiment. The antagonisms and, on occasions, open feuding, which have accompanied the Weber episode, have largely been avoided in this field. Davis's good relationship with Bahcall and the CalTech group, facilitated by their joint investments, may have played the decisive part here.

There has only been one instance of which I am aware when this largely informal way of dealing with criticism has broken down. In 1974–5, Davis received three letters from astrophysicists concerned about the possibility of ^{37}Ar being trapped in the tank (the same worry that Bahcall had back in 1968). Davis replied to these astrophysicists pointing out why such a possibility was unlikely and what sort of test he was prepared to do to check it. Two of the astrophysicists were satisfied, but the third one, Kenneth Jacobs, went ahead and published his objections in *Nature* (31). Jacobs noted that the detection chemistry was 'one of the more neglected aspects of the problem'. He put forward the hypothesis that 'the solar-neutrino problem is solely an artefact of the chemistry of the detection technique'. It is my understanding that, in the original version of his article, Jacobs had compared Davis's experiment with other famous cases in physics where there was only one experiment near the noise level which, on replication, was found to be in error. It took Jacobs a year to get his paper into *Nature* and he eventually had to drop any comparison between famous errors and the solar-neutrino experiment.

Jacobs, who had carried out an extensive search of the chemistry literature and, who had even done some experiments with chemists, despite his astrophysics background, suggested several mechanisms for trapping and also produced arguments as to why previous checks run by Davis were inadequate. A reply to these criticisms soon appeared in *Nature* (32) and Jacobs in turn published a reply (33), concluding that 'my chemical trapping solution to the solar-neutrino problem remains a viable alternative'.

It is not my intention here to go into the details of the arguments and counter-arguments between Jacobs and his critics. In any case for most respondents the issue has been resolved by yet another check which Davis has carried out (33a). Jacobs's criticisms were, in effect, brought to an end in 1976 when he failed to get tenure at the University of Virginia (an episode uncorrected with his work on solar ne trinos).

The significance of the Jacobs contribution is that it shows that it was possible for plausible arguments against the experiment to be mounted in public. Indeed Jacobs's attempt to discredit the experiment by comparing it with notorious examples of past mistakes has been a successful debunking ploy in other cases (34). On this occasion, however, it is the debunker who has the minority view.

Jacob's criticisms probably came too little and too late to have any substantial effect. In view of his marginal position and the difficulty he had in getting his article accepted, he was always fighting an uphill battle against the emerging consensus that Davis's result could be trusted.

The majority of theoreticians now seem prepared to stand by the result. In giving reasons why they believe Davis, many draw attention to his modesty. By this they mean that he has not made any great theoretical claims for his results. The theoreticians' embarassment has thus, to an extent, been saved.

This again can be seen as stemming from the joint enterprise. Just as it was important for Bahcall, in view of his past investments, that the experiment should remain credible, Davis too would have little to gain from stressing the conflict with astrophysics. The publication format further facilitated this because Davis could happily leave the theoretical consequences of his result with Bahcall. Any theoretical criticisms fell on Bahcall's shoulders, thus ensuring Davis kept his smooth relationship with the rest of the theoretical community.

The Importance of Partnership

The theme of this paper has been that in order to understand the relationship between theory and experiment we should take account of the social relations between experimenters and theoreticians. In this case I have tried to show the importance of the joint investments of credibility undertaken by both parties. It is only in the light of these investments that we can understand the reception accorded to Davis's result.

In understanding the outcome of other scientific controversies it is perhaps important to look at the relationship between experimenters and theoreticians in these terms. From my own interview data I have one other case that is suggestive. One of my respondents, J, is an experimentalist, but he also likes to do his own theory when possible. J had recently made some observations and had been approached by a theorist, L, who offered to do the theoretical analysis in return for speedy access to the results. Rather than welcoming such collaboration, as Davis had done, J refused; subsequently the credibility of his observations had come under attack. J, himself, thought that this was because of his refusal to co-operate with the theoreticians. He told me:

I'm sure that if I had gone to L, I would have had holy water sprinkled on us and thus would all be in good shape.

J took a dim view of Davis's relationship with the theoreticians, as the following extract of interview material shows:

J: I think first of all Davis is the kind of guy that can be worked on, he can be worked on by Fowler, he can be worked on by Bahcall, OK?
Pinch: Worked on in what sense?
J: They treat him just as a technician, he does measurements, they are going to do the theory. OK, I won't accept that.

We should be cautious in interpreting J's comments in too literal a manner — he has a reputation for paranoia. However, it is clear that his experience has been very different from the smooth partnership entered into by Davis and Bahcall.

Davis has always been quite happy to accept the division of labour between experiment and theory entailed within the partnership; as he told me:

This all started out as a kinda joint thing . . . and if you start that way you tend to leave these little boundaries in between. So I stayed away from forcing any strong opinions about solar models and they've never made much comment about the experiment . . . You see it's done in a broader way in high-energy physics.

It is interesting that Davis draws here on the analogy of high-energy physics where arguably there exists the most rigid division between experimentalists and theoreticians. However, in high-energy physics the division is well institutionalised and it is possible for the theorist and experimentalist to go their separate ways. In this case there was no equivalent of the pre-existing accelerator which the experimentalist could use to produce data for the theoreticians to interpret. Both groups had to work closely together to bring the detector into existence at all. This required the special partnership which I have outlined. The difference between the solar-neutrino project and other projects from the theoreticians' point of view can be seen from Bahcall's comment that:

First of all the feasibility of the experiment was a joint project. . . . A lot of times you do theory and someone else goes away and does the experiment but in my case I invested such a large amount in the experiment and . . . . I felt that, as I continued to do that, that I wanted to sell the experiment, that is to get funding for it so it would happen.

The lack of a pre-existing apparatus meant the theoretician had, in this case, to engage in more activities than usual. He had, not only to make the theoretical predictions, but also to 'market' the experiment to ensure it got funded. The economic metaphor adopted by Bahcall to describe his activities ('selling') is particularly appropriate in this case. He, and Davis, had to persuade the wider community that it was worth putting up the necessary half-million dollars.

Conclusion

Experiments such as that carried out to detect solar neutrinos are probably exceptional. Most experiments of this 'one-off' type are not as expensive. However, the special nature of the experiment and the concomitant social relationships is useful for illustrating aspects of scientific activity not usually visible in other cases. In particular the joint investments made have become explicit. There is no reason why, in principle, the investments documented here should not happen in much more mundane pieces of science. Indeed Latour and Woolgar (35) document several such cases in their study.

What I think the solar-neutrino case illustrates well is the connection between the conditions for the production of scientific knowledge (the Popperian context of discovery) and the epistemological status of the end-product (the Popperian context of justification). The virtue of the notion of credibility is that it combines what have traditionally been seen as epistemological concerns with the concerns of sociology and psychology. If scientists are regarded as attempting to maximise their credibility by making investments then the outcomes of their investments are likely to be influenced by the pre-existing investment strategies (36). Scientists, like good businessmen, choose their investment strategies carefully in the expectation of a favourable outcome which will enhance their credibility. The production of credible information — information which, in epistemological terms, is some approximation towards scientific truth — can be seen as stemming from the previous investments of credibility.

This relationship is particularly clear in the solar-neutrino case because of the huge size of the investments made by all parties (the experimeter, the theoretician and the wider community who put up the money). It seems *a priori* unlikely, with such large amounts invested in the project, that it could be allowed to fall into disrepute. The credibility of the experimental result was in a sense guaranteed by the previous investments of credibility (37).

Clearly with scientific experiments becoming more and more complicated and expensive the associated investments will be much larger. It is likely that in order to minimise risks only scientists with a comparatively large amount of previously acquired credibility will be encouraged to take part in such projects. With such projects likely to be too expensive to duplicate, scientific advance may increasingly depend on the outcome of single experiments. However, in view of the size of the investments and the lack of competition it is increasingly unlikely that the results produced in such experiments will be subject to dispute. Just as a few multi-national corporations can dominate business markets and challenges to the credibility of their products become harder, so too may the market for credible information become dominated by large and expensive projects which produce almost guaranteed credible information. Perhaps in the solar-neutrino experiment we can see something of the likely character of the physics of the future.

Acknowledgement

I am grateful to all the scientists who gave up their time to me, especially Ray Davis and John Bahcall.

Notes and References

1. I am thinking here of the work of Collins, Harvey, Pickering and Travis. See, for example, H. M. Collins, 'The Seven Sexes: a Study in the Sociology of a Phenomenon, or the Replication of Experiments in Physics', *Sociology* 9, 205–224 (1975); B. Harvey, 'The Effects of Social Context on the Process of Scientific Investigation: Experimental Tests of Quantum Mechanics', this volume; A. Pickering, 'The Role of Interests in High-Energy Physics', this volume; and G. D. L. Travis, 'Constructing Creativity: The 'Memory Transfer' Phenomenon and the Importance of Being Earnest', this volume.
2. These differences have been documented by a variety of authors. See, for example, M. J. Mulkay and A. T. Williams, 'A Sociological Study of a Physics Department', *British Journal of Sociology*, March 1971, 68–82; J. Gaston, *Originality and Competition in Science*, University of Chicago Press, Chicago, 1973; W. O. Hagstrom, 'Competition in Science', *American Sociological Review* 39, 1–18 (1974); I. Mitroff, *The Subjective Side of Science*, American Elsevier, New York, 1974; and A. Bitz, A. McAlpine and R. D. Whitley, 'The Production, Flow and Use of Information in Research Laboratories in Different Sciences', British Library Report Series, London, 1975.
3. A cross-section of philosophical articles on the connection between theory and observation can be found in R. E. Grandy (ed.) *Theories and Observation in Science*, Prentice-Hall, New Jersey, 1973.
4. See K. R. Popper, *Objective Knowledge*, Clarendon Press, Oxford, 1972.
5. The original idea was proposed by B. Pontecorvo and L. W. Alvarez.
6. Interviews with Ray Davis were conducted at the Brookhaven National Laboratory on October 17, October 22–23 and December 6, 1978.
7. K. R. Popper, *The Logic of Scientific Discovery*, Hutchinson, London 1959.
8. Bruno Latour and Steve Woolgar, *Laboratory Life*, Sage, Beverley Hills, 1979.
9. W. O. Hagstrom, *The Scientific Community*, Basic Books, New York, 1965.
10. Pierre Bourdieu, 'The Specificity of the Scientific Field and the Social Conditions of the Progress of Reason', *Social Science Information* 14, 19–47 (1975). See also, K. D. Knorr 'Producing and Reproducing Knowledge: Descriptive or Constructive?', *Social Science Information* 16 (6), 669–696 (1977).
11. E. M. Burbidge, G. R. Burbidge, W. A. Fowler and F. Hoyle, 'Synthesis of the Elements in Stars', *Reviews of Modern Physics* 29, 547 (1957).

12. Letter from William Fowler to Ray Davis, January 7, 1958.
13. Interviews with John Bahcall were conducted at the Institute for Advanced Study, Princeton, October 20–21, and December 4, 1978.
14. Letter from John Bahcall to Ray Davis, November 20, 1962.
15. Letter from Ray Davis to John Bahcall, December 20, 1962.
16. Letter from John Bahcall to Ray Davis, January 3, 1963.
17. J. N. Bahcall, 'Solar Neutrinos. I. Theoretical', *Physical Review Letters* 12, 300–302 (1964); and R. Davis, Jr., 'Solar Neutrinos. II. Experimental', *Physical Review Letters* 12, 303–305 (1964).
18. See for instance, J. C. Hardy, and R. I. Verrall, *Physical Review Letters* 13, 764 (1964), and P. L. Reeder, A. M. Poskanzer, and R. A. Esterlund, *Physical Review Letters* 13, 767 (1964).
19. Letter from Ray Davis to John Bahcall, January 21, 1964.
20. 'Erratum', *Scientific American* 212, 8 (April 1965).
21. For a discussion of the experimental reception of Weber's work see Collins, 1975, *op. cit.*, Note 1.
22. See Travis, 1981, *op. cit.*, Note 1.
23. For an informative account of the experimental possibilities in 1966 see F. Reines, *Proceedings of the Royal Society of London*, Series A, 301, 159 (1966). Tom Jenkins of the Case Institute, Ohio, had also built a detector. However, this detector never worked properly due to a large background (thought to originate from the instrument itself).
24. Davis's apparatus had been built in the expectation that he would be able to go a factor of ten below the theoretical prediction of 1964.
25. Interview with F. Reines, University of California, Irvine, November 21, 1978.
26. Bourdieu, 1975, *op. cit.*, Note 10.
27. Letter from Ray Davis to John Bahcall, February 16, 1968.
28. Letter from John Bahcall to Ray Davis, February 26, 1968.
29. R. Davis, Jr., D. S. Harmer, and K. C. Hoffman, 'Search for Neutrinos from the Sun', *Physical Review Letters* 20, 1205–1209 (1968); J. N. Bahcall, N. A. Bahcall and G. Shaviv, 'Present Status of the Theoretical Predictions for the ^{37}Cl Solar-Neutrino Experiment', *Physical Review Letters* 20, 1209–1212 (1968).
30. F. Reines and V. Trimble (eds.), *The Irvine Conference on Solar Neutrinos*, 1972.
31. K. C. Jacobs, 'Chemistry of the Solar Neutrino Problem', *Nature* 256, 560–561 (1975).
32. B. Banerjee, S. M. Chitre, P. P. Dvakaran and K. S. V. Santhanam, 'Polymerisation and the Solar Neutrino Problem', *Nature* 260, 557 (1976).
33. K. C. Jacobs, 'Jacobs Replies', *Nature* 260, 557 (1976).
33a. This test involved creating ^{36}Ar by the decay of ^{36}Cl in a tank of perchloroethylene doped with ^{36}Cl atoms. ^{36}Ar should behave chemically in the same way as ^{37}Ar, and thus the extraction of the correct number of ^{36}Ar atoms indicates that trapping is ruled out.
34. It should be noted though, that such attacks rarely appear in the literature. Harry Collins informs me that Weber's experiment has been debunked informally in this manner.
35. Latour and Woolgar, 1979, *op. cit.*, Note 8, Chapter 5.
36. A similar argument has been made in T. J. Pinch, 'What Does a Proof Do if it

Does Not Prove?', in E. Mendelsohn, P. Weingart, and R. D. Whitley, *The Social Production of Scientific Knowledge*, Sociology of the Sciences, Vol. 1, Reidel, Dordrecht, 1977, 171–215.

37. I would not like to suggest that a deterministic relationship exists. It is always possible that Davis's experiment could have lost (and indeed still might lose) credibility. The market for credible information, like other markets, can always be subject to social contingency.

THE ROLE OF INTERESTS IN HIGH-ENERGY PHYSICS:

The Choice Between Charm And Colour*

ANDREW PICKERING

University of Edinburgh

Introduction

The process through which scientists choose between competing theories has long been of interest to analysts of science, particularly philosophers, but has yet to receive as much detailed attention as it deserves from sociologists. This paper is intended as a contribution towards remedying that deficiency.

For the sociologist, an interesting way to look at scientific theory-choice is in terms of the reality of scientific concepts, objects and their relations. The problem is one of understanding how, for instance, the reality of objects in the natural world — their 'out-thereness' — can be seen as the outcome of a social process. The aim of this paper is to sketch a simple model of the social construction of 'out-thereness', and to illustrate how the model can be applied to a particularly significant episode in the history of theoretical high-energy physics (HEP).

The episode in question concerns the discovery, and theoretical interpretation, of a number of very unusual elementary particles, in the period from 1974 to 1976. A variety of theoretical models of these particles were proposed during this period — foremost amongst them the models known as 'charm' and 'colour' — and an analysis will be given of the process whereby the charm model became established and colour rejected. In this introductory section I want to explain the general form which the analysis will take; the following sections will deal with its application to the example chosen.

Professional discourse amongst theoretical physicists centres on ways of looking at the world — theories, models, idealisations of data, mathematical

* Research supported by the Social Science Research Council.

Karin D. Knorr, Roger Krohn and Richard Whitley (eds.), The Social Process of Scientific Investigation. Sociology of the Sciences, Volume IV, 1980. 107–138.
Copyright © 1980 by Andrew Pickering.

techniques and so on — and the problem of understanding the accomplishment of 'out-thereness' is equivalent to that of understanding the ways in which the components of such (often small-scale) 'world views' become entrenched in the practice of the community of theorists. In order to discuss this latter problem, some image is required of the social and cognitive structure and dynamics of scientific work, and such a schematic image — which one might call the 'interest model' — will now be discussed.

The interest model has two key concepts: that of an 'exemplar' and, of course, that of an 'interest'. Let us take 'exemplars' first. Kuhn first introduced the term in the 'Postscript' to his *Structure of Scientific Revolutions*, and the present usage of the term is based upon the quite extensive discussion he gave there (1). Kuhn used the term 'exemplar' as a shorthand for 'shared example'. He emphasised that such a shared example derives from the concrete demonstration in some practical situation of the utility of a cultural product — a new experimental technique, a new theoretical model, or whatever — and that it is precisely through such demonstrations that new concepts are related to the natural world and acquire their meanings. Particular research networks within a given scientific community are to be seen as engaged in the articulation — the working-out in practice — of particular exemplars. As Kuhn put it:

More than other sorts of components of the disciplinary matrix, differences between sets of exemplars provide the community fine-structure of science (2).

The idea of an exemplar is perhaps best clarified through historical examples — such as those given by Kuhn, and those discussed later in this paper — but a few remarks are required here, before turning to 'interests'.

Kuhn's work suggests that an exemplar may best be seen as a novel combination of cultural resources, the deployment of which constitutes a recognisable practical achievement. A question which naturally arises at this point is why one piece of work rather than another constitutes such a recognisable achievement — what, in particular, does 'recognisable' mean in this context? Consideration of this question will bring us to the concept of 'interest'. For the purposes of the present work, an exemplar can be regarded as an *analogy* drawn between some new aspect of the subject matter of the field and some other field of discourse (3). The aspect in question is conceptualised and organised by analogy with some other aspect of the field; the analogy being made concrete by the exemplary work. Thus the exemplar refers back, from the problem to be understood at the research front, to some existing body of practice. Phrased in this way, it is clear that an exemplar is an example *for some particular group* — the group which has established the preceding body of practice — and not for others. One can speak of the group or groups having expertise relevant to the articulation of some exemplar as having an 'investment' in that expertise, and, as a corollary, as having an 'interest' in the deployment of their expertise in the articulation of the exemplar (4). An 'interest', then, is a particular constructive cognitive orientation towards the field of discourse. As a shorthand description one can refer to an exemplar being so constructed that it 'intersects with the interests' of some particular group or groups.

The outline of the 'interest model' is now almost complete, but one point remains to be stressed. The description of an exemplar as an analogy tends to suggest that it is a monolithic, unitary entity, but this is misleading and as open to criticism as the monolithic interpretation often put upon Kuhn's original description of a 'paradigm' (5). The important observation here is that an exemplar is typically a multi-dimensional construct, referring back not to a single unitary body of practice, but to several, possibly completely disjoint traditions. Thus individuals can set about articulating an exemplar along one of several dimensions, according to their prior investments and interests; and, in so doing, may well acquire new expertise and interests relevant to other dimensions of the exemplar.

To sum up, then, the image of the evolution of scientific culture implicit in the interest model is the following. The research front of a scientific speciality is to be seen as broadly patterned into research networks, each network being engaged in the elaboration of a particular exemplary achievement (6). Members of a given network can be described as having an interest in creating knowledge of a form characteristic of the original exemplar. However, the research front is further patterned, at a much finer level, by the constellation of interests proper to individual researchers; this constellation being idiosyncratic and determined by the researcher's professional evolution, moving from one network to another. This idiosyncracy at the individual level allows for fluidity and the rearrangement of the pattern of networks: as new exemplars are created, new research networks can form as individuals engage in elaboration of the original achievement along dimensions appropriate to their pre-existing interests.

In outline, one can understand how the 'reality' of concepts emerges from this flux of changing networks in the following way. Firstly, consider the particular network (or cluster of networks) engaged in the elaboration of a particular exemplar. Entrenched within the practice of this network will be certain concepts central to the exemplary achievement. These concepts will be at the heart of the way in which members of the network make sense of their own and each other's work in the particular area of research. Because of this, a limited 'out-thereness' is achieved − the concepts become the relatively impersonal 'property' of the network rather than the personal 'property' of their creator. Secondly, because of the multidimensional aspect of exemplars noted above, it is possible for members of distinct networks to be engaged in the elaboration of the same concepts in different research areas. In this case, as we shall see, not only does the community of discourse about the shared concepts extend beyond a single network, but the entire practice of one network can come to be seen as important and relevant to the practice of another. Thus, the concepts originally entrenched in the practice of a single network can come to be entrenched in the practice of others, and their 'out-thereness' correspondingly increased.

One can at least imagine a situation in which all the members of a particular research specialty were engaged in the articulation of a single exemplar, or of a single cluster of exemplars related by unifying links (say, by a single explanatory theory and a unified ontology). This is the circumstance idealised by Kuhn in his idea of a community-wide 'paradigm', and it is clear that, here, scientists would speak unproblematically in terms of real objects and so on, deriving from the fundamental exemplar(s). The situation to be discussed in the case study approximates to that just described. It is, however, worthwhile to indicate in advance the differences between the actual situation and the ideal, in order both to illustrate the concept of consensus implicit in this paper, and to facilitate the introduction of a sociologically useful definition of '*ad hoc*ness'.

We will see that by mid-1976, in consequence of various exemplary achievements, the existence of charm had become entrenched in the practice of several influential networks working in a variety of research areas. In contrast, although it remained in principle possible to reconcile colour (and other alternative models) with the data, the protagonists of colour had failed to achieve *exemplary* solutions to the misfits between their model and the data. Although the responses of colour's protagonists to these misfits were logically sound, they could be described as 'sociologically *ad hoc*'. That is, they failed to intersect with existing interests within the HEP community, since they did not make any analogical connection with existing bodies of practice, and hence failed to lead to the establishment of any new bodies of practice.

Thus, by mid-1976, there existed what one might call an 'active' consensus on charm within the cluster of networks engaged in the elaboration of exemplars related in one way or another to the existence of charm. Actively opposed to this consensus were only a handful of theorists, each committed to one of a disparate set of alternative perspectives. (In fact, all of the public defenders of colour eventually abandoned their position. The ultimate residue of anti-charm theorists will not be further discussed in the case study, since this would require considerable additional technical detail and contribute no new insight into the process of consensus formation).

Finally, one can also speak of a community-wide 'passive' consensus existing on charm by mid-1976 (with, of course, the exception of the *isolated* opponents just mentioned). By that time, any physicist otherwise uninvolved in the charm-colour debate but obliged to choose between the two in the course of his research – for instance, to calculate the background contribution from the new particles to some experimental data – would naturally have chosen charm. The passive consensus implied by the existence of such a natural choice is readily understandable if one remarks that this hypothetical physicist would wish his own research product to be of utility within the HEP community at large, rather than to single, isolated, individuals.

The 'New Particles': Charm and Colour

We can now turn from the abstract sketch of the interest model to its application to an historical example. The example concerns a major development which took place in HEP between 1974 and 1976 (7). During this period several highly unusual elementary particles – the 'new particles' in the parlance of the time – were discovered, and a great deal of theoretical effort was directed towards an explanation of their properties. HEP theorists initially articulated a wide range of theoretical models of the new particles, but by mid-1976 a consensus had arisen that one of these models – known as 'charm'

— was right, and its competitors — principally a model known as 'colour' — were abandoned. The aim of the following sections of this paper will be to use the interest model to illuminate the way in which the reality of charm was accomplished, in comparison with the failure of the alternative models to achieve that status. I want first to give a broad outline and some general discussion of the developments at issue, and then to turn to a more detailed analysis in terms of the interest model. I should, however, clarify one point in advance. Several recent studies of the social construction of scientific knowledge have focussed on debates over experimental techniques: Collins, for instance, has characterised his study of the gravitational radiation controversy as a study of negotiations over what constitutes a 'working' gravitational wave detector (8). The study discussed in this paper concerns negotiations of a different kind. Throughout the period considered here, members of the HEP community treated experimental data as facts: no important negotiations over experimental techniques took place, but instead negotiations concerned how well the various theoretical models could cope with the data in the context of the existing traditions of HEP (9). With this proviso in mind, then, let me now turn to an outline of the actual events.

On November 11th, 1974, two groups of HEP experimenters, one from the East Coast and one from the West Coast of the U.S.A., announced their independent discoveries of a new and highly unusual elementary particle (10). One group named it the 'J', the other the 'psi', and by common consent it has become known as the 'J-psi'. I will return to the question of why it was unusual later; for the moment it is sufficient to note that its properties were not easily reconciled with expectations then current within the community. Within days of the discovery announcement the journals were flooded with a variety of theoretical speculations on the nature of the J-psi. Ten days after the announcement of the J-psi further experiment revealed the existence of another unusual particle — the 'psi-prime' (11) — and detailed measurements were soon made of the properties of both the J-psi and psi-prime. In the light of these observations, many of the early speculations on the nature of the J-psi quickly came to be seen as untenable, and in early 1975 only two theoretical models survived as serious contenders for the explanation of the new particles. These models were known as 'charm' and 'colour', and it is the way in which the choice was made between them that I want to discuss here (12).

The new particles had immediately become a major focus for experimental effort, and in response to the accumulating data the charm and colour models were progressively refined and articulated. In essence, one can say that each model came to be embodied as an ever more complex string of statements about the interactions of elementary particles. The individual statements comprising the string associated with a particular model were quite distinct and carried quite different associations from those of its rival, but nonetheless the protagonists of both models were sufficiently ingenious to avoid contradiction with the data: each new datum was accommodated by an appropriate adjustment somewhere in the string of statements – the adjustments, of course, differing according to the model used. Thus, at any particular time, the two models were able to give quite different explanations of the same set of observations.

This circumstance offers further support, should such be needed, to the idea that there is no such thing as a crucial experiment in science; and, from a somewhat wider perspective, constitutes a neat exemplification of the Duhem–Quine thesis, the latter being the holistic proposition that scientific knowledge is an inter-connected network and that unexpected experimental observations can, in principle at least, be accommodated by appropriate adjustments anywhere within the system (13). Contemporary philosophers of science have approached the problems posed by Duhem and Quine in a variety of ways, but in this paper I want to look at how they are handled in practice by a real scientific community (14).

In outline, consensus developed as follows. In late 1974 there was, as I have mentioned, no obvious preferred explanation for the new particles, although charm and colour were the most frequently discussed candidates (15). In the first six months of 1975 little new data of any significance appeared, but the colour explanation came to be seen as increasingly unlikely, although several individuals and groups continued to defend it in the literature and in conference talks. In July 1975 the discovery of the first of what proved to be a new family of related particles was announced, and this led to the wholesale abandonment of colour. From this time onwards only three theorists continued to advocate colour in the literature and at conferences. In the spring of 1976 a second family of related particles were discovered, which were almost universally interpreted as charmed particles, and by summer 1976 'charm [was] ready for the textbooks' (16), as one leading theorist put it. Nonetheless, the recalcitrant colour theorists interpreted this second family as coloured particles and maintained their position. It was only in the summer of 1977, when detailed measurements had been reported on members of this second family, that they concluded that 'there was no way' (17) that colour could be defended, and abandoned it.

There were thus, as I will elaborate below, three distinct 'epochs' in the establishment of charm. In the first, from November 1974 to June 1975, a loose consensus formed in favour of charm: in the second, from July 1975 to May 1976, there was a relatively solid consensus favouring charm, and alternative models — principally colour — received little attention; and in the third, from June 1976 onwards, charm was regarded by the HEP community as a whole as established (18). The changes in consensus going from the first to the second epoch and from the second to the third were quite clearly associated with important qualitative changes in the data — the successive discoveries of new families of particles related to the J-psi and psi-prime — and there is a great temptation to treat this as the entire analysis: 'the data decided', one wants to say — but this would be a mistake. It would be a mistake because, on a rather abstract level, it ignores the consequences of the Duhem—Quine thesis, and it would be a mistake because, on a quite concrete level, it ignores the fact that the colour theorists were able to hold their model immune from falsification until well into the third epoch, and, in principle, for ever.

How, then, was the choice made by the community between the competing models? In the remainder of this paper I will argue and illustrate the thesis that it was the interaction of the differing theoretical responses of the two models to the emerging data with the pre-existing matrix of 'interests' supported by the HEP community which determined the triumph of charm and the demise of colour. What I want to show is the way in which the elements of the charm model intersected with the interests of an ever increasing number of the sub-cultures of HEP, and the failure of colour to emulate this. One consequence of this style of analysis is that it is inevitably technical, and it should be borne in mind in what follows that the discussion of technical points will necessarily be over-simplified and abbreviated, not least because of the very success of charm's protagonists in intertwining their chosen model with all the most promising (and popular) theoretical lines in HEP in the early 1970's.

First some technical preliminaries. Three distinct forces are recognised as important in the world of elementary particles; in order of decreasing strength these are known as the strong, electromagnetic and weak interactions (the fourth, gravitational, force is too weak to have any perceptible effect). Most particles, for instance the proton and neutron, experience the strong inter-action, and such particles are known as 'hadrons'. A subdivision of the family of hadrons, which will be significant in this discussion, is made on the basis of their intrinsic angular momentum or 'spin': particles having integral spin are known as 'mesons', while particles having half-integral spin are known as 'baryons'. A few particles, for instance the electron, experience only the weak and electromagnetic interactions, and these are known as 'leptons'.

This paper will be mainly concerned with conjectures as to the properties of hadrons, since both the charm and colour explanations of the J-psi and its subsequently discovered relatives asserted that that was what they were. As soon as the J-psi was discovered it was clear that if it was a hadron, it was highly unusual. Quite simply, it lived too long. At the time it was the heaviest particle known (more than three times more massive than the proton), and it was well established that massive hadrons are unstable, decaying rapidly to lighter hadrons with a lifetime of the order of 10^{-23} seconds; a lifetime, furthermore, which decreases with increasing mass of the parent. The J-psi was observed to live around 2000 times longer than any straightforward estimate of its expected lifetime, and the immediate theoretical problem was to find an explanation for this.

Both charm and colour gave explanations which depended upon variants of the 'quark' model. In this model hadrons are not seen as truly elementary particles, but rather as composites of more fundamental entities known as quarks. Mesons are pictured as made up of a quark plus an antiquark, while baryons are pictured as comprising three quarks. Quarks are thought to come in several different types, and the various species of quark are distinguished by assigning them different 'quantum numbers', in just the same way as is routinely done for the hadrons of which they are constituents. Some of these quantum numbers can be understood in terms of their macroscopic equivalents — one can think of the 'spin' of an elementary particle in analogy with the angular momentum of a spinning top — but others cannot, and are best thought of as book-keeping devices used to explain the various conser-vation laws which are observed to hold in the interactions of elementary particles. Quarks are thought to carry two distinct sets of these book-keeping quantum numbers, quaintly known as 'flavours' and 'colours', and these were at the heart of the competing explanations for the new particles.

Let me give the charm explanation first. In the pre-psi era there were three established flavours of quarks – 'up', 'down' and 'strange'. The charm model asserted that a fourth flavour – 'charm' – existed, and that the J-psi was a meson composed of a charmed quark plus a charmed antiquark. Because the book-keeping rules for charm were those of simple addition, the net charm of the J-psi was supposed to be zero (the quark having charm +1, the antiquark charm –1). The charm explanation of the long lifetime of the J-psi was based on an empirical rule known as the 'Zweig rule'. The Zweig rule stated that decays of hadrons were inhibited whenever they involved the mutual annihilation of constituent quarks. This rule had been observed to hold in the few previous instances where it appeared to be applicable, and since the only way the J-psi could decay to the old hadrons was through mutual annihilation of its constituent charmed quarks, it clearly offered at least a qualitative understanding of its longevity.

Thus the charm explanation depended upon the existence of a new quark which carried a new flavour. The colour explanation, on the other hand, required no new quarks, exploiting instead the freedom of the colour quantum numbers. Quarks are supposed to come in three colours, – say, red, yellow, and blue. Colour labels combine together like vectors, and the old hadrons were all supposed to be colourless – each red quark, for instance, having its colour cancelled by a red antiquark, and so on. The colour model asserted that, for the first time, in the J-psi colour was visible; that in the J-psi the colour quantum numbers of the constituent quarks did not cancel out. Thus the J-psi was supposed to be a red particle (or blue, or yellow – which particular colour was immaterial). Hadronic colour was supposed to be conserved by the strong interactions; hence the J-psi could not decay to old colourless hadrons via the strong interactions; and hence its anomalously long life span.

These, then, are the essences of the two models, and we can now proceed to look at their respective fortunes.

The First Epoch

I will discuss the three epochs in chronological order. In the first epoch, when only the J-psi and psi-prime had been discovered, the two models faced superficially equal obstacles to acceptance. Nonetheless, the charm model outstripped its rival in popularity, and the explanation for this lies in the differing extent to which the articulations of the two models intersected with the interests of various subcultures.

The immediate obstacle to the acceptance of charm was that the Zweig rule went some way towards explaining the lifetime of the J-psi and psi-prime, but not far enough. A straightforward extrapolation of the suppression of decays, from the few old hadrons to which the rule was applicable to the new particles, led one to expect that the J-psi would decay around 40 times faster than it actually did. There were, of course, two ways of looking at this discrepancy: as one group of theorists put it, 'this is either a serious problem or an important result, depending on one's point of view' (19). Theorists predisposed to charm saw it as the latter, and those to colour as the former, but it is highly significant that there was a third, ostensibly neutral, group which was inclined to side with charm. This was the school of 'hadrody-namicists', theorists who had invented, elaborated and used the Zweig rule throughout the 1960's. These theorists had invested time and energy in the Zweig rule; they had the expertise required to see the world constructively from its perspective, and one can straightforwardly say that they had an interest in the elaboration of the rule in the fresh context offered by the new particles. As I have mentioned, the Zweig rule was supported by relatively few observations, and if one accepted charm then a striking new datum was added to the set — namely, that the rule became more effective at higher energies — and there was new work to be done. Thus the most striking mismatch between the charm model and the data could be construed as a puzzle which intersected with the interest of an existing research network, and normal science could be, and was, done on it (20).

Furthermore, the proponents of charm themselves provided a possible set of tools for attacking this particular puzzle. To understand why they were in a position to do this some background is called for. The existence of charm was volubly advocated by a group of theorists centered on Harvard even before the J-psi was discovered. These physicists were the spearhead of what might be called the 'gauge theory revolution'. Gauge theory is a particular example of a quantum field theory, and as such is seen as a possible explana-tory base for the entire subject matter of HEP. Quantum field theory in general had been in the doldrums from the late 1950's onwards, facing intransigent mathematical problems, until it was rescued by important theoretical developments in the early 1970's (21). As a result of these developments those few physicists who had retained an active interest in field theory came to realise that gauge theory in particular had many attractive features. Harvard was the most influential centre of field theoretic expertise, and throughout the 1970's theorists there (and, later, elsewhere) devoted a great deal of effort to the construction of models of elementary particle interactions consistent with gauge theoretical ideas. Again, this stream of practice is readily understood in terms of the prior interests of the theorists involved. Furthermore, as we shall see, several of these models came to constitute exemplars for the work of theorists not initially having an interest in gauge theory. What must be stressed at the outset is that gauge theorists did not confine their attention exclusively to charm, and that, since many physicists do not dissect their knowledge in the way I am presently attempting, successes for gauge theory anywhere fed-back as support for charm (and vice versa) (22).

This offers a nice illustration of the general remark made in the introduction concerning work on different exemplars sharing a common element. The point here is the following. During the period under consideration various gauge-theoretic exemplars were constructed, and the birth of any new stream of practice based on a gauge-theoretic exemplar increased the proportion of the community for whom gauge-theory constituted a central item of discourse. Gauge theory would enter the vocabulary of the theorists elaborating the model, the experimenters involved in the production of relevant and potentially relevant data, and so on. This enlargement of the 'gauge-theory speaking' community continually acted to further the 'out-thereness' of gauge theory, offering an immediate boost to the 'reality' of any new gauge-theoretic model. There was, in a very real sense, a revolution in progress in the period I am considering – and, as its most visible specific focus, charm both marked a watershed in the revolution and was reinforced by it.

To return to the story then, by mid-1974 gauge theorists had become convinced, for reasons which it is unnecessary to go into here, that for their approach to make sense – for their long-term goals in theoretical development to be accomplished – charm must exist (23). When the J-psi was discovered, they immediately interpreted it in terms of charm, and also gave a distinctive explanation of the super-Zweig rule required to explain its longevity. I will not give details of this explanation, but simply note for the moment that it was based on a simple model motivated by the gauge theory candidate for the theory of the strong interactions, now known as 'quantum chromodynamics', or 'QCD' for short. Two facets of the QCD model, or the 'charmonium' model as it was called, are relevant to the present discussion. Firstly, it made concrete predictions for the existence of yet more long-lived new particles, and I will return to this in my analysis of the second epoch. Secondly, it constituted an exemplar for work outside the charmonium programme itself. Let me explain what I mean by this. The charmonium model asserted that the charmed quark and anti-quark which compose the J-psi interact in a simple way consistent with the general structure of QCD. As such it was an example of a long tradition of 'spectroscopic' quark models. It differed from its predecessors in specifying the model parameters in terms of the expectations of QCD. There was, of course, no reason to limit the application of the model to the new particles, and one group of Harvard physicists published an extensive analysis of the spectroscopy of the old hadrons using an appropriate formulation of the new model, in which they showed how existing puzzles could be seen in a new light, how new puzzles could be created and solved, and so on (24). The new model showed the existing network of quark spectroscopists how they could enrich their approach and generate new soluble puzzles, and − in the background − the rising tide of gauge theory guaranteed that such work would be of interest to an increasing fraction of the community, and not simply within the specialist network. It intersected with the interests of quark spectroscopists − they accordingly took it up, and this work fed back, by enlarging the 'charm-speaking community', as support for the reality of charm (25).

Here we can see clearly both the analogical and multidimensional aspects of exemplars. The analogical element of the new spectroscopic quark model resided in its treatment of the quark interactions within hadrons: these were treated in essentially the same way as the interactions of charged particles within well-understood atomic systems (more on this in the discussion of the second epoch). The multi-dimensionality of the exemplar arose from the juxtaposition of at least four identifiable elements: the atomic analogy just mentioned; the gauge-theory idiom in which it was couched; the contemporary practice associated with the spectroscopic quark model; and the set of relevant data, which was redefined by the model itself. Each of these dimensions intersected with the interests of some group or groups, although, as it happened, only the dimension relating to contemporary quark modelling required any degree of sophistication, and hence it was quark-modellers (rather than, say, atomic physicists) who set about elaborating the new model.

To summarise, then: what charm did in the first epoch was:

(i) it generated a puzzle – the super-Zweig rule – which intersected with the interests of hadrodynamicists,

(ii) it supplied its own solution to this puzzle – the charmonium model – which had predictive power (and hence was welcomed by experimenters), and which intersected with the interests of hadron spectroscopists by enriching both their puzzles and their techniques, and

(iii) in a wider context it supported, and was supported by, the gauge theory revolution.

If we now turn to what colour did in the same period we will be able to gain some inkling of why the consensus moved strongly in favour of charm. There is something of a problem here since there was considerable diversity amongst specific colour models, which I will attempt to circumvent by dealing only with the most tenaciously defended variant of the model – that proposed by Gordon Feldman (of Johns Hopkins University) and Paul Matthews (then of Imperial College London, now Vice-Chancellor of the University of Bath) (26). (The third theorist mentioned earlier who continued active work on colour into the second and third epochs was Berthold Stech, of Heidelberg University. His version of the colour model differed in detail from that of Feldman and Matthews, but encountered analogous obstacles to acceptance. Where relevant I will indicate these in footnotes).

As I mentioned above, at the heart of the colour model was the proposition that the J-psi and psi-prime were manifestations of a new conserved quantum number called colour. This immediately explained the longevity of the new particles, and was, furthermore, historically dignified: the flavour known as 'strangeness' had been invented and accepted in similar circumstances in the 1950's. Thus, the colour model was, if anything, faced with fewer problems than charm when first proposed. However, it soon acquired a comparable obstacle to acceptance. Early in 1975, detailed experiment on the psi and psi-prime had revealed that photons (quanta of the electromagnetic field) were only to be found infrequently amongst their decay products. This was a considerable setback for the colour model since, straightforwardly articulated, the model predicted that decays involving photons would be the predominant mode (27). The response of Feldman and Matthews to this observation, which was known as the 'radiative damping' problem, was to equate it with the problem of the super-Zweig rule which charm generated, and then essentially to ignore it (28). They felt that the QCD explanation for the super-Zweig rule was based on unjustified approximations, and thus, even if they themselves failed to offer an explanation for the radiative damping problem there would still be no rational grounds for choice between the two models (17). Logically, this reasoning was probably correct, but it generated little support for colour. And the reason for this was that the radiative damping problem, unlike the Zweig rule, intersected with no interests whatsoever within the community.

This is an important point which requires some elaboration. I have already stressed that the essential characteristic of an exemplar is that it refers back to an existing body of practice and associated interests as well as forwards to a new area of research, and it was in the respect of referring back that charm was so successful, and colour so unsuccessful. Feldman and Mathews's first response to the radiative damping problem illustrates this nicely, being clearly *ad hoc* in the sociological sense explained in the introduction. Feldman and Matthews invoked what they referred to as the 'Feynman rule'. If one follows up the reference they give for this rule, one finds, in a paper co-authored by Richard Feynman, the somewhat apologetic introduction of an arbitrary suppression factor, designed simply to improve the fit to the data of a phenomenological spectroscopic quark model. It is to this arbitrary factor that Feldman and Matthews refer. Being arbitrary, the factor was intrinsic to no body of practice – there was no expertise involved in its use, no interests were bound up in its deployment – and thus Feldman and Matthews' response to the radiative damping problem failed to intersect with any interests within the HEP community (29). As a consequence, no new body of practice came into being around the 'Feynman Rule'; there was no enlargement of the community of colour-related discourse, and no increase in the 'out-thereness' of colour.

Thus, in contrast with charm and the Zweig rule, colour's response to the radiative damping problem was completely *ad hoc*. In terms of the generation of either interesting puzzles or new exemplars, charm had a distinct and unarguable edge over colour (30). Also, although I will not discuss it in detail here, the wider context of the gauge theory revolution favoured charm: in essence this was because the charm model as articulated by most theorists was based on fractionally charged quarks, while those theorists who related colour to their long-term interest in gauge theories did so on the basis of the unfashionable idea of integrally charged quarks (31).

The Second Epoch

For all of these reasons consensus with the HEP community moved strongly in favour of charm and against colour during the first epoch, but nonetheless the charm consensus remained tentative; at an international conference held in June 1975, Gordon Feldman recalls that around 10–15% of the submitted papers favoured colour rather than charm (17), and there were no less than four independent review talks on colour given, as compared with only one on charm (32). However, a dramatic change soon took place. In July, 1975, the discovery of what proved to be the first of a whole new family of related long-lived particles (which I will refer to as the 'chi' particles) was announced, and at another international conference held in August 1975 (at which time evidence had been announced for three such chi particles), a marked change in the balance of power was evident; Haim Harari, who gave the theoretical review of the new particles, only briefly discussed colour and concluded that 'in spite of the ingenuity that went into some of these models their gross features are incompatible with the experimental observations' (33); and James Bjorken, in his conference summary talk, described charm and the charmonium model as 'standards of reference [which] an experimentalist will naturally use to interpret his data' (34). The July 1975 announcement of the first chi particle thus marked the beginning of the second epoch, and from that point onwards Feldman, Matthews and Stech were left as the only public advocates of colour.

This transformation from the loose consensus of epoch one to the more solid consensus of epoch two is extremely interesting. The first point to be made is that, as I mentioned earlier, the charm model did predict the existence of a new family of particles. The 'charmonium' model, as the Harvard theorists called it, required the existence of five new long-lived particles less massive than the psi-prime, into which the psi-prime would occasionally decay with specified characteristics. Thus, at first glance, one is tempted to assert that the HEP community acted in accordance with some model of scientific rationality akin to that implicit in Lakatos' idea of a 'research programme' in favouring charm in the second epoch; the charmonium model, one might want to say, involved a progressive problem-shift which received increasing empirical support throughout the second epoch. In more straightforward language, one might rephrase this as that it was obvious to all concerned that the charmonium model was right. This was, I think, how the situation appeared to the majority of the HEP community, but, even so, some explanation of why certain explanations are seen to be obvious is called for, and this point requires some emphasis before I give my own analysis of 'obviousness'.

The difficulty which arises in any simple explanation of the success of the charmonium model is connected with the lack of explicit criteria of 'confirmation'. Why, for instance, in August 1975, were the three chi particles then established seen as empirical support rather than as refutation for the charmonium model which predicted five? This question is not without point, since, as we shall see, the colour model, too, led one to expect the existence of particles intermediate between the psi and psi-prime. One might answer the question with the assertion that the community was guessing that a further two particles would be discovered. This is true, but the question then remains as to which factors disposed physicists to make that particular guess. Furthermore, by the summer of 1976 two further chi particles had been tentatively identified — making up the required total of five — and hailed as confirmation of the model (35). However, these latter two particles had properties which were in quite clear disagreement with the straightforward predictions of the model, and the 'it's obvious' explanation remains problematic even taking these into account.

This objection might seem a mere quibble, in the light of the evident weight given by the HEP community to the correct prediction of five chi particles, but to indicate that the quibble must be taken seriously let me refer briefly to later developments. In the period subsequent to 1976 the charmonium model was worked out by theorists in increasing detail and with increasing sophistication, and these theorists came to conclude that at least one of the chi particles — the least massive — had properties inconsistent with the predictions of the model. They concluded that, if this particle actually was a member of the same family as the others, then something must be radically wrong with the model. At the same time a high-precision experiment was underway at Stanford to investigate the properties of the chi particle. This 'Crystal Ball' experiment, as it was known, failed to find any evidence of the lightest chi particle at the previously reported mass — but did find evidence for the 'same' particle at a considerably higher mass, much closer to the prediction of the model (36). This change in observed mass caused little surprise in the community, since the original observation had been made with very poor statistics.

This is not the place to elaborate on these later developments, but it is clear that, during the second epoch, the partially worked-out charmonium model was instrumental in maintaining the reality of some rather tenuous data, even while the data was seen as supporting the reality of the model. Hence one can only conclude that the dominance of charm in the second epoch stands in need of some explanation, and that an explanation in terms of, say, 'research programmes' and 'novel facts' would run into severe difficulties — since at least some of the 'novel facts' in question were stabilised only by the model they were apparently confirming (37).

How then is one to understand the success of the model? The explanation I will give is in terms of the intersection of interests. The forces which had been at work in the first epoch — the active streams of work on the Zweig rule and the new QCD-related quark spectroscopy, and the increasing momentum of the gauge theory revolution — could only be reinforced by any sign of confirmation of the charmonium model, and vice versa. And to these forces were added new ones.

To unravel the new sources of support for charm in the second epoch it is necessary first to outline the theoretical basis of the charmonium model. The model interpreted both the psis and the chis as bound states of charmed quarks, and it departed radically from earlier quark models in its assumption that charmed quarks are much heavier than the old up, down and strange quarks — so heavy, in fact, that within hadrons such as the psis and chis the constituent charmed quarks move very slowly (nonrelativistically) in comparison with the highly relativistic motion entailed by quark models of the old hadrons. Now, non-relativistic motion is much more tractable theoretically than relativistic motion. In particular, the charmonium model depended upon an image of a charmed quark non-relativistically orbiting its antiparticle under the influence of a central potential, in exact analogy with the atomic system of an electron orbiting a positron (the antiparticle of the electron). The latter system is known as positronium, and is one of the textbook applications of quantum mechanics to atomic physics, being almost identical to the hydrogen atom in its formal treatment. The name charmonium was coined to make explicit the parallel between the envisaged structure of the new particles and the simplest and best understood atomic structure; and the psis and chis were pictured in the charmonium model as energy levels of the charmonium system in exact analogy with the energy levels of the positronium spectrum. The charmonium model illustrates perfectly the role of an exemplar as the concrete embodiment of an analogy relating a new field of research back to an established body of practice.

The model was intuitively transparent to any trained physicist, and this had two important consequences. Firstly, whenever the model encountered a mismatch with reality the resources were available to essentially anyone to attempt to fix it up, and for others to appreciate such work. In order to calculate the charmonium spectrum one had first to specify the potential in which the quarks moved. The earliest models chose simple potentials, and as data accumulated and discrepancies were noted with the predictions, more sophisticated potentials — involving 'hyperfine' splittings — were introduced to explain them in complete analogy to the detailed treatment of atomic spectra. Given the undergraduate training of physicists and the crude statement of the charmonium model, the pattern of extension of the model to the puzzles posed by the chi particles was obvious — and as data accumulated on the chi particles it became food for an active stream of normal science (38).

This stream of normal science was one clear source of fresh support for charm during the second epoch. Another source was less direct but more fundamental: namely, the charmonium model made quarks themselves 'real'. To fully appreciate this argument requires some knowledge of the history of the quark concept, which I can only outline here. Since their invention in 1964 it had never been clear to physicists what to make of quarks: were they real objects, or were they no more than mnemonics for observed regularities? Had it proved possible to isolate a single quark and study its properties this question would have been resolved, but an extensive programme of experiment had failed to do so; quarks — if they existed — remained obstinately confined within hadrons. Theoretical models based on quarks had been enormously successful in explaining various features of the data throughout the 1960's and 1970's, but nonetheless all of these models were based on assumptions or approximations which made little sense if taken too seriously. The constituent quark model of hadron masses, for instance, was based on approximations which could not be justified in the context of the theory of special relativity – and relativity has always carried more weight in HEP than quarks.

Now, what the charmonium model did was to show that *if*, by some lucky chance, there happened to exist a species of quark which was very heavy, *then* it was possible to construct models of hadrons containing them which were not based on 'nonsensical' assumptions. No fundamental principles had to be ignored in the charmonium model: if charmed quarks were heavy, then the charmonium spectrum made just as much sense as the atomic spectra on which physicists are weaned. And furthermore, if the charmonium model worked – if it fitted the data – then quarks were just as real as electrons and positrons. Of course, this reasoning would strictly speaking only apply to the heavy, charmed quarks, but since these were to be seen as simply a new flavour of the old, light quarks, these, in their turn would be seen as real. There was thus great scope for positive feedback here. If the charmonium model worked, quarks would become real and doubts over the significance of the considerable amount of work being done on the basis of the quark model would be reduced; the entire community would be disposed to see puzzles thrown up by any variant of the model as valid and worthy of attention, and so on. It was a classic bootstrap situation in which the more one believed in and utilised the quark concept the more one was inclined to see any indication from the data as validation of the charmonium model, and the more one believed the charmonium model to have been confirmed, the more one was inclined to believed in and utilise quarks.

This massive intersection of interests is, I believe, the only possible explanation for the dramatic loss of support for colour in the second epoch. It is particularly noteworthy that those physicists supporting colour on the basis of models which could encompass both colour and charm at once abandoned the former for the latter (39). Also, in the third epoch, when charm had finally become institutionalised, all of the major retrospective review talks concentrated on the quark-charm-gauge theory nexus (40).

The activities of Feldman and Matthews in defence of colour during the second epoch only highlight the importance of the intersection of interests.

Their response to the discovery of the chi states was completely *ad hoc* in my sociological sense. They pointed out that the existence of the chi's did not falsify colour, but beyond that they had little to say. The colour model predicted the existence of coloured versions of all the old colourless hadrons. Feldman and Matthews had interpreted the J-psi and psi-prime as coloured versions of particles called 'rho mesons', and similarly they were at liberty to interpret the chi particles as coloured 'pions' and so on. Unfortunately they were unable to discuss what the masses of the chi's should be, how they related to the psi's, how long they should live – in short, all of the questions experiment could investigate (41). This was because their style of explanation was based on group-theoretical symmetry arguments and, for reasons I will not go into here, could not easily be adapted to the dynamical perspectives mentioned above which made charmonium so attractive. Thus the discovery of the chi states did not lead the colour model to intersect with any new interests – its simply remained silent on the topic – and it was stripped of almost all of its adherents by the success of charm (42).

The Third Epoch

So much, then, for the second epoch. It is now time to go on to the third and final epoch in which charm was enthroned as the real thing. Despite the success of the charmonium model in the second epoch, it could not be said it demonstrated that charm, as required by gauge theories, existed. The charmonium model only required that some new species of heavy quark existed, not necessarily carrying the specific quantum numbers associated with charm. As a dynamical model anathema to the philosophy of colour its success was quite sufficient to effectively bring about the demise of the latter, but to establish the existence of charm something more was required.

That something more was the observation of 'naked charm' – particles made up of a single charmed quark plus an old non-charmed quark and hence carrying non-zero total charm, in contrast to psis and chis in which the charm of quarks and antiquarks cancelled out. To cut a long story short, the first manifestation of naked charm was found in April 1976, in the shape of a long-lived meson known as the 'D'. The decays of this particle were seen to be highly unusual; and unusual, furthermore, in exactly the way the protagonists of charm had long predicted (43). This was enough to institutionalise charm

(44). In view of the forces at work which I have discussed earlier, and the ability of charm to provide an acceptable framework for normal science on this most recent new family of particles (45), this surely calls for no further explanation, and none will be given.

From the point of view of this paper the most interesting event in the third epoch was the abandonment of colour by Feldman and Matthews. Interestingly enough, this did not come about at once — indeed, as soon as the discovery of the D had been announced they published a paper entitled 'The Discovery of Coloured Kaons?' (46) — but by the summer of 1977 they had been worn down by the accumulating data. Their reasons for abandoning colour centred on rather technical issues, but I will attempt to give a brief sketch. In the 'coloured kaons' paper they had given definite predictions, which differed markedly from the equivalent predictions of charm, for a more massive particle related to the D. Unfortunately, subsequent experiment categorically supported charm and refuted colour. Since Feldman and Matthews were hardly in a position to challenge the fundamentals of the experimental method they sorted through the resources of their model, searching for a new candidate having the required quantum numbers to partner the D in agreement with experiment. Here they collapsed. Their only suitable candidate explained the existing observations, but also predicted phenomena which were not observed. They could have fixed this up by the invention of some mechanism, in a way analogous to that used to explain away the old radiative damping problem, but this would have been hopelessly *ad hoc*. Gordon Feldman certainly saw it as a totally meaningless manoeuvre and, as he put it, 'I made sure we were wrong . . . there was no way . . . these particles are presumably not . . . colour ' (17). Colour could have been preserved from falsification, but the cause was manifestly lost — it would have served no purpose (47).

The point to be stressed here is that by this time it made essentially no difference to the reality of charm whether Feldman and Matthews maintained their defence of colour or not. Their sociologically *ad hoc* avoidance of falsification had failed to give birth to any new streams of practice, and they had been reduced to a discourse-community of two. Quite literally, they were reduced to talking to themselves. As Professor Feldman put it: "just to be able to talk to other physicists I have to be able to speak about it [i.e. charm]" (17). In the eyes of the HEP community, the colour model was irrevocably attached to its authors, Feldman and Matthews, rather than residing 'out there' in the real world.

Summary and Conclusions

This completes my account of the establishment of charm and the demise of its principal rival, and the interpretation of this episode in terms of the 'interest model'. The concepts of 'exemplars' and 'interests' have been used to explain why the existence of charm came to be embodied in the practice of an increasing number of groups of HEP theorists, and why a similar development failed to occur in the case of colour. Through a series of exemplary achievements — giving solutions to its initial problems which were fruitful in a whole variety of directions, and tying these solutions into a gauge-theoretic framework — and the *ad hoc* failure of colour to emulate these, charm became entrenched in the practice of several sub-cultures of theoretical HEP, and in the process became real.

In conclusion, let me make three comments. Firstly, for reasons of space, this paper contains something of an omission. It has concentrated on HEP theorists and underemphasised their experimental colleagues. In fact, it must be acknowledge that the interplay between these two groups was very important in the establishment of charm. During the three epochs I have discussed, charm became central to the practice of many experimenters as well as theorists. Indeed, it was only after a determined and goal-oriented programme of experiment and analysis that the D-mesons, which set the final seal on charm, were found. Without such involvement of the experiment community in the domain of discourse it is hard to see how the reality of any theoretical construct could come about. Even so, if this paper were expanded to include the development of charm-related experimental programmes, the form of the analysis would not be altered — although some discussion would be called for of the role of theoretical models in the way experimenters make sense of their practice.

The second comment is more important, and more positive. It is that the scheme of scientific development outlined by Kuhn in the 'Postscript' to his *Structure of Scientific Revolutions* seems to work, at least in the interpretation adopted in the interest model. This point needs to be made explicit, since despite the widespread interest and controversy which have surrounded

Kuhn's work, very little attention has been paid to empirical investigation of his assertions. From the present case study it appears that bodies of scientific practice devoted to the elaboration of particular exemplars *can* be identified, and that the outcome of this episode, which has been very influential in the subsequent development of HEP, can be understood in terms of these bodies of practice. Besides the demonstration of this, the most important points to emerge from the study concern the nature of exemplars. Their defining feature is seen to be their analogical role — referring back to established bodies of knowledge and practice. It is precisely the presence or absence of such 'referring-back' which enables one to distinguish between exemplary achievements and those which I have called *ad hoc*. Finally, as the concrete embodiment of analogy, the aspect of exemplars which must be stressed is their multidimensional nature. It is only because exemplars are multidimensional constructs that one can conceive of constellations of *related* bodies of practice based upon different exemplars — and the solidity of our knowledge is clearly dependent upon the extent of such constellations.

The third comment concerns a possible direction in which the image of science implicit in the interest model may lead us, and can be introduced by reference to the work of the philosopher of science, Mary Hesse. In looking at the developments through which charm became established one cannot fail to be reminded of Hesse's network model of knowledge (48). Charm became intrinsic to the practice of the HEP community through becoming a principal focus of just such an interconnected network of generalisations as Hesse describes. Conversely, colour and the other alternative models failed because they did not become tied into the network; they floated free and continued to be identified with their creators rather than with the natural world. In this sense the interest model is a sociological counterpart of Hesse's network, setting out to understand the social dynamics underlying the network's evolution. One particularly interesting observation which comes out of the present case study concerns the role of the charm model in relation to the ambiguous data on the chi particles during the second epoch. It is clear that as theoretical models become more securely tied within the whole network of theory they can play an increasing role in the 'stabilisation' of data. Furthermore it can, I believe, be argued that this role extends far beyond that of simply removing the ambiguity inherent in data of poor statistics, ultimately to the level of stabilising experimental techniques, methods and procedures (49). It may be possible, by pursuing this line of thought, to recover Kuhn's full-blooded conception of a large-scale, community-wide paradigm, as a coherent network of theoretical and experimental practice. This would clear a path for the exploration of the associated concepts of incommensurability and revolution — an exploration which has been bogged-down for too long in philosophical debate.

Notes and References

1. T. S. Kuhn, *The Structure of Scientific Revolutions*, Chicago University Press, Chicago and London, 2nd edn., 1970, pp. 174–210.
2. *Ibid.*, p. 187.
3. The relation between exemplars and analogies has been emphasised by Margaret Masterman, 'The Nature of a Paradigm'. In I. Lakatos and A. Musgrave (eds.), *Criticism and the Growth of Knowledge*, Cambridge University Press, Cambridge, 1970. The central role of analogy in scientific thought is treated from a philosophical perspective in M. Hesse, *The Structure of Scientific Inference*, MacMillan, London, 1974. For a sociologically oriented discussion of analogical thought, see K. D. Knoor, 'The Scientist as an Analogical Reasoner: A Critique of the Metaphor Theory of Innovation', this volume.
4. For the use of 'investment' in the analysis of science, see B. Latour and S. Woolgar, *Laboratory Life: the Social Construction of Scientific Facts*, Sage, Beverly Hills, 1979, and K. D. Knorr, 'Producing and Reproducing Knowledge: Descriptive or Constructive?' *Social Science Information* 16, 669–696 (1977). Work which refers to 'interests' includes S. B. Barnes, *Interests and the Growth of Knowledge*, Routledge and Kegan Paul, London, 1977; D. A. MacKenzie, 'Statistical Theory and Social Interests: a Case-Study', *Social Studies of Science* 8, 1978, 35–83 (1978); S. B. Barnes and D. A. MacKenzie, 'On the Role of Interests in Scientific Change'; and S. Shapin, 'The Politics of Observation: Cerebral Anatomy and Social Interests in the Edinburgh Phrenology Disputes', both in R. Wallis (ed.), *On The Margins of Science: The Social Construction of Rejected Knowledge*, Keele, *Sociological Review Monograph* 27, 1979.
   As Kuhn has remarked (*op. cit.*, Note 1, 187–204) the utility of concepts such as exemplars (and, by implication, expertise, investments, interests and so on) derives from the existence of an inarticulated, tacit component of scientific practice (see M. Polanyi, *Personal Knowledge*, Routledge and Kegan Paul, London, 1973; H. M. Collins, 'The TEA Set: Tacit Knowledge and Scientific Networks', *Science Studies* 4, 165–186 (1974), and 'Building a TEA Laser: the Caprices of Communication, *Social Studies of Science* 5, 441–50 (1975)). In the present paper exemplars and interests are used as mediating concepts in the analysis of the process whereby the idiosyncratic and personal practice and experience of individual scientists is organised into a relatively impersonal system of articulated knowledge. It is this transmutation of personal experience into articulated knowledge which allows one to speak of the *social construction* of 'objects'.

5. The monolithic characterisation of a 'paradigm', and the refutation of such a concept, are typified by the approach of J. W. N. Watkins, 'Against "Normal Science"'. In I. Lakatos and A. Musgrave (eds.), *op. cit.*, Note 3.

6. 'Research network' here refers to a group of scientists sharing a common cognitive orientation, such as one might identify using the techniques of citation analysis, rather than to a group primarily identified by communication patterns.

7. The empirical data on which this paper is based derive from an extensive review of the HEP literature (technical and popular), and correspondence and interviews with around 60 leading physicists, including the main protagonists of the 'charm' and 'colour' models (see below). I have given a more extensive account and documentation of the period under consideration here in 'Model Choice and Cognitive Interests: A Case-Study in Elementary Particle Physics' Edinburgh preprint (1978, unpublished), and this will constitute part of my Ph.D. thesis (Edinburgh, forthcoming).

8. H. M. Collins, 'The Seven Sexes: a Study in the Sociology of a Phenomenon, or the Replication of Experiments in Physics', *Sociology* 6, 141–184 (1976).

9. HEP theorists and experimentalists constitute distinct professional groups. The accomplishment of the reality of objects clearly requires the involvement of both groups, and the simplest way in which this can come about is through each group regarding the products of the other as 'fact'. This is by no means always the case in HEP, but, since much of the data on the new particles was produced using *standard* techniques, solidly rooted in practice, there was little incentive for theorists to query the empirical material at their disposal. (For a minor qualification to this, see discussion of the 'chi' particles given below).

10. The discovery on the East Coast was made by a group from the Massachusetts Institute of Technology (MIT) led by Samuel C. C. Ting, working at the Brookhaven National Laboratory on Long Island. The West Coast discovery was made by a Stanford Linear Accelerator Center (SLAC) – Lawrence Berkeley Laboratory (LBL) collaboration led by Burton Richter, working at SLAC in Stanford, California. The publications announcing the discovery were, respectively, J. J. Aubert *et al.*, 'Experimental Observation of a Heavy Particle J', *Physical Review Letters* 33, 1404–5 (1974); and J.-E. Augustin *et al.*, 'Discovery of a Narrow Resonance in e^+e^- Annihilation', *Phys. Rev. Lett.* 33, 1406–7 (1974).

   Ting and Richter were rewarded for their discovery of the J-psi by the joint award of the 1976 Nobel Prize for Physics. The 1979 Nobel Prize for Physics was shared by three theorists whose work was central to the episode under discussion: S. L. Glashow of Harvard University, one of the inventors of charm and its most determined advocate; and S. Weinberg, also of Harvard, and A. Salam, of Imperial College London and the International Centre for Theoretical Physics, Trieste, who independently proposed the unified gauge theory (see below) of the weak and electromagnetic interactions, within which charm achieved major significance.

11. This particle was discovered by the SLAC-LBL group and was reported in G. S. Abrams *et al.*, 'Discovery of a Second Narrow Resonance', *Phys. Rev. Lett.* 33, 1453–4 (1974).

12. An analysis of the failure of other proposed models of the new particles would go along exactly the same lines as that to be given for colour, and will therefore not be explicitly given here.

13. For a discussion of the Duhem–Quine thesis and the philosophical problems associated with a belief in the existence of crucial experiments, see I. Lakatos, 'Falsification and the Methodology of Research Programmes' in I. Lakatos and A. Musgrave (eds.), *op. cit.*, Note 3.

14. For instance, Lakatos (*op. cit.*, Note 13) provides a normative methodology which he believes to be adequate. I will indicate below why Lakatos' technique of rational reconstruction is inapplicable to the episode under discussion here.

15. The three major rapid publication HEP journals are *Physical Review Letters, Physics Letters* and *Lettere al Nuovo Cimento*. Between them they published 62 theoretical papers submitted before the end of January 1975 on the J-psi and the psi-prime. Of these articles 24 favoured charm, 7 colour, 11 the so-called 'IVB hypothesis' which was quickly abandoned, and 14 unconventional models (the remaining 6 concerned the application of conventional techniques to the data). It would be unwise to make quantitative inferences from these numbers alone since many papers went unpublished during this period, and I base my assertion that there was no clearly preferred theoretical explanation for the new particles on interview material and the production of inconclusive contemporary review articles at the major research centres (for instance H. Harari, 'PSIchology' SLAC preprint PUB-1514, 1974 and 'CERN Boson Theory Workshop', CERN preprint TH. 1964, 6.12.74).

16. J. Ellis, 'Charm, Apres Charm and Beyond', Lectures presented at the Cargese Summer Institute on High Energy Physics, Cargese, Corsica, 5–22 July 1977 (CERN preprint TH. 2365 [1977] p. 1).

17. G. Feldman, interview, 10.5.78.

18. I will not document these changes in consensus in detail here. Since the new particles generated a great deal of excitement within the HEP community they were intensively reported in the scientific press, and one can obtained an overview of the evolution of consensus from the pattern of this reporting. Thus *Science* carried one report (**186**, 909–911 (1974)), in epoch one, which indicated that there was no theoretical consensus on the nature of the new particles, and two reports (**189**, 443–5 (1975) and **191**, 452, 492 (1975)) in epoch two which discussed only charm. The most detailed contemporary popular reporting was in the *New Scientist*; from November 1974 to March 1975 a variety of theoretical explanations were noted, but in the thirteen articles subsequently published during the first two epochs, charm was the only explanation to be discussed.

19. M. K. Gaillard, B. W. Lee and J. L. Rosner, 'Search for Charm', *Reviews of Modern Physics* **47**, 277–310 (1975); at p. 300.

20. To give some sort of quantitative feel for this, let me note that *Physics Letters* (the major European rapid publication journal) published 14 papers on the Zweig rule *per se* (i.e. treating it as a fact to which the new particles were relevant rather than as part of a putative explanation of the new particles) during epochs one and two (submission dates of these papers range from 12.5.75 to 7.6.76). I have been unable to locate any analogous papers, in any journal, devoted to the parallel problem engendered by colour (see below).

The pre-existing interest in the Zweig rule was indicated by the uneasiness manifested by the HEP community over its 'proper' name when it came to prominence in connection with the new particles. Many physicists, anxious to give due credit, began to refer to it as the Okubo-Zweig-Iizuka rule, after the three theorists who had independently contributed to the original exemplary achievement between 1963 and 1966. In a 1977 paper (Fermilab preprint Conf. – 77/76-THY) Lipkin solved the problem of eponymy thus:

> The rule forbidding [various reactions] has been credited to a number of physicists in various combinations. To avoid arguments about credit, this paper refers to the A . . . Z rule and allows the reader to insert the names of all desired friends from Alexander to Zweig. (p. 2)

In a recent letter, Professor Kalman of Concordia University pointed out to me an alternative solution: 'so many authors opposed [the Zweig rule] that perhaps the widely used term Quark Line Rule is better.' This latter title is interesting since it suggests, quite correctly, that during the late 1960's and early 1970's the rule had been extensively discussed in terms of the quark model, and hence draws attention to the great significance of the meshing of charm and the quark model (see below). However, I retain the name 'Zweig rule' because it should be emphasised that the rule was not the exclusive property of quark theorists (indeed, when Okubo first proposed it in 1963, quarks had yet to be invented).

21. The important breakthrough was the demonstration by G. 't Hooft, then a graduate student at the University of Utrecht, that gauge theories possessed a most desirable mathematical property known as 'renormalisability' (G. 't Hooft, 'Renormalisation of Massless Yang–Mills Fields', *Nuclear Physics* **B33**, 173–199 (1971)).

22. The most important independent source of support for gauge theories during this period came from the accumulating data on 'weak neutral currents', predicted by gauge theory models and first discovered in 1973. For popular accounts of the relevance of these, see 'Neutral Currents: New Hope for a Unified Field Theory', *Science* **182**, 372–374 (1973), and 'The Detection of Neutral Weak Currents', *Scientific American* **231**, 108–119 (Dec. 1974).

23. In essence, the existence of charm was the simplest explanation for the set of experimental data relating to weak neutral currents (see note 22).

24. A. De Rujula, H. Georgi and S. L. Glashow, 'Hadron Masses in a Gauge Theory', *Physical Review* **D12** 147–162 (1975).

25. For instance, O. W. Greenberg of the University of Maryland was, in the 1960's, one of the pioneers of both colour and quark spectroscopy. During epoch one he propounded colour as an explanation of the new particles. Discussing his reasons for subsequently abandoning colour in favour of charm (interview, 11.5.78) he remarked that 'QCD has made a lot of impressive successes' and cited a recent fit of baryon masses, based on the exemplar discussed here, as a 'great advance'.

26. The lack of unanimity amongst colour modellers was clearly significant in their failure to achieve objective status for their viewpoint: each variant of the model was readily seen to be proper to the individual or small group proposing it. The diversity of approaches reflected the failure of each of the groups involved to achieve exemplary solutions to the problems thrown up by the relation of the model to the data (see below).

27. This problem had become apparent by January 1975. See O. W. Greenberg's review of colour models, 'Electron-Positron Annihilation to Hadrons and Color

Symmetries of Elementary Particles', in A. Perlmutter and S. Widmayer (eds.), *Theories and Experiments in High-Energy Physics*, Plenum Press, New York, 1975.

A similar problem concerned colour's prediction of electrically-charged partners of the J-psi and psi-prime. See B. Stech, 'Broken Color Symmetry and Weak Currents', in H. Faissner *et al.*, (eds.), *Proceedings of the International Neutrino Conference Aachen, 1976*. It should be noted here that the following account will focus on those features of the data which determined the final outcome of the battle between charm and colour. In fact, some of the most straightforward predictions of the colour model related to experiments such as the production of the new particles in hadronic or neutrino-induced reactions which gave inconclusive results, especially favouring the predictions of neither model.

28. In their first paper on colour and the new particles ('Has ψ_4 Already Been Observed at Stanford Linear Accelerator Center?', *Phys. Rev. Lett.* **35**, 344–6 (1975)) Feldman and Matthews listed predominantly radiative decays as a prediction of their model, but disavowed this in a short footnote which read 'These modes are damped by the Feynman rule'.

29. One could labour this point further, but probably the following comment of Feynman and his colleagues on introducing the suppression factor in their original paper will suffice: ' . . . in a most unsatisfactory way, [we] have included . . . an adjustment factor F . . . . This is frankly just empirical fitting' (R. P. Feynman, M. Kislinger and F. Ravndal, 'Current Matrix Elements from a Relativistic Quark Model', *Phys. Rev.* **D3**, 2707 (1971)).

30. Stech's response to the radiative damping problem was to point out that if the typical radius of the new particles was large compared with the wavelength of the emitted radiation, then straightforward estimates of the rate of radiative decay would be too large, 'Thus', as he put it (private communication), 'there was an answer to the critics and no objection was raised against this answer'. However, this response also failed to coincide with any current interests, and Stech himself did not indicate how it might be amplified into a phenomenological programme; it, too, was *ad hoc*.

31. In the original formulation, given in 1964 by M. Gell-Mann and G. Zweig, quarks were supposed to carry fractional electric changes (either one- or two-thirds of the charge of the electron). Building upon the exemplary achievement of these two physicists the main line of quark theory, including gauge theory formulations, had continued to assume fractionally charged quarks. With the introduction of the colour quantum number it became possible to envisage integrally charged quarks, and, in papers published in 1973, J. C. Pati (of the University of Maryland) and A. Salam (of Imperial College London) had constructed a gauge theory model containing such quarks (see note 39). However, since there was no empirical evidence at that time favouring integrally charged quarks the majority of theorists continued to work with the fractionally charged versions. The advocacy of colour as an explanation of the new particles by Pati and Salam can be seen as an attempt to demonstrate the relevance of their approach to the 'fractional charge speaking' community.

32. A. Zichichi (ed.), *Proceedings of the EPS International Conference*, Palermo, Italy, 23–28 June 1975, Editrice Compositori, Bologna, 1976.

33. W. T. Kirk (ed.), *Proceedings of the International Symposium on Lepton and Photon Interactions at High Energies*, Stanford, 21–27 August 1975, p. 323.

34. *Ibid.*, p. 991.

35. See, for instance, the review given by B. H. Wiik, 'Plenary Report on New Particle Production in e^+e^- Colliding Beams', in *Proceedings of the 18th International Conference on High Energy Physics*, Tbilisi, U.S.S.R., July 1976, pp. N75–85.

36. I am extremely grateful to Professor James Bjorken of the Stanford Linear Acelerator Center who first made me aware of these developments. Bjorken described the situation in February 1979 thus: 'The theoretical status [of the two most recently identified chi particles] has been evolving; by now they have been firmly denounced by several of the charmonium experts I most respect . . . as not having anything to do with the charmonium model. Thus, predicting three out of five observed states [i.e. particles] may not be that much of a triumph' (personal communication). And he continued by describing the outcome of confirmation of the two dubious chi particles by the 'Crystal Ball' experiment as possibly 'leading to a new theoretical crisis'. Before the 'Crystal Ball' data became available I was able to confirm Bjorken's assessment of the situation in correspondence with two of the charmonium experts involved: H. J. Schnitzer of Brandeis University, and L. Okun of The Institute of Theoretical and Experimental Physics, Moscow (see note 38). (The Russian group had outlined their position in, 'η_C Puzzle in Quantum Chromodynamics', M. A. Shifman *et al.*, *Physics Letters* 77B 80–83 (1978)). The first indication that the lowest mass chi particle could not be found at the mass previously reported came in E. D. Bloom, 'Initial Studies of the Charmonium System Using the Crystal Ball Data at SPEAR', XIVth Rencontre de Moriond, Les Arcs-Savoie, France, March 11–23, 1979. Since then I have heard from a third charmonium expert, Professor K. Gottfried of Cornell University, who wrote: ' . . . we are now in the happy situation of not having to deal with these embarassing objects. The charmonium model is therefore in a far healthier state than it has ever been' (personal communication, April 1979).

37. For several instances of unreflective reference to 'novel facts' in connection with Lakatos' methodology of research programmes, see the essays contained in *Method and Appraisal in the Physical Sciences*, C. Howson (ed.), University Press, Cambridge, 1976.

38. The first and simplest charmonium model was constructed by two Harvard theorists, H. D. Politzer and T. Appelquist. Although they had given seminars on the model, predicting the existence of very long-lived particles even before the discovery of the J-psi, they did not submit their work for publication until the discovery had been announced; (their first paper on the model was 'Heavy Quarks and e^+e^- Annihilation', *Phys. Rev. Lett.* 34 43–45 (1975)). The model was quickly adopted by theorists all over the world, leading to a stream of increasingly sophisticated phenomenology of the new particles which continues to the present. Most intensive work on the subject has been done by E. Eichten and K. Gottfried of Cornell University, H. J. Schnitzer of Brandeis University, and a Russian group led by L. B. Okun and V. I. Zakharov of the Institute for Theoretical and Experimental Physics, Moscow. References to this work and that of many others can be found in the major review article by V. A. Novikov *et al.*, 'Charmonium and Gluons', *Physics Reports* 41 1–133 (1978).

39. For instance J. C. Pati and A. Salam (of the University of Maryland and Imperial College London) were at the time working on a gauge theory model which required that both charmed and coloured particles exist. In his first post-psi review talk in January 1975, Pati listed three possible explanations of the J-psi and psi-prime in the Pati-Salam model, two of which were essentially colour and the third charm. In his next major review, in September 1975, he discussed only one theoretical interpretation, which was essentially equivalent to charm, and from this point on he and Salam ceased to advocate colour as the explanation of the new particles. Pati's reviews are reproduced as 'Particles, Forces and the New Mesons' in A. Perlmutter and S. Widmayer (eds.), *op. cit.*, Note 27, and 'The World of Basic Attributes: Valency and Colour', in R. Arnowitt and P. Nath (eds.), *Gauge Theories and Modern Field Theories*, MIT Press, Cambridge Mass., 1976.

40. See, for instance: S. D. Drell, 'Elementary Particle Physics', *Daedalus* 1 15–31 (1977); V. F. Weisskopf, 'New Trends in Particle Physics', talk delivered at the metting of the Societe Francaise de Physique in Poitiers, July 1 1977 (CERN preprint TH. 2379 [1977]);
    L. Van Hove, "Hadrons and Quarks in High Energy Collisions', review article for a general audience of physicists to be published in Russian translation in *Uspekhi Fiz. Nauk.* (CERN preprint DG-3 [20.10.1977]);
    S. D. Drell, 'When is a Particle?', Richtmeyer Memorial Lecture, San Francisco 24 January 1978, reprinted in *Physics Today* 31 (6), 23–32 (1978);
    Y. Ne'eman, 'Progress in the Physics of Particles and Fields', *Physics Bulletin* 29, 422–24 (1978);
    V. Weisskopf, 'What Happened in Physics in the Last Decade', *Phys. Bull.* 29, 401–403 (1978).

41. Feldman and Matthews stated their position on the chi particles in 'A Case for Colour', *Nuovo Cimento* 31A, 447–486 (1976), and 'Colour Symmetry and the Psi Particles', *Proceedings of the Royal Society, London* A355, 621–627 (1977).

42. Like Feldman and Matthews, Stech felt that the existence of the chi particles did not falsify colour, but he too was unable to provide a constructive approach to them. As he put it, 'our colour model required from the beginning (*without a good theoretical framework, however*) that the effective quark masses are not fixed but dynamical . . . and give rise to a spectrum of the kind which was found' (personal communication, emphasis added).

43. G. Goldhaber, F. M. Pierre *et al.*, 'Observation in e^+e^- Annihilation of a Narrow State at 1865 MeV/c^2 Decaying to $K\pi$ and $K\pi\pi\pi$', *Phys. Rev. Lett.* 37, 255–259 (1976).

44. See the *Proceedings of the 18th International Conference on High Energy Physics*, Tbilisi, U.S.S.R., July 1976 – for instance, the reviews given by R. Schwitters (pp. B34–39), B. H. Wiik (pp. N75–85) and A. De Rujula (pp. N111–127). See also the popular scientific press of the time, for instance 'Charmed Quarks Look Better Than Ever', *Science* 192, 1219–1220 (1976); 'Iliopoulos Wins His Bet', *Nature* 262, 537–538 (1976); and 'Naked Charm Revealed at Stanford', *New Scientist*, p. 413 (20.5.76).

45. Even before the discovery paper on the D's had been submitted for publication, the Harvard group had written a paper on the analysis of the data in terms of charm. Entitled 'Is Charm Found?' (A. De Rujula, H. Geogi and S. L. Glashow,

Phys. Rev. Lett. **37**, 398–401 (1976).) this paper went into the data in 'disgusting detail' (interview, A. De Rujula, 20.3.1978) to demonstrate its consistency with the predictions of the group's 1975 paper (*op. cit.*, Note 24).

46. G. Feldman and P. T. Matthews, 'The Discovery of Coloured Kaons?', *Physics. Lett.* **64B**, 353–358 (1976). This was the last paper which Feldman and Matthews were to publish on colour. My account of subsequent developments in their position is based on interview and correspondence with G. Feldman.

47. Although he adopted a completely different explanation of the D's from Feldman and Matthews, Stech ultimately encountered exactly the same obstacle. In a paper submitted for publication in November 1976 ('Are the D Mesons Diquarks?', *Phys. Rev. Lett.* **38**, 304–306 (1977): references to Stech's earlier work on colour are to be found in this paper) he suggested that the D's could be successfully accounted for as bound states of two quarks (n.b. *not* a quark and an antiquark, as in all conventional pictures of mesons). Stech's feelings at this time seem to sum up those of all of colour's public advocates and also those who had ceased to support it actively:

> On more general grounds, however, there was little hope that the colour model would survive. In talks and conversations I pointed out that the model and the data had now become so tight that there was no freedom for excuses in case even a single prediction went wrong'. (personal communication)

And indeed, like Feldman and Matthews, he now considers colour to have been 'indirectly disproved' by the accumulating data on charmed mesons *plus* the failure to find similar additional particles predicted by his model.

48. M. Hesse, *op. cit.*, Note 3.

49. The following case-studies are relevant here: S. Shapin, 'The Politics of Observation: Cerebral Anatomy and Social Interests in the Edinburgh Phrenology Disputes', and H. M. Collins and T. J. Pinch, 'The Construction of the Paranormal: Nothing Unscientific is Happening', both in R. Wallis (ed.), *op. cit.*, Note 4; B. Wynne, 'C. G. Barkla and the J Phenomenon: a Case-Study in the Treatment of Deviance in Physics', *Social Studies of Science* **6** 307–47 (1976); H. M. Collins, 'The Seven Sexes', *op. cit.*, Note 8; 'The TEA Set' and 'Building a TEA Laser', *opera cit.*, Note 4; A. R. Pickering, 'The Hunting of the Quark', *Isis*, forthcoming, and 'Experts and Expertise: The Case of the Magnetic Monopole', *Social Studies of Science*, forthcoming.

THE EFFECTS OF SOCIAL CONTEXT ON THE PROCESS
OF SCIENTIFIC INVESTIGATION: EXPERIMENTAL
TESTS OF QUANTUM MECHANICS

BILL HARVEY

Napier College of Commerce and Technology, Edinburgh

Introduction

This paper deals with a case-study from the recent history of physics, and the general aim of the paper is to illustrate the role of a wide variety of factors, other than purely internal technical factors, in determining the outcome of this piece of scientific practice. My approach is what has been described as 'naturalistic' (1); that is, I do not wish to presuppose the existence of a code of conduct, or a set of norms, which is sufficient to account for the social behaviour of scientists. (Mulkay (2) provides a powerful critique of such presuppositions.) By the same token, a sceptical attitude will be taken towards scientists' *own* accounts for their actions; that is, such accounts will be treated as data rather than as complete explanations of behaviour.

In order to identify the effects of social context on scientific investigation, at the 'micro-level' of the individual scientist and the reception of his work, it is necessary to look in detail at the particular situation in which that scientist finds himself. Knorr has explicitly recognised the context-dependent nature of scientists' strategy, in deciding such things as what topic to study and how to present their results. Instead of postulating a specific code of behaviour, Knorr argues that scientists are fundamentally concerned with 'success', a concept similar to what some other authors have called 'making out'. The type of success desired, Knorr claims, depends entirely on the local context of the scientist:

> What counts as success is determined by the field and by the agent's position in the field . . . the notion of success is an *indexical* expression which refers us to the context of a local, idiosyncratic situation . . . success is *by and for* an agent at a particular *time and place*, and carried by local *interpretations*. (3)

Karin D. Knorr, Roger Krohn and Richard Whitley (eds.), The Social Process of Scientific Investigation. Sociology of the Sciences, Volume IV, 1980. 139–163.
Copyright © 1980 by D. Reidel Publishing Company.

This view suggests that the social and cultural, as well as the technical, context in which a scientist finds himself will influence not only the style, timing and presentation of his work but also (at least in principle) its content.

Although these views clearly open up a whole realm of possible enquiry, they also raise what seems to be a serious methodological issue. Having cast doubt on the accounting procedures of scientists, what are we to make of our own data, when we read scientists' writings and talk with them in interviews? For example, if a scientist tells us that he did X because he thought it would lead to Y, this 'reason' is itself an account, given in the (rather artificial) context of an interview and no doubt framed within the requirements of that context. It may be interpreted as a legitimation, a rationalisation, or a rewriting of history by hindsight. The same question asked by the scientist's colleague in an informal context, or asked by the interviewer some years hence, may well yield a different answer. Which is the 'real' reason?

There are at least two ways to avoid this problem. One is to concede that there are no real reasons, and that sociologists themselves are simply in the business of generating accounts according to their own criteria of reasonableness. Another, and to my mind more satisfactory, reply is to appeal to our own skills, as sociologists and as inhabitants of the everyday world, in interpreting other people's statements. Unless we accept a rather extreme solipsism, we are led to believe that it *is* possible to make sense of the world. True, the work of ethnomethodologists (4) suggests that this 'making sense' is itself a complex interpretive process − an active accounting procedure − and thus threatens to return us to the position discussed above. But at the very least, this work also points out that the problem of interpretation is not ours alone. I am well aware of the fact that I have not solved the problem. Nevertheless, it is important that we are aware of its existence. At least this awareness may stimulate our critical faculties. In the last analysis, of course, it is the reader who must judge the plausibility of my own account in what follows.

In this case-study, I shall try to make two major points. I shall first provide evidence in favour of Knorr's notion of the indexicality of success. By examining a group of physicists who became involved in a particular topic, I shall argue that these physicist's aims and motivations can only be satisfactorily accounted for if we include detailed discussion of their local social context.

Secondly, and perhaps more importantly, I shall examine the response to one particular physical experiment, both by the experimenter involved and by his colleagues within the speciality. This experiment produced rather surprising results which are now interpreted as straightforward error. What I hope to show is that this interpretation was by no means an abstract logical deduction. Instead, it came about by a complex interplay of psychological, social and technical factors. In order to account satisfactorily for this small episode in the recent history of science, I believe that we must take note of the particular context in which this experiment took place, and in which the experimenters' notions of 'success' were framed. In the last section of this paper, I shall discuss the possibility that the very content of scientific knowledge may be affected by the social context in which this knowledge was generated.

The Background to the Experiments

My case-study concerns a series of experiments which were performed over the last ten years, and which were designed to test the theory of Quantum Mechanics. Quantum Mechanics (hereafter QM) could fairly be described as a cornerstone of modern physics. Its impact and scope has been characterised in the following terms:

Never in the history of science has there been a theory which has had such a profound impact on human thinking as QM; nor has there been a theory which scored such spectacular successes in the prediction of such an enormous variety of phenomena (atomic physics, solid state physics, chemistry, etc.). Furthermore, for all that is known today, QM is the only consistent theory of elementary processes. (5)

Despite its great empirical success, many of the philosophical implications of QM have been a source of disquiet to some physicists, theologians, and philosophers since the development of QM in the 1920's. Some of these issues, such as the wave-particle duality of matter and light, and Heisenberg's uncertainty or indeterminacy principle, are well-known. Although the mathematical *formalism* of QM led to no contradiction with experimental evidence, the *interpretation* of that formalism was for some years a major focus of dissension.

In a series of debates with Neils Bohr, Einstein raised a number of objections to QM; in the course of answering these objections, Bohr developed what has come to be known as the Copenhagen Interpretation of QM (so called because Bohr and many of his colleagues worked in Copenhagen). Jammer writes:

As is well known, this interpretation is still espoused today by the majority of theoreticians and practicing physicists. Though not necessarily the only logically possible interpretation of quantum phenomena, it is *de facto* the only existing fully articulated consistent scheme of conceptions that brings order into an otherwise chaotic cluster of facts and makes it comprehensible. (6)

Nevertheless, a very large number of alternative interpretations of QM have been proposed. Different authors have perceived different philosophical flaws in QM, so that there is an enormous diversity of approaches towards reinterpretation (7).

The aspect of QM which is directly relevant to the present context is known as 'non-separability' (8). For certain physical systems, such as a pair of particles which are created simultaneously, QM provides predictions concerning the physical parameters of the system as a whole (e.g. its total mass or momentum) but provides very limited information about the properties of each individual particle. When Einstein raised this issue in 1935, arguing that QM therefore provided an incomplete description of reality, Bohr replied that for any real experiment, QM provides a full description of all that we can measure, and that it is meaningless to discuss the values (or indeed the existence) of properties which we cannot measure.

It is possible to frame Einstein's objection to QM in terms of a rival theory, which postulates the existence of 'hidden variables'. These variables would fully characterise those properties of individual particles which Bohr declared to be meaningless. Since these variables permit the analytical separation of the quantum-mechanical 'global' two-particle system into its constituent parts, they are termed 'local hidden variables' (hereafter LHV). Physicists disagree over whether Einstein had this specific sort of theory in mind, but in 1964 J. S. Bell did construct such a theory (9). More importantly, he showed that although the LHVs could not be detected directly (hence their name), they led to predictions which differed in some small respects from those of QM; specifically, QM and LHV predict slightly different correlations between the properties of the constituent parts of a physical system, such as the spin correlation of atomic particles, or the polarisation correlation of photons

(10). Thus, for the first time (11), it seemed possible, at least in principle, to perform an experimental test of a proposed alternative to QM, rather than to limit the evaluation of this alternative to philosophical or mathematical analysis. Since then, a number of such experiments have been performed. The physicists involved in this work are the subjects of this paper.

Effects of Social Context: Who Became Involved with LHV and Why?

To answer such a question fully would require unattainably detailed knowledge about every facet of the indivdiuals concerned. Indeed, as pointed out earlier, one may question the whole concept of 'real' reasons. Nevertheless, I shall try to show that the social *and* technical context of the LHV activity played a major part in selecting these individuals.

Let us examine some of the salient features of this context. In the first place, this work was experimental, and was thus different in kind from all other work on the reinterpretation of QM. Secondly, despite its possible philosophical significance, LHV could hardly be described as a highly *plausible* theory. Although the great success of QM over the past 50 years did not rule out the possibility that LHV was correct (since the theories agree in all but a few of their predictions, and no experiment had thus far probed the area of conflict) nevertheless the likelihood of falsifying QM in these experiments was not perceived by anyone involved to be very great.

This implausibility was not restricted to LHV. Nearly all the work then being done on the philosophical implications of QM, and the numerous attempts to reinterpret the fundamental basis of the theory, were seen by many physicists as having little value. For example, one author, who was himself sympathetic to such investigations, and who had made an important study of the 'measurement problem' (a major focus of interest among students of QM) prefaced his comments by noting that

the problem of measurement in QM is considered as non-existent or trivial by an impressive body of theoretical physicists. (12)

Factors such as these are highly relevant; they determined, to a very large extent, the sort of person (in psychological and sociological terms) who was likely to become involved with LHV. In the first place, the experimental nature of the work excluded a number of people who had a long-standing interest and involvement in the philosophical and theoretical analysis of QM. Such people had neither the necessary technical training, nor access to the relevant experimental equipment. This in turn meant that these people were faced with an intrusion, into their area of interest, of a new group, working with a new methodology, and obtaining results which philosophers were not fully equipped to discuss (13).

In the second place, again because of the nature of this work, interested physicists had to exert considerable efforts in order to obtain funds and specialised apparatus. In particular, one group of theoreticians had to 'draft in' an experimentalist who would not, by himself, have performed such an experiment. This event is very relevant to my next section, since the results of this experiment strongly disagreed with QM, a most surprising event. It is therefore worth quoting at length from a theorist's account of his actions:

> We went around asking everybody we had access to, who had experimental knowledge of optics, 'where can we get photon pairs which we can use for the purpose of testing LHV?' ... I called *P* to discuss the problem ... he said, we have an apparatus at our university very much like this .... Pipkin had a student, Holt, who was just beginning his doctoral work, intending to use this apparatus to look at the lifetime of an intermediate state ... We explained what was going on, why their apparatus was useful ... We had to do a lot of explaining of the motivation for our experiment ... this type of thing was very far from the concerns of Pipkin and Holt so we had to discuss the matter for about an hour or so before they became fairly convinced that we were on the track of something interesting. (14)

Clearly, access to the necessary apparatus was an important factor here, and Holt would never have become involved but for this fortuitous coincidence. Holt's recollection of his own early feelings corroborate this view:

> I thought, sure, I'll whip that off in six months then get back to some real physics.

A third important factor was the low status of 'foundations' work. Many of the experimenters claimed that this constituted a severe problem:

> I had considerable problems ... with finding a place to do this experiment. The comments you get ... for doing this hidden-variable thing. They think it's a waste of time because they already know the result ... X was very upset that I was spending too much time working on what was obviously of no importance, the results were already known, and it was crazy that I didn't believe the existing theory.

Ph.D students involved in these experiments made similar comments about their supervisory committees:

> I encountered difficulties because of what the topic was, because I had to justify to the people on my committee what was going on. They had very strong biases about the subject matter . . . whereas with other types of thesis experiments it's taken for granted that, well, lots of people are doing this, you're measuring the coefficient of such-and-such, and you're okay.

I do not claim that the LHV physicists were severly presecuted for daring to question the validity of QM. After all, the experiments themselves were *technically* respectable, and the LHV hypothesis had been advanced by a respectable theorist, based at a high-status institution (CERN). One experimenter summed up the position like this:

> B. said that my experiment was interesting, but he asked if I had a permanent position, because I would have difficulties, many people would say that my experiment wasn't interesting and that I was wasting my time. Well, I have seen some people who *could* have said this, but if I explain the problem as I see it . . . many people finally say, okay . . . T said to me, 'I would never give such an experiment to one of my students, but if one came and saw me with the same enthusiasm as you have, I would let him do it.' You see, experiments like this are a kind of a luxury. You can accept them from time to time.

Clearly, there was no grand conspiracy to suppress these experiments. Nevertheless, I believe it would be fair to say that the LHV physicists deliberately chose to enter a field which was of low prestige compared with other fields, and which was seen as very unlikely to produce surprising or informative results. Evidently, *some* factors must have overridden these disincentives.

A rather facile way of accounting for the involvement of these physicists would be to say that they simply found the topic interesting. Certainly, one would be surprised to find people voluntarily working on a topic which they did *not* find interesting. Indeed, I found in interviews that nearly everyone involved spent some time explaining their involvement in terms of interest. Apparently, people who were in favour of QM found just as much interest as those who were less convinced:

> I went into this business with the idea of disproving hidden variables once and for all.

> I got into the business with the idea that . . . hidden variables might really be there.

> I was very interested originally in the foundations of QM, simply because I couldn't understand it, and I wanted to understand it.

However, to leave the explanation at this point is inadequate. It leaves untouched the notion that scientists are morally superior disinterested seekers after truth. It may be considered slightly sordid to account for behaviour in any other terms, such as self-interest, but I do not think we can ignore other factors.

For example, it seems highly significant that nearly all of the experimenters were Ph.D or postdoctoral students. Scientists in this position may have some special criteria for 'success' not shared by more established scientists. To some extent, their choice of thesis topic is a means to an end; namely, being awarded a Ph.D. None of my interviewees felt that their LHV work had 'typecast' them. Indeed, they have now gone on to work in fields as diverse as atomic physics, laser fusion, and the psychology of perception (15).

This would appear to leave the field free for a decision in terms of interest alone. Here again, however, we must be cautions. Other criteria are also relevant. For instance, a Ph.D student requires a topic which is not beyond his technical competence, yet which allows him to develop and improve his range of technical skills, and so enhance his future employment prospects. He requires a topic which will yield worthwile non-trivial results within two or three years, yet which is something more than a routine application of well-known procedures, differing only in detail from what has gone before.

Seen in this light, the LHV experiments begin to look more desirable. The work is technically feasible, yet it can be presented as a fundamental test of one of the most important theories in physics; at the same time, it avoids the necessity for very expensive hardware or large-scale collaborations involving 20 or 30 people, in sharp contrast to fields such as high-energy physics. These factors seem to have been important for the LHV physicists. Their comments, quoted below, portray them as an opportunistic group, for whom an interest in QM may have been a necessary, but by no means a sufficient condition of their involvement:

I was in nuclear physics . . . *I was looking for a thesis project*. I always wanted to do experiments which sat on a table-top but nevertheless had some reasonable significance, and I'd always been concerned about the basis of QM . . . this seemed like a good thesis experiment.

I didn't like the idea of a high energy experiment as part of a big team, with all the politics and bureaucracy . . . The LHV experiment was technically difficult . . . I'd always been interested in QM . . . The experiment was graduate standard. *It was just luck* that I was free at the time. Otherwise I'd have done a weak interaction experiment.

I was looking for a postdoc position, or someplace to go when I finished my thesis in astrophysics, and I wanted to do something in the foundations of QM, although I didn't really have anything in mind until I read about LHV.

(Emphasis added in all three quotations.)

Another physicist, speaking before his experiment was completed, said:

From the experimental point of view it's very interesting, because I'll learn many things, I'll use some techniques that I don't know. This is very interesting for an experimentalist.

The factors discussed above (16) can be subdivided into several groups; each type of factor played some part in selecting the particular group of people who did perform LHV experiments, while at the same time excluded other people. Thus there are institutional factors (access to funds and equipment), technical factors (possession of the necessary experimental skills), theoretical factors (the status of HV theories and the recent history of QM) and socio-logical factors (the special position of Ph.D students and the criteria by which Ph.D topics are chosen). It is necessarily more difficult to locate people who were *deterred* from doing an experiment because of these factors, since by definition they are unlikely to appear in the LHV literature. However, I do know of several physicists who, at one time, planned to perform experiments, but gave up the idea because of lack of access to the necessary apparatus (17), or became involved with other commitments.

In principle, it would be possible to predict the sort of person likely to become involved with any given topic, by identifying the social and technical factors which select such people. In practice, the complexity of most social contexts makes this difficult, and the analysis must, for now, be retrospective. Nevertheless, such an analysis supports Knorr's general contention that scientists are motivated by a whole series of issues which impinge on their local situation.

Connections can also be made between the social context of LHV and other features of the LHV activity. For example, let us consider the way in which the LHV experimenters presented their work in papers addressed to a wider audience. Much stress is placed on the differences between this work and virtually all previous work on the interpretation of QM: the latter is described as "a vast inconclusive body of literature" (18) and "the concern of philosophy of science rather than of actual physics" (19), whereas the LHV

work constitutes "a dramatic change in the state of affairs" (20) and "a decisive experimental test of the entire family of LHV theories" (21). Certainly,
the LHV work was different; however, it seems clear that references to
'decisiveness' were used at least partly as a rhetorical device, serving to distance
the experiments from the earlier low-status work. The experimenters themselves recognise that their results are in fact less than completely decisive,
since a number of assumptions had to be made in order to compensate for the
limitations of the available apparatus (22). In fact, the LHV group took great
pains to spell out and analyse these assumptions. Such rigour is admirable,
but again it cannot be wholly isolated from the context; as one experimenter
put it: "In this field, publication should be done with higher standards than
you would impose on a normal physics experiment. We've got to redeem
ourselves from a generation of quacks."

Effects of Social Context: The Response to Anomalous Results

In this section, I wish to advance a stronger claim: namely, that the context
of these experiments had an important bearing on the manner in which the
results of the experiments were interpreted. I shall focus on one experiment,
performed by Holt, which apparently contradicted QM, and I shall argue that
the response to this experiment, both by Holt and by others, cannot be
explained solely in terms of technical factors.

Holt's experiment was similar in design to another experiment, performed
by Freedman and Clauser (23), which was completed a few months prior to
Holt's, and which agreed completely with the predictions of QM. Initially,
Clauser seems to have been fairly enthusiastic about LHV, and according to
his own and others' accounts, he had rather hoped to falsify QM. Clauser
described his feelings about his own results:

I was really disappointed . . . I wanted to find the fatal flaw in QM . . . there's not much
you can do to deny the result. You do the experiment yourself and that's what comes
out of it. What can you say?

Holt did not respond to his own result in this straightforward empiricist
manner. Apparently he had strong reservations about the validity of his
results as soon as they began to appear. Clauser and Freedman published
their results, whereas Holt did not — nor did he try to. Holt, and his Ph.D

supervisor, Pipkin, took a long time to decide whether or not to submit their results to a journal.

We kept flip-flopping. One of us favoured publishing, the other didn't, then we both changed our minds . . . . In the end we decided not to publish, nor to keep it a secret.

Their final decision was to produce an unpublished manuscript describing the experiment and the results (24).

In addition, although Holt's first results appeared in 1971, he did not submit his Ph.D thesis until April 1973, the intervening period being spent in a (fruitless) attempt to isolate a source of error in his experiment. Although both the thesis and the later unpublished paper describe an exhaustive series of error-tracing tests, they are written in rather different styles. This would seem to be Holt's response to the different audiences and aims of these two accounts. He told me:

The thesis was written very strongly . . . the mood I was in at that time was, if I'm going to present this, then whether I fully believe it in my own heart of hearts or not, I'm going to give it a fair presentation and not just out of the side of my mouth happen to mention that the consequences of this experiment could be very startling. I was going to make the presentation as strong as could be justified by the results . . . . In the paper, the presentation was less strong, because this was for publication, where you really want to say nothing which is going to be speculative, you want to put in the minimum that you can justify. In particular, I felt one should take the attitude, 'Look, here are our results, we are very cautious about them, we don't accept them, but we think you ought to know about them' . . . . A thesis is just a completely different thing from a refereed publication, what's appropriate for one isn't appropriate for the other.

Why did Holt spend nearly two years checking his apparatus, rather than simply stating his results then dropping the matter? He now describes this ' investment of time as virtually inevitable, to safeguard both his doctorate and his reputation:

I was very disappointed with my results . . . I don't believe QM has yet reached its outer limits . . . and also, as a practical matter, it meant that I had to spend an extra two years looking for systematic errors to make sure that anybody would believe me . . . When it came time for my final oral I was expecting a hard time, and a lot of suggestions on what could have gone wrong . . . but during those two years I had inputs from so many different quarters that just about everything had already been thought of . . . I know a lot of people have had the attitude before they knew about what I did that it was obviously just a sloppy experiment. Then they've come and looked at the apparatus and read my thesis and talked to my supervisor or me, and they almost invariably say,

'I'm really impressed that you looked at all these possible systematic errors and I can't think of anything else. Not that I believe your results, but I do believe that it was a very carefully done experiment.'

Holt also stressed the fact that he had performed two other experiments during his Ph.D research which had absolutely nothing to do with hidden variables.

I took the precaution of naming the thesis 'Atomic Cascade Experiments' and emphasising the fact that I'd done two other experiments as well that I wanted people to notice ... one of these was I think a fairly important contribution, I was fairly pleased with that result, though everyone keeps looking at the hidden variable part of the work.

At one time, while holding a very temporary post, Holt considered the possibility of repeating his experiment, and negotiations concerning this issue took place at three different locations. However, around this time, he was offered a more secure long-term post elsewhere, involving more 'orthodox' experiments. As he put it:

If you're looking for a career in physics, you can't just keep doing way-out experiments. You want to do some mainstream experiments too. People kept telling X to go out and measure a few numbers instead of doing more of these crazy experiments. It was even worse for me, since I was doing them and getting the wrong answer.

Let me summarise the alternatives available to Holt. He could have publicly disowned his result, claiming that it was due to an error – but this would not reflect well on his competence, at a stage in his career when he was looking for employment as an experimental physicist. He could have simply presented his results as he found them, and moved on to a new field – but given the surprising nature of his findings, disbelief would have been inevitable. Could this Ph.D student really have found a flaw in QM, when another group, with a very similar experiment, claimed to have found none? The possibility of error in Holt's apparatus could not be overlooked. In addition, the assessment of the work by Holt's Ph.D committee also counted for a great deal. Even after his exhaustive search for errors, Holt still expected 'a hard time' from them.

Thus, Holt's actual response was clearly a sensible one. Faced with a result which he did not believe, his actions seemed to him to be a way of minimising any damage which could be done, and of optimising the outcome of what could have been a very embarrassing episode. By showing that the error was persistent and apparently deeply-rooted in the apparatus, and by permitting other physicists to examine his apparatus, without isolating the error, he attempted, as it were, to 'defuse' the error so that it did not reflect seriously on his own competence as an experimenter. My impression from talking to nearly all the LHV physicists is that Holt has successfully presented himself as a good experimenter who had a bit of bad luck, obtained an incorrect result, yet treated that result in the correct skeptical manner (25).

However, another option *was* available to him: he could have published his results, claiming or implying that they were valid. Undoubtedly he would have received a great deal of publicity for this, and *if* he were to be vindicated, his prestige would have been greatly enhanced. But this is a very big 'if'. The central role of QM in contemporary physics, the marginality of LHV, Clauser and Freedman's result — all these factors strongly suggest that Holt's results were *not* likely to be corroborated by future experiments. In interview, Holt dismissed this possibility, claiming that he intuitively doubted his results. Given such doubts, there was little to be gained by sensationalism.

There was yet another reason for adopting a low profile: a reason which was particularly relevant for Holt's local situation. His own supervisor, Pipkin, had been involved in a similar situation in the early 1960's, when another of his students obtained results which apparently disproved quantum electrodynamics, another highly successful physical theory. This claim, which was published, was later shown to be spurious. Although Holt stresses that no pressure was exerted on him to 'cover-up' his results, this embarrassing episode, so close to home, must surely have served as a cautionary tale. What would be gained by a public fanfare? His result was still on record, and was known to the small group of physicists actively involved with LHV. Why risk having to make a retraction at a later date of a result which he doubted anyway?

In the light of his social and cultural context, it seems clear that Holt did indeed behave rationally (26). But it is not my aim to assess the rationality of physicists. The important point to be gained from this discussion, I feel, is that unless we are prepared to consider the context in which behaviour occurs, we can neither fully appreciate that behaviour, *nor* can we perceive the possibility of alternative behaviour under different circumstances. At first sight, Holt's behaviour takes on almost an air of inevitability which, I would argue, is not warranted. Faced with similar problems, other individuals might well have behaved differently. By identifying the factors which apparently guided Holt's actions, we simultaneously construct a set of parameters which may, in some sense, have played a part in determining the outcome. Different settings of these parameters may lead to different outcomes. I shall return to this point in my final section, which by necessity will be somewhat speculative.

But let us return to the *actual* outcome. As things turned out, Holt's virtual capitulation led almost inevitably to universal disbelief in his results. Over and over again I was told in interviews "Holt himself doesn't believe his result, and if the person who actually does the experiment doesn't believe it, why should I?" Scientific controversies, at least those most often studied by sociologists of science, are typically structured in terms of two opposing viewpoints; the combatants attack the work of their opponents, and defend their own work against such attacks. In so doing, arguments are elaborated, new experiments are performed, and a variety of resources are employed in an attempt to win over the scientific audience (27). By his choice of presentation, Holt virtually ensured that a controversy of this sort would not arise. What *was* the effect of Holt's result on the LHV group? Let us now turn to the response of *other* physicists to this anomalous result.

The Response of Other Physicists to Holt's Result

The discussion in the previous section might have led the reader to expect that Holt's result would have been totally ignored. However, this is not what happened. A number of physicists took an interest in Holt's work; some visited his laboratory to examine his apparatus, and some performed other experiments in an attempt to resolve the disagreement between the experiments of Holt and of Freedman and Clauser. At first sight, this may seem slightly odd. It is certainly true that the two experiments gave different results, but why were other people prepared to take Holt's result seriously enough to do further research on it, when Holt himself was apparently convinced that his result was simply wrong?

There is more than one possible answer to this question. One sort of reply would invoke the norm of 'organised skepticism' — i.e. this reply would argue that not only are scientists constitutionally skeptical about novel results, but they are equally skeptical about any attempt to dismiss such results, even if the dismissal is made by the person who actually obtained these results.

There are several difficulties with this sort of explanation. For example, it does not account for the frequency with which, as already mentioned, Holt's own dismissal was cited by interviewees as a justification for their own rejection. In addition, if such a norm of skepticism were to be applied universally, it is difficult to see how scientists would find the time to generate new results, since all errors would have to be followed up by an independent observer. The existence of categories such as 'gremlins' and 'transients' in scientists' vocabularies, which serve to account for unexplained, often temporary deviations from expected results, suggests that in practice there are limits on skepticism.

I wish to put forward an alternative explanation: namely, that belief or disbelief in Holt's result was by no means a crucial factor in the strategy of the LHV physicists. All that mattered was that Holt's result was, or could be presented as, an anomaly or a puzzle which had not been explained. Superficially this is similar to the above explanation; both accounts rest on the premise that science is a puzzle-solving activity. Anomaly generates practice. The important point, though, is that *not all* anomalies give rise to practice — hence the existence of categories such as 'gremlins'. A great many anomalies are routinely abandoned without any prolonged investigation into their causes. The decision as to whether a particular anomaly should be followed up or dismissed in a complex one, and I would argue that such a decision is not made solely on technical grounds.

As we have seen, Holt's particular position ensured that he *did* have to investigate his result in some depth. Had he not searched diligently for a source of error, and had he not been seen to have done so, he felt that this Ph.D might not have been awarded and his competence as a physicist might have been questioned. Why did *other* physicists choose to devote their time to this problem?

I believe that the answer is that they had nothing to lose and a lot to gain. They had nothing to lose because they were not responsible for Holt's result, so that if they *did* discover a trivial error in Holt's procedures, they themselves would not be embarrassed. More importantly, further experimentation could serve several functions which would not be served by simply ignoring Holt's result.

The first such function is perhaps the most obvious; namely, that the disagreement between the two experiments would be resolved. To the best of my knowledge, no-one involved in LHV favoured Holt's result, and if no further experiments had been done, it seems clear that QM would have been vindicated. Nevertheless, it cannot be denied that it would be more satisfying to have corroborating evidence.

A second factor was the credibility of the LHV enterprise. As stated earlier, some rather extravagant claims were made for these experiments. For the first time, a decisive answer to an interpretive problem would be available. Holt's result clearly does not go well with such claims. Clauser, at least, was apparently acutely aware of this fact. He investigated Holt's result by performing a similar experiment, whose results agreed fully with QM. Clauser explained his rationale in the following terms:

In the work which I and others did, we really ought to have put a great effort into getting very clean experiments to avoid criticism, and I think to some extent we were quite successful . . . the people I've been working with who have studied this have really made this thing respectable experimental physics, which it was not when we started.

A third function to be served by further investigation of Holt's result was that, like any challenging piece of work, it offered the chance to develop skills and techniques which could then be applied to any number of topics. To enlarge on this point, I shall discuss another of the LHV experimenters, Fry.

Fry first took an interest in LHV in 1970, soon after he heard about the first published proposal for an experiment. Together with a co-worker, he applied for a number of grants in 1970 and 1971 in order to purchase the necessary equipment. Unfortunately, they discovered that the apparatus they were able to obtain could not overcome certain technical problems (connected with the hyperfine structure of the mercury atom). In addition, the results of the first experiment, by Freedman and Clauser, appeared at this time. Both of these factors contributed to Fry's decision to abandon his experiment. However, Holt's result completely altered the situation. As Fry put it

I didn't have the money to get around the (hyperfine) problem and so I abandoned the experiment in 1972. Then when the Holt—Pipkin result came out, that provided enough impetus for me to get more money to buy a laser and do my experiment.

In fact, when Fry reapplied for funds in 1974, he was given money by an organisation which had rejected his application in 1970. Admittedly, his second application included substantial technical improvements, but Fry at least has no doubts that the change in the granting body's attitude was the result of Holt's findings.

The reason they gave for their first rejection was that there were already two other experiments in existence . . . of course, when they disagreed, the higher (data collection) rate of my experiment became more crucial.

Holt's result, irrespective of whether Fry believed it to be valid, thus gave him the opportunity of negotiating for funds.

Holt's experiment provided a basis from which I could argue to get some more money.

I certainly do not wish to imply that Fry had no interest in the LHV issues other than a way of getting money. He himself notes that

aside from the question of getting funds, someone had to resolve the disagreement . . . there had to be another independent experiment.

Nevertheless, I think there is some basis for claiming that Holt's result was not a crucial part of Fry's motivation, but rather provided a resource by which he could fulfill some wider aims in his work. For example, in 1973 Fry published a paper (28) on *general* applications of two-photon correlation experiments, in which he noted their usefulness in testing LHV theories, *as well as* other uses such as finding the efficiency of photon detectors and studying resonance fluorescence.

A further point: after publishing his experimental results, which were "in excellent agreement with the QM prediction . . . and in clear violation of the LHV restriction" (29), Fry made a further request for funds to improve his apparatus in order to gain more data on the LHV question, and also to perform several quite different experiments, involving two-photon correlations, along lines similar to those discussed in his 1973 paper. There is no suggestion that this application was motivated by doubts over the validity of Fry's existing LHV results. To quote Fry,

This (proposed experiment) doesn't really tell you anything new, in a direct sense . . . (in the original LHV experiment) I took data for about an hour and a half. If I took data for 300 hours, I would be able to have really small error bars, and get a really beautiful curve, and just to have that beautiful result it should be done. That alone is enough argument.

Fry's improved experiment would be more satisfying from the point of view of experimental design, but it would not tell us anything we don't already know about the status of LHV theories. It therefore seems plausible to conclude that a major part of Fry's strategy was to develop experimental techniques *per se*, and then apply them to a number of quite different empirical problems.

   A further piece of evidence is relevant. Shortly after completing his LHV experiment, Fry moved temporarily to another university in order to take part in another 'fundamental' experiment, this time to study parity violation. Like many of the LHV physicists, Fry expressed a *general* preference for such fundamental experiments rather than more routine work:

May people just go out and measure things . . . but I think it's much more exciting to do things like the hidden-variable experiment or the parity experiment.

It is important to remember that none of the LHV experimenters planned to spend their entire professional life doing LHV experiments. Indeed, many of them claimed that once it became clear that the results of the existing experiments favoured QM, it was difficult to imagine anything being gained by further tests. None of the numerous alternatives to the Copenhagen Interpretation of QM had led to realisable experimental predictions which could provide genuine tests of these alternatives. (This is also true of David Bohm's well-known HV theories — see Note 11.) Most of the experimenters therefore described their LHV work as "a one-off job". The LHV group were experimental physicists first and foremost, and hidden-variable investigators second. Their reference group, to whom they looked for recognition and future employment, was the mainstream physics community, and not the diffuse and fragmented collection of physicists and philosophers who spend a large proportion of their time on the interpretation of QM.

   It is difficult to *disprove* the view that scientists are primarily motivated by a desire to search for truth and to resolve puzzles and anomalies. But such a view merely explains the existence of scientific practice; it says nothing about why some anomalies are explored and others are not. It is for this reason that I have taken the response to Holt's experiment as a problematic outcome which requires explanation. Both Holt and the other physicists involved could have reacted differently, and I believe that it is only by reference to the particular context in which these people operated that we can provide a detailed account of their practice and of the actual outcome. To claim that different courses of action lead to different pay-offs may seem obvious. What I have tried to show here is that such pay-offs cannot be assessed solely by reference to general notions of scientific methodology; instead they are largely determined by the local context in which decisions are made.

Of course, it is by no means easy to give a *complete* description of the 'local context', and any particular reading of this context, such as my own, could always be challenged. But this is no reason to give up all attempts to understand the detailed mechanics of scientific practice; nor does it undermine the validity of the general claim that such practice is heavily influenced by non-technical, and specifically social, factors.

Social Context and the Creation of Scientific Knowledge: Some Tentative Comments

By this point, I hope to have convinced the reader that the particular social, historical and cultural context in which the LHV experiments took place had a major effect on many features of these experiments — their location, the people who performed them, the way in which they were presented, and the response to anomalous results, both by the originator of these results and by other LHV physicists.

The real question, of course, is whether or not all this is ultimately trivial. Could the outcome of the experiments — the data themselves and the conclusions drawn from them — be affected by anything other than technical criteria?

Ultimately, the answer depends on what one regards as trivial. For example, if Holt's experiment had been performed by a person of higher status, or by someone who aggressively defended its validity, this might have no effect at all on the data obtained in subsequent experiments, but it might well have led to a quite different style of debate and a different sequence of events. It is interesting to speculate about what might have occurred if Clauser, who initially hoped to disprove QM, had obtained Holt's results, and vice versa.

Clauser himself suggested that they might then have been 'at each other's throats.' This in itself might have made a substantial difference to the outcome. As discussed earlier, Holt's virtual capitulation led almost inevitably to widespread disbelief in his results. Had these results been vigorously defended by their originator, a whole range of hypotheses, 'ad hoc' or otherwise, might have been put forward to explain the apparent clash between the rival experiments. We simply have no way of knowing what *might* have happened.

One clue is available to us. Soon after Holt's result became known, he was contacted by a member of what might be termed an 'alternative science' institution in California. This group was closely involved in the parapsychology movement, and expressed interest in Holt's work. Holt did not follow up this contact − indeed his supervisor, Pipkin, informed me that one reason why they were reluctant to publish their results was because they did not wish to give encouragement to unorthodox groups who might exaggerate the significance and credibility of Holt's result. If Holt *had* been willing to invoke parapsychology to account for his anomalous results, the involvement of such groups would be classed by some observers as anything but trivial (30).

Obviously, any discussion of how things *might* have turned out, had circumstances been different, must be speculative. The justification for such speculation is that unless we are prepared to consider alternatives to the *actual* outcome, that outcome can easily be interpreted as inevitable and unproblematic. The whole process of social change within science then becomes either inaccessible to sociological analysis, or else describable only as the straightforward application of a generalized scientific methodology. Where there is controversy in science, it is relatively easy to show the existence of alternative interpretations of empirical data, each with its own sort of plausibility. Where there is no controversy, as in the LHV case, the sociologist is forced into the role of a devil's advocate, however immodest this may appear, if the scientists' interpretation is to be rendered problematic. In what follows, I shall adopt such a role, not in order to argue that the LHV group were in any sense mistaken, but to illustrate, once again, the role of the social and cultural context in determining the actual outcome.

Virtually all the discussion which took place concerning Holt's experiment was a discussion about where the error in his work might lie. As Pipkin put it

We couldn't understand why the experiments clashed. Clearly, the reasonable thing was that one of them was wrong.

For many excellent reasons, it was concluded that it was Holt's experiment which was wrong. But this decision took place within a context of shared theories and mechanisms and, equally importantly, within a context of almost total disbelief in LHV. Anyone who wished to defend the validity of Holt's result, particularly after the results of the later experiments became known, would almost certainly have had to reject some section of contemporary physics. The fact that this did not happen does not necessarily imply that it could not have happened.

For example, Clauser published a paper in 1976 (30a) in which he describes an experimental investigation of Holt's 'anomaly'. In this paper, he points out several 'possibly significant' differences between Holt's apparatus and Clauser's own partial replication. One of these is that different sorts of polarisation analysers were used: Holt employed calcite crystals, while Clauser (and all the other experimenters) employed sets of glass plates, arranged in parallel rows and aligned at the 'Brewster angle'. Now morphologically, a lump of crystal and a set of 13 or so glass plates are quite dissimilar, but functionally they are held to be identical (or at least sufficiently alike to avoid the necessity of including calcite crystals in the replication). This functional identity is derived from our current theories about the nature of polarised light; in other words, the identity is defined by the context.

(The practical equivalence of these devices was defined by the social context in a much more direct way. Clauser's lab operated on a tight budget. He already had a set of glass plates from his earlier experiment, and would not have been able to purchase a pair of calcites even if he wanted to, which apparently he did not.)

I do not wish to claim that LHVs only manifest themselves in the presence of calcite crystals, any more than I wish to claim that LHVs only show up in the presence of experimenters whose surnames begin with 'H'. Nevertheless such claims are clearly not impossible to make. Their reasonableness, or lack of it, derives from a set of tacit conventions. The risks involved in rejecting these conventions vastly outweighed the possible benefits – in this particular case. All I wish to point out is that functional equivalence is dependent on theory. The fact that, for example, mercury thermometers appear to do the 'same' job as alcohol thermometers or (less obvious) as thermocouples, only derives facticity from our shared theories of thermometry (31). The apparent solidity of material artefacts should not obscure their links with abstract theories. Let me provide another argument from the LHV activity. One LHV experiment, proposed by Aspect, is still in progress (32). It is designed to test what seems a rather radical hypothesis. The experiments to date are all static experiments: the apparatus is set up and a series of readings then taken. Such experiments do not rule out the possibility that some sort of signal is transferred from one part of the apparatus to another: this signal might contain information about the configuration of the polarisation analysers, and the photon source might then modify its output in order that the results *appear* to agree with QM. The proposed experiment would be able to detect any such subterfuge.

The results of this proposed experiment are awaited with interest by the LHV group. The hypothesis which it tests is evidently taken seriously, despite the fact that it hypothesises a new mechanism not presently known to physics. It does not account for Holt's results, but I think it does indicate that it is possible to suggest that LHVs, which by definition are unknown quantities, have special properties which make their detection less clear-cut than we might suppose.

I wish to present a final piece of evidence. This concerns the response of a number of LHV physicists to a suggestion such as the above. I asked these physicists whether there was any effect which could be present in all the experiments *other than Holt's*, and which could account for the disagreement between Holt's results and the results of the other experiments. At first, this possibility was denied emphatically, but when pressed they replied in terms such as:

I can't think of an example, but I haven't really thought about it, though.

Oh, you can always mock up a very perverse or psychotic type of mechanism.

The errors argument explains my prejudices, if you like. Obviously, someone could come up with a systematic error which goes the other way.

Some interviewees *did* suggest errors which could be present in all the other experiments, and they were indeed 'psychotic' and 'screwy' in terms of current physical theories. Since these effects would have to be present in a number of experiments, and would have to have gone unnoticed by several different people, it is not surprising that no-one takes them at all seriously. I certainly do not claim that people should. All that I am trying to show is that arguments cited by physicists as reasons for rejecting an anomalous experiment do not take the form of logically-compelling deductions from a set of timeless axioms. Science is not like that. Scientists are continually faced with decisions about where to invest their time. They study problems in which they feel there is some likelihood of gaining worthwhile results. LHV had had its chance, and it had failed to show results. Everyone agreed that it was time to move on. The possibility that Holt's results were correct was simply not plausible. But the assessment of plausibility is a complex judgement. In a different context, where someone had felt strongly in flavour of LHV, or where someone had been ingenious enough to construct an alternative account of the experimental results, the case might not have closed quite so quickly.

What role should we give to Nature in all this? Might it not simply be that QM is a correct description of the world, and that LHV is not? Indeed it could. But we do not have direct access to Nature. We approach reality through experimental practices into which we are socialised (33), practices which are located in a social context. We describe experimental data in terms of observational categories which are heavily dependent on current theories (34). Thus our knowledge about the world cannot be isolated from the social context in which that knowledge is generated.

Notes and References

1. See, for example, S. B. Barnes, *Scientific Knowledge and Sociological Theory*, Routledge and Kegan Paul, London, 1974; and David Bloor, *Knowledge and Social Imagery*, Routledge and Kegan Paul, London, 1976.
2. Michael Mulkay, *Science and the Sociology of Knowledge*: Allen and Unwin, 1979.
3. K. D. Knorr, 'Producing and Reproducing Knowledge: Descriptive or Constructive? Towards a Model of Research Production', *Social Science Information* 16, 670–74 (1977).
4. Woolgar has applied an ethnomethodological analysis to science itself. Steven Woolgar, 'Writing an Intellectual History of Scientific Development: The Use of Discovery Accounts', *Social Studies of Science* 6, 395 (1976).
5. Max Jammer, *The Philosophy of Quantum Mechanics*, Wiley, New York, 1974, p. v.
6. Max Jammer, *The Conceptual Development of Quantum Mechanics*, McGraw-Hill, New York, 1966, p. vii.
7. For a comprehensive review of alternative interpretations of QM, see Jammer, *op. cit.*, 1974, Note 1.

8. Bernard D'Espagnat, *Conceptual Foundations of Quantum Mechanics*, Benjamin, London, 2nd. edn., 1976, pp. 75–158.

9. J. S. Bell, 'On the Einstein Podolsky Rosen Paradox', *Physics*, 195 (1964).

10. In this paper, I concentrate on those experiments which involved the use of optical photons produced by atomic cascades. For details of the experiments, see J. F. Clauster and A. Shimony, 'Bell's Theorem: experimental tests and implications', *Reports on Progress in Physics* 41, 1881 (1978).

11. This is not strictly correct. An earlier experiment by Papaliolios had tested a quite different hidden-variable theory, but the test was never claimed to be decisive. For details, see Jammer, *op. cit.*, 1974, Note 1.

12. D'Espagnat, *op. cit.*, 1976, Note 1, pp. 161–163.

13. This in turn led to some interesting results. Some of the theorists attacked the whole experimental methodology, and argued strongly in favour of an alternative, explicitly speculative methodology. For details, see my forthcoming Ph.D thesis, University of Edinburgh.

14. Personal correspondence with Abner Shimony, 1977. All the statements made in this paper by LHV physicists were obtained from correspondence and interviews over a two year period. In some cases, particularly when discussing sensitive issues, anonymity was requested, and some of my quotations are therefore unattributed. The sources for all other quoted statements are made clear in the text.

15. Hagstrom found a similar lack of concern about type-casting among Ph.D physicists. See W. O. Hagstrom, *The Scientific Community*, Southern Illinois University Press, Carbondale, 1975, p. 160.

16. This list of factors may not be exhaustive. Another possible factor was the small chance of a large pay-off if QM were to be refuted. In retrospect, few of my interviewees claim to have taken this possibility at all seriously, but it is difficult to know whether this claim is coloured by what they now know about the experimental results.

17. Of course, these physicists were not merely passive pawns in all this. For example, Clauser made strenuous (and successful) efforts to find a laboratory with the necessary equipment. He moved 3000 miles, took up a post at the same institution, and slowly worked his way into the lab concerned.

18. E. S. Fry and J. McGuire, unpublished grant proposal, 1971, p. 4.

19. M. Lamehi-Rachti, *Mécanique Quantique et Théories des Variables Cachées Locales*, unpublished Ph.D dissertation Université de Paris-Sud, 1976, p. 2.

20. R. A. Holt, *Atomic Cascade Experiments*, unpublished Ph.D dissertation, Harvard University, 1973, pp. II, 3–4.

21. J. F. Clauser, M. A. Horne, A. Shimony, R. A. Holt, 'Proposed Experiment to Test Local Hidden-Variable Theories', *Physical Review Letters* 23, 880 (1969).

22. For a detailed discussion of the assumptions, see Clauser and Shimony, *op. cit.*, 1978, Note 10.

23. S. J. Freedman and J. F. Clauser, 'Experimental Test of Local Hidden-Variable Theories', *Physical Review Letters* 28, 938 (1972).

24. The initial status of this manuscript was still unclear. In later publications by Holt and co-authors, the manuscript is cited as 'R. A. Holt and F. M. Pipkin (to be published)'.

25. Given Holt's insistence that there was an error in his apparatus, and his equally

strong insistence that this error has never been identified, one might still wonder whether someone else might have been able to find the error. To this extent, a question mark remains. However, most of the LHV physicists recognised the difficulty involved in such error-tracing.

26. This does not necessarily mean that Holt *maximised* his success. Some of my interviewees claimed that in Holt's position they would have gone about things slightly differently. This might have led to a slightly more or less favourable outcome. What does seem certain is that Holt *was* concerned with gaining a favourable outcome.

27. See, for example, B. Wynne, 'C. G. Barkla and the J Phenomenon: A Case Study in the Treatment of Deviance in Physics', *Social Studies of Science* 6, 307 (1976), and H. M. Collins, 'The Seven Sexes: A Study in the Sociology of a Phenomenon, or the Replication of Experiments in Physics', *Sociology* 9, 205 (1975).

28. E. S. Fry, 'Two-Photon Correlations in Atomic Transitions', *Physical Review* A8, 1219 (1973).

29. E. S. Fry and R. C. Thompson, 'Experimental Test of Local Hidden-Variable Theories', *Physical Review Letters* 37, 465 (1976).

30. Ironically, parapsychologists *have* become involved, but they now argue that the results *in favour of* QM provide evidence to support their views. See, e.g. Jack Sarfatti, '*Towards a Quantum Theory of Consciousness, the Miraculous and God*', unpublished paper, Physics/Consciousness Research Group, San Francisco.

30a. J. F. Clauser, 'Experimental Investigation of a Polarisation Correlation Anomaly', *Physical Review Letters* 36, 1223 (1976).

31. See H. M. Collins, *op. cit.*, 1975, Note 27, p. 216; and Bill Harvey, 'Cranks and Others: Science as a Sociological Phenomenon', *New Scientist* 77, 739 (1978) (March 16th, no. 1094).

32. A. Aspect, 'Proposed Experiment to test the nonseparability of quantum mechanics', *Physical Review* D14, 1944 (1976).

33. P. L. Berger and T. Luckmann, *The Social Construction of Reality*, Penguin University Books, Harmondsworth, 1971.

34. See Bloor, *op. cit.*, 1976. Note 1.

ON THE CONSTRUCTION OF CREATIVITY: THE 'MEMORY TRANSFER' PHENOMENON AND THE IMPORTANCE OF BEING EARNEST (1)

DAVID TRAVIS

Polytechnic of North London

1. Introduction

This paper is concerned with some aspects of the construction of a now widely rejected piece of scientific knowledge, the 'memory transfer' phenomenon (2), which has been the focus of a controversy in neuroscience over the last twenty years. Most interested scientists agree that, *if true*, it would have revolutionary implications for our understanding of how the brain works. But there has been a marked polarization of beliefs over the reality of the phenomenon, and the status of the participants. The field has been variously assessed as a case of bad science, unconscious experimenter bias and 'mass hysteria' while others believe that the major proponents should be in line for a Nobel prize. Chedd, writing in the *New Scientist*, has commented:

If anyone still holds any illusions about the objectivity of science, then even a cursory glance at the brief history of the chemical transfer of memory would surely unburden them. It is virtually impossible to enter the subject, either as a participant or observer, without pre-conceptions (3).

One early feature of the field was the perception of a subversive flippancy in some articulations of the memory transfer phenomenon. In this paper I will examine part of the climate of opinion surrounding the reception of this piece of scientific creativity, specifically the aura of 'schoolboy humour', relating the perceived incongruity of the conceptual structure of the phenomenon to concrete actions and institutions within the field.

2. The 'Memory Transfer' Saga

The 'official history' of the field begins in 1953 with two psychology graduate

Karin D. Knorr, Roger Krohn and Richard Whitley (eds.), The Social Process of Scientific Investigation. Sociology of the Sciences, Volume IV, 1980. 165–193.
Copyright © 1980 by G. D. L. Travis

students at the University of Texas. Thompson and McConnell attempted to condition a simple freshwater flatworm, the planarian, to contract or 'scrunch up' each time an electric light was switched on; the unconditioned stimulus being a mild electric shock delivered through the water in which the worm was placed (4). The planarian was strategically interesting because it is the lowest organism on the phylogenetic scale to have bilateral symmetry, a primitive brain, and human-type synapses. Thus it should be the lowest organism capable of true learning (5).

Thompson and McConnell's results – indicating that the planarian could be classically conditioned – were published in the *Journal of Comparative and Physiological Psychology* (6), one of the highest status journals for animal research (7), and the mainstream of physiological psychology (8). The paper was a straightforward piece of research which caused relatively little notice, and no controversy, until later experiments made it important.

One of the peculiarities of planarian worms is that they can undergo a-sexual reproduction through fission. Thompson and McConnell had speculated about what effect this might have on the learning they had induced, and when McConnell had set up his laboratory at the University of Michigan, he performed an experimental simulation. Trained worms were cut in half across the middle, allowed to regenerate, and tested to see how much they remembered (9). Surprisingly, the animals which regenerated from the tail sections remembered as much as, if not more than, the heads (10)! This report caused a good deal of interest: apart from being an intriguing phenomenon 'as such', it also carried the implication that the memory was not localised in the brain, but distributed throughout the worms' body, perhaps in all its cells.

A third set of experiments made the research 'glamorous' and attracted a good deal of comment in the popular press. Some species of planarians – including those used by McConnell – are cannibalistic when starved. Trained worms were chopped up and fed to their hungry, untrained fellows, who did much better at their learning task than those fed on a diet of untrained worm (11). 'Food for thought' to cite a common witticism of the period.

The planarian research, including the original conditioning study, became the focus of a bitter controversy which was conducted mainly among psychologists and zoologists. The important issue was whether the worms could be said to have learned anything in the first place, rather than the question of whether the results of the experience could be transferred. As it happened, these concerns were effectively superceded for many scientists when in 1965 four research groups, working without knowledge of each other (12), published results claiming that the memory transfer effect could be produced in vertebrates (13).

No one doubted that rats could learn.

There followed a rash of attempts to replicate the phenomenon, many of which failed (14). Later, more positive results began to emerge, and by 1970 the 'hit score' in terms of experiments was 133 positive, 115 negative, and 15 equivocal (15). Since then the number of positive reports has increased more rapidly than the number of negative reports.

In 1972 a research group headed by Ungar claimed to have isolated, characterised and synthesised one of the transfer agents, 'scotophobin', a peptide said to code for fear of the dark (16). It has subsequently been claimed that the compound produces dark-avoidance behaviour in rats, mice, goldfish and cockroaches (17).

Few scientists now give the results of the field much credence, and active research has virtually ceased following the death of the major proponent, Ungar, in 1977. The failure *can now be seen* as the failure of a logical progression of experimentation related to the concept of a *molecular* code for memory (analogous to the genetic code), and most reviews adopt this construction of events. Until a difficult-to-define point in the early 1960's however, the implications of memory transfer (in planarians) were not connected to speculations about molecular memory mechanisms. From 1965 or so, a marriage was proclaimed by some proponents of the transfer phenomenon, but those concerned with molecular memory mechanisms *per se* were somewhat reluctant suitors. The memory transfer phenomenon was taken to require a molecular memory *code*, and was widely recognised as the only experimentally testable formulation of the hypothesis that specific memories are coded in specific molecules. Molecular memory *mechanisms*, on the other hand, need not necessarily imply specificity of *coding*, nor need they allow for the possibility of a memory transfer phenomenon.

One final piece of context is that initially quite separate from the planarian transfer experiments there were, in the mid sixties, high expectations that there would be some kind of advance related to the chemical basis of memory. As far as can be gathered there was a widespread feeling among those concerned with the biochemistry of memory that in the next decade or so 'something was going to happen'.

3. Structure and Ambiguity in the Memory Transfer Phenomenon

3.1. The Idea of Memory Transfer

In abstract, an experiment in the field can be characterised as comprising three phases. The initial training involves the application of a number of relatively standard procedures and practices that would be recognised by animal training psychologists all over the world. (In the case of planarian worms the situation is more complex. Obviously they had hardly ever been used in behavioural laboratories before this series of experiments, and although terms such as 'stimulus', 'response' and 'classical conditioning' denote shared cultural resources, the *detailed rules* and tacit knowledge necessary for their *agreed application* to planarians was problematic (18).)

The second phase is the extraction of the transfer factor (or a solution thought to contain the active material) from the body of the worm, or from the brain of the animal. Some protocols involved a crude homogenate of brain, others some kind of purification procedure which would concentrate, and give further information about the characteristics of, the transfer factor. Again, these are routine activities in the context of certain laboratories. Similarly, and thirdly, thousands of animals are injected every day with chemicals of biological origin, and the subjects' performance on running a maze or some other learning task recorded.

Taken separately, these are three culturally legitimate practices likely to be found in behavioural psychology, biochemistry, and pharmacology laboratories, respectively. Putting them together in the context of studying the behavioural effects of biological compounds − hormones for example − obtained from animal organs is a commonplace in some laboratories. However, linking these practices in the context of the transfer of specific memories in vertebrates produced a mixture of amazement, derision, and shock. In a loose manner of speaking, the phenomenon was 'odd'. It seemed to violate a number of assumptions about memory − it not being the sort of thing you can put through a homogeniser (a relative of the kitchen liquidiser) or hold in a test tube (19). On orthodox theory, memory should be a matter of a network of nerve cells.

Whilst it was still associated with planarians the implications of memory transfer were to a large extent *contained*. Planarians are fairly primitive organisms, and have the potential for regeneration not found in vertebrates for example. Perhaps, it was thought, memory is somewhat 'different' than in higher organisms (20). But rats are another matter all together: the vast bulk of experimental data on the biochemistry and physiological psychology of memory is from studies of the rat. The principles of memory are thought to be basically the same as in humans, at least as far as the (bio)physical basis is concerned. The memory transfer experiments on rats broke a kind of implicit inferential barrier. As a phenomenon associated with worms, memory transfer *could* be regarded as a biological oddity of limited relevance and applicability. Claiming that the phenomenon operated in rats was far more consequential. So, despite a knowledge of the worm-running experiments, the first mammalian results produced strong reactions (21).

It was as if some kind of monster (22) had been produced, a *chimera* (23) constructed out of a lion's head, a goat's body and a serpent's tail. The results had no right to exist in the conceptual space they attempted to occupy — indeed, there was no conceptual space in which they could reasonably exist (24). To switch metaphors, the memory transfer field had produced the scientific equivalent of the sewing machine and the umbrella on the operating table (25).

Professor Ernest Chain at the 1968 UNESCO – IBRO meeting vehemently deplored "wasting precious time on such *chimerical* and *ridiculous* goals when it could be spent on better founded biochemical investigations". (26)

A scientist who first heard about one of the mammal experiments during a neuroscience meeting in 1965 when the results were reported 'informally' (not by one of the researchers concerned with the experiments) commented:

X came in with a copy of *Science*, to read it, and a discussion ensued . . . I guess [it's] fair to say it sounded incredible to me, and at the same time it sounded like if it was true it was the greatest thing since soap or something . . . most people [at the meeting] I think, thought it was a bunch of crap. (27)

Another researcher noted that "there was a kind of fever in the air at the time" and felt the need to stress that in his particular group "our doubts

didn't take the form of laughing or saying 'there's nothing to it' [they] . . .
took the form of 'well we'd better see for ourselves', because the consequences
were just too important to ignore" (28).

These extracts reveal a deep seated ambivalence about the claims to have
shown the transfer phenomenon in vertebrates. There was surprise and
amazement; reactions tinged in some cases, and dominated in others, by the
possibility that this was some kind of a joke (29). That is not to say, of
course, that the scientists reporting the results were widely seen as perpetrat-
ing a hoax. Undoubtedly *some* observers felt that this was a possibility, and
there was a precedent for this opinion. Jacobson — one of the 'famous four',
who had previously worked with McConnell, commented:

I recall that when the regeneration report [on planarians] was first submitted for publication, one referee angrily professed that this was either the biggest finding or the
biggest hoax in psychology for years — and he suspected the latter to be true . . . at least
the veracity of the experimenters is no longer challenged. (30)

Jacobson's final point was somewhat premature. One scientist informed me
darkly "[at the time] I was not ready to call some of them liars . . . at a later
point I was quite willing to do so" (31).

Such accusations were in the minority. A more common reaction was to
see it as humour of cosmic proportions, a whimsicality, or sport of Nature
which had led astray those scientists who had not kept an adequate grip on
their control groups and interpretations. The ambivalence however was deep.
The results just might be true, and if so it would not pay to be left out of
"the biggest thing in memory for a hundred years" (32). Certainly many
groups of scientists went ahead and tried transfer experiments, and some
published their results in one form or another (33).

In this section I have emphasised an ambiguity in perceptions of the
phenomenon, and described the deep ambivalence in reactions to the claim
to have demonstrated the phenomenon in rats. Now there is always some
uncertainty surrounding the introduction of a new and surprising scientific
claim. What emerged here however, was that the specific ambiguity associated
with memory transfer was part of a wider structure of ambiguity which
related to a number of institutions and actions in the field (34).

In the rest of this paper I will look at one theme in the *structure* and the
source of this ambivalence, and in doing so offer a partial explanation of why

this particular piece of scientific creativity failed to become more widely institutionalised.

3.2. Funny Ha-Ha, Funny Peculiar or Creativity?

As I have described it, there was a structural ambiguity in the reception of the vertebrate experiments. Should they be taken as a joke or as a serious piece of scientific creativity? Or perhaps both? The reactions associated with this particular episode are, no doubt, symptomatic of a general question of the relations between humour, other forms of understanding, and creativity (35). This is a difficult and little-explored area, but a useful analysis is to be found in the work of Arthur Koestler, especially *'The Act of Creation'*, and *'The Ghost in the Machine'* (36). The argument proposed is that creativity in humour, science and art have a similar 'logical' pattern – the discovery of hidden similarities – but differ in what Koestler calls the 'emotional climate'. To gloss his account, the 'logical' similarity subsists in the bringing together of frames of reference in a collision (humour), in a fusion (science) or in confrontation (art). These cognitive frames are not necessarily incompatible, but in the case of humour for example, are *habitually* held apart.

Let me unpack this a little further. (In doing so I would not claim to be following Koestler closely, but freely interpreting). In the case of assimilated scientific creativity we can occasionally recapture to some extent the moment of fusion when previously unrelated cognitive elements (frameworks) were brought together in a new configuration. Krohn has given a number of detailed examples of this kind of account in his thematic paper for the conference on *The Social Process of Scientific Investigation* (37). Whether the juxtaposition of frames is eventually seen as a piece of scientific creativity by the relevant community will depend crucially on subsequent events. It *might* be reconstructed as a 'clang association' or a pitfall (38). Institutionalised creativity on the other hand will be seen to have been fruitful in terms of further research but, *at the time* of its introduction, it may have seemed absurd.

The relativity of meanings in science when 'the uncertainty of the future is visited on the past' has now been well established (39). The difference between the recognition of a potential scientific contribution as 'creativity' or 'absurdity' may not be very great, and the attribution unstable. Explanations of scientific innovation in terms of an interactive theory of metaphor stress this (40), and Barnes has noted that the introduction of a new metaphor may be indistinguishable from a category mistake (41).

This perspective blurs the sharp distinctions between creativity, the meaningful, and the absurd, seeking to uncover ways in which such attributions are constructed and maintained. Koestler's approach helps us to visualise the polyvalency of meaning extending beyond the strictly scientific into humour.

The comic, according to Koestler, is the bringing together of frames of meaning or associative contexts that are habitually held apart, so creating a surprising configuration. In some cases the juxtaposition is 'impossible' and the unstable conceptual space that is created explodes in laughter (42). One result of this can be the kind of cathartic effect that Koestler describes when the tension wrought by the conjoining of habitually incompatible frames is discharged (43). In more 'intellectual' forms of humour however, such as witticism, satire or irony (44), there can be an intention to leave a certain tension or discomfort. A further characteristic of these higher forms of humour found in the logical paradox for example, is that the interpretive work of 'seeing the joke' shades over into that of 'solving the puzzle' (45).

Let me illustrate some of these points through a series of examples. We are so familiar with statements such as 'light is a wave' that we tend to miss the literal absurdity. We know what is really meant. Other statements may be humorous *as well as* scientific: 'glass is a liquid' may be surprising and can produce a wry sense of amusement when we recognise the particular way in which the scientist is contradicting everyday categories. The humour is contingent, and separable from the scientific point. We can accept these divergent definitions of 'solid' and 'liquid', making sense of the statement according to the context. A *child* stating that 'glass is a liquid' would almost certainly be corrected.

In the particular context in which it was received, the memory transfer phenomenon in mammals was not perceived simply as a piece of potential scientific creativity. It was also seen to have some of the characteristics of a joke, and the question of appropriate reactions was problematic. The juxtaposition of frames of reference that was memory transfer in mammals was certainly surprising. It carried enormous implications that some saw as potentially fruitful, others as absurd. Seen against the background of the great expectations held by some scientists for the possibility of a molecular memory code analogous to the genetic code, the phenomenon implied a startlingly simple experimental strategy. To stretch a point, it was *such* a startlingly simple extrapolation that for some it was almost *surreal*.

But why was this so? In looking at the sources of this response most of the discussion will centre on events related to experimentation on planarians — an occupation known as 'worm running'. It was these events that structured the situation in such a way that the mammal experiments precipitated the reactions I have described.

4. The Importance of Being Earnest

4.1. Science and the Comic

One of the characteristics of an emergent specialism is the founding of a journal devoted to the area. This provides a distinctive forum, an outlet for research reports and a focus of identity which may be highly important in terms of group solidarity. So it was in the early memory transfer field — but with a difference. When McConnell's research became known through the scientific and popular press he received many requests for information (mainly from high school students) on how to obtain planarians, how to keep them, feed them, and carry out experiments. His group produced a set of mimeographed instructions and — with characteristic humour — labelled it 'The Worm Runner's Digest' Vol. 1, No. 1. This was sent out complete with a heraldic device bearing the legend 'Ignotum per Ignotius' (46). Some of the recipients took the joke at face value and sent back the reports of their experiments for publication, and so the journal was launched (47).

The masthead of *The Worm Runner's Digest* proclaimed that it was 'An informal journal of comparative psychology published irregularly by members of the Planarian Research Group'. It was also one of the small group of journals that published scientific humour (48), or as McConnell cynically put it, "it is the only scientific journal that *knowingly* publishes satire" (49). Mixed in with straight scientific reports (including experiments on planarians and later, transfer experiments on other animals) were such articles as 'A Theory of Ghosts' and 'Aversive Conditioning in the Dead Rat'. In addition to these spoofs and satires – some of them with a cutting edge, some of them schoolboy humour – there were cartoons and poems.

Later in its career the straight articles and the spoofs were separated, partly to gain respectability, and partly because some scientists complained of being unable to tell which were serious articles and which were not, until they had nearly finished the piece (50). Viewed from one side the '*Worm Runner's Digest*' (WRD) contained the humour; printed 'upside down' and starting from the 'back' cover, the '*Journal of Biological Psychology*' (JBP) contained straight scientific papers (51). In one sense this could be regarded as little more than an amusing scientific curio of no great consequence. Certainly, few of the important papers in the transfer controversy were published exclusively in the *WRD/JBP*. In the main, significant papers were published elsewhere, the *WRD/JBP* carrying modified versions or more informal accounts. In some cases 'early' or 'rough' results were reported in its pages, and in others (a small minority) the journal carried reports by those, like high school students, who would be unlikely to get a paper into an orthodox journal. But for all that, the journal did boast a normal refereeing pattern.

A number of scientists dismissed the *WRD/JBP* as 'a comic', 'a scientific joke-book', 'a scientific *Playboy*', but these comments should not be taken at face value by the sociologist (52). The journal was important in three respects relevant to this discussion. Firstly, it provided McConnell with an editorial forum (entitled 'Worms and Things . . . ') in which to comment on the controversy and articulate his views, a function that was enhanced by the two other factors. Secondly, it carried annotated bibliographies of all research relevant to the running of worms and, later, to the wider memory transfer controversy. As an information source for those interested in following the field it was a 'must'. Lastly, it was sent, sometimes *gratis*, to those involved in the research and to those who might be interested, so achieving a high penetration of the field. The *WRD/JBP* was thus an institutional sign of McConnell's position at the nexus of an informal communication network for worm running and transfer experiments. Indeed, when a group of interested scientists met in 1967 to consider replication problems in the transfer field they organized an informal reporting network, to be administered by McConnell (53).

The journal also reflects McConnell's approach to science, that it should be fun *as well as* serious, and that the deflation of pretentiousness through humour is not just compatible with, but can be part of, progress in science (54). The *WRD/JBP* is anomalous precisely in that it brings together two modes of understanding — science and humour — which if not in any formal sense incompatible, are at least habitually held apart and separate (55).

To put science — any science, not specifically memory transfer — together with spoofs and satires is to break accepted categories and taken-for-granted distinctions in a subversive manner. If the *WRD/JBP* were *just* satire and spoof it would have produced unease to the extent that the articles succeeded in showing the fatuity of some aspects of science (56). The effect of putting the subversive (57) humour with apparently straight science was, however, to produce an added dimension of unease, which reflected on the scientific articles.

The *WRD/JBP* as a social institution within the field can be seen as a concrete representation of McConnell's ideas on the relation of scientific creativity and humour. But with regard to the transfer studies, their presentation as straight research was weakened by their physical location amongst satire and spoof (58), *particularly so, given the nature of the conceptual framework of the idea of memory transfer.* The points I wish to make are these: *given* the reputation of the *WRD/JBP* institution, *any* straight piece of scientific reporting would be tinged by placing it in that context; given the particular configuration of cultural resources that constituted memory transfer the effect was multiplied. But the associative context did not in any simple way *determine* the response, for the reputation of the *WRD/JBP* institution itself was partly a concomitant of its being a vehicle for the articulation of memory transfer. It would be difficult, and unnecessary for present purposes, to disentangle this nexus and sort out which aspects were 'causes' and which 'effects'. What can be said is that a deep seated ambivalence towards memory transfer *grew up with* the *WRD/JBP* reputation: the institution acted as an amplifier.

4.2. Something Unusual . . .

I have made several claims about ambiguity, unease, violations of taken-for-granted rules, and habitually separated frames of reference. A fertile way of looking at the situation is through the perspective developed by Joan P. Emerson in her paper 'Nothing Unusual is Happening' a resource that has been used by Collins and Pinch in their study of parapsychologists, who adopt the stance 'nothing unscientific is happening' (59).

Emerson's central hypothesis is that "social interaction has intrinsic properties that naturally bias negotiations towards a "nothing unusual" stance; [and that] this bias inhibits the application of deviant labels" (60). The process of negotiation of appropriate stance in problematic situations is developed through two cameos. In the first a patient is undergoing a gynaecological examination which she sees, and reacts to, as 'something unusual', while the medical staff attempt to pass off the situation as routine, everyday, activity. In the second cameo two would-be robbers interrupt the proceedings at an all female, society 'hi-jinks' party where "[j] okes and pranks filled the evening", (61). The socialites resisted the attempted re-definition of the situation as 'serious' by passing it off as just another prank.

This is a stickup. I'm SERIOUS (one of the robbers) cried. All the ladies laughed.
One of them playfully shoved one of the men. He shoved her back. As the ringing laughter continued, the men looked at each other, shrugged and left empty handed. (62)

The gynaecologist maintains a sober medical definition of the situation: under different circumstances the robbers fail to establish that something seriously unusual is happening.

In the memory transfer saga McConnell introduced a number of anomalous elements that did not square with the tacit rules for the conduct of science. Jokes and pranks filled the *Digest*. Should the transfer phenomenon be taken as 'serious' or as 'hi-jinks'? The reception of the reports of memory transfer in mammals can be seen to hover uneasily between the two situations. Like the female participants in both cameos there was an expectation that something unusual was going to happen. One scientist commented that memory transfer was "not an unexpected development, but 'strange' " (63).

A surprising new scientific theory (or revolution) can be seen as an attempted 'hold up' of orthodoxy, but in the ambiguous situation I have described, it was not consensually clear that this was what was going on. I am not claiming that the phenomenon was taken as 'simply a joke' (prank), but, rather, that there was uncertainty. The context bore confusing signs. McConnell had acted like a gynaecologist in fancy dress. 'Nothing unusual' (unscientific) was the necessary stance if the phenomenon was to be taken in earnest, but once the fancy dress had been seen, it was correspondingly more difficult to pass off the event as a wholly serious attempt at re-definition.

Thus, one of the important tacit rules for doing science is to be seen to be in earnest.

4.3. Spoiling the Act

I have emphasised the cultural climate of humour that was associated with the *WRD/JBP*, as an index of 'not being in earnest'. In the minds of a good number of critics this was linked with a nexus of what they saw as 'social' factors that included sensationalist popular press accounts of the research, aspects of McConnell's personality, and his performance at conferences. Such interpretive accounts − 'home-grown sociology' as one respondent termed them − were extended to cover other participants, particularly those seen as important.

The truth of these attributions is irrelevant here − but for the sake of symmetry it should be pointed out that proponents used similar modes of explanation in making sense of the actions of the critics. The details of these perceptions will be explored elsewhere, but one point deserves mention. Many felt that McConnell was far too 'open' about the research. In the words of a *proponent* active in the field for some time:

McConnell talks about [the research] in a very casual and annoying way. Such as his first transfer study [in planarians] where he dropped the stuff on the floor, he scooped it up and shoved it back into the animal . . . . (64)

Asked at a conference in 1962 whether the 'RNA' injection had been tested for polysaccharides, a possible contaminant, McConnell replied:

You will forgive me if I point out that I am not a biochemist and that I have to depend on my two medical students for information on this point. (65)

Here McConnell can be seen to have dropped his guard, allowing attention to be focused on 'backstage' happenings. Being open, or 'telling it like it was', is not the same as being earnest.

In reading the laboratory notebooks of some of the other scientists involved (on both sides of the controversy) it was noticeable that unfortunate events sometimes occurred during experiments. The air conditioning broke down making the animals uncomfortable, relays failed to deliver food pellets as they ought, and some animals inexplicably fell sick. By the time the results reached the public (constitutive) forum of science these contingencies had been remedied (66). Order had been created. In these extracts however, McConnell can be seen to have allowed, if not actually encouraged, a glimpse behind the curtain while the scenery was still being wheeled into place, and this has weakened the dramatic illusion. He indulges in 'telling it like it was', and being earnest is not the same thing as being honest — nor is it as rhetorically persuasive.

Such events contributed to the possibilities of the audience adopting a 'something unusual' stance, and a further series of actions also encouraged such a definition. McConnell noted on several occasions that, in a sense, the regenerated worms could be said to have 'inherited' learning, a notion that sails perilously close to the Lamarkian Heresy. One scientist from the 'Bible Belt' of the United States described it as a "Church-burning" idea in the context of the mid-1960's, because of its association with Lysenko and the Communist Threat. McConnell's group went further with their indifference to orthodoxy by beginning a series of experiments to test the possibility of the transfer of memory through *sexual* rather than *a-sexual* reproduction, a very pointed challenge to neo-Darwinians beliefs. Perhaps fortunately, there were problems:

We got a species [of planarians] from Buckhorn Springs. Big worms. But as soon as we started training them they stopped mating. If we stopped the training they mated. It makes you wonder about the value of an education. (67)

The group made no further attempts in this direction, as McConnell explained:

The word came through loud and clear. If we succeeded we would really be in trouble. (68)

In these extracts McConnell *can be seen* to have followed a subversion strategy (69) not only in the constitutive forum, by transgressing 'cognitive and technical norms', but also by allowing backstage contingencies to show through. The latter factor is, I think, the more important. It is a violation of the 'rules' of the institution of science itself, rather than an attempted subversion of a particular theory — a process which is expected to take place *within* the rules.

Once more; one must be *seen* to be in earnest (70).

5. Structures of Interests in Reactions to the Phenomenon

I hope I have outlined the structure and established a major source of the widespread ambivalence that greeted the reports of the memory transfer phenomenon in mammals. In this section I want to look in greater detail at the slightly wider context in which the research was situated, in order to show more clearly why it could be seen to stand out as anomalous. This will involve showing why the ambiguity characteristic of the initial reception of the mammal experiments (roughly mid-1965 to the latter part of 1966) was not precipitated by the earlier planarian research. To some extent this will be a restate and more firmly ground the themes so far developed, but in doing so I will be engaging in a process that is akin to explaining an in-joke. The explanation destroys the force of the humour. The transfer experiments should now seem more serious.

5.1. The Worm Running Experiments and the Containment of Implications

I have indicated above (p. 169) that the implications of the phenomenon were to a large extent contained whilst it was associated with planarian worms. Before the experiments in higher organisms, such as the rat, most of the scientists concerned with worm running were psychologists and zoologists, and the arguments of critics were directed not so much against the notion of memory transfer itself, but the issue of whether the planarians could be said to have accomplished true learning, rather than some 'non-learning' phenomenon such as pseudo-conditioning or sensitisation. This issue related directly to the technical and conceptual competences of behavioural psychologists, for example. The reason behind the lack of criticism (by later standards) of the implied theory of a molecular memory mechanism has much to do with its *disjunction* from their main disciplinary interests. Some indeed were happy with a basically 'black box' approach of the kind associated with B. F. Skinner. What might be inside the black box of the brain was not of immediate consequence for their disciplinary practice. Others, (McConnell for example) were concerned to put a mechanism inside the black box, a practice for which there is also a time-honoured tradition in physiological psychology. (The postulation of neural mechanisms that might account for learning – which has been called 'carefree neurologising' – should not be seen as contradicting my point about the disjunction of this concern from the mainstream of psychology. It is just that the scientific culture is relatively open on this point.) Though there was *individual* commitment to particular models and mechanisms of brain function, at a *disciplinary* level there was no uniform consensus except in the most general terms. It was *then* an open – and by later standards widely ignored – question as to whether the transfer phenomenon was in fact compatible with this general perspective, or anomalous (71).

As far as the group of scientists who concerned themselves with the planarian research were concerned, there was no general disciplinary constraint motivating involvement in the memory mechanism issue in the constitutive forum. However the knowledge that the planarian research apparently *could* have widespread implications for a mechanism of learning and memory helps to account for the *saliency* of the worm running saga.

This is only superficially a paradoxical point. There was a good deal of popular press publicity which dwelt for instance on the associated Lamarkism, and which cited McConnell's speculations about the implications for human learning and memory, including the notion of 'artificial memories'. For many such extrapolation belonged in the realm of science fiction rather than science fact; and this no doubt helped to raise the temperature of the debate. However, the reaction in the formal scientific reports (72) was conducted with legitimated cultural resources. If the results could be shown to be a consequence of non-learning phenomena, or if planarians could not be reliably trained (73), then the basis for extrapolation (flights of fancy) was undercut, and the implications contained. Had the planarian results achieved a greater scientific legitimacy, then some of the implications might have been considered more seriously, as was the case with the mammal experiments. (Though even if learning in planarians had been accepted as demonstrated, it would of course have been open to scientists to find *other* reasons for denying the implications – learning and memory might be 'different' in planarians for instance.)

This background helps, I think, to account for why the implied memory mechanism does not so easily stand out as anomalous, irrespective of whether it was believed or not. To put it another way, the scientific culture within which worm running was located in the early days was such that the umbrella and the sewing machine on the operating table were just a collection of (cognitive) objects which, granted, had no special reason to occupy the same (conceptual) space, but had no special reason *not* to be together, either (74).

5.2. The Mammal Experiments and the Extrapolation of Implications

The experiments with mammals such as rats reported in 1965, led to structural and institutional changes in the field that can be related to the interests and technical competences of the scientists who then joined the research area. Many of them were *directly* concerned with the question of memory mechanisms, but few of them had any primary commitment to psychology. To be sure, many had some background or training in psychology, but increasingly this was in harness with, or secondary to, expertise in biochemistry, pharmacology, or 'neuroscience'. A separate development is that the period from the mid-1960's to the 1970's marks the creation of a much more integrated approach to the study of brain function, and the creation of what some have called 'molecular neurobiology' (75). These features were visible in the transfer research. Reviewing the field in 1971 Bryant and Petty commented that:

by 1969, among transfer-related publications for which we could determine disciplinary affiliation, only 2 of 16 were by psychologists, the rest were by biochemists, physiologists, and pharmacologists. (76)

Thus the disciplinary background against which the mammal transfer experiments were judged was different to that of the disputes over the planarian research in the early 1960's.

I will now examine two further aspects of the context of the research and the possibilities of extrapolation. Firstly, when the planarian research began, events such as the Watson and Crick papers on the structure of DNA and the coding possibilities of macromolecules were well off-stage. By 1965 the spectacular rise of molecular biology in breaking the genetic code was taken to hold enormous promise as a model for a new endeavour: cracking the brain's memory code. The atmosphere is captured by Bonner in his Presidential Address to the Pacific Division of the American Association for the Advancement of Science:

And so, brain biology is the next great challenge – the challenge to break the brain code. It will be an enormous task, but it is already clear that it can be accomplished. (77)

He also noted:

It has of course been suggested that information stored in memory is stored in the form of new RNA molecules which then contain the [experiential] data written out in RNA language. *No thought is so fantastic that the molecular biologist should not try thinking it for a while.* (78)

Bonner goes on to doubt that memory molecules exist, suggesting his own scheme. The point however is that visions of a new heroic age and funda-mental novelty were not confined to the transfer field by any means. Rather, they are part of the background against which it operated, and of relevance to its reception. On this account one might expect that the transfer phenomenon would be *readily* received — it seems to have a good 'fit' with the conceptual structure and great expectations I have outlined, at least *prima facie*. As evidence for this fit, some scientists, though critical of the experiments in the field, maintain that the idea of a molecular memory code is a reasonable, logical extension of the genetic code, deserving of serious attention. More often these days however the transfer notion is held up as a kind of *reductio ad absurdum* of the idea of molecular memory code. After Kuhn, we are familiar with the notion that the 'same' data may be seen in radically different ways, and here we have a related case (79).

The *possibility* of these divergent attributions can be seen in the second piece of context. Consider the relationships between the various theories of molecular memory mechanism described by Bogoch:

perhaps in no other scientific endeavour have so many propositions managed to appear so lacking in conflict with each other. (80)

The transfer phenomenon and its associated theoretical implications were injected into this scientific culture of 'free floating' theories. Expectations were high, but they were diffuse. Further, unlike the other notions, the transfer phenomenon was seen to have experimental consequences that were directly testable. It held the promise of an exemplar (81) on which future research *could* be based. But of more importance for present purposes, the model channelled speculations towards the implications of the notion of transferrability. A number of consequences that *can now be seen* as implicit in molecular memory mechanisms were raised in a pointed form, and these implications ran far beyond expectations. Rose, writing in the *New Scientist* noted that Jacobson's experiment (one of the first four mammal studies) was "at first sight unbelievable". Later in the same article he argued that:

it would not only mean that specific RNA coding molecules existed, but that they had an identical interpretation not only in the brains of individual animals of the same species, but *across species* as well, i.e. that a learning response always and inevitably produces a defined and unique RNA molecule with one and only one specific interpretation. The prospect of students cannibalising their teachers' RNA would suddenly become debatable. Equally, many people might have second thoughts about the virtues, of including, say, grilled beef brain, on their menu. (82)

Some took the phenomenon to imply a universal coding scheme, as if the putative transfer molecules were the physical representations of Platonic Ideal Forms. To have certain kinds of memories would be to have certain kinds of molecules in the brain. When questioned on this point many scientists were non-commital about such 'philosophical' issues, but were not unhappy, and in some cases positively agreeable with my suggestions that the transfer phenomenon could be seen as implying a molecular representation of some kind of Chomskian deep structure.

Whichever way one looks at the results they were surprising. Bonner (above) notes that cracking the brain's memory code would be an enormous task. Memory transfer arrived almost as he was speaking. Bonner called the RNA-as-memory-molecule idea 'fantastic' just as a group of scientists were proclaiming that the revolution was not only at hand, but all over bar the shouting! As I see it, diffuse expectations were un-expectedly given the possibility of concrete content, allowing extrapolation which, in some, could induce a kind of intellectual vertigo.

But this is only one view. There were, as always in science, plenty of available cultural resources with which to deny the implications, or alternatively, to recast them as reasonable. It *could* be argued that the phenomenon was false, not reproducible, non-specific, applied only to certain simple or primitive kinds of behaviour, or that the radical disjunction between cognitive (brain) and emotional (hormonal) phenomena was misplaced. Alternatively, on the grounds of *parsimony* (always a good device), one would *expect* Nature to use the same or a similar memory code in different species. And *why not* molecular 'deep structures'?

It is apparent from interviews and the literature that, while some scientists saw memory transfer as scientific creativity, others regarded it as an absurdity. There was, however, an acceptance that the phenomenon represented a 'logical' extension of informational coding themes in molecular biology. Proponents saw the inferences as perfectly reasonable. Some critics agreed, seeing it as reasonable but mistaken. For others the logic was of a twisted kind. "A sadist is a person who is kind to a masochist" captures it nicely (83).

Should memory transfer be taken to be a chimerical monster, or a new natural kind? Science is about creating the impossible, and after the surprise had faded, and the incongruity had collapsed into laughter, various groups began work on the further construction and deconstruction (84) of memory transfer. Incongruity was replaced by ambivalence, and rest was renegotiation.

6. Concluding Comments

In this paper I have sought to show how a certain structure of ambiguity grew up with the planarian transfer experiments. McConnell's violations of certain tacit rules for doing science reciprocally amplified the perceived incongruity of the transfer phenomenon, so structuring the initial reception of the mammal studies. The violations should also be seen as part of McConnell's heterodox personal approach to science, and that should not be under-valued. In Popperian terms for example, the bold and falsifiable hypotheses of memory transfer were the epitome of good science (85).

Two further sets of comments are in order: one on the notion of memory transfer, and the other on the role I have assigned to McConnell.

Firstly, I have shown in Section 5 above why the idea of memory transfer was anomalous for those concerned with memory mechanisms, and why it was not nearly so anomalous *in terms of disciplinary interests and competences* for psychologists in the worm running controversy. But most people − scientists or not − hearing of the experiments for the first time, react with humour and surprise. This is a kind of baseline to which the scientific reactions should be related.

It seems that in our culture the phenomenon is just odd. Why this should be so is, strictly, beyond the scope of this paper, but it is no doubt due in part to the fact that 'everybody knows' that memory is about impulses in an organised structure of nerve cells in the brain. We also 'know' that our memories are unique (86). In a comment on this paper Krohn has noted that the conceptual violations implied by memory transfer compare with those of Darwin's evolution/natural selection model and the discovery of animal to man disease contagion. However, much more analysis would be required to properly ground these suggestions.

To turn now to McConnell, I have described his actions as having been influential in producing a structure of ambiguity where radically divergent definitions of the situation were possible. But that is not the same thing as saying that he caused the rejection of memory transfer. Science is far more subtle than that! If the worm running saga had been played 'straight', the mammal experiments would still have produced some surprise, and even shock. No doubt there would also have been a certain amount of humour associated with the reaction (this would be expected on Koestler's analysis), but this would probably have been seen as *epi*phenomenal. What McConnell did was to attach the epiphenomenal social factor to the idea of memory transfer in a thorough-going way, and it took some time to cleave the two apart again. Indeed, the separation was never complete, and for a considerable time the atmosphere of 'not being in earnest' was available as a satirical resource for those wishing to attack the field.

What can be said is that without the comic connection, the open-ness at scientific forums, and the implicit Lamarkism; and perhaps with a more neutral term like 'transfer of response bias', the reaction would have been considerably muted. One set of resources in the rhetoric of rejection would have been denied, though others were available. That is, the ambivalence was certainly a significant factor in the rejection of memory transfer – but it was not a sufficient condition.

In examining this series of events I have attempted to remain neutral about the 'reality' of the phenomenon. Naturally, I find it unexceptionable that rational actors should hold widely divergent views. I do not want to devalue the reactions of scientists on either side of the controversy. None of them treated it as *just* a joke. Indeed there was a serious intent behind the humour. As McConnell put it:

today, Science stands fair to join Religion, Motherhood, and the Flag as a domain so sacrosanct and sanctimonious, that leg-pulling isn't allowed, levity is forbidden, and smiling is scowled at. (87)

... now perhaps you see the *Digest* for what it really is: the house organ of an anti-Scientific movement ... only when we learn to laugh at ourselves can we proceed to slaughter all those Sacred Cows and turn Science back into science. (88)

Postscript

In a long and interesting response to this paper Professor McConnell agreed with most of the points made, and emphasised the bitterness of the reactions among psychologists, to the worm running experiments, and among other scientists, to the later research on mammals.

Having been shocked to the core by responses such as those given me by Nobel Laureates, I'm sure I defended my ego by resorting to humour. Part of my wit was bitter attack. Part of it – mostly the self-deprecating type – was little more than the same 'submission" response that a young wolf shows to the pack leader when he bares his throat before the leader's teeth. I became a court jester in self-defence. (89)

In personal, psychological, terms the humour was more of an *effect* of the reception of memory transfer than a *cause*. McConnell also noted that "the humorous approach of the *Digest*, while it caused unease, did at least let us barely survive while the research went on" (90).

McConnell's reading of the bitterness of the reaction to worm running conforms to mine, and I find his personal (psychological) account both compatible with the sociological account given in this paper, and with the logic of his situation. To go any further one would need a biography to show why he reacted in terms of humour rather than in other ways, and that is beyond my compass. His comments are however a poignant reminder to the sociologist that there is always more that can be said.

Acknowledgements

It is a pleasure to offer thanks to Harry Collins, Peter Glasner and Trevor Pinch for their comments, and to the scientists who spared the time to talk to me. As is obvious, I owe a special debt of gratitude to Professor James V. McConnell of the University of Michigan.

Notes and References

1. The research reported is part of a case study carried out whilst a graduate student at the University of Bath. G. D. L. Travis, *The Sociology of 'Memory Transfer'*, Ph. D. thesis forthcoming.

   I had assumed that I had constructed this title directly from available cultural resources, but must have been unconsciously influenced by A. Koestler, *The Act of Creation*, Pan Books, London, 1969. Koestler stresses 'The Importance of not Being Earnest' (pp. 63–64) in freeing man from the rails of instinct.
2. 'Memory transfer' is the popular label for the field, but some proponents have

sought to suppress it in favour of more neutral terms such as 'transfer of behavioural bias'. The phenomenon has been rejected, but not 'disproved' of course. Even the strongest critics were virtually unanimous in their belief that the phenomenon did not exist, *and* that they could not prove the point.

3. G. Chedd, 'Scotophobin – memory molecule or myth?', *New Scientist*, 240–241 (August 1972).

4. A readable account of this and other experiments is to be found in J. V. McConnell, 'The Biochemistry of Learning', *Das Medizinische Prisma* 3, 1–22 (1968).

5. According to Hebb's theory that learning is a matter of reshuffing the connections between neurons. See McConnell, *op. cit.*, 1968, Note 4; D. O. Hebb, *The Organisation of Behaviour*, Wiley, New York, 1949.

6. R. Thompson and J. V. McConnell, 'Classical Conditioning in the Planarian, *Dugesia dorotocephala*', *Journal of Comparative and Physiological Psychology* 48 (1), 65–68 (1955).

7. D. L. Krantz, 'The Separate Worlds of Operant and Non-Operant Psychology', *Journal of Applied Behaviour Analysis* 4, 61–70 (1971).

8. J. Blundell, *Physiological Psychology*, Methuen and Company, London, 1975, p. 34.

9. The number of trials required to reach a given performance criterion is compared with the (greater) number required by regenerates of untrained worm. The differences is taken to be a measure of learning. Other control groups would normally be included in the experiment.

10. J. V. McConnell, R. Jacobson and D. P. Kimble, 'The Effects of Regeneration upon Retention of a Conditioned Response in the Planarian', *Journal of Comparative and Physiological Psychology* 52, 1–5 (1959).

11. J. V. McConnell, 'Memory transfer through cannibalism in Planarians', *Journal of Neuropsychiatry* 3 (Suppl. 1), 42–48 (1962).

12. Priority did not become a *public issue*. The publication, and more importantly, the acceptance dates are quite clear, but in interviews there was discussion about the real *quality* of the research reported, the differential *visibility* of the claims, and the fact that the results in one paper had been read at a conference in 1964. See R. K. Merton, 'Priorities in Scientific Discovery', *American Sociological Review* XXII, 635–59 (1957); 'Singletons and Multiples in Scientific Discovery', *Proceedings of the American Philosophical Society* 105, 470–86 (1961).

13. They were F. R. Babich, A. L. Jacobson, S. Bubach and A. Jacobson, 'Transfer of a response to naive rats by injection of ribonucleic acid extracted from trained rats,' *Science* 149, 656–7 (1965); E. J. Fjerdingstad, T. Nissen and H. H. Roigaard-Petersen, 'Effect of ribonucleic acid (RNA) extracted from the brain of trained animals on learning in rats', *Scandinavian Journal of Psychology* 6, 1–6 (1965); S. Reinis, 'The formation of conditioned reflexes in rats after parenteral administration of brain homogenate', *Activitas Nervosa Superior* 7, 167–68 (1965); G. Ungar and C. Ocegura-Navarro, 'Transfer of habituation by material extracted from brain', *Nature* 207, 301–2 (1965). Ungar and Oceguera-Navarro used rats as donors and mice as recipients; the others used rats only. (Later experiments involved other inter-species transfers.) As the above titles indicate, the transfer experiments in vertebrates were accomplished by injecting a recipient with a homogenate or solution of brain taken from a trained animal.

14. A sociological perspective on replication, especially in controversial areas of science, is to be found in H. M. Collins 'The Seven Sexes: A Study in the Sociology of a Phenomenon, or the Replication of Experiments in Physics', *Sociology* **9** (2), 205–224 (1975). An extension of that perspective to the memory transfer phenomenon is to be found in G. D. L. Travis 'Replicating Replication? The Case of Memory Transfer', to be published in *Social Studies of Science*.

15. The information is taken from J. A. Dyal, 'Transfer of behavioural bias: reality and specificity', in E. J. Fjerdingstad (ed.), *Chemical Transfer of Learned Information*. North-Holland, Amsterdam, 1971, pp. 219–264. The memory transfer field is an almost legendary case of problems over replication. See I. St. James-Roberts, 'Are researchers trustworthy?', *New Scientist*, 481–3 (2nd September 1976).

16. G. Ungar, D. M. Desiderio and W. Parr, 'Isolation, identification and synthesis of a specific-behaviour-inducing brain peptide', *Nature* **238**, 198–202 (1972).

17. See for example G. Ungar, 'Peptides and Behaviour', in C. Pfeffer and J. R. Smythies (eds.), *International Review of Neurobiology*, Vol. 17. Academic Press, New York, 1975, which discusses some of the other behaviour-inducing peptides. H. N. Guttman and J. R. Cooper, 'Oligopeptide control of step-down avoidance', *Life Science* **16**, 914–24 (1975) makes the claim to have isolated a further peptide 'Catabathmophobin'. Some of the conclusions of Ungar *et al., op. cit.*, 1972, Note 14, are disputed in H. N. Guttman, B. Weinstein, R. M. Bartschott and P. S. Tam, 'Reputed rat scotophobin prepared by a solid-phase procedure shown invalid by comparison with a product derived from a classical synthesis on the basis of physical and biological properties', *Experientia* **31**, 285–90 (1975).

18. For a discussion of tacit knowledge see M. Polanyi, *Personal Knowledge : Towards a Post Critical Philosophy*, Harper and Row, London, 1958. J. R. Ravetz, *'Scientific Knowledge and its Social Problems*, Penguin Books, Harmondsworth, 1973, contains a discussion of the related notion of 'craft knowledge'. See also H. M. Collins, *op. cit.*, 1975. Note 14, and 'The TEA Set: Tacit Knowledge and Scientific Networks', *Science Studies* **4**, 165–86 (1974).

19. The notion of cannibalism carries its own unsettling connotations of course.

20. Feeding a homogenate of 'trained brain' to mammals would not work since digestive enzymes would break down the molecules thought to be involved. The planarian digestive system does not break down food in this way before taking it up. It was thought possible at one time that viable 'trained' cells were incorporated into the recipient worm – more of a transplant than a transfer.

21. Some of the factors relevant to the initial containment and subsequent 'explosion' are dealt with in Section 5 below.

22. There is an extended discussion of monsters and monster barring techniques in mathematics in I. Lakatos, *Proofs and Refutations. The Logic of Mathematical Discovery*, Cambridge University Press, Cambridge, 1976.

23. I should make it clear that the 'memory transfer' field is quite distinct from the biological speciality which studies chimeras or 'genetic mosaics'.

24. In using the notions of conceptual space I am not implying a picture of pre-existing finite space waiting to be 'filled', a point made against Mulkay by Law and Barnes. I assume the geometry of conceptual space is distinctly non-Euclidian and created by the actors involved! See M. J. Mulkay, 'Three Models of Scientific Development', *Sociological Review* **23**, 509–26 (1975); J. Law and B. Barnes, 'Research Note:

Areas of Ignorance in Normal Science: A Note on Mulkay's 'Three Models of Scientific Development'', *Sociological Review* **24**, 115–24 (1976); M. J. Mulkay, 'The Model of Branching', *Sociological Review* **24** 125–33 (1976).

25. This famous image of the Comte de Lautréamont symbolised the enigmatic linking together of objects which had no previous connections with each other, in order to produce ambiguity, and 'exceptions to the physical and moral order'. This was adopted as a theme by the Surrealists, who also sought to break the distinctions between reason and absurdity, seriousness and humour. See *Lautréamont's 'The Maldoror'*, translated by A. Lykiard, Allison and Busby, London, 1970; S. Gablik, *Magritte*, Thames and Hudson, London, 1977, pp. 45–46. An alternative way of conceptualizing some of the points in this paragraph is through the work of M. C. Escher, particularly the impossible buildings, e.g. 'Ascending and Descending', 1960; 'Waterfall', 1961. Taken separately the parts seem reasonable, but the particular relations Escher produces radically alter the 'meaning', making them 'impossible'. Reproductions of the prints are to be found in, for example, M. C. Escher, *The Graphic Works of M. C. Escher*, Pan Books, London, 1978.

26. M. R. Rosenzweig, 'Discussion'. In S. Bogoch (ed.), *The Future of the Brain Sciences*, Plenum Press, New York, 1969, p. 321. Emphasis added.

27. Interview material, 1976.

28. Interview material, 1976.

29. I am not trying to argue that this was the only possible response, or to suggest that scientists perceived what was going on in terms of umbrellas and sewing machines on operating tables, any more than they perceive major theoretical controversies in terms of ducks and rabbits. However I do claim that this is a valid sociological interpretation, and that the 'happening' involved a confusion of contextual signs relevant to the application of categories such as 'scientific creativity' and 'joke'.

30. A. L. Jacobson, 'Learning in Planarians: Current Status', *Animal Behaviour* (Suppl. 1), 78 (1965).

31. Interview material, 1977.

32. Interview material, 1976.

33. Many results – probably more 'negative' than 'positive' were never published.

34. The notion of structural ambiguity has been developed from the discussions of 'systematic ambiguity' in P. Winch, *The Idea of A Social Science and its Relation to Epistemology*, Routledge and Kegan Paul, London, 1971, pp. 18–33, but also has an affinity with the notion of 'sociological ambivalence' in R. K. Merton and E. Barber, 'Sociological Ambivalence', in E. Tiryakian (ed.), *Social Theory, Value and Sociocultural Change*, Free Press, New York, 1963, pp. 91–120. "*In its most extended sense*, sociological ambivalence refers to incompatible normative expectations of attitudes, beliefs and behaviour assigned to a status or set of statuses in society" (p. 95). From this, the idea of norms and counter-norms is developed. (See also R. K. Merton, *Sociological Ambivalence and Other Essays*, Free Press, New York, 1976, Chaps. 1–3; I. Mitroff, *The Subjective Side of Science*, Elsevier, New York, 1974.) I am not here concerned with the terminology of statuses and roles; and 'polyvalence' rather than the oppositional pairs suggested by 'ambivalence' would, strictly, be more appropriate. Insofar as norms of science are implied in this paper they are treated as part of the 'social rhetoric of science' as in, for example,

M. Mulkay, *Science and the Sociology of Knowledge*, George Allen and Unwin, London, 1979, pp. 21–26, 63–73.

36. A. Koestler, *The Ghost in the Machine*, Pan Books, London, 1967; *The Act of Creation, op. cit.*, 1969, Note 1.

37. Roger Krohn's paper was circulated to participants before the conference. R. Krohn, 'The Social Processes of Scientific Investigation' unpublished paper, McGill University, June 1978.

38. J. R. Ravetz, *op. cit.*, Note 16, pp. 94–191.

39. H. M. Collins and G. Cox, 'Recovering Relativity: Did Prophecy Fail?', *Social Studies of Science* 6, 423–45 (1976).

40. In this paper I have assumed an *interactive* theory of metaphor. See W. H. Leatherdale, *The Role of Analogy, Model and Metaphor in Science*, North Holland, Amsterdam, 1964; D. A. Schon, *The Displacement of Concepts*, Tavistock, London, 1963.

41. S. B. Barnes, *Scientific Knowledge and Sociological Theory*, Routledge and Kegan Paul, London, 1974, p. 86.

42. See M. Foucault, *The Order of Things*, Tavistock, London, 1970, p. xvi for a similar point.

43. A. Koestler, *op. cit.*, 1969, Note 1, p. 88.

44. Since writing this I have come across a paper by E. Wright, 'Sociology and the Irony Model', *Sociology* 12, 523–43 (1978). Wright sees the need for a model of rationality that can handle inconsistency, misunderstanding and 'falsity' as well as consistency, understanding and 'truth' (p. 540, my scarequotes), and discusses the *joke* in terms of ducks and rabbits. Indeed, Wright seems to draw on many cultural resources that are also used in 'relativistic' sociology of science.

45. A. Koestler, *op. cit.*, 1969, Note 1, p. 90.

46. Roughly, the explanation of the known by the still less known.

47. A fuller account is given in J. V. McConnell, 'Worms and Things ... ', *Worm Runner's Digest*, 11(1), 1–4 (1969).

48. The other long running example is the *Journal of Irreproducible Results*; and closer to home there is the *Subterranean Sociology Newsletter*. Further details of these and other journals are to be found in E. Garfield, 'Humour in Scientific Journals and Journals of Scientific Humour', *Current Contents*, 5–21 (20th December 1976). Sadly, the *Worm Runner's Digest* ceased publication in 1979.

49. Interview material, 1976.

50. Interview material, 1976.

51. The relation between the science and the humour – mixed up, or back to back – can be seen as an embodiment of the relation of frames of meaning that Koestler describes. There was a homology between the structure of the idea of memory transfer and the *WRD/JBP*.

52. Though many of the scientists interviewed appreciated some of the humour, few were whole-heartedly enthusiastic about the *WRD/JBP*. On the other hand, B. F. Skinner and Michael Polanyi have been numbered among its supporters, and Arthur Koestler has written "One of the last Palinurian joys of civilised middle age is to sit in front of the log fire, sip a glass of brandy, and read *The Worm Runner's Digest*."

53. Another characteristic of the attempted institutionalisation of a new scientific

area of course. I do not mean to suggest that McConnell was the sole motivator in this institutionalisation. W. L. Byrne, then of Duke University, was especially important in arranging seminars to tackle the replicability problem, and in organising a session at the 1967 AAAS.

54. Escarpit has argued that humour in science is necessary in order to remain intellectually open — it changes the angle of view of reality. R. Escarpit, 'Humorous attitude and scientific inventivity', *Impact of Science on Society* **19** (3), 253–58 (1969). See also Koestler, *op. cit.*, 1969, Note 1.

55. This is not to deny the 'white haired eccentric scientist' and 'schoolboy humour' syndromes in science. Such 'deviations' are in the category of 'honoured exceptions' and not seen as *constitutive* of the science.

56. To the extent that satires failed as good demolition jobs they could bring the journal itself into dispute.

57. McConnell felt that the humour of the Digest was mainly 'gentle'. Reactions among interviewees (about 70) varied, from amusement and approval, through indifference to mild irritation and annoyance. Questioned about the role of the *WRD/JBP* in the controversy many felt that 'it hadn't helped', and McConnell himself was widely seen among critics to have been engaged in 'knocking' the establishment.

58. The inclusion of 'non-scientific' resources and thoughtful counter-points is not, of itself, subversive of the high-minded intentions of science. The journal *Perspectives in Biology and Medicine* for example publishes poetry between serious scientific papers. (The Autumn, 1970, issue contains M. Lipman 'Latent Thumb-Sucking — a New Chimerical Syndrome', pp. 86–97, which the author states "was taken seriously by three psychiatrists and two associate professors of medicine, and one professor of pediatrics. Two medical students laughed heartily.") As a related point, many scientific diagrams are caricatures in the sense of being 'one-sided' exaggerations designed to make a particular point. See S. B. Barnes, 'Science, Ideology and Pictorial Representation' unpublished paper read to the Conference on the Sociology of Science, University of York, September 1975.

59. H. M. Collins and T. J. Pinch, 'The Construction of the Paranormal: Nothing Unscientific is Happening', in R. Wallis (ed.), *On the Margins of Science: The Social Construction of Rejected Knowledge*, The Sociological Review Monograph No. 27, Keele, 1979, pp. 237–70.

60. J. P. Emerson, 'Nothing Unusual is Happening', in T. Shibutani (ed.), *Human Nature and Collective Behaviour*, Prentice-Hall, Englewood Cliffs, 1970, pp. 208–22.

61. *ibid.*, p. 209.

62. *ibid.*, p. 217.

63. G. Ungar, 'Introduction' to *Molecular Mechanisms in Memory and Leaning*, Plenum Press, New York, 1970, p. viii.

64. Interview material, 1976.

65. J. V. McConnell, 'Discussion'. In M. A. B. Brazier (ed.), *Brain Function, Volume 2: RNA and Brain Function, Memory and Learning*, University of California Press, Berkeley, 1964, p. 178.

66. A distinction between contingent and constitutive forums in science is made in Collins and Pinch *op. cit.*, 1979, Note 52.

67. Interview material, 1976.

68. Interview material, 1976.

69. See P. Bourdieu, 'The Specifity of the Scientific Field, and the Social Conditions for the Progress of Reason', *Social Science Information*, 14 (6), 19–47 (1976).

70. Some aspects of the humorous style of McConnell and several of his associates were occasionally visible in their reviews of the field. In reviewing a book containing a number of memory transfer papers, Brindley complained that the papers were "in several cases marred by a strange facetiousness." G. B. Brindley, 'Chemical Mnemology', *Nature* 228, 583 (1970).

71. McConnell (and others) are seen as having been contradicting the orthodox belief that memory is stored in a specific structure of neurons. Ungar's formulation is that the transfer factors (peptides, not RNA) act as signposts or chemical markers within the neural structure and that the phenomena is perfectly compatible with, but an extention of, orthodox views. The relation between these views are explored in G. D. L. Travis, 'Creating Contradiction, or why let things be difficult when with just a little more effort you can make them seem impossible', unpublished paper read to the British Sociological Association, Sociology of Science Study Group, Manchester, February 1978. For the establishment of an anomaly in physics see T. J. Pinch, 'Theoreticians and the Production of Experimental Anomaly: The Case of Solar Neutrinos', this volume.

72. While memory transfer research reports were stylistically fairly 'normal' a proportion of reviews of the field are unusual in adopting a narrative and sometimes anecdotal style. See also Note 70.

73. Bennett and Calvin published a report 'Failure to Train Planarians Reliably' concluding that the animals were [then] of little use in studies of the biochemical bases of learning. This paper is often cited as a 'knock-down of the worm-running experiments, but in interviews I did not find a single scientist who was not prepared to accept that planarians could in some sense be trained. E. L. Bennett and M. Calvin, 'Failure to Train Planarians Reliably', *Neurosciences Research Program Bulletin*, 3–24 (July–August 1964). A more detailed account of the events surrounding this paper is to be found in my paper cited in Note 14 above.

74. This point relates to the analysis to be found in R. Whitley, 'Cognitive and Social institutionalisation of scientific specialities and research areas', in R. Whitley (ed.), *The Social Processes of Scientific Development*, Routledge and Kegan Paul, London, 1974, pp. 69–95.

75. There have been arguments about appropriate titles both in what I have called the transfer field, and in the wider area of the study of the biological (biochemical, neurological, . . . , etc.) bases of learning and memory. Whitley notes this as a general feature of biology. "The difficulty that biologists, in particular have in naming their specialty attests to the ambiguity of cognitive and social structures in this field . . . . . . and may well occur in others." R. Whitley, *op. cit.*, 1974 Note 74, p. 91. See also Note 2 above.

76. R. C. Bryant and N. Petty, 'Field in Transition' [Review of Fjerdingstad 1971, *op. cit.*, Note 15.] *Journal of Biological Psychology* 13 (2) 50–52 (1971).

77. J. Bonner, 'The Next New Biology', reprinted in *Plant Science Bulletin* 11 (3), 1–8 (1965).

78. *ibid.*, p. 6. Emphasis added.

79. A *related* case, because the controversy over the transfer phenomenon does not

easily fit Kuhn's notion of a paradigm clash. See T. S. Kuhn, *The Structure of Scientific Revolutions*, University of Chicago Press, Chicago, 1970.

80. S. Bogoch, *'The Biochemistry of Memory'*, Oxford University Press, New York, 1968, p. 81.
81. See T. S. Kuhn, 1970, *op. cit.,* Note 79.
82. S. P. R. Rose, 'Is Learning Transferable', *New Scientist* 781–83 (16th December 1965).
83. Quoted in Koestler, *op. cit.*, 1969, Note 1, p. 197.
84. An excellent account of this kind of process is to be found in B. Latour and S. Woolgar, *Laboratory Life*, Sage Publications, London, 1979.
85. See K. R. Popper, *The Logic of Scientific Discovery*, Hutchinson, London, 1972. I should say that I do not in general adhere to the Popperian scheme, but I agree with the implication in this case.
86. Whether or not memory transfer contradicts these ideas, or rather scientific refinements of them, is a matter of debate. See Note 71.
87. J. V. McConnell (ed.), *The Worm Re-turns*, Prentice-Hall, New York, 1965.
88. J. V. McConnell, 'Confessions of a Scientific Humorist'. In J. V. McConnell and M. Schutjer (eds.) *Science, Sex and Sacred Cows*, Harcourt Brace Janovich, New York, 1971, pp. 8–9.
89. J. V. McConnell, personal communication, 9th September 1979.
90. *loc. cit.*

PART III

THE RESEARCH PROCESS

STRUGGLES AND NEGOTIATIONS TO DEFINE WHAT IS PROBLEMATIC AND WHAT IS NOT

The Socio-logic of Translation*

MICHEL CALLON

Ecole des Mines de Paris, Centre de Sociologie de l'Innovation

In the space of a few short years the centre of interest in the sociology of sciences has radically shifted. At first timidly, later with increasing boldness, sociologists have penetrated the sanctuary. They no longer confine their interest to a study of how institutions work, or the rules governing competition, or network or community organisation. Increasingly, they are investigating the content of science itself.

Though this change of direction now seems legitimate, and indeed irreversible, it still remains very tentative. Deeply marked by its recent past, the sociology of science still takes for granted the chopped-up, compartmentalised world the scientists are so patiently building up, being ready to distinguish, and even unhesitatingly to place in mutual opposition social factors and technical or cognitive ones (1). Concepts like social contexts of scientific research are still in common use today, proving the continuing vitality of this way of thinking. Within reality territories and domains are divided off, frontiers laid out, a priori factors of different types identified and phases obeying a specific logic enumerated (2).

However, these common distinctions are having increasing difficulty in holding out against sociological ventures. The deeper we delve into content, the more the legitimacy of black boxism seems questionable (3) and the more difficult, hazardous and arbitrary the separation of social from non-social, cognitive from non-cognitive becomes (4). The most solidly-based concepts dissolve, revealing their ambiguity. What does 'reproducing an experiment mean'? (5) What is understood by the expression 'reporting on a research process'? (6) It gradually becomes apparent that social and cognitive are inextricably entwined exactly where unravelling them seemed to present no

197

Karin D. Knorr, Roger Krohn and Richard Whitley (eds.), The Social Process of Scientific Investigation. Sociology of the Sciences, Volume IV, 1980. 197–219.

problems. The protagonists are involved in a never ending struggle to impose their own definitions and to make sure that their view of how reality should be divided up prevails. Consensuses are reached, lasting for longer or shorter periods of time, concealing balances of power. The dividing line between what is considered social and what is considered technical is constantly re-negotiated.

These struggles bedevil every moment of the research process, though they probably have the most important consequences in the very early stages when problems are being identified and the certain marked off from the uncertain. From this point of view, existing interpretations are not really satisfactory, distinguishing as they do on the one hand, identification or emergence of problems (7) on the other hand, recognition of them and their gradual legitimising until various social groups take charge of them (8). However, analysis of the struggles and negotiations pitting social protagonists against each other as they strive to define what is problematic and what is not reveals that distinctions of this type are unrealistic. During these preliminary skirmishes research problems and the groups which will take charge of them are *simultaneously* determined. Social structures and cognitive structures are defined within the same crucible. Though very different, they are both by-products of the same reaction. The study of problematisation is vital for understanding the rules governing the mysterious chemistry, the constantly renewed fusions, which permanently produce the social and the cognitive.

In this article I aim to show the relevance of this point of view, limiting myself to the study of two issues; (a) Description of the mechanisms through which reality is problematised, that is the work of what I propose to call 'forces of problematisation'; (b) analysis of the relationships between various forces of problematisation and the general mechanisms by which problems impose themselves. I shall attempt to answer these questions by describing French work on fuel cells. This research got underway in the late fifties, occupying, for a decade, a large number of research workers and technicians working within the universities, in CNRS (9) laboratories, and in research centres belonging to large firms. The work was financially and politically supported by DGRST and DRME (10). In reconstructing the development of this research, we have had access to the records of the various laboratories involved and to the complete records of the DGRST. In addition we inter-viewed the main protagonists.

An Abundance of Problematisations

The DGRST was founded in France in the late fifties, with the aim of preparing, coordinating and implementing French policy with regard to scientific and technical research. One of its first acts was to set up 'concerted actions' in which laboratories, both private and public, within industry or the University, came together for a limited time to work on top priority programmes. Each 'action' is administered by a scientific committee consisting of about fifteen experts (scientists, industrialists and officials) who take part *intuitu personae* in the work of the committee. The committee selects projects from those submitted and distributes the credits allocated to the work. The procedure used was worked out during the final years of the IVth Republic. In this way public and private research can work together and programmes rejected by traditional institutions (CNRS, universities, industrial enterprises) are more readily financed, thus facilitating coordinated and collective work on subjects that have been given top priority.

In fact, in the early sixties, the CNRS and industry left the scene vacant, the former undermined by academicism, the latter little concerned with research and innovation. The DGRST filled this vacuum. As a result, the main initial beneficiaries of the operation were those scientists whose disciplines had been misunderstood or looked down upon by both the University and the CNRS, who housed them, but gave them no real means for development. The 'concerted action' procedure fitted them like a glove; they were assured of both industrial and political support; likewise they had scope for action in the form of credits, both of which had previously been refused (11).

The above remarks are fully applicable to the research on fuel cells undertaken within the framework of the "energy conversion" concerted action, whose aim was to develop new forms of energy production. There were no industrialists on the committee responsible for pushing the programme through, the scientists intended to call the tune. They imposed their own analysis of the situation, sketched out the problems to be solved and the links between them. They decided how the work was to be divided up and coordinated. Finally they indicated what was at stake at the social, political and economic levels (12).

In the case of fuel cells, problematisation operated in three phases and reveals a wide range of possible analyses.

(1) The committee's first task was to identify interesting fields of research. The general theme of energy conversion provided an initial territory within which priority sectors had to be identified. The first discussion focussed on the definition of what was interesting and what was not. Two physicists, X and Z, were set against each other.

When he was asked to sit on the committee, X was a scientist well known within his own discipline of solid state physics. He had spent a considerable time working in a well known laboratory in the United States. Since his return he had published several articles that attracted considerable attention. At the committee's very first meeting he put forward an analysis of spheres of research that might be of interest. His argument is summarised in Table 1. At the head of each line and column the various forms of energy are indicated; electrical energy, light energy, mechanical energy, thermal and chemical energy. The columns correspond to the initial energy forms, the rows − the final forms. Each division of the table thus represents one possible method of energy conversion, for example, conversion of chemical energy into electrical energy. Each of these divisions is simultaneously and inextricably linked to various phenomena, various effects and a variety of technical devices. Some divisions are partly empty, either the devices do not yet exist, or else the phenomena have not yet been properly identified. Other divisions refer to spheres so huge that an exhaustive inventory is thought unrealistic. We shall return later to the 'logic' (we would call it 'socio-logic') underlying this table. For the moment we shall content ourselves with pointing out how it functions.

First of all the table establishes a perfectly clear frontier between what is analysed and what escapes analysis. The 'edges' of the table demarcate the reality considered relevant. This is a very general phenomenon, the construction of a black box. X has created an inside and an outside, manufacturing a local coherence. He has defined a protected territory, claimed an autonomy.

The table demarcates and defines spheres of research on the basis of categories considered obvious and quite distinct. If the table possesses its own coherence, which enables it to define a distinct universe, closed in upon itself, this is because it provides a strong framework. The energy forms can be located and demarcated. The concept of energy conversion is not called into question. Using his table, X divides up the ground, defining territories quite separate from each other. Not only does he mark off the different domains, he also

TABLE 1

Final form \ Initial energy form	Electrical	Light	Mechanical	Thermal	Chemical
Electrical	Converters Rectifiers Transformers Oscillators	Photovoltaic Photogalvanic effects	Electric machines wind tidal power currents	Thermoelectric thermo-ionic effects	Fuel cells Ordinary cells Accumulators
Light	Electroluminescence. Discharge in gases	Luminescence	Triboluminescence	Incandescence	Chemoluminescence
Mechanical	Electric machines	Crookes Radiometer ?	Simple machines; Energy storage	Thermal machines	Artificial muscle Propellant
Thermal	Static heat pumps (Peltier effect). Electric heating by arc. Dielectric heating H. F. Plasmas	Solar energy collection	Heat pumps refrigeration	Refrigerators (adsorption) Exchangers	Combustion
Chemical	Electrochemistry	Photosynthesis Radiochemistry	Chemical grafting laminating	Thermochemistry ?	(too huge) ?

shows what work remains to be done. The squares are more or less easy to fill in, more or less enigmatic. Reams have been written about the conversion of thermal energy into mechanical energy, whilst in the square chemical energy → electrical energy there is little to be said. Darkness reigns. Who at that time would have dared to claim that the functioning of fuel cells had been fully investigated? Thus are contrasted the old and the new, the more and the less problematic; fields already explored (thermal machines, electric machines) and fields that call for new investigations (fuel cells, photovoltaic effects . . .).

However, X's is not the only possible problematisation; at the same time another physicist, Z, put forward another one. Z is a product of one of the most renowned French scientific institutions: the *Ecole Normale Supérieure*. Though he is only just starting out on his scientific career, he already has considerable support behind him. He is not yet well known enough to belong to the energy conversion committee, but his reputation is sufficient for him to be allowed to explain his point of view to the scientists and industrialists concerned with fuel cells. A large scale meeting is arranged. In his speech Z lambasts X. His line of argument leads him to radically different conclusions.

Z does not even refer to the general question of energy conversion. At no point does he distinguish different forms of energy. All this is outside his field of analysis. His point of departure is electrocatalysis, that is catalysis of reactions which liberate electrons (oxidoreduction reactions). In this way he defines the sphere within which research should take place. The concept of electrocatalysis cuts short discussion just as effectively as the table proposed by X. Demarcation of this problematic field is based on a set of concepts, theories and elements which are taken for granted. Z makes specific reference to the latest developments in solid state physics, and the tools these provide for the study of electrocatalysis.

Z's problematisation is very much less structured than that of X, but it follows the same logic; a problematic field closed in upon itself, then statement of elements taken for granted and considered certain, which give the field its rigid, autonomous framework. Though Z's presentation of his problematisation remains somewhat vague with regard to details, he is able to show quite clearly how it differs from X's analysis. He considers that electrochemistry will remain in a very weak position until it has managed to extricate itself from the technological approach that is stifling it. For him the theoretical unity of the fuel cell is a myth. Though admitted and consolidated by X's problematisation, this object must be 'de-constructed'. The alternative is clear. The problem is not that of improving catalysis in fuel cells, but rather of working out the laws governing electro-catalysis in general.

(2) The committee accepted X's proposed problematisation. Fuel cells are one of the three themes given top priority. The committee instructs Y to work out a research programme on fuel cells. Y is an electrochemist by training, director of the 'Electrolysis laboratory', which is dependent on the CNRS. After a few weeks work he presents the committee with a document explaining his own problematisation. His analysis is synthesised in a table (Table 2) giving details of the lines research should follow and indicating research centres to be mobilised. How is this table organised?

TABLE 2

Themes	Interests	Research centers	Credits (F)
1. General study of kinetics of reactions to electrodes	. scientific . technical: increasing cell power	CNRS Electrolysis Lab IFP (for hydro-carbons	2 300 000 400 000
2. Study of catalysis of depolarization reactions	technical	CNRS Catalysis center IFP (hydrocarbons) CNRS electrolysis Lab	1 000 000/year
3. Research on electrodes	technical	doubtless industrialists	200 000/year
4. Research on molten electrolytes		Grenoble school	500 000/year
5. Research on internal cell resistance	technical (cell output improvement)	electrolysis Lab	500 000
6. Research on diffusion	Molten, aqueous electrolytes	– ? – CNRS Electrolysis Lab	200 000 100 000
7. Research on special electrolytes	. Semipermeable membranes . solid or immobile electrolytes	?	450 000
8. Technological research	HT cells LT cells	?	1 000 000 500 000

Firstly, the table demarcates a territory for analysis within the area of reality. This territory is firmly delineated by the outlines of a specific object, the fuel cell, and by the theoretical assumptions made about it. Y's problematisation fits perfectly within that of X. The latter had already provided a system of partitions which Y took over as it stood. The fuel cell represents a privileged object in electrochemistry, as viewed by Y. No-one and nothing could undermine this relationship. The cell is contained as a whole within electrochemistry, and vice versa. There is no overlap on either side. The wall around is a perfect fit, it is totally self-sufficient and may not be disturbed in any way.

The table defines themes for research by formulating problems (these are explained at more length in the accompanying notes). Y draws up his balance sheet, using his own organisation and formulation of problems. He draws a demarcation line between what, in his view, is known of how a cell works, and what is not known. What strikes the observer forcibly is how the fuel cell's architecture, the different elements that make it up, and the phenomena within it, all correspond closely to the aims and themes for study. There are the electrodes, the electrolyte, the catalyst. There is reference to knowledge that was widely accepted and used at that time in France by those calling themselves electrochemists (diffusion, internal resistance, depolarisation, kinetics . . .). A whole set of concepts, proposals, ways of thinking, methods of giving proof are called into play to isolate and define the darker corners of how a cell works. The areas of ignorance appear against a background of certainty, admitted knowledge and systems of interpretation (13).

We might note in passing, since this helps to explain the nature of the opposition between X and Z, that one of the most important results of this type of problematisation is the place given to catalysis. Y states that catalysis is merely a technical problem, therefore of secondary importance (Y is a fundamentalist). This is in strong contrast with Z's position. For Y the problem of catalysis will be solved as soon as the problems of kinetics, transport of reagents and optimal structure of electrodes have been elucidated. Z states precisely the opposite.

(3) The research programme proposed by Y was adopted exactly as it stood. Since a concerted action was involved he divided up the work between the various research centres, both private and public, which he thought were likely to be interested. Thus he proposed to entrust to his own laboratory

(Electrolysis laboratory) several themes of research, in particular the study of catalysis of depolarisation reactions. When the committee accepted his proposal *Y* recruited two researchers, *A* and *B*, whom he incorporated into his laboratory, entrusting the research to them. Thus *A* and *B* in their turn launched into problematisation.

Let us now leave aside what happened in the other research centres and concentrate on *Y*'s laboratory, particularly on his two researchers.

A, who is a metallurgist by training, follows straight on from *X* and *Y*'s problematisations. The technical structure of the cell is for him the furthest limit of all investigation; this is a reified object which researchers must accept. Problems must be formulated and solved within the space occupied by the electrodes, a double layer and the electrolytes, a space organised around intangible elements, whether the material components of the cell, or the concepts, laws and experimental devices which serve to decipher its workings (Tafel's law, Nernst's law, adsorption, kinetics of reactions . . .)

The problematisation *A* puts forward concerns the texture of the electrode (the reference to metallurgy is obvious), that is, the spatial distribution of pores, the distribution and forms of crystallisation of the catalysts, the path followed by the electrolyte moving towards the fuel. *A* is only interested in the electrode and the double layer surrounding it. His problematisation shows the same features as those of *X* and *Y*: (a) It gives an exact definition of the relevant field (here the electrode), and rejects the rest, to remain unexplored. As one moves away from the double layer − the fringe of electrons which surround the electrode and feed it − the shadows gradually darken and finally become impenetrable. (b) The electrode itself is seen as a system for linking up elements which are not problematised (fuel, catalyst, electrons snatched from the electrolyte . . .) During a first phase, all that is open to variation, is the spatial organisation of these elements, that is, the relationships between them.

B, on the other hand, gradually turns against *Y*'s system of division and finally arrives at a radically different problematisation from that of *A*. Taking his inspiration from *Z*, he works towards a problematisation that emphasises the problem of catalysis within an electric field (electrocatalysis). He favours recourse to concepts and methods from solid state physics. The fuel cell is no longer the inevitable point of reference. The aim is no longer to solve the problem of catalysis as defined and delineated by *Y*. *B* builds up the enquiry in another way. There is no question of electrodes and their texture, nor of diffusion of reagents. The problem posed by B is the behaviour of a hydrogen atom on a metallic surface. Under what conditions and by what mechanisms are the electrons liberated? At one stroke another world appears, other frontiers are carved out. B forces back into the shadows objects and questions which were to have peopled his sphere. He reintroduces quite other certainties, takes other facts for granted, borrows other instruments from solid state physics, quantum mechanics, nuclear magnetic resonance . . .

All these problematisations come to life, they complete each other, expose each other, join together, separate, and they all share an identical structure. In what follows I clarify just what that structure is.

General Structure of Problematisations

The various problematisations that have just been evoked employ a dual mechanism.

First of all an initial frontier is traced between what is analysed and what is not, between what is considered relevant and what is suppressed, kept silent. The problematisation carves out a territory which it then cuts off from the outside, forming a closed domain with its own coherence and logic. Through this type of operation private 'hunting grounds' are created. A division is suggested between what will be the property of scientists and what will be left for outsiders. Looked at from outside, this mechanism is no different from that leading to the setting up of a black box.

Next, a second frontier is traced between what is intangible, taken for granted, and what is problematised or unknown. In other words, in order to formulate problems and mark off zones of ignorance, protagonists necessarily take as their basic concepts, systems of interpretation and reasoning which are then given the force of certainties and thus totally escape suspicion. Problematisation does not necessarily attack previously fabricated knowledge, or established theoretical systems (14). On the contrary, problematisation must of necessity rest on elements of reality (concepts, proposals, matchings up, results . . .) which are considered irrefutable and firmly established. A protagonist never places himself completely on the side of order, nor on the side of disorder. Disorder only forms against a background of order and certainties. The latter form specific configurations which involve systems of lacunae, in their interstices lodge pockets of problematisations. Thus problematisation must also be described as a process of certification and of objectification. Conversely, to objectify involves making choices, imposing associations, deductions and, consequently leaving empty spaces, laying aside questions without a reply. The construction of reality functions like Carnot's heat cycle; using a hot source (problems) and a cold source (acquired knowledge). If one of the sources disappears, production is interrupted. Hence Figure 1.

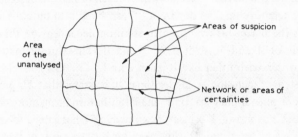

Fig. 1.

Before going any further with our analysis of the process of problematisation, let us stop for a moment and look at a few results of the type of analysis chosen.

Problematisation culminates in configurations characterised by their relative singularity. There is not *one* single way of defining problems, identifying and organising what is certain, repressing what cannot be analysed. Witness the different paths followed at the same time by X and Z, or by A and B. In this case the configurations are in opposition with each other. However, there is plenty of variety within each of these main options. Though there may be strong similarities (which enable problematisations to be grouped together) there are always differences, however slight. Each protagonist organises and problematises reality in his own original manner in keeping with his own idiosyncracies, his own background and the particular conditions in which he finds himself (15). Henceforth we shall no longer make a distinction between an actor and his problematisation. Identifying a problematisation postulates the existence of an actor.

As the cases of X, Y and A show, hierarchical relationships often exist between problematisations. Hence the idea of a *degree* of generality of a problematisation. When X proposes a demarcation of zones of research, he defines several themes which are independent one of another: photovoltaic cells, fuel cells . . . Each of these themes build up and closes around itself a specific reality which defines an area of research. The functioning of the fuel cell, which is considered problematic, must be studied as such. A statement of this type, however decisively expressed, is in no way irrefutable, proof being Z's opposition. X puts forward hypotheses, the result is not a foregone conclusion. He has his first success when Y develops his own problematisations within the territory marked out by X. Y can be said to have set up house in X's rooms (he makes his own problematisation dependent on that of X). As this is true of X and Y, so it is of Y and A. These problematisations are enclosed within each other like Russian dolls $(A \subset Y \subset X)$. Precisely because of this system of inclusion, it can legitimately be stated that X's problematisation is more general than that of Y, the latter in turn being more general than that of A. X has shown Y a black box in which Y has agreed to shut himself (the same is true for Y and A). However, this is not a result of the 'quality' of the problematisations involved. The degree of generality only indicates the extent in which the particular problematisation has been accepted as a basis for further work. It is inseparable from the balance of power set up. Y agrees to occupy the place X has prepared for him. A is equally docile with regard to Y.

The chain of inclusions could be continued in both directions. X has not called into question the general theme of energy conversion. On the contrary, his problematisation has helped to consolidate it. A has appointed assistants, technicians to whom he sub-contracts part of the operation. In theory the chain is unending. By these closing mechanisms, by allocating positions, by constructing black boxes, the chain simultaneously relates and distinguishes scientific policy and specialised research. This remark leads me to emphasise the general nature of the problematisation process. It indiscriminately affects areas which are normally considered to be scientific, technical and economic, and it actively participates in setting up these categories. X establishes close links between machines and scientific phenomena. (Thus he links the destinies of the fuel cell with those of electrochemistry). For Z the intimate interdependance of science and technology must be called into question. Thus every problematisation works out on its own account what is internal and what is external, what is scientific and what is technical, the links which should exist between the two, etc . . .

These final remarks raise new questions. How is it possible for problematisations, though different from each other, to form connexions with one another? A reply to this question will be found in a description of the special logic which problematisation obeys.

Problematic Situations and the Socio-logic of Translation

Each problematisation process results in the formation of what I propose to call a problematic situation. A characteristic feature of this situation is the specific demarcation it creates between three fields or areas: the un-analysed area, the area or network of certainties, and the area of suspicion (see Figure 1). Problems are identified and rendered autonomous; established facts are stated; links are postulated; whole sections of reality are pushed back into the shadows. The problematic situation is thus a dual process of construction and de-construction. Forms are created, outlined, recombined, questions posed. If we look at the situation from this point of view, we can legitimately call it the expression of a balance of forces. The origin and nature of the forces are of small importance. The study of their effects is sufficient: on the one hand, certainties are combined and stated, on the other hand, suspicions and queries are formulated. But how is this balance of forces created? How can we describe the work of construction/deconstruction, identification and shaping into form?

Let us first of all turn to the centre of the process, the area of suspicion. For that we must return to Y and his problematisation, as its general outline is represented in Figure 1. In the research programme that he put before the committee Y not only outlined the main problems that needed to be solved, but he also suggested which research centres might take charge of them (column 3). In addition he gave estimates of the funds that might be allocated to each theme. Thus his table has a dual message. Firstly, the one we have looked at so far which brings out the problems and the links between them. Secondly, he shows the relationships between the protagonists as well as the relationships between the problems. In fact each of the eight study areas chosen by Y is associated with interests and potential actors. We must stress that these are only proposals. Y is not certain he will be able to impose his problematisation. However, the important point is that for Y the social and the cognitive, the problems and the actors are arranged within the same structure. To each of his problems corresponds a place and a position attributed to an actor. The actor may be named, or his identity remain unknown. Moreover, the relationships between the protagonists and their positions are clearly identified through the relationships postulated between the problems. Thus, properly speaking, the cell exists in two ways: one we might call techno-scientific, the other social, for it is not distinct from the social group approached to carry out its elaboration and production. Problem definition, as practised by Y, is a highly strategic activity, aiming as it does to interest varied groups in an enterprise whose development as a whole they will not be able to control.

In what we have called the area of suspicion, which forms the heart of the problematic situation, there is no divergence between organisation of the social field and that of the cognitive field. Definitions of problems and the links between them cannot be distinguished from the work of organising fields of interests to be aggregated – witness the question marks that figure in some squares of the table. Definition of a problem implies definition of a group, even if no empirical unity can be named. Y gives shape to the social, he builds a field of positions.

We can go further. The list of problems as suggested by Y cannot be *deduced* from the state of scientific and technical knowledge (Z's active criticism provides proof of this). *It translates a determination to incorporate interests*, and to interest those who are still only potential partners. In fact Y's programme represents an attempt to mobilise social groups. I propose to call this particular logic by which problems are directly associated with groups; the socio-logic of translation (16).

Why this expression? To justify its use I need only analyse the mechanism at work. What Y is saying can be summed up thus: "I define a series of problems P1, P2, P3 ... P8 and assign them to groups G1, G2 G3 ... G8 (see Table 2). I state that a sequential solution of these problems would lead to solutions of the problem posed by X, that is how to build up and acquire scientific and technical mastery of fuel cells".

Definitions of P1, P2, P3 ... and statements of their interdependence follow a *socio-logic*. In fact to state that P1, P2, P3 ... are "logically" linked (by the problematic unity of the cell) is to state that a community of interests exists between G1, G2, G3 ... This puts forward the hypothesis that G1 will take charge of P1, G2 will take charge of P2, and that G1, G2 ... will accept the idea that a relationship exists between P1, P2 ... , that is to say that social intereaction between them is conceivable. In short, *Y* constructs a system of social interactions. We do not find on the one hand social actors, on the other knowledge. There is joint, programmatic organisation of both knowledge and of social actors. Hence the idea of a *socio-logic*.

The statement that P1, P2, P3 ... can stand in relationship postulates: (a) that a set of related significations exist for problems formulated within different territories, and (b) that the solution to a problem (mastery of fuel cell functioning) can be achieved through a series of displacements of problems. The word 'translation' corresponds precisely with these two meanings. Considered from a very general point of view, this notion postulates the existence of a single field of significations, concerns and interests, the expression of a shared desire to arrive at the same result. Though translation recognises the existence of divergences and differences that cannot be smoothed out, it nevertheless affirms the underlying unity between elements distinct from one another. Translation involves creating convergences and homologies by relating things that were previously different. In the more limited case we are examining, translation first of all assures that intelligible connexions exist between questions concerning, for example, diffusion in electrolytes, kinetics of reactions in electrodes and performance of the cell (measured by available potential and intensity of current). Proposals, results and appreciations can be converted from one to another so as to become comparable. For example, a particular modification in electrode structure and the distribution of the catalyst will react upon the operation of diffusion, the latter in turn will modify the kinetics of the oxidoreduction reactions; the result will be a variation in the intensity of current with consequences for commercial implications. Translations like these are never a foregone conclusion. They are formulated as hypotheses which will be judged convincing or otherwise, (*B*, unlike *A*, is not convinced) (17). However, simultaneously, and this is its second significance, translation emphasises the interdependence of problems. Solution of a problem depends on the prior solution of a whole series of other problems (to improve kinetics implies previously improving diffusion; achieving control of an outlet involves agreeing to study the structure of electrodes). Translation asserts the necessity for some detours, and indicates the required changes of route. The concept of the socio-logic of translation stresses that these conversions, and changes of route, are valid simultaneously for the problems and the actors. The problematic zone (or area of suspicion) is a zone of *fusion* where the cognitive and social mingle in the same logic.

The area of certainties is organised according to the principle of *fission* (not fusion). It includes and connects elements on which it confers a status of certainty. We must add, and this is fundamental, that it creates simultaneously clear distinctions between, for example, technology, science and the social. Let us return to Y. The notes that accompany his table enable one to re-construct social, technical, scientific and political reality. We find the DGRST and its policy, the budget allocated to the energy conversion concerted action, CNRS policy with regard to electrochemistry, also the double layer surrounding the electrode, Tafel's law establishing a relationship between tension in the electrodes and the density of current, Nernst's law which links tension and energy of activation. The area of certainty does not only include the cognitive and technical. It is a multiple, differentiated world composed of heterogeneous elements that are stable and identified. Y combines these previously different elements, organising them according to a logic that respects the divergences rather than cancelling them out, that reinforces various certainties and established facts rather than eroding them, and which does not call into question the final integrity of the individual elements. Respect for these elements is the price that has to be paid in the course of problematisation. Fusion only operates when surrounded by fission. But here again a balance of forces is involved. Everything seems to indicate that Y was unwilling to pay the cost of calling various elements of reality into question. He is not able, or does not wish, to alter the DGRST's policy to 'modalise' Tafel's law. He does not possess the resources to carry out the job of reconstruction. Of course, by thus revealing his lack of power he actively helps to consolidate realities like the DGRST's policy and Tafel's law. These realities have not been enunciated once and for all. They only exist as long as the protagonists take them for granted, (perhaps because the latter do not have resources with which to challenge them). Once again, we are faced with a socio-logic — not to call into question Tafel's law or the DGRST's policy means one is not willing to present a challenge. In this case the socio-logic is one of fission which respects and builds up differences and distinctions.

All we need to say here about the structure of the un-analysed is this: its structure resembles that of the unconscious. It represents what is kept silent so that the rest may be stated.

Success or Failure of Problematisation: From Consent to Resistance

We must now describe the process by which a problematic situation succeeds in incorporating interests, that is, to impose its own problematisation.

The committee asked Y to draw up a research programme on fuel cells. He puts forward suggested themes, and says which laboratories he thinks might be responsible for them. So far these are only conjectures. We have seen that underlying them was a will to incorporate interests. In other words, Y will only impose his problematisation if the groups approached agree to take part. Therefore, his success depends on the reactions of G1, G2, G3 . . . and on Y's ability to convince them and persuade them to accept P1, P2, P3 . . .

What is likely to happen? In theory several situations are possible. We may conveniently distinguish five ideal typical responses. The people to whom the problems have been assigned (P1, P2 . . .), providing they agree to play the game at all, can extend their criticisms in two directions; (a) a first subject for discussion is the formulation of the problem allotted to them. Does it fit with their own understanding of the problem? (b) Are they in agreement with the general outline of the suggested problematic situation? This means, do they agree to the sequence P1, P2, P3 . . . , the choice of groups G1, G2, G3 . . . ? Do they consider Y's problem to be unproblematic and vice versa?

TABLE 3

Reactions		Group's appreciation of the problem assigned to it	Group's appreciation of the problematic situation as a whole
Tagging along		+	+
Negotiation	1	−	+
	11	+	−
Opposition		−	−
Inertia		0	0

What is the significance of these various strategies?

Tagging along: The group approached recognises that its interests coincide with the solution of the proposed problem. Moreover, it endorses the socio-logic underlying the problematic situation which is in course of consolidation. This is Y's position in relation to X. He agrees to take charge of the cell theme, acknowledging the field of research to be a highly interesting one for electrochemistry. He does not challenge the intellectual consistency of the problematisation (classification of energy forms, confusion between technical devices and theoretical objects), nor its socio-political consistency (energy conversion is a homogeneous field of research which should be financed by the DGRST rather than the CNRS). A adopts the same strategy with regard to Y. This 'tagging along' attitude is an expression of a balance of forces which ensures, locally and provisionally at least, the total success of the problematisation. Thus it is possible to conceive of problematisations which are deduced one from another, but only so long as it is clearly recognised that deduction is never more than a successful translation.

Negotiation 1: The group approached agrees with everything except with formulation of its own suggested problem so it launches into a limited, detailed negotiation. The context as defined is not called into question; the site (18) assigned is not contested. However, specific alterations are requested. For example, within the laboratory of which Y is the head, some researchers working in collaboration with A slightly alter the way the study entrusted to them is formulated, refining and articulating it. One researcher in particular, instead of investigating the catalysis of the depolarisation reaction, concentrates his attention on the reaction itself and its mechanisms. Thus, he diverges slightly from the originally proposed study.

Negotiation 11: The group approached agrees with nothing at all, except the formulation of the problem assigned to it. In other words, it is ready to launch into the specific research proposed, but it does not intend to fit into the collective enterprise outlined, nor will it accept the suggested socio-cognitive relationships as outlined. Here criticism can operate in several fields. Social: the group approached considers the proposed agglomeration of interests unnatural. Cognitive: it considers the relationships between problems postulated are questionable. This is the opinion of the industrialists Y includes in his research programmes. They agree to the themes suggested, but refuse to cooperate, in the long term condemning the enterprise to failure (19).

Opposition: The group approached challenges the problematic situation as a whole. It actively contests formulation of the problem assigned to it, as it does the whole set of presuppositions underlying the problematisation. Z and B adopt a strategy of this type. B, for example, refuses to concentrate on catalysis of oxido-reduction reactions in fuel cells only. He shifts the question, transforming it into one specific aspect of a more general study in which the fuel cell and DGRST policy do not appear . . .

Because it is the expression of a wish to enlist a variety of groups the problematic situation leads to reactions. Through his problematisation Y invites G1, G2, G3 . . . to join his enterprise. These groups react in turn, each in its own way: A follows, B is in opposition, the industrialists negotiate . . . The translations are successful in varying degrees, the interests are only partially incorporated. The problematisation achieves support, in one place and provokes violent attacks elsewhere. A and B react . . . and this is crucial from a sociological point of view . . . because, despite themselves, they are implicated in Y's problematization. Interaction is possible between Y, A and B because they are placed by Y in his zone of fusion.

Thus, a chain of relationships, a series of shifts, and a sequence of translations are formed which induce consent or provoke resistance in the various groups. X problematises and mobilises Y who follows on. Y problematises in turn and mobilises A who also follows on. A problematises and . . . the sequence could go on for ever. However, quite a different chain of events would have been quite possible: X problematises, Y follows, B is in opposition . . . he builds up another problematic situation and begins to seek support in his turn. His growing success implies Y's failure. A beaten man, Y leaves his post at the head of his laboratory. Let us go on looking at B's career. He widens his empire, extends and imposes his translations. Never again will a problematisation like X's have a chance of success. Very often there are forks in the path, deviations, sometimes reverse reactions, even loops whereby a protagonist can be eliminated. As a result of this never-ending movement in which translations are imposed and then break up, certainties are built up and categories of reality erected. Thus our analysis is contrary to that of J. Dewey

(20) though he used concepts similar to our own. The effect of the actor's action is not to create stability and order. It is to create local instability. With the creation of such instability the possibility of autonomy arises (21).

One last point remains to be made. We have just described strategies which arise as responses to a problematisation. But in what conditions do they appear? Why does Y follow X? Why does B resist? The answer is to be found in the concept of capital though not as this is understood by Bourdieu (22). Concept is not a stock. For example, X's capital is more than his credit social relationships, prestige, and his influential position. He is more than a set of resources. Economists are well aware that identical resources can lead to different strategies, some ending in failure, some in success. Capital cannot be dissociated from the way it is utilised to incorporate interests, seek support, intervene, translate and convince. These valorisation strategies must be studied if the force of a problematisation and its power to enlist support are to be assessed (23).

Conclusion

(1) Using the concept of the problematic situation, with its distinction between zone of fusion and zone of fission, we can go beyond the natural opposition that often operates between the social on the one hand and the cognitive on the other. The analysis of problematic situations, showing how they are organised, throws light on the process by which the limits between the social and the cognitive are constantly re-defined. The zone of fusion is the crucible where practical categories are worked out, whilst in the zone of fission they are consolidated. However, it must be noted, that these cleavages are always linked to a specific problematic situation. In these conditions, surely, concepts like the *social context* must be cast aside. They fail to recognise the reality of problematisation and take for granted what is in fact at stake for the protagonists. To problematise is, among other things, to produce social context both for oneself and for others.

(2) In addition, the concept of the problematic situation makes discussion of the significance of the sociology of content possible, something which is everyone's dream. My view is as follows: It is only possible to discuss content from within a problematic situation, that is, after having defined what is considered problematic and what non-problematic. The sociologist is caught

up in the same situation as the scientist. He cannot avoid answering the question: where do the frontiers lie between what is certain and what is uncertain, between fusion and fission? In talking of content, the sociologist starts out from already existing problematisations. How in these conditions can he differentiate his enterprise from that of the scientist? This is a difficult question, but I think I have the outline of a reply. It is rare, perhaps even impossible, for a problematisation to impose itself without encountering any obstacle. Alongside it and against it, opposition and negotiation strategies spring up, even though they may well be condemned to final failure. The protagonists themselves operate an active, never ending criticism, with the result that a given problematisation is always parasitised by other problematisations (24). To parasitize, as its etymology indicates, means to place oneself alongside, to create a gulf, a difference whilst at the same time maintaining links. It also (in French at least) means to interfere with a message, to distort information. Interference can go on for ever, criticisms and reactions to them form a branching chain which is never broken — unless the parasite devours its host. And this occurs when one problematisation succeeds in destroying that which it was criticising. Sociological analysis must find its accommodation within this series of translations. The sociologist adds one more translation to those produced by the protagonists. He is a parasite living on other parasites. In this respect he is like all other actors. He cannot differentiate his enterprise in principle from that of the scientist. He differs only in that his practical focus of interest is that of translation — the sociologic of parasitisms. He is nourished by the eternally recurring parasitism he studies round about him.

Notes and References

* This research was financed by CORDES.
1. D. O. Edge, and M. J. Mulkay, 'Cognitive, technical and social factors in the growth of Radio Astronomy', *Social Science Information* X11, 25–60 (1973).
2. The classic distinction between scientific research and scientific knowledge as admitted by authors as different as K. R. Popper, *The Logic of Scientific Discovery*, Hutchinson, London, 1959; and G. Holton, *Thematic Origins of Scientific Thought, Kepler to Einstein*, Harvard University Press, Cambridge, Mass., 1973, is the vitable result of atheoretical choice of this type.
3. R. D. Whitley, 'Black-boxism and the sociology of science: a discussion of the major developments in the field', *The Sociological Review Monograph* 18 61–92 (1972).

4. B. Latour, 'Who is agnostic; what could it mean to study science?', *Sociology of Knowledge, Science and Art*, Vol. 3, Kuclick, H. (ed.) (forthcoming)

5. H. M., Collins, 'The Seven Sexes: A Study of the Sociology of a Phenomenon, or Replication of Experiments in Physics', *Sociology* 9, 205–224 (1975).

6. B. Latour, 'Is it possible to (re) construct the research process? Sociology of a brain peptide' (this volume).

7. T. S. Kuhn, *The Structure of Scientific Revolutions*, University of Chicago Press, Chicago, Ill., (1970); K. R. Popper, *Objective Knowledge*, Oxford University Press, 1973.

8. M. J. Mulkay, *The Social Process of Innovation: A Study in the Sociology of Science*, The Macmillan Press, London, 1972; D. Chubin, and K. Studer, 'The Place of Knowledge in Scientific Growth', Paper given at the American Sociological Association meetings, September, 1977. The archetypal opposition is that of K. R. Popper, *The Logic of Scientific Discovery*, Hutchinson, London, 1959; and 1973, *op. cit.* and J. Dewey, *The Quest for Certainty: A Study of the Relation of Knowledge and Action*, Minton, Balch and Co., New York, 1929. The former makes problematisation into a categorical imperative. The latter sees in de-problematisation the expression of an existential requirement (man abhors disorder and attempts to produce stability).

9. CNRS: National Centre for Scientific Research, the largest public research body in France with more than 7,000 researchers with special status, working in laboratories. The CNRS covers all scientific disciplines, being particularly orientated towards fundamental research.

10. DGRST: General Delegation to Scientific and Technical Research, formed in 1958, whose mission is to coordinate research carried out by the different public bodies and to support lines given priority. At the time we are investigating the DGRST wielded great influence within the administration.
    DRME: Direction of Research and Testing Resources, charged with coordination of Research financed by the Army Ministry.

11. R. Gilpin, *France in the Age of the Scientific State*, Princeton University Press, Princeton, 1968; P. Papon, *La Science et le Pouvoir en France*, Editions du Centurion, Paris 1979; K. Pavitt, 'Governmental support for industrial research and development in France: theory and practice,' *Minerva* **XIV**, (3) Autumn, 330–354 (1976).

12. M. Callon, 'De problème en problème: itineraire d'un laboratoire universitaire saisi par l'aventure technologique', CSI-Cordes, 1978.

13. We need only note here that established facts of quantum mechanics are ignored. The knowledge and facts used are those dating from the beginning of the century. The most striking feature is their wide diversity. They belong to the realms of physics, chemistry and thermodynamics.

14. From this point of view Mulkay's criticism of Kuhn is decisive. See in particular Mulkay, 1972, *op. cit.*, Note 8. See also G. Lemaine, 'Science normale et science hypernormale', mimeo, 1979.

15. This singularity, well brought-out by K. Knorr, 'Producing and reproducing knowledge: descriptive or constructive? Toward a model of research production', *Social Science Information* 16, 669–696 (1977) is also valid for new knowledge seeking recognition, G. N. Gilbert, 'The transformation of research findings into scientific knowledge', *Social Studies of Science* **VI**, 281–306 (1976).

16. I owe the concept of translation to M. Serres, *Hermes 111, La traduction*, Paris, Editions de Minuit, 1974.
17. An analysis of translation mechanisms needs to be developed. We simply state that it is linked to the construction of problematic situations themselves. A problematic situation de-contextualises concepts, proposals and categories, and then re-contextualises them using its own logic. Thus problematic situations permanently create metaphors. The latter's existence make translation possible (for 'metaphorisation' see R. Krohn, 'The Social Process of Scientific Investigation', unpublished paper, McGill University, 1978).
18. K. Knorr, *op. cit.*, 1977, Note 15.
19. M. Callon, 'L'Etat face à l'innovation technique; le cas du vehicule electrice', *Revue Francaise de Science Politique*, 426–447 (Juin 1979).
20. R. E. Dewey, *The Philosophy of John Dewey*, Martinus Nijhoff, The Hague, 1977.
21. See the very fine analysis of a novel by M. Tournier put forward by G. Deleuze, *La logique du sens*, Editions de Minuit, Paris, 1969.
22. P. Bourdieu, *La distinction*, Editions de Minuit, Paris, 1979.
23. M. Callon, and B. Latour, 'Unscrewing Leviathan: How do actors macrostructure reality?', Forthcoming 1980.
24. M. Serres, *Le parasite*, Grasset, Paris, 1980.

THE DEVELOPMENT OF AN INTERDISCIPLINARY
PROJECT

JAN BÄRMARK AND GÖRAN WALLÉN

University of Gothenburg

Problem and Perspective

Our objective is to draw attention to the development process within a research project, more particularly a case study of a forest project. The growth of knowledge in a research project can be seen as the result of interaction between cognitive and social factors. In order to study the interactions between intellectual, organisational sociological and psychological factors, we decided to study interdisciplinary research because we believe that it is easier to follow the interaction of cognitive and social factors directly in a project in which disciplines with conflicting paradigms, research roles and cognitive interests have to confront each other. There are differences between researchers' roles and the competence of theoreticians, empiricists, specialists and generalists which are as important as the differences between scientists from different disciplines.

In this paper we discuss, for example, the different motives of the researchers for entering the project, the basic differences in outlook and personality between empirical and theoretical scientists, and the effects of the existing academic career structure which creates a lack of solidarity within the group. Consideration of the development process within a project is also crucial to an understanding of the project. Research management approaches often imply that a project can be planned and organised once and for all in the beginning, and according to a simple goal structure. On the contrary, the organisation must be continually adapted to the development of knowledge, for example by using problem oriented groups instead of discipline oriented groups as in matrix organisations.

Correspondingly, knowledge cannot be integrated once and for all at the

221

Karin D. Knorr, Roger Krohn and Richard Whitley (eds.), The Social Process of Scientific Investigation. Sociology of the Sciences, Volume IV, 1980. 221–235.

end of the project simply by compilation of reports from subprojects. We have found that integration of knowledge is dependent on integration at different stages in the research process. Integration of knowledge in an interdisciplinary research group also implies that social integration must occur (1). Additionally, in our investigations of a number of projects we have found that it is necessary to have access to categories, perspectives and theories from the philosophy of science, sociology, the psychology of science and organisational theory. In this sense, studies of interdisciplinary science ought themselves to be interdisciplinary.

Our Methods

Our methods consisted of participant observation, close readings of reports, and interviews with scientists.

We can differentiate between three separate phases:

First, we formulated questions about problems concerning world-picture assumptions, ideals of science and research roles. The scientists, however, did not like to answer specific questions about metascientific problems but preferred to talk in general terms about their personal experiences with the project. They did not want to separate their way of handling metascientific problems from their own personal backgrounds, relations between their early interests in school, their ways of thinking and their specific interests in the forest project. They drew our attention to the importance of good interpersonal relationships in the research group as a prerequisite for inter-disciplinary cooperation and to the importance of the organisational settings for the growth of knowledge.

Second, we asked more open questions about their experiences from the project. Why did they begin on the project? What background did they have? What factors had created their way of working with science? What roles had they played in the project? etc. From these interviews we obtained a great deal of information about cognitive style, personal experiences, different perspectives on the project and about the interaction of cognitive and social factors in the project. At the same time, our understanding of the project had deepened so much that we could ask specific questions about the different scientists' contributions to the project and this led us to the third phase of the interviews.

Third, we asked specific questions about the cognitive parts of the projects, the specific investigations, different aspects of model-making, problems in the process of integrating knowledge, etc. As we got different information from different researchers we gained insight into the biological problems, model-making, etc., which enabled us to reconstruct the history of the project. Cognitive elements, for example integration of knowledge, were dependent on social factors just as were ways of cooperation during the research process.

The Forest Project

The forest project is the oldest project we studied. It started about ten years ago, and it is also the largest, including 100 researchers and technical assistants.

There were different kinds of problems in the different phases of the project, so we have found it better to present our material in chronological order with our comments in each part of the presentation (2). There were five distinct phases in the life cycle of the project:

Phase One: The Initiation Phase (August 1970–June 1972)

One of the reasons for initiating the project was a desire on the part of some researchers to develop their experiences from the International Biological Programme (IBP) in which they had taken part. Another source of inspiration was a large ecological project on the Baltic Sea on the ecosystem level, i.e. studies of the flows of energy and matter in the ecosystem, rather than of individuals and populations. Thus a ecosystem tradition began to emerge. This view had a world picture component: the ecosystem perspective, and a methodological component: ecological knowledge has to be formulated in mathematical language. The link between the world-picture and the mathematical method was computer simulation. The ecosystem perspective was intended to unify the different disciplines.

Also some researchers thought that biological in Sweden was in need of renewal because the discipline of ecology was rather descriptive, especially compared to the North American parts of IBP. They were interested in introducing more exact methods and mathematical models. There were also many young biologists who had no university position and so were available for the project. One of our informants who came into the project as a young scientist and soon achieved a leading position told us:

For me and many of my colleagues this was our last resort. We had to choose between this project or giving up an academic career. (3)

Subprojects were also initiated for doctoral students.

The forests in Sweden are very important to the economy and there were a lot of practical problems to be solved, for instance acidification of the soil, and fertilisation. The project was launched on the political level to solve all these problems by way of a large 'forestry management information system'. Ideas were borrowed from management information systems and the planning of the Apollo project. All these various motives are mirrored later on in many different goals of the project. The main part of this period was spent resolving conflicts in interests between different research bodies (4). Finally the project received special financial support from the Swedish parliament. The whole budget was about 27 million Swedish crowns (roughly 5 million U.S. dollars) for seven years.

Phase Two: Establishing the Project (July 1972–December 1973)

The project was, in this phase, mainly a cooperative project among researchers from different biology departments, some meteorologists and some data specialists. There were subgroups such as zoologists and microbiologists. The main problem was the formulation of operative goals and problems. The aim was to produce a mathematical simulation model for the coniferous forest which would show how the growth of trees varied with different inputs of temperature, water, carbon, nitrogen, etc. The model was also intended to coordinate the research work and make it into an interdisciplinary project.

At first, there were many seminars to teach the biologists systems analysis and mathematical models but many biologists found the mathematical methods difficult to learn. A single all-encompassing model was too complex to handle and they could not find any relation between the global model and their own fields. There was also some criticism that the model was a kind of black box model giving no explanations of causal processes. This was partly due to the aim of the model, which was to predict changes in the ecosystem without providing detailed explanations.

As no theoretical model that could guide the empirical investigations had been developed, the biologists went out into the field making empirical investigations on their own. At the same time, there was pressure from the research councils to start the empirical investigations at once. Both of these groups shared the conviction that 'real research' is synonymous with empirical investigation and not with tedious theoretical work making models. But there were also long delays in getting measurement equipment due to a shortage of money. Consequently, many of the earlier measurements could not be used: some had a wrong resolution of time measurement and other methods were incompatible. The whole project fell into a period of crisis during which a leadership crisis also arose.

As the first modelling approach failed, critics began to have an influence on the project and the project board was widened to a larger group including more of the empirical scientists. This large group, however, was inefficient in coordinating the project at the field level; many members of the boards felt more responsibility to their subgroups than for the project as a whole.

In retrospect, many of the scientists regretted rushing into this phase of establishing the project. It would have been better had a small group carried out theoretical investigations for a few years to prepare the whole project and to structure the empirical investigations. Such a planning period would also have made it easier to select researchers for the next part of the project. Many of the later difficulties are traceable to conflicts in this preparatory phase.

A Comment on the Psychology of Science

The reactions from the empirically-minded biologists towards systems theory are a reminder of the strong interrelations between intellectual and psychological factors. In accordance with Mitroff we found psychological differences between theoreticians and empirical scientists.

Mitroff states:

Whereas the sensation type (the empirical scientist) may be too data-bound (he tends to go on collecting data forever because he is afraid to risk a generalisation that goes beyond the available data), the intuition type (the theoretician) may be too data-free; he may spin out a hypothetical conclusion in a minute that is based on no data at all. (5)

This is exactly what we found in our project; the first modelling approaches had no empirical significance and the empirical scientists collected long series of data in order to feel assured that the amount of data was enough to cover the complex empirical reality.

Some of the scientists had previous experience from interdisciplinary science and were not wholly unfamiliar with systems theory. They could see the idea behind system thinking but preferred to work without the models. The only heuristic value in the models, according to them, was that the models helped in structuring one's own thoughts. Although the very goal of the project was to produce models of the ecosystem, there was a lot of scepticism among many of the researchers.

The research leaders had not taken into account that learning systems theory is more complicated than just learning a new method or technique. The use of systems theory implies the adoption of new kinds of intellectual resources with new world-picture assumptions, preconceptions about science (criteria of knowledge, epistemology, etc.) and new research roles. Many of the scientists were not used to abstract reasoning in mathematical models. Their interest in attending seminars in order to learn a new 'paradigm' soon faded. They were interested in empirical investigations, measurements and the process of handling a lot of empirical data. So, instead of adopting new perspectives, they continued their research in the traditional manner.

At the beginning of our studies we unconsciously adopted the project leaders' view on the project. The project leaders had the most clearly articulated conception of the whole project and it was much easier for us to talk in terms of methodological problems and about research management problems to them than about what happened on the research field levels, for instance plant physiology, to scientists. Thus, in the beginning we thought that the more empirical scientists' refusal to learn systems analysis methodology and to take into account the global perspectives of the project was irrational. But later on, we changed our perspectives to that of the participants and realised that the models were too far removed from field work, so the previous competence of the researchers could not be fully exploited. The cost of learning a new competence was too high and was worthless as a skill when they had to return to their original disciplines after the project. Some scientists came from disciplines in which mathematics and statistics were looked upon with suspicion.

Phase Three: *Empirical Dominance* (*January 1974–December 1975*)

Problems of cooperation coupled with the difficulties mentioned above led to a reorganisation of the project in 1973. Various preconceptions about science were represented in the project. The first approach to making a global model of the ecosystem implied the construction of a mathematical model in theoretical biology which could be used for forestry management.

This preliminary model of the ecosystem was used to define certain problem areas (such as gas exchange, litter fall, consumption). However, the model was not developed to the point where it could be used to put forward specific questions. But these problem areas did form a basis for a change from cooperation between disciplines to problem-oriented groups and it was useful for planning purposes and for empirical work. For some time it also stopped the battle over resources between the disciplines.

At the beginning of this phase, the empirical researchers thought that this reorganisation would provide the working conditions which had been lacking and that they would have more opportunity to plan their own work. This change initiated the third phase of the project, with empirical dominance. The project was so large that it was impossible to steer the subgroups towards integrative work which led to a situation in which the actual field work was not particularly interdisciplinary. At the same time, the data measurement equipment at Jädraås, experiment-station, had begun to work. The technical equipment was considered to be one of the most important parts of the project and it was hoped that the multitudes of data could shed some light on the problems with the models and that a data bank would be created from an 'undisturbed forest' to be compared later with data from forests outside the experiment area. A lot of automatic measurement equipment was used and a special computer was used to steer this equipment and record the data. Integration was done at the planning level, on the theoretical side for the whole project and for the empirical work on an intermediate level in the problem-oriented groups.

Naturally, there were also advantages for the relative freedom of the empirical researchers, for instance the unexpected discovery of the fact that the production of bio-mass in the roots of the trees was twice as large as had been anticipated. The main steering effort in this phase then, consisted of a reorganisation into research-problem-oriented groups. A secondary effect of this was an emerging gap between empirical and theoretical work. These organisational changes also reflected integration over the borders of disciplines and disintegration of empirical and theoretical knowledge. In a few cases, however, a spontaneous integration of field work did occur. The experimental station at Jädraås offered a creative atmosphere for informal discussions and planning of further research projects.

Phase Four: Modelling (1976–1978)

In this phase, most of the empirical work went on as before but the modelling work was more successful than it had previously been and modellers began to demand empirical data. The first modelling attempts were aimed at making a global model of the pine-ecosystem. At the beginning of 1976 the idea of a global model was abandoned and a family of partial and more detailed models were produced. These latter models were closer to field work and the more traditional knowledge about growth in plants. These models were at first based on empirical data from literature because the data from the project did not have the same resolution in time measurement or did not fit in other ways, and also due to delays in delivery.

Views still vary on the relationship between partial and global models:

In the beginning I thought it was easier and more attractive to have a model which could be stretched to the big perspectives and also could be used for the small perspectives . . . . I have realised that this is very difficult for practical reasons and, not least for reasons of data technology, that this global-modelling work is very demanding and laborious.

Today there is a very negative attitude towards working with complex models because it is very difficult to follow their biological relevance. (3)

New kinds of models were built to answer specific questions and some applications were investigated, for instance the effects of acid-rain from burning oil on a forest ecosystem. From this we might hypothesize that in some cases successful solutions to practical problems could be found by using problem-oriented models without a purely scientific background. The term 'applications' would thus be misleading. As we have mentioned, there were a number of efforts to make a global model of the ecosystem. At the end of the project the researchers approached the model building in a new way: they began to use models as 'instruments' and not as 'maps' of reality. This led to an acceptance of radical simplifications of the models, for instance a reduction of the numbers of variables. As a consequence, a plant stand model for the growth of biomass in a 150 years perspective could function as the desired global model.

On the organisational side a special group and subprogramme were established for modelling and data-systems work. Thus, the previous gap between empirical and theoretical work now had an organisational manifestation. This group was later replaced when the project board was reorganised into a smaller group, from twelve researchers representing the problem groups to five who worked closer together.

Different modelling approaches, from a global model to submodels, from partial models to a global model and finally, expansion of one submodel to a global model, but not encompassing all the partial models, are in one sense an iterative kind of integration (6). In retrospect, different modelling approaches are not mutually exclusive and it seems that the first modelling approach was a necessary prerequisite to the second, etc. The transition of different modelling approaches can therefore be seen as quite rational. But the researchers themselves felt that it was due to failures in the earlier modelling approaches.

The integrational factors in this phase were thus: partially overlapping models, iteration in the sequence of different modelling approaches and, on the organisational side, a special working group for the development of knowledge. Among the disintegrational factors was the increasing complexity when different partial models are connected together. The conflict between theoretical and empirical work also grew deeper.

Some Consequences of the Division of Work

As the scientists were not interested in adopting the systems model, a division of work between modellers and empirical scientists took place. For some scientists this implied that their research roles were diminished, from their point of view, to mere data-delivering for the project. Furthermore, the data were used in such a manner that their producers could not recognise them when they appeared in the wider context of the model. This led to problems of a social nature. At the end of the project this matter was considered and the researchers responsible for data-collection were also allowed to take part in later work.

The process of delivering data was looked upon in different ways by modellers and empirical scientists. The modellers needed data quickly for their work. The empirical scientists, on the other hand, were eager to get longer series of measurements in order to get data which could fulfil their criteria of knowledge. The criteria of the empirical scientists were not taken from the modeller's paradigms but came from their own disciplines with their data-criteria.

You have to have large series of data, which take time to handle statistically in order to confirm reliability. This side has been underrated. (3)

For some scientists, the task of being a data deliverer was thus problematical. Time and again they had to choose between the demands for fast results for the project, and their own demands, which were to continue a productive line of research by continuing to do experiments and take measurements.

We didn't like the methods that were supposed to be used for the first data needed in the project. We wanted to work out our own methods and had to fight very hard to do so because it would then take time to get any data at all. (3)

For other scientists, the research role as data deliverer was not a negative experience. These scientists, on the other hand, had very vague ideas of the general goals of the project. There was a lot of scepticism and uncertainty between the two main group of scientists, the modellers and the empirical scientists.

Many of the empirical scientists look upon us as some kind of flagship of figurehead sitting at the prow, making the wave glimmer in the sunshine, but think there is no concrete need for us in the practical scientific work. This view is rather common among many of the empirical scientists.

There has been some difficulty for the project leaders to understand why certain empirical data are needed and to get enough money for this. It is not a matter of only saying that we want to have the data by a certain day and we except you to deliver it. Methods of obtaining the data must also be found. For some of the physiologists it took perhaps one year to get the equipment in order.

It often happened that we in the process of making models had a shortage of certain information .... . The measuring programmes were perhaps often too heavy. We have several examples that show that they actually should have been cut off. It is a question of encroachment on the individual scientist .... . This must be said to be a weakness of the project, there should have been better interaction between model and reality.

I have made up my mind at this time that I will only work with things I find meaningful. And if that does not suit the project? That is of secondly importance to me. (3)

These kinds of problems exemplify a more general problem in directing a large scale project. It is necessary to direct and coordinate the different investigations and at the same time, the more the project leaders direct, the smaller the opportunity for innovation by the participants.

Phase Five: Synthesis, Generalisations and Applications (1979–1980)

In the last phase, knowledge was integrated on the intermediate level in producing synthesising reports. We think that there are certain dangers in synthesising models afterwards, but then of course, this part of the project is not finished yet. In putting together pieces of knowledge there is a risk of missing system effects, for example new qualities could appear in the whole system which could not be found in the parts.

In the modelling work, the partial models could be connected. Output from one model could be used as input in the next one. But some factors are treated as constant and the latter models are not connected to the former. The modellers admit that some system effects could appear but they think that if these were anticipated the models would be too complex. One important system effect has appeared and caused a lot of trouble and discussion. It was found that knowledge about the 'mechanism of photosynthesis' was not necessary on the system level of the growth of a whole tree. Of course, it is necessary that photosynthesis occur but the trees are 'good at photosynthesising' so this is not a limiting factor for the growth, on the contrary, external factors are dominant. Research on photosynthesis is overly ambitious in terms of the goals of this project.

The Role and Competence of the Generalist

In interdisciplinary groups problems arise in understanding one another's language and preconceptions about science. In order to master problems such as these and to bridge the gap between specialists, a new kind of researcher-role is required, the role of generalist. He is to function as a link between the scientists in the group, leading discussions about ideas, coordinating scientists

and investigations, editing reports and sometimes functioning as a research
therapist solving psychological problems in interpersonal relations within
the group. In other words, the generalist must have an understanding of
the cognitive as well as the social problems of research. In many projects,
organisation and administration are so closely bound to methodological
problems that the generalist must also be skilled in administration. The necessity for generalists, however, may simply be the effect of lack of integration
in the research team. We have found in our interdisciplinary projects that
different kinds of generalists can develop in a given group.

First we can speak of generalists in a restricted sense. About half of the
scientists in the ecological project never worked in interdisciplinary groups
but they had the opportunity to meet scientists from other fields of research
and to learn new methods and perspectives. Here, the generalist is familiar
with different approaches although he does not usually overstep his own. In
one sense, the generalist is and must be a specialist. He must be well acquainted
with some field of science. One way to create generalists of this kind is to
let scientists oscillate between research within their own discipline and
participation in interdisciplinary groups. The generalist must develop competence within his own discipline in order to have a solid basis to stand on.

Second, competence as a generalist may involve the ability to create
models of data from different areas of research, for example mathematical
models. In this case, the role of generalist is based mostly on an integrating
methodology. This created some problems when the biologists felt that their
field was being intruded upon:

The data people have done a lot of work. They have done a lot of biology without
discussing it with the biologists. They have studied biology literature, etc. It is one thing
to study the literature in order to discuss a subject with us biologists, but quite another
to work within biology without asking the biologists, and that atmosphere can become
tense.

It is one thing to learn the fundamental concepts, and another to try to evaluate the
physiological work. I don't think that the data people have the competence to do this
in the same way a biologist would. They don't have the feel for it. (3)

Third, in some projects, as in the forest project, there is no strong integrative
process, but there are many coordinated subprojects. Most of the integration
of knowledge must be done at the end of the project. The generalist's function is to provide a synthesis of information from different subareas. To be

able to do this, the generalist must know the relationship between the different problem areas and have system theoretical competence.

We speak of two kinds of generalists. First we have the people who only have the mathematical skills. But in order to handle ecosystem problems it is necessary that you have the interest in and the knowledge of biological problems at the right system level. (3)

The person who said this meant that many of the specialists could not understand that simplifications are inevitable when changing perspective from parts of the tree and partial processes to, for example the level of growth of the whole tree.

Fourth, the role of generalist could involve coordinating projects. Since the organisation of a research project must be adjusted to the development of knowledge, for instance work groups according to problem areas in the project, the project leader must have scientific competence in the field. But the generalist, as a research coordinator, must also stimulate the researchers to cooperate and take responsibility for the integration process. In this project many of the researchers felt no responsibility for the general goals of the project, so it was very important that the project management kept the project together cognitively and administratively. Being a generalist can be the same as having the competence to work as a consultant in different kinds of interdisciplinary groups and handle general methodological, psychological and sociological problems. Metascientific competence is important in order to introduce discussions about paradigmatic questions such as world pictures, assumptions about causal factors, ideals of science, the role of researcher, etc. This has been a part of our own tasks when studying the projects.

Conclusions

(1) Our objective here is to draw attention to the development process within a research project. In order to get a realistic concept of knowledge, to find out what the 'real problems' are and to find the right scientists for the project, a preparatory phase is essential. In the forest project the lack of theoretical preparation led to a lack of coordination between theoretical and empirical investigations. As the problems and knowledge change, the organisational forms have to be changed as well. Much of this dynamic planning can only take place through close co-operation on the research field level. More formal

meetings on an intermediate or project level were experienced as boring, and as disturbing to the researchers in their work.

(2) Knowledge cannot be integrated once and for all at the end of a project simply by compilation of reports from subprojects. We have found that integration of knowledge is dependent on integration at different stages in the research process. Integration of knowledge in an interdisciplinary research group also implies that social integration must occur.

(3) Many research administrators and scientists tend to have a simplified and overly rationalistic picture of the research process. In the forest project, the research board had underestimated the social and psychological factors such as interests, cognitive styles and academic career. This led to few cases of co-operation during the project. So the main part of the integration of knowledge had to take place at the end of the project. The consequences were social problems among the scientists and a low degree of integration.

(4) There are differences between different researcher roles and the competence of theoreticians, empirical scientists, specialists and generalists which are as important as the differences between scientists from different disciplines. These groups of scientists have different interests and cognitive styles and this must be taken into consideration in order to attain co-operation. This has implications for measuring standards, relationships between models and reality, etc.

Notes and References

1. Different possibilities of integration of knowledge are discussed in Jan Bärmark and Göran Wallén, *Knowledge Production in Interdisciplinary Groups* (Report no. 37 in series 2, 1978, Department of Theory of Science, Univ. of Gothenburg) and Jan Bärmark and Göran Wallén, *The Interaction of Cognitive and Social Factors in Steering a Large Scale Interdisciplinary Project* (paper presented at the International Conference of Interdisciplinary Research Groups, Reisenburg, April 22nd–28th, 1979). Report no. 41 1979, Department of Theory of Science, Gothenburg.
2. The presentation is based on interviews and internal reports from the project; see Folke Andersson, *Development, Coordination and Administration of an Integrated Ecosystem Project* (paper prepared for the workshop 'Initiation of and training for integrated projects', Wenner-Green Center, Stockholm. 770509-10, organised by the Colloboration Committee of Northwest European Research Councils (NOS) (mimeo)) and Per Anders Bergman, *Development of a Large-scale Research Project*, FEK-report 5, Stockholm, 1975.

3. Quotations from our interviews.
4. It was difficult to formulate precise goals and they were also in conflict with each other in parts, see Bärmark and Wallén, *op. cit.*, 1979.
5. See Ian Mitroff, *The Subjective Side of Science*, Amsterdam, Elsevier, 1979, p. 168.
6. This manner of integration has been brought to our attention by Fred Rossini *et al.* in *Frameworks and Factors Affecting Integration Within Technology Assessment*, Georgia Institute of Technology, Atlanta, 1978.

PART IV

WRITING PUBLIC ACCOUNTS

DISCOVERY: LOGIC AND SEQUENCE IN A SCIENTIFIC TEXT (1)

STEVE WOOLGAR

Brunel University and McGill University

The work of this paper is part of a more general exploration of the viability of an ethnomethodological approach to understanding science. I have argued elsewhere that ethnomethodologically inclined approaches to the study of science should provide useful insights into the nature of the activities which constitute scientific practice. In particular, an examination of some of the standard objections to ethnomethodology shows them to be misguided, in that they are based on an overly narrow conception of the range of phenomena with which ethnomethodology can deal and on an intractable definition of the legitimate substance of sociological inquiry (2). However, a full assessment of the value of ethnomethodology for understanding science can only be made in relation to the fruits of empirical inquiry (3). The argument of this paper is divided into two parts. In the first part, an analytic perspective informed by ethnomethodological thinking is located in relation to the debate between rationalist philosophy and the strong programme in the sociology of knowledge. This debate is taken as the basis for an examination and clarification of the position that a fruitful understanding of the nature of scientific inquiry must eschew many of the features of both philosophical and sociological perspectives on knowledge production. An attempt is also made to explicate the central assumption of the analytic perspective: that of isomorphism between presentational context and scientific concepts. The second part of this paper offers a tentative analysis of one aspect of the practical activity of scientific investigation: the accomplishment of a discovery as related in a scientific text.

Karin D. Knorr, Roger Krohn and Richard Whitley (eds.), The Social Process of Scientific Investigation. Sociology of the Sciences, Volume IV, 1980. 239–268.

1. Rationality and the Strong Programme in the Sociology of Scientific Knowledge

Although there is now widespread agreement that it is both possible and desirable to analyse the social processes of scientific investigation, this general formulation conceals a number of different positions as to the precise form which adequate analysis should take. Even Merton's early work could be said in one sense to have concerned social processes of scientific investigation, although current writers would probably argue that this is stretching the applicability of the phrase to bursting point. This is not what they had in mind at all! A more exact version of what is required depends upon one of the more celebrated claims of recent work in the sociology of science, that analysts should look more carefully at the cognitive content or substance of scientist's work (4). In other words, a thoroughgoing sociology of scientific knowledge must concern itself, for example, with the way in which social interests affect the construction and use of the minutiae of esoteric mathematical proofs, or with the way in which particular knowledge constructs constrain scientific action. However, much current controversy hinges on the extent to which precepts about the truth or falsity of the knowledge under study should enter into analysts' explanation. Parties to this controversy can be denoted as the 'rationalists' on the one hand, and the supporters of the 'strong programme' on the other (5). In order to contrast the philosophical and sociological perspectives of these parties with the kind of analysis I shall be recommending, it is necessary to give a brief exposition of the positions of 'rationalist' and 'strong programmer'.

The rationalists can be characterised as a body of thinkers strongly influenced by traditional philosophical commitments to epistemological realism. That is, they are committed to the view that there exists a world of material things which do not depend for their existence on the fact that some mind is aware of them. Translated into more sociologically familiar terms, this means that the truth or otherwise of the matter is independent of the presence of social actors. In Popper, we find knowledge products preserved in the social equivalent of a hermetically sealed domain: the third world (6). Knowledge thus constituted is independent of the knowing subject. Bhaskar suggests that the removal of mankind from the face of the earth will not affect the existence of physical laws. Without man, he suggests, there would continue to be tides: gravity would continue to operate (7). None of the rationalists go so far as to argue that the presence of social actors is entirely irrelevant. After all, knowledge objects are undeniably used and manipulated by human agents. The rationalists are thus prepared to permit sociological investigations of science which confine themselves to relationships between knowledge handlers. Rationalists' eyebrows are raised when it is claimed that such social relationships determine the form and content of truth. And there are howls of anguish when it is further claimed that an understanding of the social determination of knowledge should proceed independently of the truth or falsity of the knowledge in question.

The perpetrators of this last outrage are, of course, the strong programmers. One of their central methodological imperatives is that analysts should not be swayed by the truth status of the knowledge under consideration: Barnes urges us to be naturalistic (by which I shall here take him to mean 'non-evaluative') (8); Bloor asks that we be impartial (9). This would be uncontroversial but for the insistence of the strong programme that sociologists concern themselves with the substance of scientific knowledge. Since the substance of scientific knowledge is traditionally the domain of philosophers of science, who can be characterised as attempting to expose the internal logic of scientific arguments, it is perhaps not surprising that the intrusion into this territory by non-philosophers causes consternation. If these non-philosophers wield a methodological armory which explicitly denies the relevance for their explanations of attempts to specify the rationality or truth status of knowledge, consternation is likely to be redoubled.

An exhaustive examination of the range of different positions adopted in this debate is well beyond the scope of the present paper. For present purposes, the relevant facet of the rationalist critique of the strong programme is the assertion that any attempt to conduct investigations into the nature of knowledge from a truth neutral standpoint is *absurd*. This absurdity appears to hinge on the fact that such a perspective starts by ruling out certain questions which are relevant from the point of view of the rationalist philosopher: rationalist philosophical study of knowledge requires *ab initio* some specification of truth content. In any case, it might be said by rationalist philosophy, it is simply *impossible* to maintain a truth neutral standpoint: assumptions about the veracity of objects in the real world will inevitably be smuggled into the analysis, if only because we adopt a realist standpoint in the course of confrontation with the 'objects' of our world. The strong programmers would presumably reply that this does not invalidate attempts to push analysis as far as possible from a relativistic viewpoint; that the truth status of knowledge is not denied by the strong programme, it is merely suspended for research purposes. Yet there is one aspect of the rationalist argument which is not satisfied by this reply. As both analysts and members we are inevitably tied to a structure of discourse which includes the use of modalities, the achievement of objectivity, the assessment of what really is the case and so on. To the extent that we are constrained in our use of available language resources, we will inevitably reproduce the rhetoric of realism. To me, this suggests the importance of a venture which attempts critically to examine the nature of this rhetoric.

This dispute between rationalist and strong programmer hinges on the fact that while both are committed to understanding the nature of scientific knowledge, the former approach presupposes a style and form of adequate explanation which is qualitatively different from the latter. Put another way, the debate between the rationalists and the strong programme is a debate over the nature of adequate explanation. So long as explanation depends on assuming truth status, there is no room for the strong programme; so long as questions of truth status are ruled out of court by sociological elucidation of the strong programme, there is no place for the rationalist (10). It is, of course, possible to imagine that at some future date, this dispute might be said to be 'resolved': from the point of view of parties to the debate, it might be apparent that the argument of one or other side 'had prevailed'. As a practical matter, the issue would thus be reckoned to be closed. In principle, however, arguments of the kind outlined will always be available to potential protagonists. It is therefore important to distinguish between the 'resolvability' of the debate as a practice accomplishment and the essential 'irresolvability' of the debate in principle.

Having established a tension between competing parties to a controversy, the stage is set for the introduction of the author's resolution (11). However, this author's attempt to resolve the tension is not an attempt to resolve the argument between rationalist and strong programmer. In other words, my interest is not the practical task of establishing the ascendancy of one or other position. Instead, I shall try to alleviate tension by suggesting that resolution of the debate, or even alignment to one or other position is of little consequence for a fruitful understanding of scientists' activity. The discussion requires refocussing so that arguments between strong programmers and rationalists are subject to critical appreciation. From this vantage point it is possible to see a congruence between this dispute and those which constitute scientific practice. The analyst's task is not to resolve such disputes, but rather to develop an appreciation of their form and currency.

The argument can be expressed differently as follows. Science is an essentially practical activity, in the course of which participants themselves engage in negotiating the character of the phenomenon with which they are dealing. That is, scientists can be seen to be routinely concerned with questions about what exactly the thing is that they have got, whether or not they *really* have got something, whether or not that thing would make its presence known under different circumstances, and so on. The activity of science thus comprises a practical concern with issues which we meet in slightly different form in the discussions of professional philosophers and sociologists. The similarity between the practical concerns of working scientists and proponents in the debate between rationality and the strong programme in the sociology of knowledge is particularly striking. As has been argued elsewhere at length the practice of everyday laboratory work comprises continual disputes, strategies and arguments at a local level (12). The occurrence of these actions is emphatically not limited to occasions of 'controversy' in the usual sense of the term. Instead, participants display a constant and routine concern to settle or deal with matters which, in the universe of discourse associated with professional academia would be characterised as being of profound epistemological significance. Laboratory practice thus involves participants' attempts, on the one hand, to establish the reality of truth of a phenomenon which they claim their actions to be about or related towards, and on the other hand, to specify a variety of sociological circumstances or factors which 'explain' the scientific work with which they are familiar. I see in these activities of laboratory scientists a microcosm of the debate between rationalists and the strong programmers described above: in an important sense, practising scientists variously and interchangeably take the position of rationalist or of strong programmer (13). The major difference, however, is that the adoption of one or other argument is not merely a matter of academic indulgence. Rather, the position taken appears to have immediate and significant practical consequences: "If the existence of *this* particular substance can be established (as a practical matter), it is then possible to pursue *this* strategy for further work". Or, alternatively: "If we can demonstrate the dubious social circumstances in which *this* claim was made, it is possible to discount it for purposes of our next experiment".

The wide range of different forms of explanation in which scientists engage includes both the establishment of truth status of items of knowledge and the identification of extant social factors or circumstances. In the latter regard, their efforts to characterise the behaviour and knowledge claims, both of themselves and others, variously follow the form of structural, functional and hermeneutic explanations familiar to social scientists. This also means that participants are rabid imputers of social motives and interests. They find evidence of social interests at work in a diverse collection of instances of scientific practice. Moreover, it is clear that the work of imputing social interests is recogniseably a defeasible activity for participants. That is, they frequently pay attention to (and attempt to forestall) the ever-present possibility of explanations which propose an alternative set of motives, intentions, socio-political world views, attenuating circumstances or prevalent cosmologies as the primary influence on knowledge construction (14).

Thus far, I have suggested that the debate between rationalist and strong programmer is irresolvable except for practical purposes, that scientific practitioners engage in reasoning practices similar to those of parties to the debate, and that scientists are mindful of the essential inconcludeability of their reasoning practices. These observations together suggest the importance of examining the nature of the practical reasoning engaged in by scientists. Instead of contributing directly to the debate between rationalist and strong programmer, it may be more fruitful to investigate the practical management of either or both positions (or of the debate between these positions) as found in the activities of scientists (15). For sociologists, in particular, I am recommending that instead of adopting the perspective of the strong programme, we recognise that modes of reasoning essentially similar to those constituting the strong programme — including activities such as the attribution of motives or interests, the specification of social context, the search for causal influence and so on — both characterise and have significant consequences for scientific work. Thus, the practical reasoning activities of scientists provide an alternative focus for our attempts to further our understanding of the 'process of scientific investigation' (16).

Scientists' practical reasoning comprises a wide range of activities amenable to investigation; the analyst can profitably turn to the use of evidence, interpretation of data, argument and so on. He can find these activities in the actions, conversations, seminar discussions, conference presentations, inscriptions, recordings and writings of scientific work. For purposes of illustration I have arbitrarily chosen to concentrate in this paper on the last of these activities – the writing of scientists. More specifically, I shall examine participants' practical management of the notion of 'discovery' by considering the character of discovery as made available in a scientific text. Thus, the particular aspect of scientific practice studied here is the work of accounting through textual organisation. Before proceeding with the analysis, however, it is necessary to review the basis for assuming the availability of 'discovery' in a text.

Isomorphism

Collins' study of replication in physics makes a persuasive case for the need to look at scientists' practical actions in fine detail (17). Collins argues that in negotiating what counts as an adequate (or competent) replication of an experiment, participants in the field of gravity waves were deciding upon the list of culturally relevant variables. In other words, the substance of negotiation concerned which factors should or should not be taken as affecting the detection of the phenomenon under consideration. Collins points out that in so delineating the relevance of candidate variables, participants were engaged in specifying the nature of the phenomenon. That is, there is an essential congruence between negotiating what counts as a good experiment and negotiating the character of the phenomenon. For present purposes the argument can be expressed rather differently: both the existence and character of a particular phenomenon can be established through the negotiation of interested parties; the out-there-ness of a phenomenon is accomplished in establishing its properties (18).

Collins argues that in order to recognise the phenomenon as the upshot of social construction, it is important to monitor contemporaneously the process of negotiation. For sociologists, this is most obvious in terms of controversy, in the aftermath of which, the social contingency of fact construction is said to be difficult to retrieve. It is at this point that facts appear to take on a life of their own, passing into a realm of existence beyond the immediate research of human agency and managing to disassociate themselves from all traces of their production (19). In another sense, however, the work of establishing the facticity of a phenomenon does not end with the settling of controversy. On each and every occasion that participants refer to a fact they do so in such a way that the facticity of the phenomenon is re-established. In referring to a thing, work is done to sustain its fact-like nature, or to say it differently, to pass off the thing as being a fact. It is precisely this work, this continual reaccomplishment of a phenomenon as a fact, which makes the task of the sociologist so difficult. For it is this work, this continual re-expression of facticity, which hinders sociological reconstruction.

My point is that is possible to extend Collins' argument. For Collins, the negotiation of what counts as a good experiment is the same as negotiating the actual character of a phenomenon. The present suggestion is that the practical expression of, or reference to, a phenomenon both recreates and establishes anew the existence of the phenomenon. In describing a phenomenon, participants simultaneously render its out-there-ness (20).

The issue of congruence between practical expression and the nature of a phenomenon arises in an article by Dorothy Smith (21), in which she examines the text of an interview purporting to describe how a girl came to be defined by her friends as mentally ill. The central assumption of Smith's analysis is that there is an essential congruence between the notion of mental illness and the way the text is organised so that this notion is made available to the reader:

The method of analysis assumes that the structure of the conceptual scheme 'mental illness' which the reader uses in recognising 'mental illness' is isomorphic with that organising the text and hence is discoverable 'in' it (22).

The assumption of isomorphism has certain components which I take to be implied, although not explicitly suggested as necessary, in Smith's usage. The assumption seems to suggest that there is no sense in which we can claim that the phenomenon of mental illness has an existence independence of the means of its expression (23). This has two immediate implications. Firstly, it makes nonsensical any attempt to arbitrate on the actual existence or otherwise of phenomena. This is a question which any attempt to understand practical reasoning simply has to bracket (24). Secondly, the only way to recover the character of a phenomenon is to examine the work which is carried out by participants in effecting or bringing off its existence. This position has several parallels in the work of both linguists and ethnomethodologists. For example, in his classic work of the 1930's, Bloomfield argues that it is wrong to infer the presence of 'concepts' on the basis of scientific speech utterances. He argues that the 'inner goings on' of scientists are simply unverifiable and hence unavailable to us (25). In addition, terms such as 'ideas' are merely misnomers for linguistic events:

the term 'idea' is simply a traditional obscure synonym for 'speech form' (26).

More recently, Garfinkel has pointed out the essential interdependence between the recognisably achieved objectivity of accounts and the socially organised occasions of their use (27). A reformulation of this position appears in McHugh and, significantly, is quoted by Collins as an expression of the "epistemological stance" which underlies his argument (28).

We must accept that there are no adequate grounds for establishing criteria of truth except the grounds that are employed to grant or concede it − truth is conceivable only as a socially organised upshot of contingent courses of linguistic, conceptual, and social courses of behaviour (29).

It thus appears that the assumption of isomorphism between textual organisation and the achieved existence of a concept (in Smith's case 'mental illness') is no more than a particular case of well known epistemological position. Although it is usually thought to be in the nature of an epistemological standpoint that it is undemonstrable (30) it is worth considering certain observations which lend support (if not substantiation in any strong sense) to this assumption. Let me relate two examples of observation from a recent ethnography of laboratory practice (31).

In the course of interaction with members of the laboratory, it was suggested by the observer that members' work could be best understood as an obsession with literary inscription; that practising scientists devoted the majority of their activity towards accumulating and juxtaposing a series of figures, traces and diagrams in a manner not entirely dissimilar to the traditionally understood mode of literary production. The response of laboratory members was that the observer had made the usual mistake of sociologists of science in failing to recognise the true significance of the scientific papers;

that these were merely a means of communicating, or effecting the transfer of facts reported in them. When the observer asked for elucidation of the nature of these facts, he found that the scientists provided elucidation in the same terms as those contained in the papers. That is, the scientists employed the same kinds of persuasive device, organisation of rhetoric and so on as they used in the papers. The scientists were unable to account for the existence of phenomenon which they argued the papers to be about, except by using the same forms of expression deployed in the papers. Needless to say, the observer remained unconvinced that it was possible to demonstrate the existence of facts except through the devices of literary organisation which scientists claimed were simply a means of talking *about* those facts. Facts were not available except by virtue of their literary organisation.

On several occasions during the same investigation participants would refer to past episodes of great scientific achievement. Frequently, they would tell the story using the format 'one day so and so had an idea'. However, if the story was subjected to detailed scrutiny, it was possible to reveal a plethora of social circumstances, chance meetings, guesswork and strategical manouevres which made up the situation referred to by tellers of the story. It thus appeared that 'having an idea' was used as a means of shorthand summary in participants' retrospective accounting. In other words, participants' organisation of social circumstances, etc., in their story-telling provided for the gloss: 'an idea occurred'.

These examples suggest that it is not possible to retrieve the character of phenomena (specifically, this includes 'ideas', 'concepts' and 'facts') independently of their presentational context (32). As a corollary, if we wish to understand what for participants counts as a phenomenon, we are obliged to investigate the organisation of presentational context which makes a phenomenon available to them.

2. Analysis

About the Data

In my analysis, part of the text of Professor Anthony Hewish's nobel lecture address is taken as data and reproduced below (33). Hewish and Sir Martin Ryle were jointly awarded the Nobel Prize for Physics at the end of 1974.

The Nobel citation named Ryle for services to the development of radio astronomy and Hewish specifically for the discovery of pulsars (34).

DATA

−5   PULSARS AND HIGH DENSITY PHYSICS
−4   Nobel Lecture, December 12, 1974

−3   by

−2   Antony Hewish
−1   University of Cambridge, Cavendish Laboratory, Cambridge, England

0 Discovery of Pulsars

1   The trail which ultimately led to the first pulsar began in 1948 when I joined
2   Ryle's small research team and became interested in the general problem of the
3   propogation of radiation through irregular transparent media. We are all familiar
4   with the twinkling of visible stars and my task was to understand why radio stars
5   also twinkled. I was fortunate to have been taught by Ratcliffe, who first showed
6   me the power of Fourier techniques in dealing with such diffraction phenomena.
7   By a modest extension of existing theory I was able to show that our radio stars
8   twinkled because of plasma clouds in the ionosphere at heights around 300 km, and
9   I was also able to measure the speed of ionospheric winds in this region. (1)
10   My fascination in using extra-terrestial radio sources for studying the
11   intervening plasma next brought me to the solar corona. From observation of the
12   angular scattering of radiation passing through the corona, using simple radio
13   interferometers, I was eventually able to trace the solar atmosphere out to one
14   half the radius of the Earth's orbit. (2)
15   In my notebook for 1954 there is a comment that, if radio sources were of
16   small enough angular size, they would illuminate the solar atmosphere with suffi-
17   cient coherence to produce interference patterns at the Earth which would be
18   detectable as a very rapid fluctuation of intensity. Unfortunately the information
19   then available showed that the few sources known were more than one hundred
20   times too large to produce this effect, and I did not pursue the idea. This was sad
21   because the phenomenon was discovered by chance, about eight years later, by
22   Margaret Clarke long after I had forgotten all about my comment. She was involved
23   with a survey of radio sources at Cambridge and noticed that three particular
24   sources showed variations of intensity.

My general objective is to discern what for participants counts as a discovery (35). I shall employ the assumption of isomorphism between textual organisation and the notion of discovery, and examine those features of textual organisation which provide for the reading of the lecture: "a discovery took place". It is important to note that it is this retrospective reading, as opposed to the contemporaneous reading: "a discovery is happening", which is the focus of concern in the data at hand. To understand more fully the way in which participants' accounting procedures provide for the occurrence of discovery as it happens, we require a different kind of data (36). The present text can be though of as a "celebration" of discovery rather than a claim to discovery. In the present text events in the past are rendered consistent with the idea of a discovery having happened.

Although a number of devices have been recognised as playing a major part in textual organisation (37), the organisation of textual presentations involving discovery makes use of a special combination of these devices as well as certain devices hitherto not recognised. As a way of setting up the analysis, I can do no better than adopt Smith's formulation of the analytical problem. In the following paragraph, I repeat her presentation verbatim, except where my substantive concern with "discovery" (rather than "mental illness") has necessitated some changes of wording (38).

Science can be thought of as one agency of social control with institutionalised procedures for assembling, processing and testing information about the observation of phenomenon so that it can be matched against the paradigms which provide working criteria of class membership. In analysing the text below, my quest is for those features of textual organisation which provide for rules or procedures for representing phenomenon as belonging to the class of "discovery". The account purports to be and can be recognised as a report of a discovery. Recognising in events the "fact" that a discovery has occurred involves complex conceptual work:

It involves assembling observations from actual moments and situations dispersed in time, organising them or finding that they can be organised, in accordance with the instructions which the concept provides. A simple, immediate and convincing recognition of a fact at this conceptual level implies that much of the work of providing events with the appropriate conceptual order has already been done. All that the reader/hearer has to do is to (find) in those events, or rather that account of events, the model which enables her to classify them (39).

An account which is immediately convincing is one which forces the classification of events as a discovery and makes any other difficult. And if it does, then the events (or the account of them) must already display the order which gives them the shape of the fact to the reader/hearer. In analysing this account as an account of a discovery I am, I argue, recovering the structure of the conceptual model which is made use of in recognising that that is what it is.

Preliminary Instructions

Certain features of textual organisation can be understood as initially providing the reader with instructions for making sense of the text with which he is faced. In the Hewish text, we can find three examples of such preliminary instructions.

(a) The Setting

Gusfield argues that the setting of an article, for example, in a 'serious' journal, establishes a claim for the text of the article to be taken seriously; it should be read as authoritative fact rather than fiction (40). In other words, readers are asked to orient to a range of vetting procedures which they could imagine having taken place before the story was allowed to appear in its current setting. Tacitly, the judgement of (presumably expert and hence reliable) others has preceded the reader's own assessment of the authority of the text. Before even beginning to read the text, the reader is faced with the choice of concurring with this expert evaluation or dismissing its authority out of hand. In the present example, the designation of 'Nobel Lecture' (1.−4) (41) and the institutional affiliation of author (1.−1) constitute a setting which provides for the authority of the text (42).

(b) Headings

Headings, typically in the form of titles or sub-titles establish the category of attributes and actions which follow. More precisely, a heading acts as a reader's guide to understanding the sense and the relevance of the terms which are set out in the subsequent text. The instructions made available by the heading are: interpret all that is said below in relation to meanings appropriate to the substance of the heading (43). In addition, headings can do the work of a summary, especially in the absence of any formal abstract. This means that a heading can act as a representational device, indicating that there is a part which is separable from the whole, that the text is actually *about* something which can be distinguished by the reader from the elaborate morass of language in which it is located. In other words the reader is told that the significance of the text can be separated from the wider body of the text. The heading 'Discovery of Pulsars' thus tells the reader what to look for in the subsequent text and how to interpret the relevance of the words which make up that text. As a fairly obvious example, 'stars' (l. 4) is to be read as part of a collection which we might call 'Scientific investigation of astrophysical phenomena' and which includes 'laboratory' (l. −1), 'discovery' (l. 0), 'pulsars' (l. 0, l. 1), 'research' (l. 2) and so on (44). This eliminates other possible understandings of the relevance of stars, simply because the reader is unable to find members of another collection which might, for example, include 'fame', 'fortune', 'show-biz', 'television' and 'Hollywood'.

(c) *Textual Opening*

The importance of textual openings is now well known. In the scientific report examined by Gusfield it was noticed that the first paragraph established a 'tension' between two points of view (45). Immediately at the beginning of the paper the 'denouement' is given, thus providing the reader with the author's solution to (or resolution of) the established tension. In Smith's terms, an assertion advanced in the opening sentences of a text provides instructions for the reader to understand further parts of the text as being about or supporting that assertion. Like headings, openings provide at least one member of a collection which the reader can use to make sense of the rest of the discussion. Unlike headings, however, openings do stronger work in that they establish or assert the 'conclusion' to the argument of the text. It is not just that openings provide a convenient system of categorisation for making sensible reading. They additionally instruct the reader to relate the contents of the text to a system of categorisation which is presented as the answer or solution to the phenomenon or events described in the text. In Smith's data, "I was actually the last of her close friends who was opening willing to admit that she was becoming mentally ill" acts as an instruction that all the things subsequently related in the text be interpreted in terms of the categorical scheme 'mental illness'. Naively, we might expect a series of facts to be presented, on the basis of which the reader can decide what to make of them. In fact, the solution asserted at the outset encourages the reader to relate all subsequently described events to this solution (46).

In the present data, we have "The trail which ultimately led to the first pulsar began in 1948 when . . . " (l. 1). I suggest that this does some of the work described by Smith (and by Gusfield) and additionally provides for reader's work of particular importance for the notion of discovery. Firstly, the assertion of the solution or conclusion ("the first pulsar") encourages readers to understand all subsequent description in terms of its relevance for this solution. To paraphrase Smith again, the problems presented by the account is not to find an answer to the question "what do all the events described here indicate?", but to find that this collection of items is a proper puzzle to the solution "the discovery of pulsars" (47). The 'reasonableness' of the solution follows from the reader making sense of described events in terms of the solution. Secondly, this in turn suggests that the construct "the first pulsar", in explaining a collection of otherwise inexplicable events, has a character rather different from any of the events. It is not just another event; it is something which explains these events. Hence, the solution is an entity of a different order from the events and in this sense is independent of them. Thirdly, the independence of this entity is reinforced by the fact that some motion is required in order to get at it. We would suppose that an entity of our own creation might be fairly readily at hand at the time when it was first noticed as existing. But "the first pulsar" is to be understood as having had a pre-existence, a quality of *out-there-ness* which required that it be *approached*. I shall focus first on features of the text which reinforce the independence or out-there-ness of the phenomenon. Subsequently I shall examine how the particular plausible means of approaching this phenomenon suggested to the reader is that of following a trail or path.

Externalising Devices (48)

As externalising device provides for the reading that the phenomenon described has an existence only by virtue of actions beyond the realm of human agency. In this case, externalising devices provide for the reading that pulsars are neither the product nor the artful creation of scientists; scientists came upon these objects rather than creating them. The dilemma is that the author should be trusted as teller of the tale, but at the same time should not be seen

as intruding upon the object. Gusfield suggests that the identification of the
role and institutional affiliation of the author establishes the reader's trust in
the author (49). In terms of my earlier comments, the setting can provide for
this trust. The scene of the action is then externalised by the use of the quasi-
passive voice:

I was able to show (l. 7)
I was also able to measure (l. 9)
My fascination . . . brought me to the solar corona (l. 10–11)
I was eventually able to trace (l. 13)
In my notebook . . . there is a comment (l. 15)
patterns . . . which would be detectable (l. 17–18)
the information then available showed (l. 18–19)

This kind of formulation is extremely common in the text. It provides for (and
reinforces) the reading that events occurred independently of the author's
involvement which was relatively incidental to the steady accumulation of
knowledge. The sustained usage of this device gives rise to an almost coy
picture of the scientists as 'fortunate bystander' or 'lucky witness'. To appreciate the importance of this device it is instructive to substitute alternative
expressions wherever the quasi-passive is used. Whereas in other circumstances
it might be quite appropriate, for example, to use 'I showed' instead of 'I was
able to show', the sustained use of the active voice makes the present account
read quite differently. More exactly, the active voice provides for the reading:
"These objects (pulsars) were artfully constructed by the teller of the tale".
At once, this conflicts with the expectancies and interpretations set up by the
initial textual opening. What manner of objectivity could be claimed for the
research process such that the claimed *inevitability* of the outcome results
from the merely *idiosyncratic* manoeuvres of the researcher?

Of related importance is the notion of community. Membership of a
community is invoked in the sense that human agents comprise a residual
category separated from the realm of objects. To restate the author's dilemma,
he has to display himself as a member of the community, with no privileged
epistemological access to the realm of objects, and yet he has to show himself
as a reporter of the nature of objects in that external realm. The quasi-passive
emphasises that the world of external objects has impinged upon him and
that all that happens in the course of path following is the result of external

circumstances rather than of his own volition. The invocation of community membership can be read as a demonstration that the "author has no special vantage point or viewpoint compared with the audience" (50). This means that any other member would arrive at the same conclusion, given the same circumstances. The notion of community membership is commonly invoked by the use of the royal 'we' (51). In this data, 'we' appears infrequently (but consider "We are all familiar with . . . . " (1. 3—4). Nonetheless, there is frequent citation of 'things we all know' which provides for a reading of the author as member of a community whose action results from the community's knowledge of the external world; his action is again thoroughly non-whimsical. In lines 1—3, for example, the author's first introduction to a communally defined problem is related. The problem can be read as belonging to a community (52) by identifying "research team" and "general problem" as members of the same collection (53). The coincidence of the author's joining the research team and his becoming interested in a problem can be interpreted as a 'natural' occurrence given the available tie between 'research team' and 'problems'. In lines 5—6, for example, the introduction to communal knowledge is brought about by a teacher. Had anyone else similarly been provided with this access to technique, they too would have been able to make the consequent steps (54).

The externality of the events described in the text is in part provided for, then, by the use of passive formulations and by the invocation of community membership. At the same time the text is clearly about the author's individual part in the events leading up to the discovery. The solution to this particular aspect of the author's dilemma is the portrayal of the *coincidence* of the inevitability of unfolding events with things which happened to the author. In part, of course, the passive formulation achieves this: it is only by virtue of the combination of circumstances essentially beyond his control that he was permitted to pull off one or other particular event. For example, in line 13, "I was eventually able to trace" can be read as happening as a result of events allowing him this possibility. Concidence is more obviously provided for right from the start of the text, in lines 1—2: "The trial which ultimately led to the the first pulsar began in 1948 when I joined Ryle's small research team . . . " I have already made a case for the way in which the objectivity (out-there-ness) of the phenomenon is provided for. In the following section, I examine the objectivity assigned to the trail which leads to the phenomenon. Given this objectivity, any event obviously involving human agency (such as joining a research team) is to be read as a coincidental rather than constitutive occurrence.

Pathing Devices

One of Kuhn's most significant, but often neglected points is that scientists' descriptions of scientific episodes are a source of considerable obfuscation to sociological and historical understanding of science (55). The source of such obfuscation is not simply that scientists are poor historians, nor just that they tend to confuse scientific and historical accuracy. More fundamentally, the marked tendency towards etiological structure found in scientific discourse reflects the fact that scientists routinely engage in establishing relationships between current work (or knowledge) and past events. One important consequence of this is scientists' insistence on portraying work as the latest in a long line of cumulative development (56). It is this picture of development with which Kuhn takes issue. According to Kuhn, sociological and historical evidence can be adduced to provide a picture of cyclical development, which contrasts with the linear-cumulative model found (especially) in scientific textbooks. Of course, much sociological and historical capital can be made of the fact that uncritical reliance on linear-cumulative descriptions can lead to an 'erroneous' understanding of the way science 'actually' develops. More importantly for present purposes, this reliance neglects consideration of a central feature of scientific investigation: the way in which participants render events as stemming, or following on from past events.

I shall refer to one aspect of the work done by scientists in accomplishing connections between events as the use of pathing devices. While providing for a reading of the out-there-ness of pulsars, it is also necessary to relate how this independent entity was 'captured', how its existence was brought within the realm of scientific knowledge. The pathing device portrays the capture in terms of a path followed by the capturers. In Smith's data we find "My recognition that there might be something wrong was very gradual" (57). "That something might be wrong" is the independent solution which readers are asked to use as a way of ordering the facts described. In addition, the acquisition of this solution is set up as a *process*. The reader is encouraged to orient to textual events as part of a process of gradual realisation. Significantly, this asks us to suspend our assessment of the facts until they have all been told. It is therefore inappropriate to query the 'oddness' of individual items of behaviour described in the text. Instead, we are told to look for the combined and *cumulative* effect of all the events (aspects of behaviour), and for the adequacy of the achieved categorisation of this cumulative effect.

In a similar way, line 1 of the pulsar data provides for a reading of "coming upon the first pulsar" as a process. The process is to be understood as cumulative in that it involves following a path ("trail"). This in turn provides instructions to the reader that all that follows should be understood as leading up to the discovery. We are asked to suspend critical evaluation of items mentioned in the text and to understand that the first section be read not for itself but as 'providing the background' or 'acting as a lead-in'. This means, for example, that if the account were being narrated, it would appear inappropriate to interrupt at, say, line 11 to raise a question about the 'solar corona'. The narrator could well rebuff a reader/hearer's interruption by explaining that the piece about the solar corona would become relevant later, that he was 'just giving the background' at this stage and that the main point of the story is the discovery of pulsars. Such an interruption is unlikely to occur, I suggest, precisely because readers are encouraged to notice line 1 as providing the instructions: "The first fifty or sixty lines are simply intended as introduction, as sketching out the background to the story, the real point of all this is yet to come, so that queries about items in this section are irrelevant or uncalled for" (58).

The pathing device in line 1 acts as a strong constraint on the way the reader interprets the text: the apprehension of the phenomenon as a discovery is to be understood by way of an account of the approach to, or capture of, the 'first' pulsar. At the same time, the initial statement about the path-like nature through which textual events must be understood, requires and finds reinforcement as the story unfolds. The instructions made available by the initial pathing device are restated throughout the text. This is done by re-presenting the events, not as 'any old collection' of events, but as a properly and sequentially connected series of events. Whereas the pathing device provides instructions for finding a link between the story's beginning and its (already asserted) conclusion, other devices establish for the reader that this link comprises an adequately connected sequence of events.

Sequencing Devices

The importance of sequential organisation in texts is recognised by Smith as follows:

The ordering of events in the narrative constructs the objectivity of the fact, the items which might serve to suggest the opposite are not only relegated to the background, they are also not constructed in the same way. They are merely as it were lying about. A careful search may identify them, but the work of bringing them into order must all be done by the reader/hearer (59).

Sequential organisation thus acts as a 'cutting out' process, whereby other potential paths and other potentially relevant events are backgrounded. The reader is encouraged to concur with the relevance of described events for the sequence in which they are located. Irrelevant events, in particular false leads, red herrings and blind alleys, are either excluded or are not tied to subsequent events (60).

Textual items can be read as connected or tied together if they can be found to belong to a common category or collection of items. I suggested earlier that this was the way that headings provided for the relevance of textual items. If we now extend this mechanism to activities and events, we can see how connections are provided for. For example, the connection between joining a research team (l. 2) and having a task of understanding something (l. 4) is made 'obvious' and hence incontrovertible by the location of a collection which includes both the former event and the latter activity. The strength of the tie between 'the task of understanding' and 'joining a research team' is reaffirmed not simply because 'everyone knows' that the task of understanding goes on in research teams, but also because the 'work of research' simultaneously provides the interpretative scheme whereby the particular sense of the activity of 'understanding' is established. Similarly, the reader can find ties between the 'task' of understanding and later activities such as being "able to show" (l. 7), being "able to measure" (l. 9), "studying" (l. 10), and being "able to trace" (l. 13). All these descriptions of action can be assigned a sensible meaning (that is, they can be understood) if that meaning concurs with the meanings of other members of the same collection: the sense of showing, measuring and so on is determined in terms of the nature of the task of understanding. At the same time, the nature of the task is elaborated and refined by the meanings given to these activities. The sense of individual activities and events thus depends on their location in a common collection of relevancies; their common location for purposes of assigning sense thus goes hand in hand with their connectedness.

Although membership ties provide for the interconnectedness of events and activities, and although these connections are suggestive of order (for example, we take the sense of joining a research team that precedes assuming a task as part of that team) it is possible to specify certain features of the text which establish a sequential relevance for these connections.

Events and activities can be read as sequentially ordered by virtue of their textual juxtaposition. Events can thus be read as being related in time, even though no specific reference to date or time is made. For example, "My fascination in using extraterrestial radio sources for studying the intervening plasma next brought me to the solar corona" (l. 10–11). Events previously related (for example, the measurement of ionospheric wind speeds – line 9) become events which happened before the author's first mention of another event (coming to the solar corona). In some cases, activities are specified as having occurred 'at a certain time', where the nominated time acts as one member of a collection of previous and subsequent time points. Events can be read as having an order by understanding the sense of their associated accompanying time points in relation to other members of the same collection. Consider, for example, the following three phrases:

In my notebook for 1954 there is . . . (l. 15)
the information then available . . . (l. 18–19)
about eight years later . . . (l. 21)

Fairly obviously, we can use the 'then' as a time referent to establish a sense of simultaneity about the availability of information noted in lines 18–19 and the making of a comment in 1954. This simultaneity also justifies the presence of lines 18–20: the contents are taken to be relevant to the current stage of the path being described. In addition the temporal tie between the two sentences provides for the second as an elaboration of the first. In this particular case, moreover, the elaboration also acts as a justification for not following a particular course of action on the basis of the 1954 notebook comment.

In a similar way, events can be read as having occurred in a sequence if they can be seen to be tied to explicit dates. In the text we can find "1948" (l. 1), "1954" (l. 15), "1965" (l. 42 and 49), "July 1967" (l. 59), "August 1967" (l. 71) and so on. The appearance of these dates in order throughout the text provides a chronological backcloth, upon which related occurrences are displayed. More importantly, events and descriptions are tied into this chronological framework so as to furnish a history involving minimal gap or overlap. For example, the dates in line 4 and line 1 establish the scope of the historical scenario: little will concern the reader that occurred before 1948 or after 1974. Line 1 also establishes the relevance in following lines of things occurring since 1948. By line 15 ("1954") six years worth of "background to the discovery" (l. 0 and l. 1) have been covered. Significantly, the coverage of these six years appears thoroughly adequate: at no point does the reader feel that an unjustified leap has been made by the author, that insufficient information has been provided to fill out what went on in (say) 1950, or that too much has been said about these years such that a reference to 1954 constitutes 'backtracking'. This effect is in part due to many of the devices already noted. Just as the heading, textual opening and pathing devices ask a reader to assess the significance of items (such as 'solar corona') in terms of 'what is to come later', so too are the contents of lines 1–15 to be understood as things which happened between 1948–1954 which are relevant to the (pre-established) purposes of this story. The strength of this effect entails a subtle inversion: lines 1–15 become "all that needs to be said about what happened between 1948–1954" and the completeness of the account is established as 'good enough'. The story then proceeds by the tied relevance of events in 1954 to those of the preceding six year period: for example, pre-1954 work associated with the solar atmosphere (l. 13) has a relevance in terms of the 1954 notebook comment about the solar atmosphere (l. 16).

Sequencing devices thus provide for the connection of described events and activities. The connectedness of these events and activities is to be looked for by the reader in the context of a pathing device which asserts the existence of a route to be followed. Thus, in the connectedness of events and activities the reader can find a cumulative relevance: the events and activities are not merely connected sequentially, they are constitutive of the route being followed.

Logic

Logic can be generally thought to be concerned with the rules of valid inference. As one popular dictionary definition puts it, those who try to following the rules of logic aim to distinguish

inferences whose premises really entail their conclusions . . . from those whose premises do not. (61)

The issue arising here is that of the adequacy of connection between one state X_1 (described in the above definition as a premise) and another state Y_1 (referred to as a conclusion). If X_1 'really' entails Y_1, if a connection can be seen to hold between X_1 and Y_1, if Y_1 can be seen to result from X_1 rather than from any other X_2, and if it is Y_1 rather than any other Y_2 that results from X_1, then the relationship between X_1 and Y_1 can be said to be logical (62).

Of course, there is no explicit claim in the text that the discovery process was 'logical'. That is, there are no explicit attempts to justify connections between successive stages of the discovery process using the kind of schematic representation just employed. This is perhaps not surprising in that we recognise a Nobel lecture as the occasion for celebration-of-having-made-a-discovery rather than for attempting-to-establish-a-claim-to-a-discovery. If anything, the legitimacy of an already established claim enjoys reinforcement rather than renewed scrutiny on the occasion of this lecture address. Yet I suggest that the text still stands as a report of a logical inquiry in the sense that participants can be seen to have proceeded in a correct fashion.

This reading is made possible by virtue of all the features of textual organisation outlined above. The reader is asked to concur with the authority of presentation, to interpret textual events and actions both as being about some external phenomenon and as giving rise to this phenomenon. In addition, the externality of this phenomenon is to be approached by way of a process of path following, in which the relevance of individual items is seen not for themselves, but as steps on the way towards the phenomenon. The intrusion of the author in this process is minimised by various externalising devices. The sequential nature of the procedure is further provided for by a variety of features which demonstrate connectedness. In terms of the above schematic representation, Y_1 can be understood to be entailed by X_1 if Y_1 is a subsequent state (rather than just any other state), if Y_1 is a next mentioned event or activity by which the continuing sense of a developing story is to be retained, if the nextness of Y_1 can be read as another step towards the already asserted (and hence pre-existing) conclusion to the story, and if the particular sense of Y_1 is to be found by reference to a collection of events and activities of which X_1 is a member.

The total effect of a whole series of $X_1 - Y_1$ connections is that of 'cutting out' alternative ways of reading the text. It is not impossible to find other events (X_2, Y_2) in the text. But their sense and connectedness is not easily established: they are not woven into the text in the same way. Thus the possibility of $X_2 - Y_1$ (or $X_1 - Y_2$) relationships is neither explicitly entertained nor provided for by their organisational presentation in the text. In this manner, alternative ways of *reading* are cut-out or background. But such is the congruence between the reader's means of understanding the path-like nature of the report and the means of understanding the path-like nature of the discovery process, that alternative ways of *proceeding* in the investigation are also cut-out or backgrounded. Thus it is hard to find alternative ways of 'coming to the problem', 'setting up the crucial experiment', 'seeing the link between one observation and another', and so on. The reading most compellingly provided for is that of an investigation which displays care and orderliness in its execution: participants have proceeded in a manner that has allowed them to infer conclusions about the existence and character of a phenomenon on the basis of observational premises.

3. Conclusion

In the first part of this paper I described a debate over the ways of studying knowledge between rationalist philosophers and 'strong programmers'. Although this debate is in no way exhaustive of the variety of positions adopted in philosophical and sociological perspectives on knowledge production, its description provided the basis for suggesting that alignment to such perspectives is (at least) an inappropriate strategy for the fruitful understanding of the process of scientific investigation. I argued that the form and currency of the activities which characterise this debate are to be found as a crucial constituent of scientific investigation. In other words, the work of science involves scientists in continual monitoring activity, in attempts to specify truth status on the one hand and in searches for the presence of the social on the other. This point is perhaps particularly salient for adherents to the "strong programme" in the sociology of scientific knowledge: those sociologists whose main analytic objective is the revelation of social circumstances in science tend to miss consideration of the way in which scientists' routine invocation and attribution of social factors and interests is crucial to their work.

Practical reasoning in sciences encompasses a wide variety of activities. In the second part of this paper I illustrated the analytic perspective developed above in relation to just one type of activity, namely the work of textual organisation whereby a particular scientific accomplishment is reported. In the particular case of an account of a discovery, a number of features combine to make available to the reader a picture of the discovery process as a path-like sequence of logical steps towards the revelation of a hitherto unknown phenomenon. The perspective adopted here might be profitably developed and extended to an examination of a much wider range of scientists' accounting practices.

Notes and References

1. I would like to thank a number of people who helpfully commented on an earlier draft of this paper. These include Peter Halfpenny, Karin Knorr, Roger Krohn, Bruno Latour and Michael Lynch.
2. S. W. Woolgar, 'What Can Ethnomethodology Tell Us About Science As A Topic?', Paper presented to Werner-Reimers Stiftung conference, Bad Homburg, 4–7th January 1979 and to BSA Sociology of Science Study Group, London, 13th February 1979.
3. In terms of its concern with issues of practical reasoning, fact production and the use of the documentary method of interpretation, ethnomethodology would appear to have a clear relevance for those interested in the nature of scientific inquiry. This relevance is implicit in the early work: H. Garfinkel, *Studies in Ethnomethodology*, Prentice Hall, New Jersey, 1967; issues more explicitly related to scientific work are raised in articles such as those by H. C. Elliot, W. W. Sharrock and D. H. Zimmerman in R. Turner (ed.), *Ethnomethodology*, Penguin, Harmondsworth, 1974. Most recently, scientific work has enjoyed extended and detailed treatment at the hands of a growing body of interested ethnomethodologists. See especially, M. Lynch, *Art and Artifact in Laboratory Science: A Study of Shop Work and Shop Talk in a Research Laboratory*, Ph.D. diss., University of California, Irvine, 1979; also M. Lynch, 'Technical Work and Critical Inquiry: Investigations in a Scientific Laboratory', Paper presented at conference on 'The Social Process of Scientific Investigation', McGill University 19–21st October, 1979.

4. Some of the earliest proposals to this effect can be found in S. B. Barnes and R. G. A. Dolby, 'The Scientific Ethos: A Deviant Viewpoint', *European Journal of Sociology* 11, 3–25 (1970); M. J. Mulkay, 'Some Aspects of Cultural Growth in the Natural Sciences', *Social Research* 36, 22–52 (1961); R. D. Whitley, 'Black Boxism and the Sociology of Science: a discussion of the major developments in the field', *Sociological Review Monograph* 18, 61–92 (1972).

5. The terms in which the debate is reported here derive from contributions to the seminar series: 'Rationality and the Sociology of Knowledge', Balliol College, Oxford, Summer term, 1979.

6. K. R. Popper, *Objective Knowledge*, Oxford University Press, Oxford, 1972.

7. R. Bhaskar, *A Realist Theory of Science*, Leeds Books, Leeds, 1975, p. 10.

8. B. Barnes, *Scientific Knowledge and Sociological Theory*, Routledge and Kegan Paul, London, 1974; *Interests and the Growth of Knowledge*, Routledge and Kegan Paul, London, 1977.

9. D. Bloor, *Knowledge and Social Imagery*, Routledge and Kegan Paul, London, 1976.

10. A sociological explanation of the dispute between rationalism and strong programme might fashionably proceed by attributing to each party a difference in 'interests'; differences in style and form of explanation, together with a fundamental difference in interests, would amount to the incommensurability of rationalism and the strong programme; since adequacy of explanation will depend in some complex way on the interests of the inquirer, it follows that any particular explanation will remain fundamentally inadequate as far as the other party is concerned. This line of argument might also account for differences between the strong programme as portrayed by rationalists, and the strong programme as described by its adherents.

11. See my comments below derived from the analysis by J. Gusfield, 'The Literary Rhetoric of Science', *American Sociological Review* 41, 16–34 (1976).

12. B. Latour and S. Woolgar, *Laboratory Life: The Social Construction of Scientific Facts*, Sage, Beverly Hills, 1979.

13. This is not to say that practising scientists are particularly 'good' or 'bad' sociologists (or philosophers). Rather, the suggestion is that they engage in essentially similar forms of 'practical reasoning'; that their competences with regard to basic explanatory skills (for example, invoking causes, attributing motives) are no different from those of sociologists (or philosophers).

14. For purposes of making the analogy between the constructive work of scientists and that of the strong programmers, this last formulation pays insufficient attention to the work of scientists in establishing whether or not *any* social circumstances are present. Although, intuitively, we might expect scientists only to be concerned with social factors when the work of science 'goes wrong', it is possible that such an assumption detracts attention from continuous implicit monitoring by scientists of the potential intrusion of social factors.

15. This shift in focus amounts to a redefinition of the explanandum, a manoeuvre which, from the point of view of protagonists to the debate outlined above, might be thought of as something of a 'Pyrrhic victory'. The cost is that of seeing knowledge production from the perspective of either philosopher or sociologist, and yet the manoeuvre opens up possibilities of investigation relatively free from (or at least respectful of) the constraints (for example, inconcludeability) of this kind of debate.

16. The term 'social' may appear conspicuously absent from this last phrase. Its absence is intended to denote my reservations about the practice of premature "conceptualisation of actions in social terms." For an elegant discussion of the way in which some sociological arguments 'fill out' analysis by the introduction of 'disengaged' analytical apparatus see Lynch, *op. cit.*, 1979, (Note 3).

17. H. M. Collins, 'The Seven Sexes: A Study of the Sociology of a Phenomenon, or the Replication of Experiments in Physics,' *Sociology* 9, 205–224 (1975).

18. In terms of the example of the discovery of pulsars referred to below, it was only possible to know that pulsars existed when you knew something about what they were. Of course, the *amount* that needs to be known about a phenomenon before its existence can be claimed to be (or accepted as) genuine is a crucial issue for scientists. In the case of pulsars, participants' prevarication on this point was extensive. See S. W. Woolgar, *The Emergence and Growth of Research Areas in Science with Special Reference to Research on Pulsars*, unpub. Ph.D. diss. University of Cambridge, 1978.

19. A point pursued at length in Latour and Woolgar, *op. cit.*, 1979, (Note 12) Chap. 4.

20. There are some similarities here with the argument of what Attewell calls the 'radical situationist' wing of ethnomethodology (P. Attewell, 'Ethnomethodology Since Garfinkel', *Theory and Society* 1, 179–210 (1974)). In particular, Attewell cites the work of Zimmerman and Pollner (for example, D. H. Zimmerman and M. Pollner, 'The Everyday World As a Phenomenon'. In J. D. Douglas (ed.), *Understanding Everyday Life*, Routledge and Kegan Paul, London, 1971, pp. 80–103.

21. D. E. Smith, 'K Is Mentally Ill', *Sociology* 12, 23–53 (1978); previously published as 'K ist geisterskrank. Die Anatomie eines Tatsachenberichtes'. In E. Weingarten, F. Sack and J. N. Schenkein (eds.), *Ethnomethodologie: Beiträge zu einer Soziologie des Alltagsleben*, Suhrkamp, Frankfurt, 1976.

22. *Ibid.*, p. 23.

23. By 'notion of mental illness' I refer to the particular notion or version of mental illness made available to and used by the reader in making sense of the text. The programme is *not* that of attempting to specify the 'essence' or 'universal character' of mental illness.

24. It is important that Smith's argument is not understood as an application of 'labelling theory'. Smith does *not* claim, for example, that what was 'actually not' mental illness was given that label by reason of accounting practices. Rather, those practices are constitutive of the phenomenon. For a critique of 'labelling theory' from an ethnomethodological perspective see M. Pollner, 'Sociological and Common Sense Models of the Labelling Process'. In R. Turner (ed.), *op. cit.*, 1974, (Note 3), pp. 27–40.

25. L. Bloomfield, 'Linguistic Aspects of Science', *Philosophy of Science* 2, 499–517 (1935).

26. L. Bloomfield, 'Language Or Ideas', *Language* 12, 89 (1936).

27. Garfinkel, *op. cit.*, 1967, (Note 3).

28. Collins, *op. cit.*, 1975, (Note 17).

29. P. McHugh, 'On the Failure Of Positivism'. In Douglas, *op. cit.*, 1971. (Note 20), pp. 337–354.

30. Certainly, Smith (*op. cit.*, 1978, Note 21) makes no attempt to substantiate her assumption of isomorphism.

31. Latour and Woolgar, *op. cit.*, 1979, (Note 12).

32. Cf. D. C. Anderson, 'Stories and Arguments: Narrative Assembly and Contrastive Characterisation as Contributive Features in the Local Organisation of a Sociology Text', unpub. paper, no date.

33. A. Hewish, 'Pulsars and High Energy Physics'. In *Les Prix Nobel En 1974*, The Nobel Foundation, Stockholm, 1975, 69—79. For reasons of space, the analysis focusses on the first 24 lines of this text.

34. Woolgar, *op. cit.*, 1978, (Note 16a) pp. 79 ff.

35. For purposes of present analysis, I have no interest in the 'accuracy' of the data. That is, I am not concerned to establish whether or not the lecture address is an adequate portrayal of the actual facts of the matter. This might be a legitimate line of investigation in another context, although there are strong arguments for suggesting that the actual facts of the matter are essentially irretrievable in any incorrigible sense (see, for example, S. W. Woolgar, 'Changing Perspectives — a chronicle of research development in the sociology of science'. In J. Farkas (ed.), *The Sociology of Science and Research*, Akadémiai Kiadó, Budapest, 1979, pp. 421—437). Here I have no wish to evaluate Hewish's claims, to downgrade the achievements alluded to in the lecture nor to detract from the perceived significance of his scientific work. This declaration is necessary for two reasons. Firstly, it seems that almost any attempt to examine a document (or any other artifact) without wishing straightforwardly to build upon, or use 'the facts which reside in the document' is greeted with suspicion. It is assumed that if the analyst does not accept the factual status of the document, he must be questioning its veracity. To repeat, my motive is not evaluative. Secondly, in the particular case of pulsars, much controversy followed the initial announcement in 1968 of discovery and was rekindled by Hewish's subsequent receipt of the Nobel Prize. See Woolgar, *op. cit.*, 1978, (Note 34). Here I am not examining the lecture address for evidence bearing on this dispute.

36. An analysis (along similar lines to the one here) of contemporaneous discovery accounting practice could attempt to discover how much needed to be known about a 'thing' before its existence could be taken as genuine (see Note 18). In the present text, the retrospective character of the account reveals the discovery as something that was on the cards all the time (even from 1948 — see below).

37. Anderson, *op. cit.*, no date, (Note 32); Gusfield, *op. cit.*, 1976, (Note 11); Smith, *op. cit.*, 1978, (Note 21). The attentive reader will notice that I gratefully employ many of the terms and expressions used by these authors.

38. Where the wording remains entirely unchanged I have acknowledged this by quotation.

39. Smith, *op. cit.*, 1978, (Note 21) p. 26.

40. Gusfield, *op. cit.*, 1976, (Note 11).

41. Line references to annotated text.

42. My usage of 'provides for' is recurrent in the subsequent analysis and merits some elucidation. By saying that a feature of textual organisation 'provides for' a certain reading, I mean simply that a certain interpretation or set of meanings is made possible. This is not to claim that this is the only reading which might in practice be arrived at, nor am I able to cite evidence categorically demonstrating that 'most people' did read it this way. Rather, my aim is to specify the characteristics of the

text which could lead to one particular and plausible reading. In the present context, it remains possible, for example, for a sceptical reader to notice lines −4 to −1 as merely an *attempt* to legitimate the whole story, 'knowing full well that this is just the kind of dubious tactic which people at that institution (l. −1) would employ'. An analysis of this alternative reading is possible, but would be complicated by the need to specify the source and applicability of a reader's 'knowledge about the use of tactics'.

43. In more formal ethnomethodological terms: the indexicality of all followed terms can be repaired by selecting that sense compatible with the collection of senses implied by the heading.

44. This scheme is loosely adopted from H. Sacks, 'An Initial Investigation of the Useability of Conversational Data for Doing Sociology'. In D. Sudnow (ed.), *Studies in Social Interaction*, Free Press, New York, 1974, pp. 31−74.

45. Gusfield, *op. cit.*, 1976, (Note 11).

46. The circularity of this scheme can be thought of as somewhat similar to assuming the answer in a mathematical proof.

47. Smith, *op. cit.*, 1978, (Note 21) p. 37. In a similar way, Garfinkel shows how the documentary method of interpretation can involve a search for the proper sense of questions to which answers are offered: Garfinkel, *op. cit.*, 1967, (Note 3) p. 90.

48. As will become clear, it is possible to think of what are described here as 'devices' in terms of the 'modalities' referred to by Latour and Woolgar, *op. cit.*, 1979, (note 12) Chap. 2.

49. Gusfield, *op. cit.*, 1976, (Note 11).

50. *Ibid.*, p. 21.

51. See M. Roche, 'A Durkheim Reader: Rules for Loud Speech and Silence', *Writing Sociology* 1, 9−23 (1976).

52. In this text, membership of *a* community appears to be more important than specifying *which* community in this text. It is noticeable, for example, that the "we" of line 3 is different from the we implicit in "small research team" (l. 2).

53. Cf. W. W. Sharrock, 'On Owning Knowledge', pp. 45−53 in Turner (ed.), *op. cit.*, 1974, (Note 3).

54. Although for reasons of space it is not possible to pursue this here, it would be instructive to examine the consequences of textual organisation of community and of the relationships established in the text between the actors depicted as participating in the discovery. The textual presentation of contributions made by assistants would be of particular relevance in the context of a subsequent dispute over which individual should rightfully be accredited with the discovery: the 'anyone else' of this last sentence has a special significance in the terms of this dispute. See Woolgar, *op. cit.*, 1978, (Note 34) Chap. 3.

55. T. S. Kuhn, *The Structure of Scientific Revolutions*, Chicago University Press, London, 2nd edition, 1970, pp. 1−9.

56. In the course of an extended study of the emergence and growth of research areas in science, requests for interviews were made to over 40 participants who had worked on pulsars during the five years after the announcement of their discovery in 1968 (see Woolgar, *op. cit.*, 1978, Note 34). In many case, the first reaction of these participants was that "it all began in the 1930's" or "to know about pulsars you really need to go back to the work of Baade and Zwicke before the war". The

accounts of some observers make an explicit case for linearity of development by excluding the relevance of certain sociological variables. See, for example, M. N. McMorris, 'The Ancestry of Pulsars', unpub. paper, University of West Indies, 1973.

57. Smith, *op. cit.*, 1978, (Note 21) p. 28.

58. Although, of course, there are no 'explicit' or 'literal' instructions to this effect.

59. Smith, *op. cit.*, 1978, (Note 21) p. 37.

60. Gusfield argues in a general way that because the comment on or significance of results appears at the end of a sequence: problem-methods-results-conclusion, the conclusion appears as the culmination of the use of methods in order to produce results. Gusfield, *op. cit.*, 1976, (Note 11) p. 19. Although both Smith and Gusfield describe the important effect of sequencing devices, neither specify in detail how sequences are provided for.

61. A. Bullock and O. Stallybrass (eds.), *The Fontana Dictionary of Modern Thought*, Fontana, London, 1977, p. 355.

62. Of course, this is not necessarily exhaustive of the requirements of logicality: conditions for adequate entailment are endlessly programmatic. That is, we can always imagine further conditions that could be specified as necessary for adequacy: for example, that Y_1 is not just another descriptive version of X_1, that Y_1 'really is' distinct from X_1 and so on. It follows that any instance of 'having been logical' is a practical accomplishment involving the repair of inconcludability by invocation of ad hoc and etcetera clauses.

CONTEXTS OF SCIENTIFIC DISCOURSE: SOCIAL ACCOUNTING IN EXPERIMENTAL PAPERS*

NIGEL GILBERT

University of Surrey

and

MICHAEL MULKAY

University of York

Almost all analysis in the sociology of science has involved attempts to describe scientists' social actions and 'technical' beliefs. For example, much effort has been devoted to investigating whether scientists, in the course of their research, act in a detached, impersonal, universalistic manner and whether these forms of action are required for the regular production of valid scientific knowledge (1). Other investigators have sought to provide definitive descriptions of the 'main features' of particular scientists' beliefs as a preliminary to explaining the beliefs as having been moulded by the actors' socially derived interests (2). In recent years, however, there has been a growing although by no means widespread recognition that neither social action nor technical belief in science can be identified unequivocally for the purposes of sociological analysis (3). This is because it has become increasingly clear that different scientists can and do give quite divergent, yet equally plausible, accounts of the 'same' act or the 'same' belief; and that particular actors tend to alter their accounts of their own and of others' actions and scientific ideas as they respond to new social situations (4). As a result, some sociologists concerned with the study of scientists' meaningful actions, as distinct from scientists' 'behaviour', have come to see that meaning does not reside in the actions themselves but in the context-dependent procedures of social accounting whereby actions are interpreted. It has also become increasingly clear that scientists' beliefs, as distinct from the variable context-

* Research supported by the Social Science Research Council, grant HR 5923.

Karin D. Knorr, Roger Krohn and Richard Whitley (eds.), The Social Process of Scientific Investigation. Sociology of the Sciences, Volume IV, 1980. 269–294.
Copyright © 1980 by D. Reidel Publishing Company.

dependent formulations which scientists produce, are inaccessible to the sociologist. Consequently, a few sociologists have begun to focus, not on the description of scientific action or belief itself, but on the ways in which scientists construct varying accounts of their actions and beliefs in different social settings. We intend below to use this approach in order to begin to provide a sociological analysis of experimental research papers.

We will bring research papers within the scope of sociological analysis by showing that they are, at least in part, a form of social account. Our central claims are: that when scientists write experimental papers, they make their results meaningful by linking them to accounts of social action and collective belief; that the accounts of social action and collective belief presented in the formal research literature employ only part of the repertoire of social accounting used by scientists informally; that these formal accounts seem to be constructed in accordance with a traditional conception of scientific rationality; that this version of rationality exists alongside other views of scientific rationality; and that these other views are excluded from the realm of formal discourse. By showing how scientists selectively portray their social actions and beliefs in the course of formal publication, we will begin to reveal how scientists themselves create that appearance of impersonality, detachment and universality which sociologists have customarily regarded as literally descriptive of social action and technical belief in science.

Full-length experimental papers are usually divided into the following separate sections: Abstract, Introduction, Methods and Materials, Results, Discussion. Although we believe that all these sections involve some kind of social accounting, we will concentrate upon Introduction and Methods and Materials sections. We will first of all present some passages from research papers to show that they do contain accounts of their author's actions and to draw attention to the way in which these actions are presented. We will then compare these formal accounts with those given informally in interviews by the same scientists. This comparison enables us to demonstrate that the two kinds of account differ dramatically in several respects and to offer some suggestions as to why this is so.

The evidence presented below is taken from interviews which we have carried out with 34 biochemists working in one specific problem area. Each interview lasted from 2 to 3 hours and was taped and transcribed in full. In preparation for each interview, we read and discussed at least two of the interviewee's published papers and, in many cases, considerably more than that. Thus, in addition to our general reading in this area of research, we have closely examined in the region of 100 published papers. This is much too large a number to be analysed in the kind of detail attempted here. In the sections which follow we have, therefore, concentrated on material from just two interviews and on one published paper by each interviewee. The reader should not forget that evidence will be required from many more research papers and from other research areas in order to establish any degree of generality for our conclusions. In addition, although our analysis is comparatively detailed, it will need to be supplemented by even finer examination of smaller sections of text. We hope subsequently to extend the analysis in both these directions. The present study is just a beginning, an attempt to take a little further the very few previous studies of this aspect of scientific accounting (5).

The points we intend to make below do not involve any deep appreciation of the technicalities of biochemistry. The reader should not be deterred, therefore, by his failure to understand completely the quotation from an introduction to a research paper which begins the next section. We use only four quotations with such a high level of technical content and only two of them need to be understood by the reader in any detail. Both these quotations are followed immediately by a 'layman's gloss'.

Social Accounting in Introductions

Introduction A

A long held assumption concerning oxidative phosphorylation has been that the energy available from oxidation-reduction reactions is used to drive the formation of the terminal covalent anhydride bound in ATP. Contrary to this view, recent results from several laboratories suggest that energy is used primarily to promote the binding of ADP and phosphate in a catalytically competent mode (1) and to facilitate the release of bound ATP (2, 3). In this model, bound ATP forms at the catalytic site from bound ADP and phosphate with little change in free energy.

A critical test of this proposal would be to measure energy-dependent changes in binding affinities at the catalytic site for adenine nucleotides. However, such measurements are complicated by the fact that mitochondrial membranes have numerous binding sites ... An inhibitor that specifically prevents substrate binding at the catalytic site would prove very useful since it would allow binding events directly involved in catalysis to be distinguished from other processes that require bound adenine nucleotide ...

An indication that the new phosphorylation inhibitor, efrapeptin, might bind at the catalytic site comes from studies with aurovertin . . . .

In this paper, we report the results of studies on the mode of inhibition of oxidative phosphorylation by efrapeptin . . . It is difficult to accommodate these results in a single mechanistic scheme involving a single independent catalytic site for ATP synthesis and hydrolysis. As will be discussed, the data are more easily interpreted in terms of a multiple interacting site model, such as the one recently proposed by C, D and E.

Layman's gloss A

ATP is one of a class of complex molecules called nucleotides. It is biologically important because it is a major source of energy in living organisms. ATP is formed by the combination of ADP and inorganic phosphate. The overall process whereby ATP is formed is called oxidative phosphorylation. The energy required for its formation (or catalysis or synthesis) is thought to be generated through a series of linked oxidation-reduction reactions. The point made by this author in the first paragraph is that, whereas many biochemists have believed that the energy produced by these oxidation-reduction reactions is used to bind together ADP and phosphate, there is now good evidence showing that this binding occurs at specific sites with little expenditure of energy. He refers to a new model of oxidative phosphorylation in which the free energy is used, not to *make* ATP, but to *release* it for physiological purposes.

He then goes on to state that this model could be tested by measuring the relevant binding affinities. However, this task is complicated by the fact that the membranes of mitochondria, which are complex intracellular particles within which these processes occur, have numerous binding sites in addition to that where ATP is formed (the catalytic site). Efrapeptin is then identified as a substance which appears to act only on the catalytic binding site and which should help the experimenter to make observation of that site alone. Finally, the author claims that the results obtained with efrapeptin are inconsistent with older views of ATP formation and are best interpreted in terms of an extended version of the new model mentioned in the first paragraph.

Many commentators have drawn attention to the way in which scientific papers are written in an impersonal style, with overt references to the actions, choices and judgments of their authors being kept to a minimum (6). In this respect the introduction, about half of which is reproduced above, is typical of scientific writing. Although three other scientists are referred to by name in the full text, there is in every instance a rapid return to less personal formulations and the authors themselves only appear once through their use of the pronoun 'we'. At various points in the exposition verbs usually associated with human agency are employed, but we often find them combined with some non-human 'agent'. Thus, 'recent results' are said to 'suggest certain possibilities', and 'studies with aurovertin' are said to 'indicate others'. Despite this impersonal style, which minimises explicit mention of social actors and their beliefs, it is clear that parts of the text implicitly offer accounts of the actions and beliefs of the authors and of their specialised research community. To this extent the introduction has a definite, albeit partly obscured, social component. We wish to suggest that the authors use the introduction to establish the significance of their findings at least partly by the way in which they organise the social element in their text.

If we consider the opening sentence we see that it is not a statement about the physical world, but about the customary nature of certain beliefs among a number of biochemists. This sentence could equally well have been written by a sociologist, trying to construct an interpretative analysis of social action in a research network. This similarity exists because the sentence *is* part of a subtle and purposeful social analysis. For the beliefs in question are presented in a way which enables the authors to contrast them unfavourably with those of another group of scientists, to which the authors themselves belong. What is particularly noticeable about the first sentence is how the beliefs which it summarises are prepared for immediate rejection. Thus, instead of presenting the central idea as a reasonable, though inconclusive interpretation associated with at least some experimental evidence, the authors choose to describe it as mere assumption. Furthermore, no supporting literature is cited. The impression is subtly conveyed that, although this idea may have been around for a long time, it has no firm scientific foundation and is not to be taken seriously.

The nature of the opening sentence prepares us to expect and to welcome the contrasting view which the second sentence reveals. Clearly the reader, as a scientist, is expected not to favour unsupported assumptions, but only views based on hard data. Consequently, in the second sentence the authors tell us that it is 'experimental results' which suggest a significantly different state of affairs from that previously assumed. They do refer implicitly to particular actors, when they use the phrase 'several laboratories'. But the authors do not formulate their argument, as they could have done with at least equal accuracy, in terms of two or more groups of scientists producing different experiments along with plausible yet divergent interpretations of those experiments, but in terms of one group's *results* undermining the other group's *assumptions*. Although in sentence two the conclusions deriving from these results are presented simply as suggestions, they are described more strongly in the third sentence as constituting a model; that is, a systematic

explanatory scheme with, as the next paragraph makes clear, a central proposition which can be put to the test. References are given for this model, in
case the reader wishes to check its content or its empirical support. Thus, in
the course of three or four sentences, the authors have conveyed a strong
impression, at least for readers unfamiliar with the topic, that the paper to
follow is based upon a well established analytical position which constitutes
a major advance on prior work. They have done this, not directly by means of
biochemical data, but by characterisation of scientific belief within their
social network.

The formal account of collective belief offered by these authors would have
been regarded as misleading by many of the scientists we interviewed. For
many of them, at least informally, were highly critical of the model advanced
in this paper and in particular expressed dissatisfaction with its supporters'
failure to provide empirical clarification of the physical mechanisms involved.
We put this point to the senior author during the interview (7).

1. *Interviewer*. The most frequent criticism of the idea of conformational coupling that
people have talked about is that it doesn't tell you anything about mechanism. How
would you respond to that comment?

Author A. I'd say they were right. We always feel a little embarrassed when we talk
about conformational change. Because its a vague sort of thing. But I think it is an
important idea. The data seems to indicate that you need energy to release ATP from the
enzyme ... I agree that it is aesthetically unpleasing not to have a very detailed account
of what's happening. If it *is* an energy driven conformational change, that change will
never, not in our lifetime anyway, be described in very discrete steps. (29–30)

In this passage Author *A* qualifies his formal description of the merits of the
model he is advocating, in response to our version of the informal comments
of other researchers. This shows clearly, not only that other scientists would
probably have introduced these results quite differently, but also that a quite
different account could have been given by the authors themselves of the
state of scientific belief within the social network under consideration.

In order to show that the research paper considered so far is not unique,
let us look at another introduction.

Introduction B

The chemiosmotic hypothesis (1) proposed, *inter alia*, that each span of mitochondrial respiratory carriers and enzymes covering a so-called energy-conservation site (2) is so arranged that $2H^+$ are translocated across the mitochondrial inner membrane for each pair of reducing equivalents transferred across that span. Evidence in favour of this value of 2.0 for the ratio of protons translocated to reducing-equivalent pairs transferred (i.e. $\rightarrow H^+/2e^-$ ratio) has come mainly from one type of experiment. In this, the length of the respiratory chain under study has been altered by changing either the oxidant or the substrate (3, 4).

In the present paper we describe an independent method for measurement of the $\rightarrow H^+/2e^-$ ratio per energy-conservation site. The same substrate (intramitochondrial NADH) and oxidant (oxygen) is used throughout, but the number of energy-conservation sites is varied from one to three by using mitochondria from variants of [a particular yeast] with modified respiratory chains. We conclude that the $\rightarrow H^+/2e^-$ ratio is 2.0 per energy-conservation site.

Layman's gloss B

This paper is concerned with the series of oxidation-reduction reactions which are believed to occur in the membranes of mitochondria. This series of reactions is referred to as the respiratory chain. It is the respiratory chain which is taken to generate the free energy required for the formation and/or release of ATP. The author takes it for granted that this energy is furnished by a gradient of protons (H^+) which is created across the mitochondrial membrane by the action of the respiratory chain. He also takes it for granted that protons are carried across the membrane by pairs of electrons ($2e^-$) at three sites. The issue which he addresses is: How many protons are carried across at each site by each pair of electrons, i.e. what is the $H^+/2e^-$ ratio?

In the first paragraph, he states that a figure of 2.0 has been obtained previously by means of experiments in which the number of sites in the chain has been varied by changing the substrate (the reagent which donates the protons and electrons to the chain) or the oxidant (the reagent which receives the electrons after the protons have been transported). This is possible because some substrates and oxidants operate at different points in the chain.

In the second paragraph he states that he has also obtained a ratio of 2.0 per site, using the same substrate and oxidant, but employing mitochondria from three different strains of yeast with respiratory chains of varying length. Later in the paper he states that these mitochondria have chains with either one site, two sites or the full three sites.

This introduction seems straightforward and unproblematic. A quantitative aspect of a major hypothesis is first identified. The authors point out that, although this part of the hypothesis has been experimentally confirmed, only one kind of experimental design has been employed. An alternative technique is then briefly described. And the introduction ends with a statement that this new technique produces the same results as previous experiments and therefore provides further support for the hypothesis. In what sense does this passage involve social accounting? In the first place, an account is being offered of the state of belief among those scientists concerned with the proton/electron ratio. Although it is not stated explicitly, it seems to be implied that there are no negative experimental findings which need to be considered and little, if any, disagreement about the scientific meaning of previous findings. Indeed, it is this form of presentation which enables the authors to depict their own results as primarily a contribution to experimental technique: 'In the present paper we describe an independent method for measurement of' the relevant ratios. Their actual observations can be treated as basically unproblematic, because they are portrayed as merely confirming what competent researchers already know. As a result, attention is directed to the novel techniques used to obtain these expected observations. In this way the author's contribution to knowledge, and thereby the meaning of their work in the laboratory, is defined by the manner in which the existing state of belief about this ratio is construed.

The content of this introduction differs considerably from the discussion of the paper in the interview. For instance, the senior author stressed informally that previous observations of these ratios were by no means widely accepted.

2. *Author B.* . . . . There's always criticism of one method. There are very few methods that are bomb-proof . . . . What we did was another way of doing it . . . .

Interviewer. So there were people at that time who were casting doubt on *P* and *Q*'s figures?

Author B. You bet there were. And not merely on the *figures*, but on whether it happened at all. [Certain people] said, 'It just doesn't happen. There are no protons ejected'. (13–14)

In the introduction, no hint is given that the ratio mentioned in the text had been strongly criticised or the previous methods put in question. Whereas in the previous introduction the position of those opposed to the authors is briefly characterised in adverse terms, in this introduction it is entirely ignored. Author *A* presented his results as furnishing a test of and further support for a model already clearly superior to the previous, poorly worked out approach; even though informally he accepted other scientists' reservations about the central ideas of the model and their doubts about its empirical foundation as entirely reasonable. Similarly Author *B* depicted his results as an advance in method; even though he was well aware that many scientists doubted whether previous observations were correct and even whether the phenomena which he was supposed to be measuring actually existed. Thus the characterisation of collective belief appears to vary from one scientist to another. In addition, each scientist offers quite different versions of collective belief in formal papers and in informal interviews. Thus in both these introductions an account of the current state of collective belief is fashioned which makes the authors' contribution seem much less problematic and open to alternative interpretation than it does in ordinary discourse.

What Is Left Out of the Formal Account

A style is adopted in formal research papers which tends to hide the author's personal involvement; and the existence of opposing scientific perspectives seems either to be ignored or to be referred to in a way which emphasises their inadequacy, when measured against the 'purely factual' character of the author's results. As a consequence of such systematic accounting, the author's findings begin to take on an appearance of objectivity in the formal text which is significantly different from their more contingent character in much informal accounting. This formal appearance is strengthed by the rigorous suppression of certain other features which appear frequently in informal accounting. In particular, reference to the dependence of experimental observation on theoretical speculation, to the degree to which experimenters are committed to specific theoretical positions, and to the influence of social relationships on scientists' actions and beliefs, is regularly eliminated as scientists move from informal to formal accounting (8).

Consider, with respect to the relationship between theory and data, the following statements made by Author *A* during his interview. In these two quotations he is describing his reaction some years before to the central idea of the model mentioned in Introduction *A*, when it was first suggested to him by the head of his laboratory.

3. He came running into the seminar, pulled me out along with one of his other post docs and took us to the back of the room and explained this idea that he had . . . He was very excited. He was really high. He said, 'What if I told you that it didn't take any energy to make ATP at the catalytic site, it took energy to kick it off the catalytic site?' It took him about 30 seconds. But I was particularly predisposed to this idea. Everything

I'd been thinking, 12, 14, 16 different pieces of information in the literature that could not be explained, and then all of a sudden the simple explanation became clear . . . And so we sat down and designed some experiments to prove, test this. (8)

4. It took him about 30 seconds to sell it to me. It really was like a bolt. I felt, 'Oh my God, this must be right! Look at all the things it explains'. (14)

In the formal paper we are told that experimental results suggested a model, which seemed an improvement on previous assumptions and which was, accordingly, put to the test. In the interview, however, we hear of a dramatic revelation of the central idea of the model, which was immediately seen to be right, which revealed existing data in a new light and which led to the design of entirely new experiments. The author mentions in the interview that this major scientific intuition came to the head of the laboratory when he was 'looking over some old data'. But the essential step which so excited those concerned was conceptual and speculative rather than empirical and controlled. It was the act of perceiving new meanings in data that were already familiar. Furthermore, when the authors of the introduction refer to 'results which *suggest* a new model', they cite precisely those results which were, according to the informal account, actually produced *as a result* of the intuitive formulation of the central idea of the model. It appears, then, that the actions involved in producing and establishing the model are characterised quite differently in the formal and the informal accounts. Whereas in the former the model is presented as if it followed impersonally from experimental findings, in the latter the sequence is reversed and the importance of unique social events clearly revealed.

The formal and informal accounts also differ in their treatment of the author's degree of commitment to the model. No explicit mention is made in the introduction of the author's prior involvement in the model's formulation. And the impression is given that the author is engaged in subjecting the model to a detached, critical test. Informally, however, significantly different statements were frequently made.

5. When I arrived here, I thought that the clearest way of demonstrating that energy input served to promote ATP dissociation from the enzyme rather than the formation of a covalent bond, would be to show a change of binding affinity for the ATP upon energisation. Everything up to that point had been kinetic evidence . . . and I felt some nice good thermodynamic data would help. (31)

6. It is a kind of shocking idea. 'Hey, everybody has been taught it takes energy to make ATP and now you are going out preaching it doesn't take energy to make ATP, it takes energy to get it off the catalytic site.' It was hard to sell . . . I personally think that its not proven, but I think its pretty close. (19)

In quotation five, scientist *A* does not describe himself as testing the model or trying to disprove it. Rather he portrays his actions in terms of looking for new kinds of evidence to furnish additional support. Similarly, in passage number six he stresses that, although only the smallest degree of uncertainty existed in his own mind, it was difficult to convince other scientists, who had not shared that initial revelation, that this model was required by the available evidence. Several phrases used by the author in the interview, varying from 'Oh my God, it must be right!' and 'its pretty close to being proven' to 'some nice good thermodynamic data would help to demonstrate it', seem to imply that he was fairly strongly committed to the model. Yet in the formal account, he chooses not to refer to his own involvement in the formulation of the model and to imply a considerable degree of critical detachment: 'A critical test of this proposal would be to measure . . . '

The last phrase in quotation three, to the effect that he designed experiments 'to prove, test', the model, suggests that, informally, the interviewee did not distinguish clearly between testing and proving the model. The following additional passages illustrate how, in informal talk, he tended to approach the issue of testing theories. In quotation seven, he is referring to his own work following on from that presented in the paper under discussion here. In quotation eight, he is talking about the response of one of his opponents to critical tests of *his* theory.

7. *Interviewer.* Do you see your current work as testing out the alternating site model or filling in details?

Author A. I think, well no. We *may* come up with additional data for the alternating site. But basically the aim is just to learn something about the catalytic site and not to test this further. (35–36)

8. He's tenacious . . . He's trying to accommodate data that doesn't agree with it by constructing a fairly complicated explanation. I think eventually he's got to give it up because I think its probably wrong. What he does is, and this is not a bad type of technique, I'm not criticising him for it, when he hears something that doesn't agree with his ideas he tries to find an explanation. The problem is that he's constructed such a complicated explanation for this, that the whole thing should be dismantled and he should start again. (24)

We can see from these passages that, informally, the speaker did not insist that experimental work has to put the researcher's theoretical framework to the test and that he was even willing to accept as legitimate what he saw as a dogged, *ad hoc* defense of a false theory. In view of his uncertainty as to whether the work reported in the paper under study was or was not devised to test the model, and in view of his acquiescence in quite different versions of research strategy, the reference in the introduction to carrying out a critical test can be seen to be a somewhat selective use of terminology. In a context other than that of the research paper, it would have been quite appropriate to have characterised the same actions quite differently; for example, as an attempt to prove an interpretative speculation to which the author was strongly committed.

We have seen that Author *A*, in informal discussion, recognises that his adoption of this particular model of ATP synthesis was brought about by his experiences in a specific laboratory and by his close contact with a particular group of colleagues. This recognition of how social relationships influence the course of individual scientists' research is hidden from view in the formalised paper. Thus Introduction *A* refers simply to the fact that 'several laboratories' had produced results which supported 'the model'. Only by consulting the references could the reader observe that only two laboratories seem to have been involved and that the author's presence as a co-author of one of the cited papers shows him to have been a member of one of these laboratories. Yet in informal discussion, the author stressed how significant was the period in that laboratory to his research career and how he has retained strong social links with the members of that laboratory and with their research.

9. I went to *C*'s lab. He had a very profound influence on me. That was really where I was educated. (4–5)

10. We were struggling with it. My students and I had all these diagrams all over and I wonder what would have happened if we hadn't gotten something in the mail. I wonder if we would ever have stumbled on it ourselves; probably not. But I got a preprint from *C*; the *C, D* and *E* paper, in which he proposed two cooperative catalytic sites and as soon as I saw it I liked it . . . This hadn't been published and we had the advantage of knowing it before it came out. *C* was very kind and kept us up with what he was doing (33–4).

This intellectual indebtedness and informal contact, which form natural topics for ordinary discourse (9), are not revealed in the introduction. The final paragraph of the introduction simply states that the empirical results which are to follow are difficult to assimilate by means of traditional assumptions and that they are more easily interpreted in terms of the model proposed by *C, D* and *E*. The strong social connections among those involved remain covert. A 'literal reading' of that final paragraph would be along the following lines: that the author carefully examined the compatability of their results with the major theoretical positions available in the literature and were led to conclude that one theory was shown to be clearly superior to the others in the course of an impartial appraisal. However, the account given informally is dramatically different. In the first place, the speaker had already decided whilst in *C*'s lab that the traditional view was inadequate and he never seriously considered interpreting his results within its frame of reference. Secondly, his experimental design was based on *C*'s original model, which he himself had played a part in formulating. Thirdly, his acceptance in this paper of the revised version of this model proposed by *C, D* and *E*, would have been impossible without fairly direct informal contact with *C*. Once again, it is clear that a certain element which is prominent in the informal account is left out of the formal introduction. There are, of course, bound to be differences of some kind between the informal and the formal accounts, if only because the former can be detailed and discursive whereas the latter are required to be brief and concise. Consequently, simply to show that differences exist does not itself take us very far. However, we have begun to show that these differences are not random, but systematic and meaningful. Certain clearly identifiable ways of characterising social action, which are treated as normal in ordinary discourse, are consistently omitted from formal accounts; whilst other, opposite, attributes are emphasised. The underlying rationale whereby informal accounts are transformed in the course of formal accounting will become clearer in the next section.

Social Accounting in Methods Sections

The existence of social accounting in experimental papers is most obvious in the sections on 'methods and materials'; for these sections consist mainly of highly conventionalised accounts of what the authors did in their laboratories in the course of producing their empirical results. The following quotes reproduce parts of the methods sections of the two papers discussed above.

These sections are typical of the great majority of experimental papers in this area of biochemistry.

Methods Section A

Heavy beef heart mitochondria were prepared by the method of *E* and stored in liquid nitrogen. Well coupled mitochondrial particles were prepared by a modification of the procedure of *F*. These particles were used to prepare inhibitor-protein-depleted particles by centrifuging under energised conditions according to the method of *G* . . .

In order to establish that ADP formation is the only rate-limiting step in our spectrophotometric assay for ATP hydrolysis, the following test was performed for each preparation of assay medium. Hexokinase and glucose were added to give a rate of absorbance change equal to or greater than that of the fastest ATP hydrolysis activity to be measured. The amount of hexokinase was then doubled, and the assay medium was considered adequate if the rate of absorbance change doubled . . .

Methods Section B

(A particular strain of yeast) was grown in continuous culture under conditions of glycerol limitation (H and B) or sulphate limitation (I and B). A variant of this yeast that does not require copper and has a cyanide insensitive terminal oxidase (J and B) was grown in continuous culture in a copper extracted medium (H) . . . Harvested and washed cells (H and B) were converted into protoplasts and mitochondria isolated as described by K. Protein was determined by the method of L. Measurements of respiration-driven proton translocation were made with the apparatus described by M and B in 1.0 ml of anaerobic 0.6m-mannitol . . . Polarographic measurements of P/O ratios were performed as described by N, by using the experimental conditions of B . . .

There is insufficient space here for a full analysis of methods sections. We shall, therefore, simply try to illustrate some general points which are related to the discussion above. One of the most noticeable features of these passages is the way in which the specific actions of the researchers in their laboratories are expressed in terms of general formulae. Constant reference is made to methodological rules formulated by other scientists; and many of the authors' actions are not described at all, but are simply depicted as instances of these abstract formulae. This is sometimes so, even when the authors recognise that they have actually departed from the original formula. Thus not only do we find, 'mitochondria were prepared by the method of *E*', but also, 'particles were prepared by a *modification* of the procedure of *F*.' Where the author's laboratory procedures are seen as introducing new practices for which existing rules do not provide, these practices are themselves presented as rule-like formulations as in the second paragraph of Methods Section *A*, which can then be used by other scientists in the course of *their* work. Informally, the principle which was usually said to guide authors in writing methods sections was that they should provide enough information for other scientists to repeat the authors' relevant actions and get the same results. As Author *B* stated: 'In the *Biochemical Journal* they have a separate section and you have to give sufficient detail there to enable any competent scientists to reproduce your experiment'. Thus the form of accounting used to depict scientists' actions in methods sections seems to be more or less explicitly an attempt to extract certain invariant dimensions from the unique, specific actions carried out by particular researchers in particular laboratories and to embody these dimensions of action in general, impersonal rules which can be followed by any competent researcher.

Methods sections, then, appear to be formally constructed as if all the actions of researchers relevant to their results can be expressed as impersonal rules; as if the individual characteristics of researchers have no bearing on the production of results; as if the application of these rules to particular actions is unproblematic; and as if, therefore, the reproduction of equivalent observations can be easily obtained by any competent scientist through compliance with the rules. In the course of informal talk, however, each of these notions is continually undermined. For instance, it is regularly noted that exact compliance with another's methods and exact replication of their results is virtually impossible.

11. When you write the paper which says how you did it, the ground rules are that you write it in such a way that other laboratories could reproduce your work and your conditions. Now that of course is impossible. There are all sorts of things that you don't know about, like 'finger factor', the local water, built-in skills, which you have taken for granted. But you try and do it anyway (Author *B*).

Or as another respondent put it:

12. Ideally, the scientific paper should make it possible, assuming that a library is available, for a Martian to come and do your experiment. But that's largely wishful thinking (Author *O*).

Thus scientists themselves are well aware of the gap between the formal appearance of methods sections and what they see as the practical realities of research.

Methods sections give the impression that the application of methodological procedures is a highly routinised activity, with little room for individual initiative and variability. Informally, however, scientists stressed that carrying out experiments is a practical activity requiring craft skills, subtle judgments and intuitive understanding (10). They talked of particular researchers having 'good hands' or 'a feel' for laboratory work.

13. You get a feel for what you need. I can tell you a story about this. I went to the workshop once to get something made. There was no way they could do anything for me for a week or a month. They were making something for Dr. X. I said 'What are you making for Dr. X?' 'Dr. X requires his water bath to operate at 36.5°C and *nothing else*'. And they were having a hard time actually. I said, 'That's ridiculous'. And I consulted with Dr. X and he produced this paper showing that in this experimental protocol, they'd worked at 36.5°. It didn't matter a damn really, whether it was 35° or 40°, as long as you stayed roughly where you were. Dr. X was not an experimenter and no longer does any. If you are an experimenter you know what is important and what is not important (Author B, 24).

When discussing laboratory practice informally, authors emphasised that dependence on an intuitive feel for research was unavoidable owing to the practical character of the actions involved. For such actions cannot be properly written down. They can only be understood satisfactorily through close personal contact with someone who is already proficient.

14. How could you write it up? It would be like trying to write a description of how to beat an egg. Or like trying to read a book on how to ski. You'd just get the wrong idea altogether. You've got to go and watch it, see it, do it. There's no substitute for it. These are *practical* skills. We all know that practical skills are not well taught by bits of paper. Could you write a dissertation on how to dig your garden with a fork? Far better to show somebody how to stick the fork in and put your boot on it. (Author B, 26).

In addition, scientists pointed out that many aspects of laboratory practice are traditional; in the sense that they are done because they are customary and are assumed, without detailed analysis, to be adequate for the task in hand.

15. *Interviewer.* One of the things we find difficult in reading those papers is understanding just *why* you have done certain things or used certain chemicals. Is there a convention about that?

Author B. The convention is that you normally use what you used last time round. You don't want to change. Let's take an example. We want to suspend mitochondria in some medium. Now if you put mitochondria in water they swell and burst. So they need support. Why did we use 0.6 ml? 0.6 ml is about right. Why did we use mannitol and not sucrose or something else? Well, because somebody in Japan 10 years ago had published the first paper on making mitochondria and he used mannitol. I don't know *why* they used mannitol. They may have been given it. Or they may have found it was better. Or maybe it was what they started with and they didn't want to change. So that's why we used mannitol. We saw no good reason to change from the original recipe. And 'recipe' is the right word. It's like cooking (Author *B*, 18).

As a result of their emphasis on the role of customary practice and on learning by example, it is not surprising that many authors said that it is often extremely difficult to specify in full those aspects of their research actions relevant to the production of their results. For so much of their knowledge and skill is tacit. Even when it is possible for a scientist to work out from the formal paper what, for practical purposes, counts as a repetition of another's methods, unless he is working on something very similar it is likely to 'take him an awful long time. Because there are so many mistakes you can probably make, I suspect. And I wouldn't even know what they are, you see, that's the snag. They'd be things I'd take for granted' (Author *B*, 20).

Scientists who belong to the same research network do, of course, often succeed in translating the content of formal methods sections into effective laboratory practice. But when these formal accounts of scientists' actions pass outside the small, specialist community to scientists who do not share the same background of technical assumptions and who have not experienced close personal contact with its members, this process of translation becomes much more difficult. Although the formulations contained in methods sections appear to be impersonal and independent of social context, they can only be put into practice by those who have participated intimately in the social life of the relevant social grouping.

16. One is telling the general reader very roughly how the experiments are done and the specific reader, that is anyone else who is working in the same field, which of the things he already knows about you have chosen to do. I mean, it would not enable an intelligent scientist in another field to set about doing those experiments . . . (Author *N*, 28)

17. From my own experience of trying to read back old papers, it can be a nightmare sometimes, trying to work out what they actually did . . . People outside the field don't even know where to get the reagents from. If I look at a paper in molecular biology, where they're using all these fantastic antibiotics, I wouldn't know where to start unless they listed the sources of supply . . . (Author *B*, 16).

It is clear, then, that the accounts of scientists' actions which appear in the methods sections of research papers differ radically from the accounts of the same actions offered informally. Whereas the formal methods section contains highly abstract versions of scientists' research activities in the form of impersonal rules, with no attempt to specify how these rules are interpreted in practice in particular instances, scientists' informal accounts emphasise that these rules depend for their practical meaning on the variable craft skills, intuitions, customary knowledge, social experience and technical equipment available to individual experimenters. It is also clear that, to varying degrees, scientists themselves are aware of the divergence between their formal and informal accounts of laboratory practice. They are aware that what they regard informally as crucial aspects of their actions are entirely omitted from the versions given in research papers. They stress that the ostensible objective of methods sections is unattainable and they imply that the meanings given to the rule-like formulations employed in methods sections vary in accordance with readers' membership of specific social groupings. Indeed, one can go further than this and show that scientists sometimes explicitly depict the accounts of social action given in research papers as 'artful accomplishments' and that scientists themselves theorise about the interpretative processes involved. In the next section, we will look at some of the comments of our two authors which seek to explain the divergence between informal and formal accounting.

Scientists' Accounts of Their Accounting Procedures

The author of the first paper examined above gave the following rationale for the formulation of social accounts in research papers.

18. Everybody wants to put things in the third person. So they just say, 'it was found that'. If its later shown that it was wrong, you don't accept any responsibility. '*It* was found. I didn't say I *believed* it. *It* was found'. So you sort of get away from yourself that way and make it sound like these things just fall down into your lab notebook and you report them like a historian ... Of course, everybody knows what's going on. You're saying, 'I think'. But when you go out on a limb, if you say 'it was shown that' or 'it is concluded' instead of 'we conclude', it should be more objective. It sounds like you are taking yourself out of the decision and that you're trying to give a fair, objective view and you are not getting *personally* involved. Personally, I'd like to see the first person come back. I slip into it once in a while. '*We* found'. Even then I won't say 'I'. I'll say

'we' even if its a one person paper. Can spread the blame if its wrong (laughs) (Author *A*, 57–8).

The aspect of accounting on which this speaker focuses is the use of impersonal formulations and the tendency to minimise the author's personal involvement. The reason he gives for this stylistic convention is that it enables the author to avoid responsibility for errors. Yet he appears almost immediately to contradict this explanation, when he suggests that everybody is aware of what is going on, that scientists recognise the conventional nature of this denial of responsibility. In our interviews, there is an enormous amount of material showing that researchers are, in practice, held personally responsible for published mistakes. It is clear that when scientists *read* papers, they translate the impersonal conventions of the formal report into their informal vocabulary. Nobody is ever misled into thinking that, because the research report made little or no mention of human agents, no researchers were actually responsible. Thus the rationale offered by this interviewee is unconvincing. Moreover, it gives little promise of providing analytical purchase on the range of material we have presented in previous sections.

Our second author also emphasised the impersonal character of research papers. But his central point was that scientific papers have this characteristic because they are devised in terms of a particular conception of scientific rationality.

19. I think the formal paper gets dehumanised and sanitised and packaged, and becomes a bit uninteresting. In some ways I like the old ones, where a chap says, 'I did this and it blew up in my face' . . . Some of the charm was certainly gone.

Interviewer. Why do you think that is?

Author B. One is a myth, that we inflict on the public, that science is rational and logical. It's appalling really, its taught all the way in school, the notion that you make all these observations in a Darwinian sense . . . That's just rubbish, this 'detached observation'. 'What do you *see*?' Well, what *do* you see? God knows, you see everything. And, in fact, you see what you *want* to see, for the most part. Or you see the choices between one or two rather narrow alternatives. That doesn't get admitted into the scientific literature. In fact, we write history all the time, a sort of hind-sight. The order in which experiments are done. All manner of nonsense. So the personal side does get taken out of this sort of paper. Maybe its felt that this isn't the place for it to be put. I don't know . . . Sometimes you get more of the personal side in reviews. Some of them are quite scandalous actually, once you can read between the lines.

Interviewer. Do you think there would be any disadvantages in allowing that sort of thing back into the formal literature?

Author B. I don't know. It depends what the purpose of the literature is. If the purpose of the literature is to describe what you did, why in scientific terms you did it – I mean, not because you want to do some bloke down or you want to advance your own career or get a quick paper out just because there's a grant application coming up soon. All these are valid reasons, but they're never admitted to. If the publishing reason is to present the science, what you did and what the conclusions were, then there really isn't much room for the emotive side. If I'm writing a paper [I don't say] 'I don't think that Bloggins understands electro-chemistry because he's a dum-dum'. I might say, 'This was overlooked by Bloggins *et al*'. I won't say *why* I think they overlooked it. I'm afraid its *gone* and its not going to reappear here. Probably it shouldn't reappear. I guess it re-appears in other places. And we still *know* what's going on. We just don't make it public (Author *B*, 32–3).

Like the previous speaker, this scientist stresses that researchers can 'read between the lines'. For example, they will read Bloggins' paper bearing in mind that he is, in their opinion, a dum-dum. In other words, they translate the formal text into their more extended informal vocabulary. However, the explanation he offers for the existence of two vocabularies is slightly more developed than that of Author *A*. In the first paragraph, his central claim seems to be that when scientists construct research papers they reinterpret and re-order their prior actions so as to make them appear to fit an inductivist version of scientific rationality. This interpretation is consistent with the material we have presented above (11). For we have shown in some detail how these two researchers eliminate from their formal accounts any reference to those personal, social, contingent aspects of their actions which feature so prominently in their informal talk; how laboratory practice is presented as governed by impersonal routines; and how data are apparently removed from dependence on human judgment or theoretical commitment. All of these features are highly appropriate to the inductivist conceptions of 'letting the facts speak for themselves'. In the first paragraph of quote 19, scientist B begins to formulate, in a very preliminary fashion, an alternative conception of scientific observation and rationality which is intended to be more suited to the content of his informal repertoire. But he fails to take this line of thought very far beyond the basic assertion that science in practice differs considerably from the conception embodied in research papers. Moreover, in the second paragraph he clearly returns to the more traditional view of science and scientific rationality. When he says that 'if you publish in order to present the science, there isn't much room for the emotive side', the speaker seems to have forgotten what he had just said about scientists 'seeing what they want to see' and constructing acceptable, non-emotive versions of their actions after the event. It is as if this speaker has at his disposal two rather different vocabularies for giving accounts of scientific action and belief, and that each vocabulary implies a different conception of scientific knowledge and rationality. In this passage B generates an apparent inconsistency by moving suddenly from one form of discourse and one conception of rationality to the other.

It is impossible to use the material presented in this section to reach any strong conclusions. What we wish to do instead is to use this material as a springboard, from which to make certain analytical suggestions. We suggest that social accounting in the formal domain is carried out in accordance with a traditional version of rationality. Within this perspective, genuine scientific knowledge is seen as being built up unproblematically by means of accurate, reproducible observation of the natural world. Observation is conceived as the act of recording the 'unembroidered evidence of the senses' and is regarded as reliable only in so far as it can be repeated 'identically' by 'everyman', that is, by any neutral, unprejudiced and technically competent person. It is allowed that scientific thought sometimes goes beyond the experimental facts, but such controlled speculation is seen as being guided by clear criteria of rationality. Accordingly, observational differences and differences of interpretation are seen as being due necessarily to the encroachment of non-scientific or non-technical factors; in other words, to the influence of personal or social factors, which are deemed to be separable from and irrelevant to the de-personalised propositions and practices of science.

There is much evidence in our transcripts that this traditional view of scientific knowledge is familiar to scientists and that it is frequently used by them. This conception of scientific rationality would lead scientists to dissociate their knowledge-claims from personal and social elements, to depict their research actions in terms of impersonal rules, to stress the autonomy of data, and so on, in exactly the way we have seen that they do in the realm of formal discourse, because to do otherwise would put their claims in jeopardy. Thus, it is reasonable to suggest that this idea of rationality is dominant in formal scientific accounting; that it is firmly institutionalised within the system of scientific publication; and that it is the systematic use of a suitable vocabulary of accounting that produces the conventional characteristics that we have observed in experimental papers.

Informally, however, this version of rationality, although still of major importance, is by no means so all-pervasive. Scientists not infrequently challenge the appropriateness of this conception of science in the course of informal talk. They also regularly employ a vocabulary of social accounting which differs radically from that used in formal papers, in that such elements as personal commitment, the priority of theoretical insight, intuition and practical skills, and so on, are seen as essential to the process of knowledge production and are routinely mentioned in describing the course of events. Few experimenters have thought reflexively enough about their informal interpretations of social action in science to have devised a coherent alternative to the institutionalised view. Nevertheless, they do translate the contents of the formal literature into their informal repertoire, in order to make them meaningful in practical terms. As a result, they are aware of the gap between that literature and what they regard as the realities of research.

In the light of these suggestions, we can begin to understand why our respondents found it difficult to provide consistent answers to the interviewers' questions about research papers. For they were being asked to talk informally about and offer informal justifications for their formal vocabulary. Given that this latter vocabulary is based on a fairly coherent view of scientific rationality, we would expect that its use within the formal context would be entirely consistent. However, we would also expect that it would inevitably generate interpretative problems when used as part of the full, and much more diverse, repertoire of informal resources. These interpretative problems are hardly noticeable in the course of fast-moving, everyday discourse. But when the discourse is recorded and examined in detail, we can observe the tendency for speakers to produce what seem to be somewhat contradictory claims. Author A offers an informal explanation of the style of research papers which stays close to the traditional view, in that the use of impersonal forms of expression is treated as having a real influence on scientists' understanding of science. Within a few sentences, however, he points out that in practice nobody takes these appearances seriously. Similarly, Author B moves uneasily between, on the one hand, repudiating all that is excluded from research papers as unscientific and unimportant and, on the other hand, criticising research papers for giving an unrealistic impression of how science actually operates. Thus, in their attempts to interpret the character of research papers, both authors can be seen to move between two rather discrepant views of scientific discourse as they themselves vacillate between two vocabularies of scientific discourse.

It seems, therefore, that the preliminary analytical suggestions we have offered in this section may throw some light on scientists' own attempts to theorise about scientific accounting as well as helping to make sense of the divergences between informal and formal accounting documented above. Our main suggestion has been that in the formal domain social accounting is carried out by authors, editors and referees in terms of one internally consistent, traditional version of scientific rationality and its associated vocabulary. Informally, however, a much wider vocabulary is used and more than one view of scientific rationality is implicit in social accounting. By comparing these two realms of scientific discourse and by examining the complexity and diversity of informal accounting, we have begun to see how the conventional characteristics of the formal domain are socially accomplished.

Concluding Remarks: Contexts of Scientific Discourse

Although sociologists and philosophers have accepted that there are 'irrational' as well as 'rational' actions in science, there has been a tendency to treat these two classes of action as quite distinct and to allocate them to separate social contexts. Intuition, speculation, idiosyncracy, personal commitment, social interest, and so on, have been seen as characteristic of acts undertaken in the context of discovery or in the private phase of scientific work. But in the public conext of verification or testing, these elements have been thought to be largely eliminated and replaced by impersonal, technical actions and judgments (12). In several recent studies, however, it has been shown that this distinction between independent contexts of action is difficult to maintain (13). Scientists appear not to abandon their personal commitments, their 'biases and prejudices', when writing up their own results; nor, it seems, do they regard other scientists' personal and social attributes as necessarily irrelevant to evaluation of the cognitive and technical claims presented via the public media of science. The formal claims in the research literature are interpreted and given meaning in the course of private reflection and informal discussion, where the contingent factors supposed traditionally to be separated from the constitution of scientific knowledge come clearly into play.

It is misleading, therefore, to treat as independent the realms of discovery and testing or the private and public phases of research. Nevertheless, although these concepts do not reflect genuine differences of social action in science, they do correspond quite closely to systematic differences in scientists' *discourse* about action. Thus we suggest that the notion of 'contexts of scientific action', which has been the source of much unprofitable debate, should be replaced by the notion of 'contexts of scientific discourse'. It is not that the character of scientists' actions changes radically as they move from having ideas to testing those ideas. What changes is the way in which scientists choose to portray their actions, as they engage in differing social relationships. The material presented above amply illustrates this latter point.

We showed that experimental papers do contain accounts of social action and of collective belief. However, the social element is partly hidden by authors through the use of an impersonal style of writing and by a tendency to underplay the diversity of scientific opinion, thereby giving the misleading impression that the interpretation of experimental findings is not socially variable. The effect is to make the authors' claims appear relatively unproblematic.

We then showed that there are systematic differences between the accounts of social action and belief in research papers and those provided by the same authors informally. Thus experimental data tend to be given chronological as well as logical priority in formal accounts; although informally these same data may be described as following on from a speculative insight. Similarly, the author's own involvement with and commitment to a particular analytical position is not mentioned in research papers, nor his social ties with those whose work he favours, although informally these may be emphasised and their influence on the author's view of scientific issues clearly recognised. Laboratory work is characterised in the methods sections of research papers in a highly conventional manner, as instances of impersonal, procedural routines which are universally effective. Informally, however, this kind of characterisation is frequently repudiated and great stress is placed on the impossibility of expressing methods verbally, on individual researchers' practical dexterity and personal intuition, on close contact with skilled practitioners, and on the need to *interpret* methodological rules in accordance with tacit knowledge.

Scientists are themselves aware that writing research papers involves social accounting and that their formal versions of their acts differ systematically from their informal accounts. Nevertheless our respondents were somewhat confused in their attempts to make sense of the divergence between the social content of formal papers and their informal, everyday interpretations which, naturally enough, they take as representing 'what really happens'.

We have suggested that not only are there systematic differences in social accounting but also different conceptions of rationality in different contexts of scientific discourse. A traditional view of scientific rationality is generally available among scientists as an interpretative resource. This view of rationality and its associated social vocabulary are firmly institutionalised within the formal organs of scientific communication. In contrast, in the course of everyday discourse, a much wider repertoire for social accounting is employed and alternative versions of scientific rationality are frequently suggested or implied.

If these suggestions are broadly correct, they direct our attention away from attempts to characterise scientists' social action as such, towards a concern with exploring how and why scientists produce varying versions of their actions. They also imply that several longstanding questions in the sociology of science are unanswerable in their customary form; for instance, whether or not scientists' actions are predominantly universalistic and whether or not action in the context of verification differs from that in the context of discovery. But most important of all, the analysis offered here begins to throw some light on the social procedures by means of which researchers construct the public discourse of science so that it appears to have the attributes of impersonality, objectivity and universality that have come to be widely accepted as characteristic of a 'genuine scientific community'. We have been studying some of the processes within science whereby the features which have provided the basis for taken-for-granted knowledge about science are socially produced.

Notes and References

1. A sample of such work is in J. Gaston (ed.), *The Sociology of Science*, Jossey-Bass, San Francisco, 1978, Part 1.

2. B. Barnes, *Interests and the Growth of Knowledge*, Routledge and Kegan Paul, London, 1977.
3. I. Mitroff, *The Subjective Side of Science*, Elsevier, Amsterdam and New York, 1974.
4. M. Mulkay, 'Interpretation and the Use of Rules: the Case of the Norms of Science'. In T. Gieryn (ed.), *A Festschrift for Robert Merton*, Transactions of the New York Academy of Sciences, Series III, 39, 1970; G. Nigel Gilbert, 'Being Interviewed: A Role analysis', *Social Science Information*, forthcoming.
5. J. Gusfield, 'The Literary Rhetoric of Science: Comedy and Pathos in Drinking Driver Research', *American Sociological Review* 41, 16–34 (1976); K. Knorr, 'From Scenes to Scripts: on the Relationship between Laboratory Research and Published Paper in Science', unpub. Vienna: Institute for Advanced Studies and Scientific Research, 1978; N. Mullins, 'Rhetorical Resources in Natural Science Papers', unpub. Institute for Advanced Studies, Princeton, 1977; B. Latour and P. Fabbri, 'La Rhetorique de la Science', *Actes de la Recherche en sciences sociales*, Fevrier 1977.
6. G. N. Gilbert, 'The Transformation of Research Findings into Scientific Knowledge', *Social Studies of Science* 6, 281–306 (1976); Knorr, *op. cit.*, Note 4.
7. Both the papers we examine here had two authors. We interviewed the senior author in each case. It is these senior authors that we will refer to as Author *A* and Author *B*.
8. We are clearly assuming here that informal accounting in interviews is similar to informal talk between scientists. For some evidence indicating that this is so, see our *Accounting for Error* (unpub.). Nevertheless, this point does need further study.
9. Although Author *A* recognised the importance of this relationship with *C*, he nevertheless maintained informally that he accepted *C*'s theory because it was the best theory. Even in informal discourse, social factors are not usually portrayed as determining correct scientific belief. Incorrect belief, however, is another matter. See *Accounting for Error, op. cit.*
10. W. Hagstrom, *The Scientific Community*, Basic Books, New York, 1965; J. Ravetz, *Scientific Knowledge and its Social Problems*, Clarendon Press, Oxford, 1971.
11. P. B. Medawar, 'Is the Scientific Paper a Fraud?', *The Listener*, 377–8 (September 12th, 1963).
12. J. Ben-David, 'Organisation, Social Control and Cognitive Change in Science', in J. Ben-David and T. Clark (eds.), *Culture and its Creators*, University of Chicago Press, Chicago, 244–65 (1977); H. Zuckerman, 'Deviant Behaviour and Social Control in Science', in E. Sagarin (ed.), *Deviance and Social Change*, Sage, London, 1977, 87–137; H. Reichenbach, *Experience and Prediction, An Analysis of the Foundations and Structure of Knowledge*, University of Chicago Press, Chicago, 1938.
13. H. Collins and T. Pinch, 'The Construction of the Paranormal: Nothing Unscientific is Happening', in R. Wallis (ed.), *On the Margins of Science*, University of Keele Sociological Review Monograph 27, 237–270 (1979); M. Mulkay and V. Milic, 'Sociology of Science in East and West', *Current Sociology* (forthcoming), 1980; Mitroff, *op. cit.*, Note 2.

PART V

THE CONTEXT OF SCIENTIFIC INVESTIGATION

THE CONTEXT OF SCIENTIFIC INVESTIGATION

RICHARD WHITLEY

Manchester Business School, University of Manchester

Introduction

Much of the literature surveyed by Roger Krohn in his draft (1) that served as the theme paper for this volume deals with instances of scientific investigation which resulted in major discoveries. The basic concern of most studies of scientific — and other — forms of creativity has been to understand how certain major advances in understanding come about. Generally the cognitive success, and indeed the nature, of the innovation has not been questioned or seen as socially problematic. Rather, attention has tended to be focussed on the psychological dimensions of invention while the social processes by which discoveries came to be seen as such and culturally legitimated have rarely been examined. Similarly, the pattern of social organisation of scientific work has usually been taken as irrelevant to scientific creativity. Discoveries have been assumed to be self evident and interest restricted to how particular individuals came to find them.

Furthermore, this literature usually only deals with developments that have come to be seen as major discoveries, creativity and research are tacitly assumed to be associated — or at any rate only interestingly so — with great success in the sciences. The study of scientific investigation is here reduced to the study of how a small number of unusual individuals developed major innovations in certain fields, creativity leading to "failure" is rarely explored and the bulk of research conducted by scientists is ignored. By focussing almost entirely on a small number of abnormal and infrequent psychological processes, most of the literature on processes of research and scientific creativity treats the intellectual and institutional context of scientific investigation as irrelevant to its understanding and hence conceives it as being essentially asocial and ahistorical (2).

297

Karin D. Knorr, Roger Krohn and Richard Whitley (eds.), The Social Process of Scientific Investigation. Sociology of the Sciences, Volume IV, 1980. 297–321.
Copyright © 1980 by D. Reidel Publishing Company.

In direct contrast to this literature, the empirical papers in this volume largely address themselves to what, since Kuhn, we have come to regard as normal science. The relatively routine, everyday activities of people termed scientists are the focus of most of the case studies reported here. The glamorous, Nobel prize winning research is by-passed to deal with the *ad hoc* contingencies faced by journeymen scientists in their pursuit of "profit" and recognition. Additionally, the main interest of many of these studies is on how results come to be accepted as such − or rejected − and how accomplishments are negotiated rather than with how great ideas were developed by particular individuals. It is the social process of making judgements and resolving disputes which claims the attention of most of the authors here. They are concerned to highlight the socially contingent nature of scientific activity and its consequences rather than to assume that knowledge can be taken for granted as the outcome of the work of a few gifted individuals.

This contrast in approaches to the study of scientific development is partly a consequence of changes in assumptions and presuppositions underlying the social study of science as briefly outlined by Woolgar (3). It is also, though, a consequence of major changes in the way science − or what is seen as science − is conducted and organised. Wherever the professionalisation of scientific work is seen as originating (4), there is little doubt that the scientific labour force has expanded considerably since the second world war and that while much of this expansion has occurred in state and business laboratories it has also occurred in what is traditionally termed 'pure' science. Furthermore, the development of applied science on a large scale cannot be treated as irrelevant to the development of scientific knowledge in the universities and academies, partly because it provides a labour market for the expanded Ph.D programmes and also because the priorities institutionalised in such non-academic organisations affect work done in 'pure' fields as has been shown by several recent papers (5). The boundaries between academic science, industrial science and governments have become less clear and obvious than they were which has led some observers to talk of the deinstitutionalisation of science (6). Scientific work has become an activity carried out by large numbers of people in a variety of institutional settings. Each of these has different objectives, but they all share the common property of organising science. Whatever the realities of science before the Second World War, there is little doubt that to view contemporary scientific work as an activity pursued by independent scholars in the interest of truth would be a gross misapprehension. Science today is a highly general umbrella term which covers a vast range of activities conducted by a large number of qualified personnel in a variety of work organisations for a variety of purposes. To see it as the work of a small number of geniuses acting in isolation would be myopic.

It could, of course, be argued, as some philosophers have done, that 'real' science is still that set of activities, and resultant knowledge, carried out by a few elite scientists in relatively autonomous institutions while 'normal' science is not really science at all. Aside from the obvious problem of deciding where the boundaries between real and unreal sciences are to be drawn, and on what basis, it is by no means clear that the day to day activities of the elite are much less mundane than those of other scientists, nor that they are much less likely to occur in highly structured work organisations. The development of large teams of experimental scientists, extensive division of tasks and full time research administrator roles in the highly recondite field of particle physics (7) suggests that "real" science is organised science rather than the work of a few intellectuals putting basic questions to nature's test. To reduce contemporary science to the activities of a small, cohesive and largely self generating scholarly community of equals is to pay nostalgic respect to past ideals rather than to undertake a serious analysis of scientific development.

Given the generality and diffuseness of activities covered by the generic term "science", and the range of organisations in which such activities are carried out, it is not surprising that the question of how scientific investigation differs from other forms of investigation — and indeed what, if any, are the unique qualities of science as a form of understanding — is not directly addressed in the studies published here. Concerned rather to demonstrate the everyday nature of scientific work than to identify its unique character, these case histories highlight the contingent aspects of scientists' judgements and decisions, their dependence upon organisational and resource constraints and the pervasive influence of competition for recognition and rewards in the development of scientific 'careers'. Indeed the occupational label 'scientist' could be reduced to a prestigious title sought by members of that occupation as a means of legitimating organisational autonomy and monopolisation of knowledge production by a privileged group, just as some see the term 'professional' as a disguise for a successful middle class trade union. Science has become desacrelised and returned to the world of profane motives and activities. Or, rather, science as an ideal standard of cognitive worth and basis for making judgements has become so generalised throughout industrial societies that its connections to scientific practices and judgements has attenuated to such an extent that the official myth of science seems irrelevant to contemporary scientific concerns. The very success of science as a means of establishing knowledge about the world has resulted in its extension over so many areas and into so many new concerns that its institutional specificity and distinct character as an activity and as a form of understanding have become less clear cut. The successful establishment of 'the scientific method' as the means of dealing with cognitive problems – whatever their sources and complexity – has so extended the scope of fields amenable to scientific analysis, and hence the range of applications of that method, that its particular character and constitution have become diffuse and unclear. By claiming the preeminence of the method of science as manifested in physics or chemistry, and extending it to other fields of study so that in principle all phenomena are subject to it, the term has become so abstracted from the context of any one activity and generalised across so many fields that it has become reduced to highly abstract and vague injunctions which bear little relation to scientific practices. It is not surprising that many scientists in the more established fields prefer to leave discussion of this topic to philosophers and neophyte sciences whereas in previous periods it was a matter of some considerable moment among natural philosophers.

Insofar as science is today defined by its 'method', this is largely an institutional definition of general norms and presuppositions as reified in textbooks and educational curricula rather than being instantiated in everyday research. Unique qualities of scientific investigation in practice – if there are any – are not located in the very general institutional concept of science. Indeed the variability of research practices in different fields, and of criteria for making collective judgements, is clear from the studies published here, which themselves do not stray much beyond laboratory science. Rather than seeking particular features of scientific investigation, perhaps it should be doubted if there is any coherence to research work in different fields such as would justify the assumption that there is some distinct social activity termed scientific investigation. It is not insignificant that nearly all the case studies in this volume are studies of people who define themselves, and are defined by others, as scientists who are working in large organisations on a range of problems for a range of purposes. Rather than looking for the essential char-acteristics of scientific research, these authors have accepted the dominant institutional definition of scientists and examined them at work constructing knowledge. Science is seen here as an accomplishment of people accredited as scientists in the course of mutual negotiations and conflicts rather than as the outcome of a distinctive pattern of investigation (9).

However, the rejection of the notion of a distinct type of investigation being scientific — or, at least, the manifest difficulty in ascertaining the particular qualities involved — need not imply that scientific work is dis-organised and predominantly structured by *ad hoc* contingencies. Instead it directs our attention away from the search for the essential features of scientific investigation *per se* towards an understanding of how particular investigations are patterned and organised in different sciences. Once it is agreed that research can take a number of forms, and is a social process rather than simply following universal methodological dictates, then the processes governing the conduct of research in different fields and their consequence for the development of scientific knowledge become a legitimate topic for sociological study. The manifest plurality of the sciences in terms of phe-nomena studied, methods of approach and criteria involved in the assessment of knowledge claims, and the failure of empiricist attempts to formulate general criteria of scientificity for all scientific knowledge, necessitate the development of a framework for analysing how research is organised in different fields and how patterns of organisation change.

In making sense of scientific development in the contemporary sciences, the context of research is obviously a crucial aspect and variations in its structure can be related to variations in research practices and their integration into different fields. This context can be seen as an organised arrangement of the sorts of background factors involved in many of the case studies published in this volume such as Pickering's 'cognitive interests', Knorr's 'resources', Callon's 'aggregation of interests' and the general citing of availability of apparatus and technical staff and other organisational constraints and cultures. These factors affect the everyday judgements of scientists and hence the sort of research which is carried out and the evaluation of its products. Consequently, their organisation and structure constitute the framework within which scientific work is conducted and made sense of. The structure of intellectual and other resources patterns the sort of research scientists both wish, and are able, to conduct and the ways in which results are understood. Different structures of these resources imply different patterns of research and therefore different paths of scientific development. In the rest of this paper I shall discuss what seems to me to constitute the major elements of the research process and this organisation as a way of ordering and understanding the structure of the everyday contingencies of scientific investigation (10).

The Intellectual Context of Research

The intellectual context of research is here considered as that abstracted set of norms and procedures which both govern and constitute what is done to what phenomena, in which cognitive setting, and how it is understood. It consists of the cognitive structures which, on the one hand, represent what is known and, on the other hand, constitute the resources with which to change and develop what is known. A particular scientific field, in this view, is constituted by the procedures which are required to develop knowledge in it so that rather than seeing scientific knowledge as a static structure which is fixed and permanent, it is viewed as a process of acquiring and changing understandings. To do research in a given field is therefore to use the procedures and intellectual resources that constitute it. This use of intellectual tools is itself guided by the particular arrangement or organisation of procedures which characterises the structure of the field and by higher order norms or preferences which order sciences. Particular combinations of available procedures will be preferred to others, and consequently research will develop along certain lines rather than in other directions. However, scientific fields do, of course, vary in their type of organisation and so, too, their patterns of development. The sorts of relations that obtain between the intellectual tools of a particular field − and their own degree of standardisation and formalisation − structure the sorts of scientific investigation that will be conducted and the interpretation and use of their outcomes. Patterns of research, such as those discussed in the case studies in this book, are, I suggest, to be understood in terms of particular arrangements of intellectual resources which order and integrate possibilities and results. Making sense of scientists' activities in different fields involves an understanding of how the intellectual components of that field are structured and mutually ordered such that it seems reasonable for a particular topic to be pursued in a particular way and the outcomes to be understood in certain ways which impinge upon other work so as to alter the collective self understanding of the field.

The ordering of appropriate topics or intellectual concerns to be pursued by scientists in a given field implies that the cognitive space or domain of the field is structured and bounded sufficiently clearly for research problems to be identified as being in it rather than part of another domain. Although the degree of boundedness and clarity of the cognitive space may vary – as between, for example, memory transfer and solar neutrino research – a minimal extent of cognitive structure delimiting the domain of the field is necessitated for it to exist at all. Research issues and foci are 'interesting' or 'relevant' or 'hot' in some intellectual context which makes sense of them in terms of more general concerns and problems which form the basis of identity of a scientific field and so 'contribute' to that field. So one intellectual component or resource involved in any research is the definition and delimitation of a particular domain of phenomena as constituting a field to which the research is oriented. This component can be termed 'domain assumptions'.

These domain assumptions vary in generality, abstraction and scope. The search for interesting and useful analogs of somatostatin described by Latour is clearly a more restricted and specific activity than the search for theoretical models in particular physics as discussed by Pickering. Fields differ similarly as the distinctions between specialisms and disciplines and research networks or areas indicate. Sometimes domains and their constitutive assumptions are seen as hierarchical in that lower order concerns and problems are derivative from more general and abstract ones, as sketched by Callon in his discussion of fuel cell research programmes, but this is not necessarily always the case and a heterarchical model is probably more appropriate (11), not least because the particular structure of conceptual networks can then be empirically investigated rather than assumed. Different sciences exhibit different arrangements of domain assumptions and there seems no good reason to assume, as Shapere (12) does, that 'sophisticated' sciences all exhibit the same structure. Indeed, Shapere requires domains to have a greater degree of conceptual closure for them to be accorded the label 'scientific' than seems necessary. The degree of closure is not simply a matter of 'sophistication' or the 'primitive' state of a science but is a characteristic that varies between fields and changes within fields over time. It is an outcome of social processes and strategies as emphasised by Callon and not simply the instantiation of 'progress'.

Domain assumptions form the background to a particular piece of scientific work which locates it as being 'interesting' within a broader intellectual context. During the course of the research process they may change, in that what seemed interesting in one context no longer is so but now is relevant to other concerns. As Pinch points out, Davis's essential problem domain was the experimental detection of neutrinos but in the course of developing the apparatus for detecting solar neutrinos he had to integrate this concern with theoretical nuclear astrophysics, and indeed could not make sense of the experiment without involving assumptions and models from that domain. Although the experiment was still in the domain of nuclear chemistry in a technical sense, its 'interest' in a broader sense was clearly in the domain of stellar astrophysics.

The specification of a cognitive domain of interest which implies some ordering of research topics or issues sets constraints – however loosely – on how such topics are to be conceptualised and worked on. Certain ways of formulating research problems will be seen as appropriate and others will not. The formulation of research topics in parts of physics, for example, has to follow certain rules if such research is to be accepted as competent contributions to those fields. Harvey's discussion of researchers studying hidden variable theories and their views of what constitutes 'real physics' highlights this point. Nevertheless, some diversity of conceptual approaches to research issues is possible even in highly structured sciences such as physics and it seems sensible to differentiate between intellectual norms distinguishing and constituting scientific fields and those which deal with the formulation of research topics and their conceptualisation. These latter can be termed formative procedures.

The way in which a particular topic is conceptualised will obviously have implications for how it is approached and worked upon. Only certain procedures and technical manipulations will be seen as appropriate or meaningful given a particular formulation of the problem. As Pinch shows in his discussion of the solar neutrino experiment, it was largely Davis' close collaboration with theoreticians in arriving at an 'appropriate' experimental design which ensured general legitimacy for his results and led to their being accepted by theoreticians as contradicting existing models. Although the term 'techniques' tends, in English, to imply some physical system of transformation rather than more general ways of working on materials, it seems a useful way of labelling this set of procedures, especially if its theory infused nature is borne in mind, as in Bachelard's concept of 'phenomeno-technics' (13), and as exemplified by Pinch's account of the solar neutrino experiment. Techniques, then, are viewed here as the sets of procedures which are available for working on topics formulated in particular ways in particular domains in the sciences.

The outcomes of working on research issues are not, of course, totally determined by the particular arrangement of input procedures. Consequently, judgements are required to make sense of results in the light of existing concerns and assumptions. These judgements can be viewed as developments of interpretative norms which are connected — in varying degrees — to dominant conceptions of the field and appropriate conceptual approaches. Again, however, particular interpretative norms are not uniquely determined by any particular arrangement of domain assumptions, formative norms and techniques so that we can usefully distinguish them analytically as a separate intellectual component or resource involved in research. Interpretative procedures are the means by which individual scientists and collectivities decide what the outcome of a particular piece of research is, and how its significance for other work is to be assessed in terms of more general concerns. Many of the case studies in this book provide examples of how such norms are developed in negotiations over the meanings of results in different fields.

The Organization of Intellectual Resources

These four components, or set of procedures, seem to me to form the minimum number of analytically distinguishable elements of scientific investigation although further sub divisions are clearly possible, as I indicated in the case of domain assumptions. Processes of research in different sciences, or in the 'same' field in different periods, can be compared and contrasted in terms of different arrangements and features of these procedures — the intellectual organisation of scientific fields. The particular ways in which research is conducted obviously depends upon the available resources and their inter-relationships or organisation which can be characterised on a number of dimensions.

Work procedures in general have been analysed in various ways, although most sociological analyses stem from Weber's discussion of formal bureaucratic rules. Dimensions such as formalisation, standardisation, configuration, centralisation, etc. have been developed and various measurement procedures applied to them, most notably perhaps by the 'Aston' school and its progeny (14). From a different viewpoint, Randall Collins has suggested that scientific disciplines should be viewed as an organisation exhibiting "a regular division of labour and relatively stable forms of influence or control" (15). He further proposes that disciplines can be arranged "along a continuum of forms of organisational control" which seems to be a matter of consensus and coherence of work practices and theories. While I am dubious about the general applicability of the Kuhnian model to all the sciences, and Collins is singularly imprecise in his use of the term 'discipline', this sort of approach to the analysis of science offers considerable sociological scope and is clearly compatible with most of the case studies in this book.

A preliminary way of developing some of the dimensions used by writers on organisations for analysing scientific investigation is to distinguish between fields where the interdependence and interconnectedness of research procedures is high from those where there are a number of alternatives available for use with any particular intellectual resource and work can be validly carried out using a variety of combinations.

Related to this is the clarity of formulation and firmness of characterisation of the intellectual resources of scientific fields. I have already referred to Travis' discussion of the openness of the scientific culture with regard to memory transfer research in planarians. This openness enabled the worm runners to make significant claims without substantial opposition or contradiction. The fluidity of the cognitive space concerning memory transfer in the 1950s was considerable so that, as Travis suggests, the implications of a number of phenomena and approaches were not especially in mutual contradiction or conflict. This fluidity, or relative low degree of clarity and firmness of domain assumptions, enabled a plurality of procedures and formative norms to coexist without much overt disagreement. In contrast, most areas of physics and chemistry exhibit strongly formulated domain assumptions and other norms and these are often mutually implicative to a high degree so that particular approaches and techniques are required by a particular topic and interpretative norms are strongly connected to the initial formulation of the problems. It is usually fairly clear in such fields whether a given topic is 'in' a particular area and whether it has been 'correctly' studied and appropriate conclusions drawn from the outcomes. In other fields where these four sets of norms are not so clearly expressed and mutually connected, both scientists and observers have some difficulty in deciding which field a given piece of research is relevant to, and how its correctness could be assessed. Indeed, the question of its domain may appear peculiar, except in the most general sense (16).

These two related dimensions can be summarised as the degree of formalisation of intellectual norms and procedures, on the one hand, and the degree of their interdependency and integration on the other hand. Formalisation is here meant in a somewhat broader sense than that used by the Aston School in their studies of organisational structures (17). Rather than referring to the use of written procedures and instructions it is intended to encompass the degree of definiteness of intellectual procedures, which may be written down or largely tacit, so that it is clear when mistakes have been made. The more formal are procedures and norms, the easier it is to identify them, differentiate them from other resources and be clear about their appropriateness and correct means of application and use. Generally, highly formal procedures restrict what can be done and how it can be done 'correctly' and so are likely to have relatively strong implications for the use of other procedures. Fields with formal domain assumptions, for instance, will restrict the range of formative norms governing the development of appropriate research topics and the use of technical procedures for working on them. The interdependence of intellectual resources in such areas of scientific research will, therefore, be considerable. In this sense a high degree of formalisation implies a relatively high degree of interdependence. However, not all the resources available in a given field need be equally strongly formalised and not all the possible interconnections between them need be equally direct or restrictive. For example, the way in which a particular domain of scientific research is delineated may be relatively weak and imprecise, in that its boundaries are not especially clear and do not directly specify what topics are part of it, nor how they should be formulated and yet technical procedures may be strongly linked to the way any particular topic or problem is developed and, at the everyday level of research practices, the interpretation of the outcomes may be relatively straightforward even if their implications for the broad domain of, say, cancer, are not so obvious (18).

Where the degree of interdependence is high in a given field so that the development of a particular topic is clearly within or without its boundaries, and it can be assessed in terms of its relevance and importance to the domain of the field, we would expect certain techniques to be clearly appropriate and the results to be relatively easy to interpret in terms of the domain assumptions. Strong interdependence implies high formalisation and in an extreme instance the degree of cognitive closure would be so great as to leave little ambiguity and scientific judgements would be relatively routine. Scientific research in this instance would be so 'normal' as to be programmable as in, for example, routine chemical analysis. In most sciences, though, as indicated by the cases reported in this volume, choices are still required of scientists and decisions have to be made about how to proceed. Nonetheless, those choices are structured by the organisation of cognitive resources in individual fields and by characterising this organisation in terms of the degree of formalisation and interdependence we can begin to understand how scientific investigation varies between various fields.

The Institutional Context of Scientific Investigation

As several papers in this volume emphasise, patterns of everyday research are strongly influenced by organisational and institutional contingencies; the particular ways in which intellectual resources are combined and used reflect what Latour terms the 'material and local circumstances' of the laboratory. An understanding of processes of scientific investigation involves, therefore, an analysis of how resources are organised, reproduced and changed, the institutional context structures possibilities and priorities so that certain patterns of research develop and not others. The 'opportunistic tinkering' mentioned by Latour occurs within distinct institutional orders so that some activities and arrangements of intellectual procedures are more feasible and fruitful than others. In the rest of this paper I shall briefly discuss some of the major aspects of the institutionalisation of research procedures in the contemporary sciences (19).

A fundamental way in which intellectual norms and procedures are institutionalised in research practices is in the form of intellectual commitments and skills. For a given scientific field to reproduce itself as a distinct area of scientific investigation, some commitment to its domain assumptions must be maintained and skills for such investigation inculcated into scientific practitioners who have the resources required for pursuing topics 'in' that field. Just as procedures may vary in their degree of formalisation, so too may the degree and scope of intellectual commitments differ between fields and the specificity of any particular set of research skills to a particular area or range of topics vary. Furthermore, the organisational basis of allocating material resources and scientists' time – i.e. employment opportunities and priorities – may not fully overlap with the domain assumptions of particular fields and, indeed, may constitute alternative criteria for topic selection and conceptualisation. Much research conducted in full time research laboratories, as evidenced by many of the papers here, is not obviously 'in' any particular university based discipline or speciality and, indeed, may deliberately set out to negate such boundaries in favour of different audiences and priorities.

The particular ways in which intellectual resources are institutionalised in a given area structure the sort of research that is carried out, how it is conducted and how it affects other work. Without commitments to topics and approaches in an area and the relevant skills and resources required to work on them, that area will simply disappear as Fisher's analysis of invariant theory illustrates (20). However, commitments may conflict, both among themselves and with the priorities institutionalised in the reproduction of skills and availability of resources, so that scientific work can take a number of directions without any clear development path emerging immediately. Such conflicts are predicated upon the intellectual resources of a field being sufficiently clearly developed – as Travis suggests – and their domain of application being mutually recognised. Where a particular cognitive space is relatively weakly bounded or interests in it are not well defined, overt conflict and competition are not very likely to occur. Scientific investigation in these situations is likely to focus on particular techniques and skills rather than on highly ordered topics and relevant criteria. Domain assumptions will be only weakly connected to research topics and outcomes.

The development and reproduction of intellectual commitments and, skills are results of the scientific education and training system, the structure of job opportunities and 'careers' (21) and the system of publication and recognition. Obviously, commitments to particular norms and procedures develop initially through the system of formal instruction and training in secondary and higher education. It is largely in educational institutions that identities of 'scientist' and, later of belonging to a particular science and discipline are formed. These identities imply general commitments to certain ontological and epistemological beliefs held to be constitutive of 'science' and of particular disciplines as well as to a given domain of interest. They also, as Kuhn and, in a different way Ravetz (22) emphasised, imply the acquisition of skills which are appropriate for the development of research in the discipline. Educational institutions thus form the basic commitments of scientists in nearly all fields, and constitute the fundamental unit of social and cognitive identity in the sciences which is one reason why the term 'discipline' is usually understood to refer to units of organisation in universities (23). Equally, of course, conflict over how these units are formed and bounded is endemic because they affect the supply of new recruits to the 'disciplines' and hence commitments to pursuing particular fields of research and hence the future existence of those fields. Without the opportunities of inculcating interest in a particular field, and the development of basic skills for work in it at an early stage of the research training process, the future of the field remains doubtful. Control over curricula, admissions and assessment in undergraduate departments of universities is thus a crucial part of the reproduction of scientific fields. Equally, the monopolisation of this initial phase of research training by the universities in most industrial countries gives these institutions a dominant role in scientific development (24).

While undergraduate instruction remains an important part of the development of intellectual commitments and skills, it is, of course, by no means the most crucial phase in many sciences. The development of the Ph.D degree as the trade union ticket for obtaining academic posts and access to research positions and facilities, has effectively downgraded the first degree in many countries although this process has occurred at different rates in different fields and in different national academic systems. By insisting on this degree as the basic requirement for conducting research, universities have maintained their control over the development of commitments and skills, although increasingly Ph.D research is being conducted outside university departments in full time research laboratories funded by the State and other bodies. Usually, within the general commitments and skills developed at the undergraduate level the Ph.D degree focusses upon more specific topics and develops more circumscribed skills. Generally, postgraduate research builds upon interests and capacities instilled during the first degree and so ready access to a large pool of competent graduates through control over an undergraduate department is of considerable assistance in ensuring continued recruitment to a particular area (25).

The extent to which a Ph.D implies commitment to a given field within a discipline varies, as Harvey's discussion of the students involved in research on hidden variables shows, and such commitment may be very tenuous in the case of sciences with weakly formalised and integrated norms and procedures. However, the skills acquired during the Ph.D process – and subsequently as a post doctoral fellow in some fields – can be expected to have a major impact upon the directions pursued by scientists. Where these skills are clearly interdependent with particular domain assumptions and other norms, then commitment to working in that field will be greater than in a situation where cognitive boundaries are weakly formalised and integrated. A further point to be noted here is that not all – and perhaps increasingly fewer – Ph.D topics and approaches are clearly located 'within' a particular discipline as institutionalised in undergraduate curricula. The more research is conducted outside university departments, the more likely is this separation of undergraduate identities and boundaries from Ph.D research to become manifest.

The development of certain research skills during Ph.D and post doctoral research implies some commitment to particular ways of formulating problems and ways of working on them, as well as to some means of interpreting outcomes. While these may be very specific and narrow, especially in highly formalised and integrated sciences, they will form the basis for more general commitments to formative, technical and interpretative norms which will direct research foci and approaches. In this sense the research conducted for the Ph.D degree will exercise major influence on future work and the organisation and control of Ph.D topics in a discipline will have major consequences for the development of particular areas. Where Ph.D students are warned off certain problems, or find difficulty in finding supervisors, commitments are unlikely to develop and interest in such areas will decline. The marginality of the work on hidden variable theories emphasised by Harvey in this volume is demonstrated by the determination of most experimentalists to do 'mainstream' physics after their Ph.Ds and not 'crazy' experiments.

The availability of Ph.D topics and encouragement of particular fields of study in a science will depend upon the general structure of the discipline and its institutionalisation in terms of university posts and other resources. The particular skills and interests reproduced during Ph.D training, that is, are a function of priorities and goals in the discipline and how these are manifested in particular departments in terms of staff interests and skills, and the availability of materials, technicians etc. In disciplines where intellectual norms and procedures are relatively highly formalised and integrated, particular areas and topics will be clearly more interesting and important than others and particular ways of approaching, working on them and interpreting the results will be clearly more appropriate than others (26). In this situation, Ph.D students are likely to be channelled into examining certain topics and developing certain skills in working on these and so commitments to particular domains and approaches will be strongly reproduced while others will be largely ignored except by a few 'deviant' students and supervisors such as, perhaps, those comparing hidden variable theories with orthodox quantum mechanics. Specialisation of topics and approaches is likely to become quite high among Ph.D students in such subfields and this in turn will restrict the general applicability of the skills acquired by these students which will reinforce existing hierarchies of topic areas and conceptual approaches. As this process of specialisation and differentiation of tasks and research topics continues, the results of much research will be only tenuously connected to disciplinary goals and objectives. As domains — and associated interpretative procedures — become narrower and more specific, their relations to broader concerns will become attenuated and sub-fields and sub-sub-fields will develop a fair degree of autonomy from the parent discipline so that the precise relevance of much research will be difficult to discern. Equally, the discipline itself will become more fragmented as specialisation proceeds and loyalties become more focussed upon lower levels of intellectual organisation and everyday research concerns are more and more specific. The extent to which the contemporary disciplines of physics and chemistry still direct and integrate research in the same way that they did in the nineteenth century seems limited (27).

On the other hand, where intellectual norms and procedures are less clearly formalised and interdependent the hierarchisation of domains and approaches is less obvious. Here Ph.D students will not be directed into 'hot' areas so much and so commitments and skills will not become so concentrated. To the extent that priorities are less clear cut, and how to pursue them less obvious, Ph.D research will be less highly organised and structured in terms of disciplinary norms and be more susceptible to "local" influences and exigencies. Research will be less clearly "theory driven" and diverse approaches to topic selection and formulation possible. The development of commitments and skills among Ph.D students in such fields will be correspondingly varied and different sets of intellectual procedures manifested in Ph.D theses. While Ph.D topics may be equally specialised in these sciences as in more formalised ones, their formulation will be less clearly specific and a wider range of technical approaches appropriate. Also, the relevance of the results will be less clear for any given set of domain assumptions and may well become seen as broader in scope than any single area. In general, because cognitive boundaries are fairly fluid and not strongly tied to particular approaches and techniques, Ph.D students will develop broader competencies which are more generally applicable, than those working in formalised and integrated sciences. In this sense, Ph.D research in relatively unstructured fields will not be so restrictive in determining future areas of work. Skills will tend to be generalised across a range of phenomena and a multiplicity of different skills will be appropriate in analysing any particular phenomenon (28).

The formal system of education and training develops general commitments to particular fields of research and the skills appropriate for conducting research on certain topics and phenomena. Manifestly, though, it does not determine totally the sort of research that is pursued, nor how that work is made sense of in terms of general concerns. Most of the studies in this volume indicate a variety of social, intellectual and organisational categories affecting scientists' judgements about what to do and how to do it. One of the most obvious of these is simply the provision of employment opportunities and research facilities in particular fields and for particular purposes. While the dominant form of employment remained university based and largely organised around the ideal of the international scholarly community, the specific details of employment structures and resource provision could reasonably be considered subsidiary to the overall organisation and priorities of the scientific field and its 'establishment', at any rate in the more integrated and formalised areas. With the development of scientific research in non-university controlled organisations, which not infrequently have specific purposes set by non-academic institutions, this procedure becomes less justifiable. This is especially so in fields of research which are relatively weakly formalised and integrated so that competing ways of ordering priorities can have considerable impact on the topic pursued and the interpretation of results. Where disciplinary boundaries are not particularly strong and clearly connected to hierarchies of 'interesting' problems and 'correct' conceptual and technical approaches, the establishment of research laboratories providing employment and resources for particular social goals will have greater impact on the sort of work undertaken by scientists than in disciplines with more rigid intellectual structures (29). In general, the multiplicity of employment opportunities for researchers in a variety of organisations, which may be oriented around mutually contradictory and conflicting principles and goals, reduces the degree of integration of intellectual norms in particular disciplines. Patterns of scientific investigation are not so fully structured by disciplinary priorities but rather become the result of a complex set of interrelationships between work organisations, educational structures and cognitive norms. Intellectual fields consequently become less clearly ordered and bounded, the meaning of any particular piece of research for a given area of concern or interest is less clear when potentially competing principles of work organisation are institutionalised in the form of employment opportunities focussed on a plurality of goals. Criteria of relevance and interest become more open and varied than the Kuhnian notion of 'puzzle solving' suggests.

The growing importance of goal directed work organisations in scientific development has, of course, become increasingly recognised (30) although the extent to which they structure commitments and hence research practices has not perhaps been overly emphasised. In some cases they provide intellectual foci and identities which are unlikely to have occurred without formal provision of employment and facilities (31). At the very least they direct attention to particular topics and concern at the expense of others and to the extent that they organise researchers in particular ways and combine or differentiate sets of skills and commitments, they determine how phenomena are conceived and worked upon as Callon's discussion shows. Simply bringing scientists with particular commitments and skills together in a single employing organisation structures orientations and approaches. The importance of these 'local' circumstances is especially notable in relatively decentralised and unintegrated disciplines such as those discussed by Knorr and Latour. In physics they may be less crucial although still not negligible.

The other major aspect of the institutional context of scientific investigation, and the one that has received most attention from sociologists studying scientific communities, is the recognition and reward system. The selection of topics and preferred methods of approach has usually been seen in terms of priorities and criteria institutionalised in particular reward structures. Although reworked from a rather different perspective, many of the papers here adopt a similar focus in their invocation of investment strategies and rates of return to individual scientists. Specific pieces of research are undertaken primarily with a view to gaining recognition or "credit" among the international scientific community in this approach, and hence particular patterns of scientific investigation are to be accounted for in terms of the structure of the intellectual market (32).

These structures vary in their degrees of formalisation and integration between scientific fields and so scientists have varying extents of discretion in seeking audiences for their work and hence in the selection of topics and methods of approach. Those in relatively weakly structured fields, where domain assumptions are not strongly formulated and integrated with particular procedures for delineating and ordering topics and techniques, will have a number of journals available for publicising their work which are not strongly mutually ordered in a prestige hierarchy. The particular topic they choose to work on, and the way they work on it will be related to the outlet selected but that decision in itself will be more open than in sciences where prestige hierarchies are more strongly established, such as physics. Journals can be seen as means of institutionalising intellectual commitments in that they reproduce in their own practices, and in their interrelations, the structure of norms and procedures which characterise particular areas of concern and work in the sciences. Given the 'public' nature of the scientific enterprise in general, and the intimate connections between journal publication and rewards and hence scientific 'careers' in most fields, the operation and organisation of scientific journals are key aspects of the organisation of the sciences in general, and of particular patterns of scientific investigation. Journals signify commitments to particular areas of concern and instantiate procedural norms. They thus both reflect the structure of scientific fields and reproduce them.

By structuring cognitive space and functioning as guardians of procedural norms, scientific journals organise commitments and skills developed in educational systems and employed in research organisations. Research that is unpublished is, on the whole (33), research that has not been done with respect to the public system of science and hence cannot form part of the corpus of public knowledge. Consequently, the existing set of journals in a science constrain and direct research topics and ways of working on them. The development of new domains of investigation and/or novel procedures for working on them frequently, therefore, necessitates the formation of a new journal, especially in highly structured and integrated fields. Commitments and skills, then, are ordered by the priorities and preferences established and reproduced in journal policies and their interrelations.

More generally, we can say that the recognition system as a whole, of which journals constitute a crucial part, directs scientists' attention to particular topics and approaches and hence structures patterns of scientific investigation. This is not by a simple exchange of rewards for valuable commodities, though. Rather, the meaning, significance and consequences of a piece of research are functions of the general structure of norms and commitments that constitute the system of recognition in a particular scientific field or number of overlapping domains. Recognition here involves interpretative norms which make sense of – to varying degrees – research outcomes in terms of domain assumptions and procedural norms. The meaning and importance of knowledge claims are established with reference to some general and appropriate means of working on them – or sets of them – and so recognition locates particular results in particular intellectual contexts. Where this is difficult or impossible, in that relevance criteria cannot link particular descriptions of results to established concerns, recognition cannot be awarded. The recognition system, therefore, involves the establishing and dissolving of links of relevance between cognitive objects in the assessment of individual scientists' contributions to certain fields of concern. It also, of course, orders these fields of concern themselves in terms of more general criteria and domains of interest. By institutionalising relevance criteria and forming the basis for reward allocation, the recognition system manifests and expresses a particular network of connections between intellectual resources which order scientists' priorities and constitute the basis for their judgements. In this sense it directs the commitments and skills developed by the educational system, and combined in various employing organisations, along particular paths of scientific development.

In sciences, where intellectual norms and procedures are highly formalised and interdependent the recognition system locates and evaluates contributions with low degrees of ambiguity. It is usually "obvious" to which area or domain a particular piece of research is a contribution, and the relative importance of it will also be fairly straightforward to assess. However, the increasing specialisation and differentiation of subfields may make the tracing of implications of knowledge claims throughout an extensive network of concerns and understanding difficult, and the integration of distinct domains into a discipline, or some such similar general unit of concern, impossible. Recognition of contributions to the discipline, then, becomes derivative of contributions to the dominant and exemplary sub-discipline or 'speciality' such as particle physics, although the precise implications of such contributions throughout physics may be uncertain. The recognition system here fragments into a number of sub-units which are organisationally linked through the educational system, but whose cognitive interconnections are not always clear.

In less highly structured fields, it is not always obvious to what concern any individual piece of research is relevant, nor how it is to be assessed in terms of 'correct' procedures. With fluid and weakly formulated domain assumptions, which do not have strong implications for particular topics and techniques, the interpretation of results with references to particular intellectual concerns, and assessment of their importance in general, will be tentative and liable to revision. A plurality of possible relevance will be possible and historical revisions of evaluations of previous research more probable than in more structured sciences. Consequently, recognition will be less clearly an outcome of contributions made to an individual area of study and may be frequently revised. Audiences for certain kinds of work, and hence recognition from particular sets of scientists, are unstable and mobile so that reference groups for research topics are different to locate except in general organisational, or largely common sense, terms. In these fields multiple connections between intellectual resources abound and are not strongly ordered so that contributions are recognised in a variety of different ways which need not necessarily be mutually compatible. The changing reception to the work on memory transfer in planarians and in rats discussed by Travis illustrates this point. In general, the contrasts drawn here are illustrated by the accounts of physics given by Harvey, Pickering and Pinch when compared with the work discussed by Knorr, Latour and Travis. By and large, audiences and relevance criteria are clearer and more stable in the former accounts than in the latter cases. Also hierarchies of topics and the evaluation of 'success' are relatively sharply defined in physics.

Conclusions

These papers, and other studies of scientists at work, demonstrate the highly contingent nature of much scientific work and of judgemental processes. What becomes recognised as scientific knowledge is the outcome of complex social processes which are not reducible to an algorithm, and which are themselves subject to change. In fields which are commonly regarded as the most scientific it is quite clear that judgements are made in the context of patterns of social and intellectual organisation and cannot be adequately understood without locating them in that context. These patterns vary in different fields and also differ over historical periods, they constitute the framework for scientific research and provide the basis for constituting scientific knowledge at any particular point. Consequently, their structure forms the basis of the organisation – and its changes – of scientific knowledge. The various ways in which intellectual commitments are organised and institutionalised in the various sciences constitute the resources for research and for making sense of the outcomes of such work. Strongly bounded and integrated norms will lead to certain forms of investigation and not others, their results will be organised in particular ways. The organisation of intellectual commitments constitutes the structure of knowledge in a science and, through the particular way it is socially institutionalised, directs research along particular lines to modify that structure and develop it. It represents – or is – the cognitive order and provides the norms for extending that order through further work which may transform it. Where the principles – or dimensions – of organisations differ in scope and nature, then the directions of future development are open and liable to a variety of influences. The context of scientific investigation, in the sense used here, locates the apparently highly contingent and *ad hoc* nature of much scientific work in a broader framework which enables us to make sense of research practices and their consequences for scientific knowledge. That is, the norms and meanings which organise a scientific field at once represent the structure of knowledge in it and govern processes of developing and modifying it.

Notes and References

1. Roger Krohn, 'The Social Process of Scientific Investigation', unpublished paper, McGill University. Most of the literature discussed by Krohn is written by psychologists and/or famous inventors.
2. An interesting exception to these strictures is Ian Mitroff's, *The Subjective Side of Science*, Elsevier, Amsterdam, 1974.
3. In his paper in this volume. Where no specific reference is given to an author in this paper, I am referring to her/his contribution to the present book.
4. Depending on the definition adopted, this is usually taken to be in the French Academy and later educational institutions or in the reform of the Prussian universities and the rise of the research laboratory. See, for example, the chapters by Crosland, Hahn and Farrar in M. P. Crosland (ed.), *The Emergence of Science in Western Europe*, Macmillan, London, 1975; R. Hahn, *The Anatomy of a Scientific Institution*, University of California Press, 1971; R. Steven Turner, 'The Growth of Professorial Research in Prussia, 1818 to 1848 − Causes and Context', in R. McCormmach (ed.), *Historical Studies in the Physical Sciences* 3, 137−182 (1971); E. Mendelsohn, 'The Emergence of Science as a Profession in Nineteenth Century Europe', in K. Hill (ed.), *The Management of Scientists*, Beacon Press, Boston, 1964. For a historian's attack on overly sociological notions of the professional scientist see S. F. Cannon, *Science in Culture*, Science History Publications, New York, 1978, Chap. 5.
5. Much of this analysis has been conducted under the rubric of 'goal directed' science as in, for example, W. v. d Daele, W. Krohn and P. Weingart, 'The Political Direction of Scientific Development', in E. Mendelsohn *et al.* (eds.), *The Social Production of Scientific Knowledge*, Sociology of the Sciences 1, 219−241 (1977), and the papers by Johnston and Jagtenberg, Küppers and by Weingart in W. Krohn *et al.* (eds.), *The Dynamics of Science and Technology*, Sociology of the Sciences, II, 1978.
6. As in, e.g. E. Mendelsohn and P. Weingart, 'The Social Assessment of Science: Issues and Perspectives', in E. Mendelsohn *et al.* (eds.), *The Social Assessment of Science*, USP Bielefeld, 1978.
7. This well known phenomenon is discussed in a number of places including J. Gaston, *Competition and Originality in Science*, Chicago University Press, 1973. See also D. J. Kevles, *The Physicists*, Knopf, New York, 1978 for a historical account.
8. The importance of alternative conceptions of science in the development of a distinct 'discipline' is illustrated in Roy Porter's *The Making of Geology*, Cambridge University Press, 1977.
9. This acceptance of dominant institutional meanings is realistic for those wishing to study scientists' everyday practices in constructing knowledge. It need not, though, and should not, imply an acceptance of those meanings as unproblematic. As an institutional reality the sociological demarcation of science from other meaning systems requires investigation − particularly in its historical context. The apparent collapse of philosophical attempts to formulate absolute criteria for distinguishing scientific knowledge from non-scientific knowledge should encourage sociological accounts of how particular conceptions of science have become entrenched and

reproduced in particular institutional contexts and their relations to research practices accounted as 'scientific'. W. v. d. Daele has sketched part of such an account for 17th century English science in his 'The Social Construction of Science: institutionalisation and definition of positive science in the latter half of the seventeenth century' in E. Mendelsohn *et al.* (eds.), *The Social Production of Scientific Knowledge*, Sociology of the Sciences 1, Reidel, Dordrecht, 1977.

10. In distinguishing between the intellectual resources for, and the institutional context of, scientific research, I do not intend to reproduce the social/cognitive distinction criticised by Callon and Latour in their papers here. Intellectual structures *per se*, do not constrain research but their institutionalisation in particular organisational arrangements does and these patterns vary between the sciences and in the 'same' science in different periods. Consequently, it seems essential to be able to identify the major components of such intellectual structures so that differences in their organisation can be analysed.

11. As briefly discussed in H. Nowotny, 'Heterarchies, hierarchies and the study of scientific knowledge', in W. Callebaut *et al.* (eds.), *Theory of Knowledge and Science Policy*, Communication and Cognition, Ghent, 1979.

12. D. Shapere, 'Scientific Theories and their Domains', in F. Suppe (ed.), *The Structure of Scientific Theories*, University of Illinois Press, 1974.

13. Although Ph.D topics are by no means always 'within' the cognitive space delineated by a particular undergraduate degree.

14. See D. S. Pugh and D. J. Hickson, *Organisational Structure in its Context*, Saxon House, Farnborough, 1976 and D. S. Pugh and C. R. Hinings (eds.), *Organisational Structure: Extensions and replications*, Saxon House, Farnborough, 1976. Three types of task interdependence — pooled, reciprocal and sequential — with different means of coordination are discussed by James Thompson in his *Organisations in Action*, McGraw Hill, New York, 1967, which focusses rather more on the way work is differentiated into tasks and controlled.

15. Randall Collins, *Conflict Sociology*, Academic Press, New York, 1975, p. 493.

16. Certainly this was the reaction of many scientists in biomedical fields in our study of scientific specialities. Cf. A. Bitz, A. McAlpine and R. Whitley, *The Production. Flow and Use of Information in Research Laboratories in Different Sciences*, British Library Research and Development Division, London, 1975.

17. Pugh and Hickson, *op. cit.* 1976, Note 15, p. 32.

18. Cf. Bitz *et al. op. cit.*, Note 17.

19. Some historical aspects are discussed in R. Whitley, 'The Rise and Decline of University Disciplines in the Sciences'. In R. Jurkovich *et al.* (eds.), *The Nature of Interdisciplinary Research*, Rotterdam, 1980.

20. C. S. Fisher, 'The Death of a Mathematical Theory: A Study in the Sociology of Knowledge', *Archive for History of Exact Sciences* 3, 137–159 (1966).

21. It is not clear what exactly a scientific 'career' consists of; Randall Collins reduces it to the sequence of contacts a scientist has in his professional life, (*Conflict Sociology*, Academie Press, New York, 1975, p. 514) which establishes his fame. Generally, it seems to refer to little more than a set of accomplishments which are only ordered chronologically. Rather similar to the vague yet frequent usages of 'career' in managerial contexts, the term is pervasive without being especially enlightening in science.

22. J. R. Ravetz, *Scientific Knowledge and its Social Problems*, Oxford University Press, 1971, pp. 76–144.

23. Although historians tend to focus more on conceptual consensus and integration as in, e.g. S. F. Cannon, *Science in Culture*, *op. cit.*, 1978, Note 1, Chap. 4; R. McCormmach, 'Editor's Foreword', in R. McCormmach (ed.), *op. cit.*, 1971; and R. H. Silliman, 'Fresnel and the Emergence of Physics as a Discipline', in R. McCormmach (ed.), *Historical Studies in the Physical Sciences* 6, 137–162 (1974). However the conceptual level at which such integration is supposed to constitute a discipline remains obscure.

24. Some of these points are developed in their historical context in R. Whitley, *op. cit.*, 1980, Note 20.

25. Although Ph.D topics are by no means always 'within' the cognitive space delineated by a particular undergraduate degree.

26. The hierarchy of specialisms in physics is a well known instance of this point. Cf. W. O. Hagstrom, *The Scientific Community*, Basic Books, New York, 1965, and D. J. Kevles, *The Physicists*, Knopf, New York, 1980. The centralisation of resources and facilities characteristic of modern physics is facilitated by the highly formal means of communication, i.e. mathematics, and is by no means universal in the contemporary sciences. The more tacit, fluid and informal are craft procedures – as is arguably the case in 'configurational' fields – the less likely are disciplines to conform to the model of physics. Cf. N. Elias, 'The Sciences: towards a theory' in R. Whitley (ed.), *Social Processes of Scientific Development*, Routledge and Kegan Paul, London, 1974.

27. Indeed, whether they function in the same way at all with reference to current research practices seems dubious. For a discussion of 19th century physics see the literature cited in Note 24, R. Whitley, *op. cit.*, 1980, Note 20.

28. These points are further discussed in the context of a study of laboratories in different sciences in R. Whitley, 'Types of science, organisational strategies and patterns of work in research laboratories in different scientific fields', *Social Science Information* 17, 427–447 (1978). See also, R. Whitley, 'The Sociology of scientific work and the history of scientific developments', in S. S. Blume (ed.), *Perspectives in the Sociology of Science*, Wiley, New York, 1977.

29. An obvious example of this is the field of cancer research in contrast to, say, physics but many biological research organisations offer similar instances. See Bitz *et al.*, *op. cit.*, 1975, Note 17, and B. Latour and S. Woolgar, *Laboratory Life*, Sage, London, 1979 and the papers by Latour and Knorr in this volume.

30. Cf. literature cited in Note 5 and the well known 'finalisation' thesis.

31. As can be argued for the emergence of 'oncology', cf. J. Sadler, *Elites in Science: a study of elites in relation to the cognitive structure and social organisation of cancer research*, unpublished M. Sc., thesis Dept. of Liberal Studies in Science, Manchester University, 1976.

32. This is especially emphasised by P. Bourdieu, 'The Specificity of the Scientific Field and the Social Conditions of the Progress of Reason', *Social Science Information* 14, 19–47 (1975).

33. Preprints in high energy physics have become accepted as almost as good as papers published in journals provided they come from one of the very small number of internationally recognised centres.

INDEX OF NAMES

Aristotle 5, 21
Arnheim, R. 5, 21

Bachelard, G. 303
Bahcall, J. 86, 87, 88, 89, 90, 91, 92, 96, 97, 98, 99, 100, 101, 102, 104
Bärmark, J. xii, xv, xx
Barnes, S. B. 172, 188, 241
Bartlett, F. C. 6, 21
Bell, J. S. 142
Ben-David, J. xxii
Bhaskar, R. 240, 264
Bjorken, J. 122, 136
Bloomfield, L. 247, 265
Bloor, D. 241, 264
Bogoch, S. 182, 193
Bohm, D. 156
Bohr, Niels (Institute) 89, 141, 142
Bonner, J. 181, 182, 183, 192
Bourdieu, P. 82, 96, 104, 216
Boring, 5, 7
Boyle, R. 16
Brillouin, L. 70, 72
Bryant, R. C. 181, 192
Burbidge, E. M. 85, 104
Bylebyl, 17, 18

Callon, M. xii, xiv, xxi, 52, 53, 71, 299, 301, 302, 312
Cameron, A. G. W. 84, 85, 91
Carnot, S. 207
Chain, E. 169
Chedd, G. 165, 187
Clauser, J. F. 148, 151, 152, 154, 157, 158, 159
Collins, H. M. 53, 71, 104, 176, 186, 245, 246, 247
Collins, R. 304
Cooper, W. 37, 52
Cowan, 80, 83

Crick, 181

Dante, A. 27
Darwin, 184
Davis, R. 80, 81, 83, 84, 85, 86, 87, 88, 89, 90, 91, 92, 93, 94, 95, 96, 97, 98, 99, 100, 101, 102, 104, 302
Dewey, J. 215
Duhem, 4, 113, 114

Einstein, A. 4, 21, 141, 142
Emerson, J. P. 175, 176
Erasistratus, 12

Fabricius, 16
Feigl, H. 4
Feldman, G. 120, 121, 122, 126, 127, 128, 129
Feyerabend, P. 3, 4, 28, 61
Feynmann, R. P. 96, 121, 135
Fischer, G. H. 9, 10, 21
Fisher, C. S. 307, 318
Fowler, W. 84, 85, 86, 87, 88, 89, 90, 98, 99, 101
Freedman, S. J. 148, 151, 152, 154, 162
Fry, E. S. 154, 155, 156, 163

Galen, 11, 12, 13, 14, 15, 18
Garfinkel, H. 247, 263
Gibson, J. J. 5, 7, 8, 15, 21
Gilbert, N. W. x, xii, xiv, xv, xvi, 12, 22
Glasner, P. 186
Gombrich, E. H. 3, 5, 6, 7, 21
Gordon, G. xxii
Gusfield, J. 251, 252, 253, 254
Hagstrom, W. O. 82, 104
Hall, A. xv
Hanson, N. R. 3, 4, 5
Harari, H. 122

Harre, R. 49, 51
Harvey, W. viii, x, xii, xiv, 3, 11, 12, 13
14, 15, 16, 17, 18, 19, 20, 53, 209,
302, 315
Heisenberg, 141
Hesse, M. 29, 51, 130
Hewish, A. 248, 249, 251
Holt, R. A. 144, 148, 149, 150, 151,
152, 153, 154, 155, 156, 157, 158,
159, 160, 161
Hoyle, F. 85, 104

Iben, I. 88

Jacobs, K. C. 62, 72, 99, 100
Jacobson, A. L. 170, 182, 187
James, R. C. 13
Jammer, M. 142, 161
Jastrow, 5

Kellogg Radiation Lab. 87
Knorr, K. D. viii, x, xii, xiv, xvi, xix, xxi,
53, 63, 71, 139, 140, 141, 299, 312,
315
Koestler, A. 29, 51, 171, 172, 185
Krohn, R. 184, 190, 297
Kuhn, T. S. 3, 4, 5, 21, 108, 109, 110,
129, 130, 131, 182, 256, 296, 308
Kuzmin 81

Lakatos, I. xxi, 50, 52, 123
Lamark, xvi
Latour, B. x, xi, xii, xv, xvi, xviii, 53,
71, 82, 83, 84, 103, 301, 312, 315
Leeper, R. W. 7, 21
Lipkin, B. S. 8, 21
Lodahl, J. xxii
Lysenko 178

Matthews, P. 120, 121, 126, 127, 128,
129
May, M. T. M. de x, xi, xix, xxi
McConnell, J. V. 166, 170, 173, 174,
175, 176, 177, 178, 180, 184, 185,
186
McHugh, P. 247, 265
Merrifield, R. B. 63, 72
Merton, R. K. 240

Minsky, M. 6, 21
Mitroff, I. 225, 235
Mottelsohn, B. 89
Mulkay, M. J. x, xii, xiv, xv, xvi, 3, 20,
139

Necker, J. A. 4, 21
Nernst, 205, 212

Pagel, W. 16, 17, 18, 19, 22
Palmer, S. E. 5, 8, 9, 21
Petty, N. 181, 192
Pickering, A. x, xii, xiv, 299, 301, 315
Pinch, T. J. xii, xiv, xviii, xx, 53, 176,
186, 302, 303, 315
Pipkin, 144, 149, 158
Polanyi, M. 3
Popper(ian), K. R. 78, 82, 103, 104, 240
Porter, P. B. 13, 22
Prigogene, I. 70, 71, 72

Quine, W. V. 51, 113, 114

Ravetz, J. R. viii, xiii, xxiv, 308, 319
Reines, F. 80, 83, 94, 95, 104
Rose, S. P. R. 182, 193
Rosenfeld, A. 8, 21
Rubin 4
Ryle, M. 248, 249, 255

Safan-Gerard, D. xxii
Seares, R. D. 86, 88, 90
Serres, M. 70, 73
Shapere, D. 301, 318
Shimony, A. 3, 20
Skinner, B. F. 179
Smith, D. 246, 247, 250, 252, 253,
256, 258
Stech, B. 120, 138
Stengers, I. 70, 71, 72

Tafel 205, 212
Thompson, R. 166, 187
Toulmin 3
Travis, D. xiv, 93, 304, 307, 315

Ungar, G. 167, 176, 187

Wallen xii, xv, xx
Watson 181
Weber, M. 99, 303
Whitteridge, G. 16, 22
Woods, A. 37, 39, 52
Woolgar, S. W. viii, x, xi, xii, xiv, xv,
    xvi, xviii, 71, 82, 83, 84, 103, 256

Zweig, G. 116, 117, 135

INDEX OF SUBJECTS

American Chemical Society 94
Anti-Neutrino 81
Aristotelian 16, 18, 19, 20
'Art and Illusion' 5, 6
Atomic Energy Commission 88, 90

Bartlett-model 6
Bielefeld Conference ix
Bio-Chemical Journal 283
Bohr, Niels, Institute 89
Boring's 'Young Girl-Old Woman' 5, 7
Brewster Angle 159

Cal-Tech 85–89, 91, 96–99
Celebrated Exemplars 4

Duhem-Quine Thesis 113, 114

'Ecological Approach to Visual Perception', The 7
Edinburgh School, The xvi

Ferric chloride 46, 47, 48
Feynman rule 121, 122
Fischer's Man-Girl Figure 11

Gestalt perception 9
Gestalt psychology xix, 10
Gestalt switch 15, 17
GHRH (Growth Hormone Releasing Hormone) 54, 55

HEP (High-Energy Physics) 107, 111, 112, 114, 117, 121–123, 126, 128–130
'Heterogeneous Reasoning' xi

International Biological Programme (IBP) 223
Isomorphism 245–246

I.S.A. World Congress ix
Interaction between Theory and Data in Science: 3–20
Notes and References 20–23

Journal of Biological Psychology (JBP) 174–177
Journal of Comparative and Physiological Psychology 166

Laboratory Life xviii
Local Hidden Variables (LHV) 142–148, 151–166

McGill University xxiii
Manchester University – Department of Liberal Studies of Science xxiii
Metaphor-Theory of Innovation 25

Nature Jacobs/Davis Criticisms 100
Neutrinos 84, 99
New Scientist 165, 182

Physical Review Letters 90
Popperian 82, 103, 184
Popper's World 78

Qualitative logics xi
Quarks 115, 116, 122, 124, 125, 126, 127
Quantum chromodynamics (QCD) 119, 121, 124
Quantum mechanics (QM) 139, 141–152, 154–164

Ravetz's Paradox viii

Scientific American 91
Social Science and Humanities Research Council of Canada xxiii

Social Science Research Council 107, 269

Social processes of scientific investigations 171

Solar – neutrinos 79, 80, 81, 83, 84, 99–104

'Somatostatin' 54, 55, 56, 65, 67, 68, 69

'Structure of Scientific Revolutions' 108, 129

Tafel's Law 212, 213

The Scientist as an Anological Reasoner: 25–50

    Notes and References 50–52

    Time magazine 91

Theoreticians and experimenters 77

Theory-ladenness 3, 28

University of Indiana 87

University of Michigan 186

University of Texas 166

University of Virginia 100

Worm Runner's Digest (WRD) 173–177

Zweig rule 116, 117, 118, 120, 121, 124